Housing Needs
and Policy Approaches

Duke Press Policy Studies

Housing Needs and Policy Approaches

Trends in Thirteen Countries

Edited by Willem van Vliet—
Elizabeth Huttman and
Sylvia Fava

Duke University Press
Durham, 1985

© 1985 Duke University Press
All rights reserved
Printed in the United States of America
Library of Congress Cataloging in Publication Data
Main entry under title:
Housing needs and policy approaches
(Duke Press policy studies)
Bibliography: p.
Includes indexes.
1. Housing policy.   2. Housing policy—Developing
countries. 3. Housing—Social aspects. I. Van Vliet—,
Willem. II. Huttman, Elizabeth D., 1929–
III. Fava, Sylvia Fleis, 1927– . IV. Series.
HD7287.H68 1985   363.5'8   85-4549
ISBN 0-8223-0587-9

Contents

List of Tables and Figures

Tables

Figures

Preface

For more than a decade now, the annual convention of the American Sociological Association has served as a framework for bringing housing researchers together in an Ad Hoc Group on Housing and the Built Environment. The meetings of this group, which puts out a newsletter three times a year to about 250 people, have fulfilled a valuable communication function. However, in an effort to include a greater number of housing researchers from outside the United States and Canada and to introduce a broader comparative perspective, Elizabeth Huttman and Sylvia F. Fava petitioned the Executive Committee of the International Sociological Association (ISA) for session space at its ninth congress in Uppsala, Sweden, in 1978. Eventually, three sessions were organized, which were very well attended and in which fourteen countries were represented. An edited selection of the papers that were given was subsequently published (Ungerson and Karn, 1980).

The ISA again responded positively to a request for sessions on housing at its Tenth World Congress held in Mexico City, in 1982. Interest for these meetings was great; more than forty people, representing seventeen countries in North America, South America, Europe, Africa, Asia, and Australia, participated in the sessions, which drew considerable audiences. The present volume consists chiefly of selected papers that were initially prepared for these meetings and subsequently revised, in several iterations, in response to detailed comments and suggestions by the editors. Some chapters, however, were written especially for this book.

The organization of the volume reflects a structure outlined in the introductory chapter that follows. The introductions to the composite parts also elaborate the dominant themes and link them to specific chapters. Therefore, only a brief overview of the contents is offered here as a general guide to readers.

Part I details current trends in household formation in a number of Western countries, trends that prevail in many advanced industrialized nations. The authors consider housing needs of different household types, including extended families, female-headed households, and families with children. In Part II the focus shifts to the role that governments have played in providing housing needed by groups such as those identified in Part I. The chapters by Newton and Wulff; Dansereau, Divay and Godbout; and Forrest and Murie analyze government interventions in the housing market in Melbourne, Montreal, and Britain and share some remarkably similar conclusions about the nature and implications of these interventions. The overall perspective of centrally organized housing systems is supplemented by a chapter by Van Vliet—, who compares the private housing preferences of young people in Israel with that country's public policy; the user perspective of government housing in the United States, Sweden, and Australia is taken up by, respectively, Anderson and Weidemann; Genovese; and Kilmartin. Part II concludes with a comparative overview by Huttman of postwar public housing policies in Western Europe and Scandinavia.

Part III focuses on different approaches to the provision of housing in less-developed countries. Here, political and economic realities necessitate a diminished role of the central government, and there is a greater reliance on self-help housing arrangements. Reviews by Gulati and Valladares of a number of relevant issues in this regard are supplemented by rare inside views of squatter housing in India (Sandhu) and Egypt (El-Messiri). A chapter on slum housing in Indonesia points to the need to coordinate housing aid programs and the potential of local participation in construction as two issues with a broader significance for housing policy in other less-developed countries.

Finally, Part IV considers the societal context of housing. As emphasized in the first chapter, we see a range of demographic, political, economic, cultural, and other factors impinging on housing policies, and these policies have different implications in different sociospatial contexts. In this connection, the notion of segregation becomes important, and along these lines Grunfeld, Ylönen, and Den Draak are concerned with antecedents and implications of the intertwining of the social and spatial organization of housing. Pugh deals with a different facet of the societal context of housing as he considers Norwegian housing policies within a broader framework of national socioeconomic policies oriented toward establishing equity.

Of their selection of papers presented at the Ninth World Congress of the International Sociological Association in Uppsala, Sweden, in 1978, Ungerson and Karn (1980) wrote in their introduction that the wide range of countries from which their papers emanated permitted an examination of how housing issues and policies relate to societies as a whole. As we point out in the following chapter, the current volume further encourages such contextual analysis of housing policies by its broadened international scope and the specific foci of its chapters.

The Editors

1

Housing Needs and Policy Approaches: An Overview

Willem van Vliet— and Sylvia Fava

Social research on housing concerns a broad array of policy issues along various dimensions and at various levels, ranging from equity in national subsidy programs to trends in regional dwelling supply to popular participation in local development to individual residential choice. Accordingly, research is conducted in a variety of settings. Researchers may be found in traditionally organized academic departments (e.g., sociology, economics), in multidisciplinary entities, and in research institutes that may be independent, semigovernmental or affiliated with a university. Other researchers come from professional backgrounds such as urban planning and architecture. In addition, many investigations are carried out in ministries of housing or similar bodies. In Third World countries, housing research is often sponsored by the United Nations and large international foundations and agencies.

Considering the great variety of research contexts, it comes as little surprise that the outcomes of research have been scattered, rather than cumulative. Academic housing researchers typically are either the only people with such interests in their department or the only representatives of their discipline in a multidisciplinary unit. Consequently, they seek out diverse audiences and report their findings in many different journals. Furthermore, results from research conducted under government auspices are often presented in documents that receive only limited circulation. In short, the dissemination of findings has been difficult.

The situation sketched above has been problematic because it provides researchers with limited opportunities to compare their findings. Such exchange is extremely valuable, however, because it enables the identification of common trends and facilitates the formulation of policy approaches to specific issues whose underlying more generic factors would not otherwise be manifest. The present volume is prompted by this hiatus in the literature. Unlike other recent housing publications more narrowly concerned with economic issues (McGuire, 1981) or the situation in the United States (e.g., Sternlieb et al., 1980; Pynoos et al., 1980; Montgomery and Mandelker, 1979; Fish, 1979; Montgomery and Marshall, 1980; Hartman, 1983), this book contains perspectives from six continents selected to illustrate, generally with original empirical data, dominant themes in social research on policies regarding housing supply and demand worldwide.

Transition

The need for comparative housing research is relatively recent and it has emerged in the transition from unselfconscious form making in housing to self-conscious form making (Alexander, 1964). The following historical sketch describes how this transition added new dimensions to the quantity and quality of housing demands and at the same time increased the need for government involvement in the provision of housing.

In preindustrial times, and even today to some extent in the less-developed countries, the inhabitants of dwellings, the designer, and the builder were one and the same person or members of a small social group. The process of so-called unselfconscious construction was guided by covert procedural rules which produced physical settings integrally linked to their sociocultural context on the one hand, and to physical and technological constraints on the other. The unspoken rules, as well as their products, evolved incrementally over an extended time. The builders were close to their materials and techniques of construction. They usually inhabited the shelters they produced and subsequently altered them, as required by their changing needs. In short, the unselfconscious building process was one of iterative, systematic responses, integrally linked to the requisites of slowly evolving housing needs (Studer and Van Vliet—, in press).

In contrast, the self-conscious building process is characterized by environmental needs which change more frequently and more abruptly and which are increasingly multivariegated. The responses to these needs involve the contemplated and synoptic use of specialized skills and the large-scale adoption of advanced technologies, over-coming physical constraints. Social and administrative distance sepa-rates the users of the environment from the producers (Lipman, 1969), as they form organizational entities such as tenant and homeowner associations, architectural firms, development corporations, and build-ing companies.

Clearly, housing is intricately interwoven with sociopolitical, eco-nomic, and technological factors constituting the societal context, and the transformation from unselfconscious to self-conscious construc-tion finds its genesis in a radical alteration of what had been an enduring societal configuration. The principal instigating force behind this change was the Industrial Revolution. Mechanization of agricul-tural production decreased the labor force in the countryside, while the introduction of industrial production created a need for unskilled labor in urban centers. This change in the economic structure resulted in a massive migration from rural to urban areas and a concomitant demand for housing. The newcomers differed in many respects from the old-time urban residents. Migrants were generally younger than existing residents, usually male, unmarried, and from a wide geo-graphical area and diverse origins. The size and demographic compo-sition of the migrant flow also affected the prevailing political struc-ture—for example, people no longer had to take oaths to become city burghers—and a type of administration that was less elitist and more plebeian emerged (Weber, 1958). Further technological advances made possible the mass production of clothing and the opening up of for-merly isolated regions. Mass communication media such as newspa-pers, radio, television, and film contributed at a later stage to the enormous increase in variations on previously stable and standard patterns of social life (Firey, 1957).

New housing demands

These developments fostered emancipation from economic and social constraints, resulting in greater social and geographical mobility. The differential distribution of these benefits manifested itself in more differentiated housing demands by groups who could self-select (Bell, 1958) their housing environment according to their preferences and weaker groups largely dependent on government aid. Thus, the demand for housing took on new dimensions with regard to both the quantity and quality of needed dwellings.

In addition, recent life-style and demographic changes in more-developed countries (e.g., the rise in dual-earner families and non-family households) have, in conjunction with certain economic and political trends, generated a different set of priorities in regard to the types of housing that are needed and the location of housing relative to a new spectrum of life chances. For example, the traditional residential suburb, once thought ideally compatible with a "familism" life-style, is no longer congruent with the needs of employed mothers with young children who, in the United States, make up the fastest growing segment of the labor force; women worldwide tend to prefer socially and functionally integrated neighborhoods, typically featuring a mix of public services, rental housing and links through the public transportation system with jobs, shops, day care centers, and other community facilities (Stamp, 1980; Mauduit and Raimond, 1971; Fava, 1980; Weiss, 1980). The emerging life-styles also express themselves in demands for procedural and legislative changes. Concerns in this regard relate to, for example, the taxation of employed wives and practices of mortgage lending institutions in dealings with single parents (Roistacher and Young, 1980; Card, 1980; Shalala and McGeorge, 1981).

Changing housing preferences express themselves not only at the community level, but also with respect to the types of dwelling units needed. There is, for example, a growing demand for small dwellings by young people who leave their parents' homes at an earlier age, elderly people wishing to live independently, and divorced people. Recent U.S. census data are illustrative of these trends: the number of female-headed family households increased by 72 percent between 1970 and 1983 (U.S. Bureau of the Census, 1983); the number of nonfamily households during the same period rose by 88 percent (ibid.); average household size declined from 3.14 in 1970 to 2.73 in 1983 (ibid.). The chapters in Part I zero in on some of these groups, to which others could be added. An implication of these demographic and life-style changes is a mismatch between actual supply and demand. For example, in 1975 the stock of five-room dwellings exceeded demand in the Federal Republic of Germany, while there was a shortage of three-room dwellings for which demand is projected to increase by 25 percent before 1990, paralleled by a 40 percent increase in demand for two-room dwellings; a clear misfit between supply and demand, even though on an *aggregate* level supply and demand do match (Marschalk, 1982; in Chapter 1, Ash presents similar data for Britain). These trends may also be observed for most other advanced industrialized nations (United Nations, 1983). On a more general level, the implication of these developments is a plurality of user groups articulating specific and different housing demands.

A matching housing supply requires a central authority with distributive and coordinating responsibilities regarding the allocation of scarce collective resources. The type and extent of such government involvement varies according to level of economic and technological development and demographic patterns identified later and illustrated by chapters in Parts II and III.

Less-developed countries

While homelessness (Hopper and Cox, 1982; United States Department of Housing and Urban Development, 1984) and squatting (e.g., Priemus, 1983; Draaisma and Van Hoogstraten, 1983) do exist in the more-developed countries, housing problems are generally less related to the availability of housing and more to accessibility and quality. In less-developed countries, the sheer magnitude of the demand for shelter overshadows qualitative aspects of housing need. In Africa, the United Nations estimates that, on the average, for each housing unit built in a city, ten new families migrate from the rural areas. The worldwide urban housing deficit is increasing at a rate of four to five million units annually.

Turner (1976) and others questioned early the ability of less-developed countries to meet the acute housing shortages by instituting a centrally organized system producing inexpensive public housing on a massive scale. Many governments have vacillated between using deep subsidies to provide very few units at truly low cost and spreading available funds thinly over many houses, most of which would be beyond the means of the great majority of the ill-housed. In addition, low-cost projects have tended to become filled by people with connections to officialdom, without regard for actual need (Peattie, 1982).

In response to the failure of governments to provide needed housing, squatters have "self-built" their housing (Van der Linden, 1982), creating "marginal" settlements, known under various names, with very large populations: 25 percent of the population in Rio de Janeiro; 33 percent in Lima; 35 percent in Manila; 37 percent in Kuala Lumpur; 46 percent in Mexico City; 48 percent in Lusaka; 70 percent in Casablanca (Dwyer, 1975; Lea, 1980). People studying or working in these settlements have dispelled myths that their population is economically unproductive and socially disorganized (e.g., Mangin, 1973; Conway, 1981; Perlman, 1976). Policy makers in less-developed countries have increasingly favored an approach to housing that seizes on popular initiative; self-help housing came to be seen as a solution rather than a problem. Accordingly, housing development programs now tend to focus on the provision of minimum infrastructure (site-and-services) and basic washing and toilet facilities (wet core). The Office of Housing and Urban Development of the U.S. Agency for International Development directs its current efforts along these lines, with at present $2 billion in loans outstanding within its Housing Guarantee Program, its principal instrument to assist less-developed countries in the provision of housing (U.S. Agency for International Development, 1982).

Attempts to eliminate the disorder and irregularity of uncontrolled settlements, while retaining the dynamism of spontaneous building, mean, in essence, the establishment of a structure of rules and incentives for channeling private investment, keeping government involvement at a minimum. The financial implications of this approach may be such that those at the low end of the income spectrum still cannot afford the resulting housing. These and other problematic facets of sponsored self-help housing have been analyzed by Peattie (1982; see also the chapters in this volume by Gulati and Sandhu) and more radical critics who situate the housing problem within a much broader structure of inequalities associated with the capitalist mode of production. These critics charge that the provision of sites-and-services is simply a palliative designed to prevent interference with a dominant capitalist economy and to defuse demands by the urban poor for a fairer share of national resources; to them, reliance on self-help housing simply means the exploitation of cheap labor (e.g., Lea, 1980; see also the chapter by Valladares). However, while systematic evaluations are still sporadic, two recent studies do show benefits of government-sponsored self-help housing, both in objective terms (Stepick and Murphy, 1980) and according to residents' subjective reports (Burns, 1983). Moreover, immediate housing pressures are likely to propel self-building further, at least in the short run.

Government intervention

The preceding discussion indicates that housing needs usually cannot be met by exclusively local efforts. In more-developed countries, as well as in those that are less developed, the provision of adequate shelter requires involvement of supralocal authorities in regard to needed building materials, organizational and technical expertise, and financial resources. In the transition from unselfconscious building to self-conscious building discussed earlier, the production and consumption functions of housing have changed. Transactions in the free market fail to provide vulnerable groups with proper shelter. Since disadvantaged groups often make up a large proportion of the population and contribute significantly to the reproduction of labor, there are pragmatic reasons for governments at least to overcome inefficiencies of the market mechanism. Chapters in Parts II and III illustrate some of the forms that such government involvement may take. Donnison and Ungerson (1982) have distinguished several levels of state responsibility regarding housing, ranging from minimal interference, through the provision of social housing with an orientation to equality, to comprehensive planning, production, and management of a nation's housing stock. Others (e.g., Fish, 1979; Yearns, 1979) have chosen chronological periods to describe the historical evolvement of the government role in housing.

The notion of housing policy stages is attractive; countries could be classified accordingly and anticipate their future needs and required responses. However, such a classification would not be unlike a Procrustean bed; it is doubtful that housing policies universally follow a path of progressively greater government responsibility, from endeavors based on organized philanthropy to comprehensive intervention aimed at providing equal opportunities for attaining prevailing housing norms, as Carmon's (1981) analysis suggests has been the case in Britain and the United States. Housing policies evolve in the interstices of demand and supply, both of which are closely related to demographic trends, available resources, and level of technological development; housing policies also evolve in the context of shifting power allegiances of stakeholders in a particular political system (Roweis, 1983). Hence, the extent of government intervention in housing varies according to a configuration of dynamic factors. Fainstein (1980) has noted how similar housing policies in the United States, Sweden, and Western Europe have differed significantly in consistency and extent of support, largely because of different institutional, ideological, and political contexts. Similarly, the type of intervention may include direct construction, land acquisition, and the provision of basic infrastructure, as well as more indirect measures like regulation of building codes, zoning ordinances, taxation, and subsidization.

Differences in the type and extent of government intervention in housing reflect different rationales for becoming involved. Classifying these rationales is a political activity, colored by one's ideological leanings. Thus, what some liberal observers see as attempts to provide housing for the poor and efforts to eliminate unsanitary conditions (True, 1979), are viewed by more radical observers as manipulations by the state, which, as an instrument of the ruling class, develops policies intended to avoid social unrest and to insure stability of a capitalist economy (Gordon, 1977). Likewise, housing construction, considered by some as an effort to relieve crowding and to alleviate housing shortages, is interpreted by others as simply an expedient economic lever to regulate levels of unemployment and inflation.

Whatever one's ideological inclination, it is clear that housing policy needs to be seen in the context of a broader societal framework. This more encompassing approach is evident in recent polemical writings concerning the nature of urban theory (e.g., Saunders, 1983; Paris, 1983; Kirby, 1983; cf. Mellor, 1977) and in chapters in this volume which illustrate that housing may be used as an instrument in conjunction with other economic and social policies to develop new towns (Sandhu; Van Vliet—); to revitalize inner cities (Den Draak); to decrease socioeconomic inequities (Pugh); to effect population distribution (Ylönen; Grunfeld; Van Vliet—) and integration (Grunfeld; Van Vliet—); and to provide incentives for private initiative (Forrest and Murie), to name but a few examples.

Ideological differences pervade the housing literature in more- as well as in less-developed countries. There exist, for example, widely divergent interpretations of homeowner policies in the west (Noto, 1980; Kemeny, 1981; Lundqvist, 1984) and site-and-services programs in the Third World (Lea, 1980). It is beyond the scope of this chapter to analyze the various ideological perspectives that currently prevail or even to identify them in any detail; some viewpoints are amplified in chapters in Parts II and III.

Housing goals often are closely interdependent with other goals that are ranked higher in the hierarchy of political and economic priorities. Housing goals, therefore, tend to be couched in vague terms like the "decent home and living environment" promised to all Americans by the 1949 U.S. Housing Act. Without adequate operationalization, such goals circumvent accountability questions. Moreover, little attention is commonly given to the specific mechanisms and conditions required for the implementation of stated goals (Schneider, 1982). Nevertheless, below we make a global distinction with respect to government involvement in housing.

Quantitative and qualitative concerns

At a minimum level, public policy is directed at the provision of an adequate aggregate number of dwelling units; at a higher level, the concern shifts to disaggregate concerns and qualitative aspects, for example, the needs of specific groups, location, and affordability (Economic Commission for Europe, 1980; U.N. Department of International Economic and Social Affairs, 1976; U.S. Congress, Joint Economic Committee, 1978). A quantitative orientation does not necessarily mean that the government itself becomes actively involved in construction as is the case in collectivist economies such as those in China, Cuba, and the Soviet Union (Barkin, 1978; Sawers, 1978). Rather the government may, as Carmon (1981) suggests, take responsibility for creating conditions required to attain a certain housing production. In this process it may provide noncompetitive and indivisible public goods such as electricity, water, sewer, streets, and other infrastructure necessary to support a housing development. It may rely for housing production on housing associations (e.g., Denmark, West Germany, The Netherlands), municipalities and local authorities (e.g., Ireland), or private construction by corporations (e.g., the United States, France) or individual builders, as in many less-developed countries.

A preoccupation with quantitative housing production is typical for many less-developed countries today, and it was dominant in responses to housing shortages caused by war destruction and the baby boom in Western countries. However, housing construction has strongly declined in European countries (Harloe, 1980), and in the United States housing starts have also decreased (U.S. Bureau of the Census, 1983). Consequently, some analysts foresee the possibility of selective housing shortages for these nations in the near future (e.g., Sternlieb and Hughes, 1983; U.S. Congress, Joint Economic Committee, 1980; Economic Commission for Europe, 1980), although opinions differ with regard to the preferred approaches to construction (Kain, 1983; Vint and Bintliff, 1983).

Government interference regarding qualitative aspects of housing is, as a rule, indirect through legislative measures concerning taxation, subsidies, and regulation. In this context, housing policy is concerned not only with new construction but also with the existing housing stock. In countries that have adopted this more comprehensive approach there is generally a strong organizational or programmatic linkage between government and lending institutions; the chief policy tools have been financial rather than administrative (Donnison and Ungerson 1982). Thus, governments have targeted a variety of grants, loans, subsidies, rent controls, and other incentive policies, in various combinations, at renters, individual homeowners, building firms, and small businesses to upgrade the quality of housing, to make housing more accessible, or to revitalize older residential areas (e.g., Varadi, 1982; Downs, 1983; Ghorra-Gobin, 1983; Tucker, 1983; see also the chapter by Den Draak and the chapters in Part II). The forms of these policies are currently being debated (ibid.; Quigley, 1980; Straszheim, 1980; Kain, 1983), and views also diverge regarding the beneficiaries of subsidies (for example, renters or owners), whether subsidies should be aimed at new construction or rehabilitation, and regarding the spatial scale of a program (i.e., scattered individual households that qualify, a renewal area, or even an entire new town).

Other issues concern the time frame of subsidies and their entry level in the housing system. Some suggest that subsidies should be targeted at middle-class households who will purchase new dwellings and vacate less expensive accommodation for lower-income groups. This filtering process is predicated on the assumption of a homogeneous housing market with a sufficient vacancy rate to permit mobility chains. In reality, segmentation is often the case, so that disadvantaged groups remain trapped while already affluent groups benefit (e.g., Bourne and Hitchcock, 1978; Marullo, 1983).

Summing up the discussion so far, we have described the need for comparative housing research as emerging from the changing relationships between housing supply and demand. We have pointed out how housing is closely linked to a broader societal context and how a transformation of this context has added new qualitative and quantitative dimensions to housing problems, increasingly requiring an allocative and coordinating role of a supralocal authority. Several approaches to government involvement were identified. Let us turn now to some issues that will demand attention in the years to come. What follows is not intended as an exhaustive list or a complete agenda; rather these are a number of issues that appear salient at the present time.

Research and policy issues

To begin with, the chapters that follow and the recent literature point to substantive, theoretical, and methodological tasks for social scientific researchers. Given the continuing strain on housing budgets, interest in the evaluation of assistance programs will likely increase. Such evaluations, which may take the shape of cost-effectiveness or cost-benefit analyses, as well as client-oriented studies, are the order of the day in the more-developed countries and are becoming more prevalent in the less-developed countries (e.g., Wegelin, 1978; Burns, 1983; Stepick and Murphy, 1980). Generally, there will also be a continuing need for studies of sociobehavioral implications of housing. Economic waste and social and individual malfunctioning resulting from ignorance or neglect of the users' perspective have been amply documented for the United States (e.g., Yancey, 1971; Gans, 1959); the significance of the link between social life and the housing environment has also been established for Europe (e.g., Genovese, 1975), the Soviet Union (Andrusz, 1980), and the Third World (Brolin, 1972; Grenell, 1972). The recently established International Housing Research Network is an expression of interest in basing the planning, design, and management of housing environments on environmental quality indicators obtained from residents themselves.

In a related vein, there will be a need to study the interplay between the aggregate supply of housing and the disaggregate nature of demand as different and new user groups articulate different and new needs without being able to build up political constituencies with adequate bargaining power (Sternlieb and Hughes, 1983). The emergence of a plurality of stakeholder groups also will likely prompt greater attention for parapolitical and informal processes (Cherki, 1976) and open-ended, dialectical decision-making procedures (e.g., Mitroff et al., 1983), as well as increased skepticism regarding traditional rational approaches (Faludi, 1983; Healey, 1983). In addition, current concerns among social scientists regarding their relations with citizens (e.g., Chavis et al., 1983) and policy makers (e.g., Keren, 1983; Zube, 1982) will make housing researchers more attentive to the utilization of their findings.

On a theoretical level, the debate regarding the role of the state will continue and likely intensify as theoretically derived positions are subjected to empirical and historical tests (Green, 1982; Bollinger, 1983). Here there is perhaps less need to add to existing formulations than to develop conceptual frameworks for comparative analyses to validate, refute, or adjust current viewpoints (e.g., Masser, 1980). The need for new methodological approaches is closely tied in with the substantive and theoretical questions identified above. These questions point to both objective and subjective evaluation studies of program effectiveness and residential quality and to comparative research based on cross-sectional as well as longitudinal analysis. Another methodological development is an increasing emphasis on programmatic approaches based on qualitative research (Peattie, 1983); these approaches are based on a commitment to intervention and the premise that qualitative information from key informants in the housing process is central to housing practice.

While the above partial agenda for research applies to more-as well as less-developed countries, there are important differences regarding policy. These differences are based, in part, on population differentials such as crude birthrate, age distribution, life expectancy, and urbanization, all of which have significant implications for housing demand. In addition, there are, of course, large differences in levels of economic and technological development, bureaucratic apparatuses, and available resources. Therefore, in less-developed countries there is likely to be a continued reliance on self-help housing and on ways to fortify popular initiatives (Lea, 1980). To avoid some of the shortcomings of site-and-service programs to date, governments may explore possibilities to introduce greater flexibility in the package that is offered. Greater choice for residents would not be restricted to the extent and type of services provided but would extend also to location, lot size, and financial arrangements. In some cases, reform of unwieldy government bureaucracies and fundamental institutional changes will be necessary to gain better control of housing costs. Above all, it is essential that housing policy not be separated from broader issues of economic development.

In more-developed countries the policy trends are more emphasis on rehabilitation and inner-city revitalization (see chapter by Den Draak; Gale, 1984); encouragement of homeowners to carry a greater share of their housing cost; and less willingness to support public and rental housing (see chapters by Ash; Forrest and Murie; Newton and Wulff; and Dansereau, Divay and Godbout). Disenfranchised groups (e.g., migrant workers and female-headed households) are increasingly placed in public housing, usually the least attractive stock which could not be sold off, exacerbating their stigmatization (Harloe, 1980).

These developments will mean greater hardships for renters (Downs, 1983) and disadvantaged groups who cannot compete for housing in a market from which protective devices are being withdrawn and replaced by regulations with uncertain distributional impacts.

Housing and development: Theory and ideology

This chapter has not adopted a particular ideological position but has identified various housing issues and trends analyzed and described more fully in the chapters which follow. We have distilled some questions, widely shared by housing researchers and policy makers internationally, and reflected the diversity of answers that are being developed. Two dominant themes emerge: the various forms of state (non)intervention in the provision and allocation of housing and the emergence of highly differentiated housing markets as an indirect expression of other state policies and objectives. In the broadest context, inequalities in housing within nations and between the more-developed and the less-developed nations can be viewed as instances of dependency or world system theory. Simply put, these theories hold that national and urban development must be understood on the basis of a region's position in the economic hierarchy. Third World development must be examined as part of Third World dependence on the core industrialized nations whose global corporate enterprises determine the international flow of labor, jobs, and raw materials needed in the provision of housing and economic development generally.

Dependency and world system theory owe much to Gunder Frank (1969) who, in his work on Latin America, distinguished three dominant perspectives on national and regional development. First is the ideal-typical method. It presents an index of the qualities of a well-functioning metropolis and, following this, considers from this standpoint what is missing in the underdeveloped region. The difference between the two is the development program. Horowitz's work with Parsons' pattern variables and Rostow's theory of growth stages are examples of this approach. A second perspective originates in anthropology and is concerned with the diffusion of innovations and desirable features of the prospering metropolis. Third, there is a sociopsychological approach which focuses on the acculturation of modern values and beliefs; a typical example would be McClelland's work aimed at inculcating achievement motives in Indian businessmen.

The just-described three approaches to development have been criticized by Frank and others for reinforcing dependency relationships rather than eliminating them. Dependency and world system theory have been advanced as alternative theoretical perspectives, directing attention to underlying basic economic structures and processes of production, consumption, and transaction. Critical observers have noted the lack of specificity in dependency theory in linking the international division of labor to the internal structure of cities and the development of housing classes (Chirot and Hall, 1982; Friedmann and Wulff, 1982). However, some analysts have recently begun to address these issues for less-developed societies (Portes and Walton, 1981: 88–91) and more-developed capitalist nations (Agnew, 1981).

The major perspectives on development are associated with different ideological positions. The ideal-typical, the diffusionist, and the sociopsychological approach are generally propagated by theorists who favor conservative or liberal views. Conservatives tend to argue that the state serves nobody's interest and approve of government intervention only to the extent that it enhances an efficient functioning of the free-market mechanism; liberals rather see the state as serving everybody's interest and they accordingly advocate an active role of the government. As do the conservatives, however, liberals remain firmly within the parameters of a dominant capitalist economy (Gordon, 1977). Dependency theorists embrace more radical views according to which the state serves only the interests of the ruling class. In their analysis, a fundamental restructuring of resource allocation mechanisms and social and economic institutions regulating the availability of and access to housing is required.

It should be noted that few radical alternatives have been set forth. Contrasts with capitalist societies tend to be sketchy and stereotyped, and to lack strong empirical underpinnings. In fact, recent rare in-depth studies of allegedly socialist housing markets in the Soviet Union, Poland, and Hungary document major social inequalities between city and countryside and among occupational groups in cities —with party functionaries, the military, and technocrats receiving the best housing (Hegedus and Tosics, 1983; Szelenyi, 1983), even though allocation is by state bureaucracies rather than by market forces (Hirszowicz, 1980; Szelenyi, 1981a).

Finally, we must note the question of whether Third World development lies most appropriately in following Western (and also Soviet) models of populations who are densely housed in large industrial cities. Both capitalist (India) and socialist (China, Cuba) nations have attempted to distribute manufacturing plants more evenly between urban and rural locations, aiming to stem migration to large cities and also to achieve local self-sufficiency in food production, manufactured goods, medical care, and other services (Barkin, 1978; Cell, 1980; Kwok, 1982; Sawers, 1978). These efforts at genuinely new development models and settlement patterns are relatively recent, and they have only begun to be assessed for India and China (Murphey, 1980).

We hope that the presentation of the detailed chapters in this volume will help readers to evaluate the several perspectives described. Such an evaluation should facilitate the formulation of research needed next.

I

Housing Needs: Implications of Household Composition

Introduction
Shirley Foster Hartley

In the more industrialized nations of the world, both household composition and changing life-styles have significantly altered the needs and desires for specific types of housing. Some of the changes in housing needs are the result of long-term trends, while others appear as short-term discontinuities that are more difficult to anticipate by both the government and private housing sectors. For instance, even with the massive commitment of the British to provide public housing and even construct whole new cities, the growth in aspirations has led to public dissatisfaction with the number and quality of housing units available, as Joan Ash reports in chapter 1. Recent housing supplies in Britain and the United States have reached a new high, yet problems remain with the unmet desires of young adults for separate housing units, of parents who want more rooms for growing families, and of single parents and the poor and elderly who have difficulty finding housing units that are not obsolete or dilapidated by current standards. Ash points out that the answer is not doubling up, by way of extended family households or communal life-styles; rather an increased supply of independent housing units would seem to be the solution most desired by the population. Her overview of the many housing problems found in Britain today shows how the variety of housing needs in the more advanced nations has increased.

The housing needs of a number of special population groups, identified by Ash, are examined in greater detail in subsequent chapters. Gaunt, for example, concerns herself with the extended family. She presents findings on intergenerational contact and mutual aid in Sweden, and she points to implications regarding family functioning and housing requisites. The research reported by Gaunt indicates that, although two-thirds of all households in Sweden consist of only one or two persons, most of these people prefer to live near members of the extended family. The number and frequency of contact with members of the extended family and mutual aid among them is inversely correlated to the distance between housing units. To avoid the isolation of individuals and nuclear family units, housing policy should accommodate the emerging pattern of large extended family networks consisting of residents of many small separate households who want to live near other family members. The Swedish case may be instructive for the future, since its demographic trends are representative of developments in many advanced nations.

Marans and Colten focus on families with children in the United States. Using data from a national survey of both renters and managers of rental units, they report effects of rental housing policies on families with children. Their findings indicate that the proportion of rental units available to parents with children decreases as the number of children increases and that the proportion of dwellings unavailable to families with children has increased from one in six in 1975 to one in four in 1980. These results are clear evidence of the need to review critically current restrictive rental practices against families with children in rental housing.

The rapid expansion in both the number and proportion of households headed by women in the United States and many of the industrialized countries is a trend that is likely to continue into the future and that demands special attention from housing policy makers. In chapter 4, Ahrentzen reports on the housing problems of low-income women who are single parents. She examines the rent burden (as a proportion of total income), crowding, the problems of searching for adequate housing in safe neighborhoods, and the problems of meeting the objective needs of this increasingly large segment of households. As in the other chapters, there are implications here for government intervention in the housing market, raising a set of issues which are discussed extensively in Parts II and IV of this volume.

Housing problems often result from broad demographic trends that give rise to issues such as those discussed in the following chapters. The significance of these demographic trends is not always recognized by housing policy makers. For instance, the postwar baby boom, more pronounced in the United States than in many other industrialized countries, resulted in a near doubling of the number of adults aged twenty to twenty-nine in 1980, as compared to 1960. When one adds to the doubling of numbers the increased desire of young adults for independent housing and the postponement of marriage, the demand for single-person housing units jumps dramatically—indeed, between 1960 and 1978 there was a sevenfold increase in the number of young persons living alone.

The trend toward cohabitation, still only about 4 percent of all marital units, is not cancelled out by the opposite effect in the housing market of marriage at a later age. The housing desires of young adults have increased, so that the difficulty of finding really desirable housing may contribute to the postponement of marriage. During cohabitation young couples may manage in a small apartment, but they want a house or larger apartment with patio or yard when they marry.

The lower birth rates of the last fifteen years in the United States mean that family size and household units are smaller than in the past. Rising expectations and increased standards of living, however, have meant that families often desire larger rather than smaller detached homes. The research reported by Ahrentzen indicates the overwhelming preference of low-income single parents for separate houses. The ideal of a home of one's own prevails even among low-income renters. On the other hand, lower birth rates in the more-developed countries mean that the future need for housing will not be nearly so great as in the less-developed nations where birthrates are two to four times higher. In these countries, different policy approaches to the provision of housing are indicated, as discussed in the editors' introduction to this book and illustrated by studies in Part III.

There are other population differentials with implications for housing: in the poorer nations, children and teens make up over half of the population; in the more developed nations, the proportion of those over age sixty-four is often four times greater than in the less-developed nations. Lower birthrates contribute even more than increased life expectancy to the higher proportions of elderly in the more advanced nations. The problem of housing for the elderly is, therefore, very different. Elderly singles in the United States, for instance, now comprise one-third of all single person households and one-half of all single female households. The seven- to eight-year gap in male/female life expectancy and a reluctance to give up independence and to live with others creates a shortage of housing for elderly singles and others with whom they compete in the housing market. Problems for formerly relatively affluent elderly persons may be associated with their attempts to maintain family homes that are too large for their needs and that therefore create a financial burden. The problems are acute for the very poor elderly, and they will grow worse as larger cohorts of middle aged progress to the later years.

Female-headed households are often among the most impoverished in the United States. The number of families maintained by women increased dramatically between 1960 and 1980, from 4.5 to 11.3 million. In the 1980s, the women who maintain these families are generally younger, more likely to have children, more likely to be divorced or never-married, and more likely to be black than their 1960 counterparts. In her study, Ahrentzen found a lower average income and a far greater rent burden for this group than for the two-parent control group, yet the trends of increased proportions of births out of wedlock and the rising divorce rates remind us that increases rather than declines in housing units needed by this group may be anticipated. In addition to the simple provision of dwellings, their location with regard to the community services and facilities needed by these vulnerable population segments is critically important.

The population growth of the last thirty years, combined with rising expectations and relatively high effective demand, has made for a clear shift from relatively large family housing units to smaller, often single person, dwellings for both young and older adults. In the more-developed countries, there is an interactive effect of housing supply and effective demand. Without increasing affluence, many older persons and teens or young adults could not afford to live alone, but, as the number of these independent households increases, those unable to afford such a life-style feel even more deprived than their monetary circumstances alone would indicate. Furthermore, as the demand for small units increases, it will be more difficult for those who are handicapped in any way—by children, physical disability, age, lack of employment or income—to compete for such units. The chapters that follow illustrate the sometimes precarious housing situation of these special population groups; Parts II and IV detail government responses and Part III focuses on approaches adopted in the Third World, which faces different problems in population and economic development.

2   The Effects of Household Formation
     on Housing Needs in Britain

     Joan Ash

Abstract. This chapter reviews trends in household formation in the
United Kingdom and examines to what extent the housing needs of
different household types are met by public policy. With official statistics and findings from user studies, the author shows how the substi-
tution of rented public housing by owned private dwellings results in
an annual shortfall in housing production in relation to household
formation (see also chapter 5 by Forrest and Murie). The conclusion
discusses emerging housing options and policy considerations.

Trends in household formation

The trend to a greater increase in the number of households than in
the number of people is of long duration in Britain (Hole and Pountney, 1971). Between 1961 and 1971, the population increased by 5.3
percent and the number of households increased by 14 percent. In the
next decade the population increase fell to .6 percent and the household increase to 5.5 percent, but household increase relative to population increase was three times more during 1971–81 than during
1961–71.

At the first census count of households, in 1911, the average household size was 4.5 people. Recently, 1971–77, the average household
size fell rapidly, from 2.91 to 2.71 persons and then more gradually, to
2.64 people in 1981. The average household size has also diminished
in the United States; it was only slightly higher in 1978 (2.81) than in
Britain in 1977.

The main cause of the reduction in average household size and multiplication of households is the growth of single-person households, which increased by 58 percent from 1961 to 1971, amounting to 59 percent of the total increase in households in England and Wales. In the next decade the increase continued but fell to 15.6 percent, which still constituted the greater part (56 percent) of the increase in households (Great Britain, Department of the Environment—hereinafter DOE—1977, Part I, table 1.10, and OPCS, 1982). The proportion of single-person households in 1981 was 21.8 percent of all households, not far off the 25 percent in the United States.

The greater part of the increase in single-person households from 1961 to 1981 was due to the increase in pensioner households (men aged at least sixty-five years and women sixty years), the proportion diminishing somewhat from 42 percent of the total increase from 1961 to 1971 to 34 percent from 1971 to 1981.

From 1971 to 1981 the proportion of persons of pensionable age increased by 10 percent, but the growing proportion of elderly single-person households was due mainly to greater longevity. The proportion of elderly people living on their own increases with age. Among those aged sixty-five to seventy-four, 14 percent of the males and 38 percent of the females live alone. The proportions increase to 37 percent of the males over eighty-five years of age and the 54 percent of the females. The proportion of females is higher because of their greater longevity. Seventy-nine percent of males aged sixty-five to seventy-four years and 35 percent of those aged eighty-five or older live with their spouse, as do 49 percent and 9 percent, respectively, of females. The rest of the elderly, 9 percent of males and 17 percent of females, nearly all live with relatives (Central Statistical Office, 1983).

The habit of the elderly to live as independent households is probably too well established to alter. Most people think that old people should not expect their children to look after them, and elderly parents appear to agree (Tinker, 1981). Many people have close ties with elderly parents, however, and like to live near them, and some people feel an obligation to accommodate a sole elderly parent in their own home, particularly when the parent is frail. Easier access to home-ownership and public housing, as explained in a following section, has also helped the elderly to maintain a separate household.

Usually, young single people lack the means, which the great majority of the elderly have acquired at some time in their lives, to enable them to set up separate households, but the habit of mature adults leaving home is long established (Hole and Pountney, 1971), and it has

Table 2.1 Proportions (in percentages) of never-married men and women aged 20–24 heading households.

		England and Wales		England	
		1961 (Census)	1971 (Census)	1977	1981
Men	20–24	2.8	7.6	14	13
	25–29	9.0	17.0	25	32
	30–34	11.7	23.4	31	38
Women	20–24	3.7	9.0	14	13
	25–29	9.1	19.7	30	29
	30–34	13.8	25.6	32	36

Source: Great Britain, Department of the Environment. *Housing initiatives for single people of working age,* 1982, table B.

recently become more prevalent in younger age groups as a result of the rise in disposable income. The proportion of never-married single people aged twenty to thirty-four in the population increased by 31 percent from 1961 to 1980, but the number of men of that age living as independent households increased by 364 percent and the number of women by 251 percent during this time. (table 2.1).

In the United States there has been a similar increase in households consisting of single people of all ages; the rate of increase of young single person households aged fourteen to twenty-four in the United States 1960–78 was somewhat greater than in Britain 1961–81.

A further increase in the number of households is resulting from the fission of nuclear families by divorce and separation. The British divorce rate seems likely to soon equal the American rate. The number of divorced men and women in Britain increased about fivefold 1961–80 (DOE, 1982a).

The divorce rate is the main cause of the increase in single-parent families, which grew from 8.4 percent of all families with dependent children in 1971–73 to 12.1 percent in 1980–82, not far off the proportion, 13–15 percent, in the United States. In Britain, 10.7 percent are single mothers, and 1.4 percent are single fathers; 6.7 percent of the lone mothers are divorced or separated, 1.7 percent widowed, and 2.3 percent single (Office of Population Censuses and Surveys—hereinafter OPCS—1983).

The baby boom of the late 1950s and early 1960s also increased the number of married-couple households, as in the United States, despite recent postponement of marriage because of economic conditions. The proportion of married couples living as part of another household was 2.3 percent in 1977 (DOE, 1977, part I, table 1.10), rather more than the proportion, 1.4 percent, living with parents in the United States in the seventies. Improvement in economic conditions enables a greater proportion of married couples to have homes of their own. From 1961 to 1971 the "concealed" couples fell by more than a quarter of a million, over half the total in 1961. Thirty-three percent of the couples aged twenty or over who married in or before 1955 were without a home of their own two years after marriage in contrast to only 7 percent of such couples who married 1971–75 (Holmans, 1981). Currently the number of married couples doubling up with relatives is probably increasing because of an estimated shortfall of 30,000–40,000 dwellings a year, representing 14–19 percent of the total output required to keep up with the needs of new households, without allowance for more single persons constituting separate households.

The long-term reduction in the total period fertility rate has resulted in a smaller number of children per family. Within the long-term trend there have been fluctuations. Most recently, the rate fell from 2.1 (replacement rate) in 1973 to 1.65 in 1977. After a rise to 1.9 in 1980, it fell again to 1.78 in 1982 (OPCS, 1983b).

The trends in household formation during the past two decades have produced a more complex pattern of needs, principally due to household fission. Many more of the youngest adults are setting out from the family home before marriage. Marriages dissolve more often, and, even when remarriage forms new households, there are intervening periods when couples who have been living in one home have a demand for two. More lone parents are bringing up children. At the end of the housing cycle, there are many more very old people who live alone.

The trends show a similarity to those in the United States, which is remarkable, considering the difference in average personal disposable income per head. This suggests that, above a particular level of affluence, marginal changes have similar effects.

Quantitative housing need

The increase in households since the first census in 1801 and the increase in average personal disposable income per capita created suf-

ficient effective demand for house building to keep up with the growing population but not until the thirties with the growth of households. The total number of dwellings first exceeded the total number
of households in 1938. Most of the 1931–39 gain was wiped out by the
cessation of house building during World War II, but, when large-scale
house building could be resumed after 1951, substantial gains were
achieved in the dwelling-household ratio. (DOE, 1977, part I, tables 1.5
and 1.11)

In 1870 the average personal income per capita was 56.3 percent of
the 1938 level. After 1951 income grew more quickly, and by 1975 it
had reached 188 percent of the 1938 level, but a substantial minority of
households had incomes which were too low to afford separate or
sanitary homes. The state became concerned with housing conditions
as part of the sanitary movement to create conditions which would
allow the masses to survive in crowded towns, but by 1914 public
housing in England and Wales amounted to only .25 percent of the
total stock of housing. The Exchequer started subsidizing houses for
the working classes after World War I, as this appeared to be the most
practical means of providing the "homes fit for heroes" which Lloyd
George had promised. By 1938, the proportion of households in public
housing in England and Wales had risen to 24 percent (DOE, 1977, part
I, table 1.23). In 1981 in Great Britain, 31 percent of households rented
homes owned by local authorities and new town development corporations.

Even the subsidized rents were not within the means of the very
poorest, but now housing benefits help people with low incomes to
pay their rents, whether they occupy publicly or privately owned
property. Nevertheless, the poor still pay a higher than average proportion of their income for housing. Households in the lowest fifth of
incomes in 1980 paid 23 percent of their income for housing, compared to 13 percent in the highest fifth (Department of Employment,
1981).

Rent control for privately owned property, started after demonstra-
tions and strikes as a result of increasing rent during World War I, has
also enabled households with low incomes to live independently. But
rent control has also inhibited the development of new privately
owned rentals for the mass market, and it has recently encouraged the
sale of privately rented property to owner-occupiers. Private rentals
decreased from an estimated 58 percent in England and Wales in 1938
(DOE, 1977, part I, table 1.23) to 13 percent in 1981 (OPCS, 1982).

Homeowners also receive assistance from the Exchequer in the form of tax relief on the interest paid on mortgages. This tax relief now amounts to considerably more than the Exchequer subsidies for public housing and rent rebates and allowances. Before 1914 all classes rented their homes, and it is estimated that no more than 10 percent of the housing stock in England and Wales was owner-occupied. Rising incomes, easy terms for mortgages, and the scarcity of private rentals have been responsible for the increase in homeownership to 56 percent of the stock in 1981 (OPCS, 1982). Homeownership has continued to increase, despite high interest rates, because it has proved to be the best form of saving in times of inflation. The higher the rate of interest, the greater is the tax relief.

Higher personal incomes, car ownership, and motorways have stimulated the growth of second homes. The effect of second homes on villages where they predominate has worried local residents, and second homes have suffered from arson in South Wales. By 1977, the total number of second homes in England was about 120,000, amounting to about .7 percent of the stock of housing (DOE, 1978a).

The latest information on the relation between households and dwellings (table 2.2) shows a crude surplus of 400,000 dwellings in 1977 over households, but in fact the stock of available dwellings was insufficient to meet the existing need. A total of 729,000 homes were vacant and unavailable because they were second homes, were in the course of rehabilitation, or were awaiting sale or assignment. Since about 200,000 homes were shared, 429,000 additional homes would be required to meet the needs of existing separate households. Still unmet would be the needs of the 149,000 married couples and the 104,000 lone parents who were part of other households.

Since 1979, the rise in interest rates and economic recession have reduced the production of houses for the market; public housing development has been particularly affected by the government's policy of cutting public expenditure since housing was planned to bear three-quarters of the cutback, although it accounted for only 7 percent of public expenditure 1979–80.

The year 1981 was the first peacetime year during the past half century when the annual net increase in stock fell behind the number of dwellings required to accommodate the net increase in households. From 1979 to 1982, public housing completions fell by half and market housing fell by 14 percent. The poor are bearing the brunt of the recession, both by further limitation of access to sound housing and

Table 2.2 Dwellings and households in England, 1977 (in thousands).

	December 1977
Dwellings	
Total	17,224
Vacant and second homes	729
Shared	199
Households	
Total	16,824
Multiperson households sharing	187
One-person households sharing	341
Margin of dwellings over households (crude surplus)	400
Concealed households	
Married couple	149
Lone parent	104

Source: Great Britain, Department of the Environment, *National dwelling and housing survey,* 1978.

by reduction of income through unemployment. In particular, young married couples who cannot afford to become homeowners will have to continue to share accommodation.

Qualitative need

Space standards

New building in both public and private sectors for the last fifty years has been concentrated on three-bedroom houses, but the latest information relating households by number of people to the number of bedrooms in the dwellings they occupy showed that only 17 percent of households consisted of four people and 7 percent consisted of five people in 1977. Consequently there was a shortage of accommodation with less than or more than three bedrooms (figure 2.1).

There is particularly a shortage of small dwellings on the market. Only about three percent of home owners' accommodation in 1977 was in one-bedroom dwellings (DOE, 1978a). A small dwelling costs more per square foot because it has to contain all the plumbing services and outside walls are in greater proportion to the overall space. Space standards per person in a one-person dwelling must necessarily be higher than for larger households. Nevertheless, young single

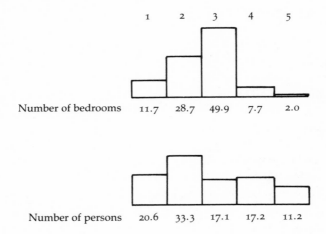

Figure 2.1 Households by number of bedrooms and persons, in percentages (*Great Britain*, Department of the Environment, National Housing and Dwelling Survey, 1978).

people who have had good jobs for a few years can afford to buy small homes; their difficulty is finding them. Single people who need independent accommodation but who cannot afford to buy and do not qualify for public housing have no alternative but private rentals which, when furnished, are the worst value for money spent on housing. Two-thirds of households' accommodation of privately rented dwellings in 1977 was occupied by single people, mostly under sixty years of age (DOE, 1978a).

Since 1977, the mismatch between household size and dwelling size has worsened in the private sector because the completion of one-bedroom dwellings has not kept up with the increase of one-person households and because more small elderly households are occupying family houses. The public sector makes better provision for small households; with about a third of the housing stock, it provides about half of the one-bedroom dwellings, mostly occupied by elderly households.

Nearly 10 percent of the whole housing stock in 1978 had four or more bedrooms and 11 percent of the households had five or more people. Nevertheless, a quarter of the large families did not have enough bedrooms (DOE, 1978a). Many of the large homes on the market are beyond the means of large families. Neither can the needs of large families be met in the public sector, where dwellings with four or more bedrooms amount to only about 6 percent of the total (DOE, 1978a).

In general, space standards have greatly improved in the past few decades. The average number of persons per room in England and Wales was .91 in 1921 and it fell to .58 by 1971 (Housing Policy Review part I, table 1.16). The proportion of households living at densities of about 1.5 persons per room was 11.5 percent in 1931 and 1.4 percent in 1971 (DOE, 1977 part I, table 1.13).

Over the past century, working-class and middle-class homes have become much less differentiated by size (Burnett, 1981). Middle-class families no longer accommodate servants, and they need labor-saving homes. Working-class people no longer generally have to cook, eat, live, bathe, and dry the washing in one room, nor do their children have to share bedrooms with parents, lodgers, or adult siblings of the opposite sex. But the improvement of average space standards in the past two decades has not resulted from more spacious accommodation for families but from the greater number of one- and two-person households and from the occupation of family housing by elderly small households.

Increase in the size of homes since the 19th century has been due mostly to the enlargement of nonhabitable areas such as garages, storage spaces, utility rooms, and bathrooms (Hole, 1965). Until 1950 there was little improvement in the overcrowding of large families (Hole and Pountney, 1971), and they are still the most overcrowded of all households.

Qualitative needs by type of household

Family households. The aspiration to own a home for raising a family is high. A 1977 survey showed that, of young people under twenty years of age, 80 percent expected to become home owners (BMRB, 1977). Home ownership is the most common and lucrative form of saving when there is inflation, and the independence it gives is also valued. The type of family household which has the highest proportion of home owners is the household consisting of three or more adults (56.5 percent), followed by the small family with children and two to four people (53.2 percent) and the large family with children and four or more people (51.9 percent) (DOE, 1978a).

Married women who are not gainfully employed have been found to spend 6.5 hours a day in housework, employed married women spend 4.3 hours, and married men 1.4 hours. Wives spend more time outside the home and husbands spend more time in the home and on household chores than they used to (Young and Willmott, 1973). Both expect modern homes and equipment to relieve them from household drudgery. Coal fires have been replaced by gas and electric heating, and central heating in households increased from 37 percent in 1972 to 60 percent in 1982 (OPCS, 1983a), though fireplaces are again much in demand. But private developers often lack the skill to design small houses which fulfill occupiers' needs for an easily run, comfortable, and pleasant home. For instance, kitchens are often too small to accommodate all the labor-saving domestic machinery now available; they are not designed to facilitate the serving and clearing of family meals, nor do they allow an adult preparing meals to keep an eye on small children in play areas. Living areas are not designed to allow different activities within the household to take place simultaneously —in particular to allow an alternative to watching television (MHLG, 1961).

With government encouragement, volume builders have recently developed low-cost "starter" homes for families with low incomes, who have until now been expected to rely on public housing. These homes do not usually have amenities such as central heating and they are much smaller than those built previously for first-time buyers. For instance, a two-bedroom starter home could have floor space of about 50 m^2 (538 sq. ft.), only about half the floor space of a three-bedroom semi-detached house which would have been bought by first-time buyers in the 1960s. Starter homes are tolerable if their occupiers do not stay too long on this first rung of the ownership ladder, but the recession which caused the reduction in space and amenity standards may reduce or remove earnings, with the result that a couple are trapped in a small starter home. When they start raising a family they will be much constrained by lack of space for normal activities, for the usual inventory of furniture, and for storage. When times are more prosperous and families can move to homes which meet their needs, starter homes will make a useful contribution to a better balanced supply of houses by increasing the proportion of small dwellings.

Another method which has been introduced to help families and other households to become homeowners is "shared ownership," administered through nonprofit housing associations which until now have been funded by central government through the Housing Corporation to provide an alternative form of subsidized housing to local authorities. A "sharing" owner gets a mortgage for part of the cost of a house (from 25 percent), pays rent on the rest and is expected to eventually "staircase" up to full ownership. The space and amenity standards in houses built for shared ownership compare favorably with those of starter homes.

The local housing authorities' main aim has been to provide sound housing for parents who cannot afford market prices for reasonably good housing so they can bring up the next generation. The family households with the highest proportion renting from local authorities are large families and small families (39.5 percent each) followed by large adult households (32.5 percent) (DOE, 1978a).

Most of the houses which local authorities have provided for families are admirable. There are now no mandatory space standards, but a modern three-bedroom local authority house usually has a floor space of about 85 m^2 (915 sq. ft.). Many parents, however, have not found the high flats which have been allocated to them by local authorities suitable for bringing up children. Although only 33 percent of local authorities' dwellings are flats, the proportion in London reaches 66 percent (DOE, 1977, part III, table VII.6). Thus, in London and some other cities, local authorities cannot allocate dwellings to families with children without putting them into flats.

In addition to strains which are caused by dangers to and constraints on children (Littlewood and Tinker, 1981), families have suffered from the poor physical condition of some blocks of flats due to building defects and lack of maintenance funds. These conditions, together with local authorities' allocation policies (Karn, 1982), have sometimes led to vandalism and the stigmatization of estates. About one-fourth of a million dwellings, 5 percent of local authority stock, mostly in high-rise projects, are difficult to let.

Flats which are unpopular with families are now being turned over to students, other young people, and the elderly wherever possible, and they are being sold to developers for rehabilitation and sale on the market. Some blocks have been physically and socially rehabilitated for use by council tenants, including some with children. In some areas, local management has been restored. The cooperation of estate managers, workers, and tenants in planning and carrying out improvements has been promoted by consultants commissioned by the Department of the Environment in pilot projects (Power, 1982). Several blocks were too far gone for rehabilitation, however, and they have had to be demolished. Altogether, hundreds of millions of pounds have been wasted on public housing intended to eliminate housing shortages quickly and cheaply but without due regard for sound methods of construction and management, consumer needs and preferences, or cost (Ash, 1980).

Single people of working age. The tenure preference of people under sixty who were living alone in 1978 was 70 percent for home ownership, 21 percent for renting from a council, and 3 percent for renting from a private landlord (DOE, 1982a). At that time, 36.3 percent of these households were homeowners, 23 percent rented from a council, and 38.2 percent rented from a private landlord (DOE, 1978a). From 1977 to 1981, the proportion of never-married men heading households in England who owned their own homes increased from 22 percent to 32 percent, and never-married women owners increased from 13 percent to 17 percent. In comparison to other owner-occupiers, a higher proportion of the never-married owner-occupiers with mortgages who are under thirty occupy a larger proportion of flats and a smaller proportion of detached and semi-detached houses (DOE, 1982a).

The access by single people to ownership of small dwellings which they can afford is now being extended by volume builders who have identified a market for small "solo" or "studio" flats from 27 m^2 (291 sq. ft.) and are including such small dwellings in their starter home developments. Some one-person flats are sold furnished; such people as male divorcees and mobile young people do not have or want to acquire furniture.

Twenty-three percent of the households made up of single persons under sixty live in council dwellings and they occupy 5 percent of council stock (DOE, 1978a). Access of such single people to council housing is limited because the usual allocation systems give higher priority to families and to elderly single people. Also, single people can only gain the right to be housed if they are homeless in very exceptional circumstances. Consequently, there is an acute problem of lack of accommodation for those who are single and homeless in London and in a few other cities. The available hostels cannot cope with the demand and some are as dreadful as in the time of Dickens.

Most single homeless people are not "down and outs" but simply people who cannot find a place to live (Drake, O'Brien, and Biebuyck, 1981). More single-person households under sixty years (11 percent) share accommodation than any other type of household (DOE, 1978a), and they would prefer not to. In a survey of working age people who live as one-person households in shared accommodation, 46 percent said that they definitely wanted a self-contained dwelling, 28 percent would prefer it, and only 24 percent preferred to share (DOE, 1982a).

Housing associations allocated 11 percent of their accommodation to single persons under sixty in 1977 (DOE, 1978a), and the proportion is probably higher now. They provide small hostels for the minority who need some support, such as young people who have been brought up in children's homes and people with mental and physical problems. Sometimes these hostels are linked to groups of small dwellings, to which hostel residents can eventually move. Nearly half of privately rented furnished accommodation is occupied by single-person households under sixty. This housing category also contains most of the shared dwellings. Local authorities, housing associations, and cooperatives also provide cluster flats, following a DOE project demonstrating how the various needs of single people can be met (DOE 1971, 1974, 1978). Furnished and cluster flats have proved difficult for local authorities to manage.

The proportion of young single people who are tenants of private landlords has decreased, while the proportion in council and housing association dwellings has increased (DOE, 1982a). Some local authorities have had surplus or hard to rent housing which they have allocated to single people; some have decreased their discrimination against the single, although they do not have sufficient suitable stock to meet demand and insufficient means to build new homes for all the singles in need. Housing associations have been increasing their accommodation for singles, and grant-aided housing cooperatives have grown to about 300 in England, with about 8,000 dwellings and 1,400 members. Their members are mostly young single people, and over half their property is old housing which has been rehabilitated (Housing Corporation, 1981). A very few of these grant-aided co-ops are full communes, but there were about 100 small independent communes in Britain in the seventies (Rigby, 1974).

The elderly. The elderly have a much better prospect than young adults of access to local authority and housing association dwellings. Elderly people who need housing are given priority in the allocation of local authority dwellings and in the provision of accommodation to the homeless, and large charitable housing associations have concentrated on providing housing for the elderly. About half of the households in housing association dwellings are elderly single-person households or couples (Bird and Palmer, 1979); 43 percent of the former and 33 percent of the latter live in local authority dwellings.

At present, the proportion of elderly households who are home-owners is not particularly high. Thirty-nine percent of single-person households are homeowners, whether they are under or over sixty. The general increase in the proportion of homeowners is working its way up the age groups and is likely to result eventually in higher rates of ownership among the elderly. The proportion of homeowners among households consisting of two adults under sixty is now 64 percent, and the proportion of couples with at least one adult aged sixty is 55 percent (OPCS, 1983a). The latter have elderly members who are on the average younger than the single-person elderly households.

The possession of a house with sufficient market value to allow an exchange without sacrifice of quality, and possibly with enhancement of income, gives elderly owners freedom to move into an apartment or a smaller house or to a better environment. There is a movement of the elderly to seaside resorts and particularly to the south coast, the "Costa Geriatrica," where there is the largest concentration of the elderly in the country.

When elderly people cannot trade in their homes to advantage and when their incomes are low, homeownership can bring problems. One problem is that they cannot easily unlock some of the capital in their homes in order to supplement their incomes. A more serious problem is when they occupy old houses in bad condition which they cannot afford to repair or heat adequately. The householders who live in property of unsatisfactory condition tend to be poor, elderly and long-established. Even with publicly funded grants, 40 percent of the owner-occupiers would have had to contribute a sum equal to their annual income to achieve a satisfactory standard in their homes (DOE, 1978b).

When incomes are low, adequate heating may be more than elderly households can afford, and then the danger of hypothermia is at its greatest. Government statistics have shown that between October 1981 and March 1982 646 people died from causes associated with hypothermia, and 85 percent of these were aged sixty-five or older. It is believed that these statistics underestimate the actual extent of hypothermia (Age Concern, 1983).

Several local authorities are making special efforts to help the elderly poor improve and insulate their homes, adding loans to the public grants already available, but local authorities' staff levels are now strictly controlled, and they often cannot afford to allow suitably sympathetic staff to spend the several hours necessary with an old person to explain what can be done and to help with the implementation of the agreed package for home improvement.

Voluntary organizations, building societies and housing associations are now undertaking projects for the improvement of the homes and financial condition of the elderly. These special projects usually uncover some horrific housing conditions among the elderly, showing that their basic housing needs are still not fully met. Such projects help the elderly borrow money for repairs and improvements on the security of their homes, obtain all the public grants they are entitled to, and make arrangements for contractors to undertake improvement work. In some cases, incomes can be increased through "home income plans," based on taking out a mortgage. Housing associations now also offer a new small leasehold home for the elderly homeowner who wants to move.[1] The proceeds of the sale of the homeowner's previous home go toward the cost of the lease.

The increasing proportion of the elderly led to the prospect of much higher public expenditure on institutional care for the elderly, which they themselves want to avoid if possible and which is much more costly than providing easily run and easily heated housing. A preferable alternative has been developed by local authorities and promoted by the Department of the Environment: "sheltered" housing provides individual small dwellings, now usually self-contained and normally in the form of one-story houses or apartments which are linked by walkways or corridors. A warden lives on the project in a dwelling connected by an alarm system or intercom with each dwelling. There is a common room for lunch clubs and social activities and a common garden. The warden sees that residents get the services they need, and promotes mutual support and social activity among the residents. The warden and other staff are now being trained to avoid maternalism and to respect and promote the independence of the residents. The number of sheltered dwellings increased rapidly from 35,000 in 1963 to more than 300,000 in 1979. The main benefit felt by the residents is from modern, comfortable, warm, and easily run dwellings (Butler, 1981).

Housing associations supply about 20 percent of the sheltered dwellings, and most of the rest are supplied by local authorities. Sheltered housing is now being developed for the market. One developer has found that his initial projects, on the south coast, went so well that he is building sheltered housing for sale throughout the country. Sheltered leasehold homes for the elderly are being provided by housing associations.

Since there is not enough sheltered housing to meet needs and since many elderly people do not want to move, a few local authorities are developing sheltered conditions for the elderly in their existing homes. A district warden and intercom or alarm system are provided. The warden visits the elderly who wish to come into the project and ensures that they get all the public services to which they are entitled.

Conclusions and policy options

During the past decade, an accelerated rate of household formation has been accompanied by an economic recession which has affected the output of both the housing market and the public sector. Between 1976 and 1982, the annual output of dwellings dropped to almost half, and the condition of the existing stock sharply deteriorated.

Both the Labour governments (1974–79) and the Conservative governments (1979—) have relied on the private market to provide for a substantial proportion of the need for additional dwellings. Housing output for the market fell while each of the parties was in power. High interest rates and economic insecurity inhibited both supply and demand, despite the advantage of owning inflation-proof residential property. The governments of both parties provided tax relief on mortgage interest which mitigated the burden of high interest rates according to the borrowers' means (the greater the means, the higher the proportion of tax relief on borrowing).

Since 1974, both Labour and Conservative governments have cut public expenditure on housing as part of a general policy to restrain overall public expenditure, but the Conservative governments have been much more committed to the reduction of public housing and the extension of homeownership than previous Conservative governments. Between 1979 and 1983, public housing expenditure was cut by 50 percent and another substantial cut is expected. Annual public sector completions fell to just over a third of the 1975–79 average.

The policy option adopted by the current government is to proceed in the direction taken by the United States (Karn, 1983): to rely on the private market as much as possible and to reduce public housing to a small fraction of the housing stock. This policy is being applied not only through reduction of public expenditure but also by sale of council dwellings, by raising council rents to encourage movement into homeownership, and by starter and shared ownership schemes.

This policy will be much more difficult to apply in Britain than in the United States, since there is a much larger section of the population in Britain which is on or near the poverty line and which cannot afford to buy a home. As unemployment has increased so have rent arrears and mortgage arrears. There are already serious problems of deterioration of the housing stock which arise from the lack of means of homeowners to keep their homes in good repair.

The Exchequer is already forgoing much more in tax relief than the public funds devoted to housing directly. Homeowners are helped with their mortgage interest payments by welfare allowances when their income is inadequate. If the cost of homeownership increases much more, homeowners will have to be included in the housing benefit scheme, which at present rebates rent according to income. If the full housing market option is followed in Britain under present circumstances, the state might have to devote more funds and tax relief for the provision of essential shelter than for provision of funds for public housing, which in fact shows an overall real rate of return of 2.5 percent, higher than the return on gilt-edged securities (Kilroy, 1982).

The political effects of any ruthless application of the market option could well result in policy modification. There are differences in housing policy within each political party as well as between the parties. Labour councils in areas which impeded tenants' rights to buy their council homes at heavy discounts proved an electoral liability. National Labour leaders have in fact never opposed homeownership in principle, but they emphasize the need for sufficient public rentals for those who cannot afford to buy. Labour leaders are now formulating a more forthright commitment to the support of homeownership with an eye to the next election, while a radical section of the Labour party looks forward to a time when publicly owned rentals can be accessible without waiting lists and when applicants can choose the dwellings they want. But if personal incomes are unlikely to be sufficient in the forseeable future to make a much higher proportion of market housing a realistic prospect, public resources are also unlikely to be sufficient to provide and maintain a public sector where housing can be allocated according to need and at the same time be available to satisfy general demand.

The most feasible policy option is to return to a more effective form of the pre-1979 consensual mixed private and public housing economy with a flexible balance of public and private housing according to different patterns of demand and need in different parts of the country. Renting and owning are alternatives which appeal differentially according to income, stage in family cycle, and life-styles, and any state support of housing should be equitably distributed between them. More effective use could be made of public housing funds if subsidies and tax reliefs did not go to people who do not need them. Also, grants for the improvement of private property should be more discriminating and concentrated on the worst property which is worth saving before it reaches the point of no return.

In public housing, bureaucratic control of details of housing management should be further slackened to allow more control by tenants through local associations and cooperatives. Surplus revenues from council rents, which are now used to keep down local taxes on property, should be pooled so that they can be used where housing need is greatest.

The argument that Britain can afford neither to maintain its existing stock of housing in reasonable repair, nor to build sufficient new dwellings to house new households does not have a sound economic base. Britain is still one of the wealthiest countries in the world, despite its failure to match the progress of a few other countries. Investment in housing in 1978 was already comparatively low, 3.2 percent of the British gross domestic product. France was investing 6.5 percent and Germany 5.9 percent; in Europe and North America, only Portugal had a lower level of investment than Britain (United Nations, 1978). Public expenditure on housing amounted to only 7 percent of all state expenditure in 1979–80. If Britain returned to higher levels of public investment and expenditure, and resources were better directed as suggested, means would be sufficient to prevent the deterioration of the household/dwelling ratio and to maintain the old housing stock in reasonable condition.

3 | United States Rental Housing
Practices Affecting Families
with Children: Hard Times for Youth

Robert W. Marans and
Mary Ellen Colten

Abstract. This chapter presents the results of a national study of exclusionary rental policies which affect children. Data from a national survey of renters and the owners or managers of their rental units document the nature, extent, and magnitude of exclusionary policies, the attitudes of renters toward living near children, and the effect that these policies have had on American families. The study shows that exclusionary practices against children have increased in the past decade. The findings suggest that exclusionary practices pose a real problem for many American families.

Introduction

Throughout the 1970s, rising construction costs and high interest rates in the United States made homeownership an unattainable goal for large numbers of young families and single-parent households. While some families have moved in with parents or other family members, most have entered the rental housing market. During the same period, there has been an increase in the numbers of families and individuals without children—e.g., elderly persons, divorced and widowed individuals, and voluntarily childless couples—many of whom do not want the responsibilities and burdens of homeownership.

As the demand and competition for rental housing increase while its supply remains relatively constant, landlords can afford to cater to the interests of certain groups and to exclude others. Older persons, except for the very poor, represent one group that is being catered to by residential developers, housing managers, and landlords, whereas families with children have often been targeted for exclusion from the rental housing market.

This chapter summarizes the arguments set forth by proponents of restrictive practices in the rental housing market which impact on households with children. It then reviews several studies conducted in selected communities throughout the United States that attempt to document exclusionary policies and the experiences of affected parties. Next, national data are presented on the nature and extent of restrictive rental practices and the attitudes of renters and apartment managers. The chapter concludes with a plea for periodic and systematic monitoring of housing practices as they affect families with children.

Background

Local studies and anecdotal evidence suggest that renters with children are often confronted with exclusionary or discriminatory policies affecting children. These policies may exclude children; may limit their numbers, ages and sexes; may restrict families with children to certain buildings in an apartment complex or to certain floors of a building; or may limit families by charging higher rents or requiring a larger damage deposit if children are present in the household. Opponents of exclusionary policies contend that these policies place a burden on families with children, that such families are forced to look longer for housing, to pay higher rents, and to live in less desirable neighborhoods in lower quality housing units.

Unlike that for race and sex discrimination, no national legislation exists which prohibits discrimination against children. Only a handful of states have legislation on their books which prohibits child exclusion, and most cities do not have ordinances to prevent it. The policies that do exist often are enforced weakly, if at all. Renters may not even be aware of them, and government officials may not be available to pursue complaints; when complaints are pursued, punishment imposed on violators is minimal.

Those who protest exclusionary policies assert that, while landlords ought to be able to protect their own interests and those of their present tenants, exclusion of all families with children constitutes true discrimination, since it is based on the assumption that all families with children are undesirable.

Exclusionary practices affect not only the families with children but many such practices also have deleterious consequences for the community. For example, an ordinance in Santa Monica, California, prohibiting child exclusion practices notes that "arbitrary discrimination against families with children leads to the decline of neighborhoods, closure of schools, and reduction of recreational services." Similarly, a study in Atlanta, Georgia, concluded that exclusionary policies have a serious impact on school enrollments and racial balance (Reid et al., 1979).

Indeed, critics of exclusionary policies have asserted that enactment of these policies is motivated, at least in part, by efforts to practice racial discrimination. Since minority families with children are overrepresented in the rental housing market relative to their proportion of the population, minorities are disproportionately affected by exclusionary policies concerning children. The evidence suggests that these policies may also serve to further concentrate minorities in certain areas of cities. Local studies in Dallas and Atlanta, in fact, have indicated that discrimination against children is associated with racial patterns. Neighborhoods in those cities which are occupied by predominantly minority group members have a significantly smaller proportion of units which exclude children than do neighborhoods which are predominantly white (Greene, 1978; Reid, 1979).

It is also agreed that the failure to prohibit discrimination against children constitutes a legal loophole which allows sex discrimination since female-headed households are also overrepresented in the rental housing market. Ironically, the data suggest that female heads of household are, in fact, very reliable tenants (Anderson-Khlief, 1979).

Others have noted that local ordinances often encourage the exclusion of children. Some municipalities have ordinances which restrict the number of bedrooms allowed in multiple unit dwellings and, at the same time, enforce codes which limit the number of persons who may occupy a unit of a given size. Calvan (1979) has suggested that these policies are designed to control educational spending in certain areas. Such policies often force families to either rent larger, more costly units, to seek more spacious housing with lower rents and of lower quality, or to purchase very small dwelling units of inferior quality. In effect, the policies constitute a governmental value judgment based on the belief that less crowding in lower quality housing is preferable to more crowding in higher quality units. It is obviously debatable whether or not this is an appropriate area for governmental intervention.

Landlords argue that almost two-thirds of rental households have no children and thus only one-third of rental units need be available to families with children. While this makes sense in theory, it does not necessarily work well in practice, since young families, recently married couples, and single parents from recently disrupted marriages are more likely to be presently searching for housing than older child-free persons. In the face of exclusionary practices, these groups with children will be able to rent only a portion of the already small number of vacant units.

Still another side of the picture is the perspective of owners and managers of rental housing who argue that children are destructive, and therefore renting to families can result in higher maintenance and insurance costs. They also point out that elderly tenants and others with no children in the household have a right to live removed from the noise, activity, and clutter of children and often exercise that right by deliberately selecting units in places which exclude children. However, members of households without children have been notably absent from the debate over this issue, so landlords have taken the role of expressing their presumed preferences. In fact, there has been no systematically collected information about the actual desires of families without children and the extent to which exclusionary policies play a role in their selection of housing.

Local area studies

Several community studies have attempted to assess the extent and impact of exclusionary policies. The Fair Housing Project (Ashford and Eston, 1979) examined child exclusion rates and types of age restrictions in five California cities: Fresno, Los Angeles, San Diego, San Jose, and San Francisco. By surveying rental listings in major newspapers, data were obtained on rent levels, number of bedrooms, whether the apartment was furnished or unfurnished, and the number of units in the building. San Francisco has a local ordinance prohibiting exclusion of families with children and thus the exclusionary rates there were comparatively low. In the four other cities, however, between half and three-fourths of all units surveyed would not permit children of any age. When size of the rental unit was held constant, median rents were higher for places which accepted children. Census and local housing surveys and plans revealed that families with children in those cities are more often inadequately housed, an effect which is particularly significant for female-headed and minority households. In another study conducted in Dallas, researchers found that more than half of the apartments listed in the yellow pages of the telephone directory exclude children and that another 12 percent restrict the ages and number of children allowed (Greene, 1978).

The California and Texas studies focused on a particular segment of the rental market, i.e., advertised apartments or apartments listed in the phone directory. Since a significant portion (one-third) of rental units are single-family homes and many rental units are duplexes or in small buildings and are unlikely to be listed in phone directories, the studies most likely explored the situation primarily for larger apartment buildings or complexes.

A third study in six metropolitan areas of the United States administered questionnaires to people who experienced problems because of restrictive rental housing policies (Greene and Blake, 1980). Respondents were persons who voluntarily answered a public service announcement on television and radio and reported their experiences with restrictive practices. The 554 respondents were a diverse group, but female heads of households and minorities were particularly burdened.

Finally, a recent study in metropolitan Cleveland (Benson, Jacobson, and Margulis, 1981) used survey data to estimate the proportion of rental units which restricted families with children. Among the non-elderly rental housing units, more than 20 percent placed restrictions on families with children, whereas 28 percent of all rental units in the region had some type of restriction associated with it.

These studies were prepared in growing or established communities where the rental housing market was tight and the problems for families with children were particularly noticeable and salient. While the data strongly suggest that exclusionary practices may be an obstacle for many families with children in specific locations, no systematic data were available until recently on the extent to which this is a nationwide phenomena.

A national survey

During the winter of 1980 a survey was conducted by the Survey Research Center of the University of Michigan in order to determine for the nation as a whole the extent and nature of policies and restrictions which limit the ability of families with children to find suitable rental housing. Although the study was motivated in part by the results of local area studies, it was not intended to confirm or refute their findings. Rather its purpose was to identify the magnitude of the problem nationally and to examine factors which might be associated with different policies.

The survey addressed four major questions: (*a*) What are the rental policies that restrict children and how extensive are they? (*b*) What types of rental units are most likely to be restricted? (*c*) Are restrictive policies increasing? and (*d*) To what degree are the housing opportunities of families with children limited by various restrictive policies?

The study also explored the extent to which families with children feel that they experienced discrimination or difficulty in finding suitable housing because they have children. Data were produced on the extent to which renters without children, including older people, seek and demand rental housing which excludes or limits children and how managers justify restrictive policies. The attitudes and preferences of tenants and managers were also examined in order to ascertain the perceived basis for policies and to estimate the impact of possible legislative change.

Procedures

The data were obtained through telephone interviews with 1,007 renters in a national probability sample of rental housing units and 629 owners or managers of those units.[1] The sample of rental units was obtained through a selection of randomly generated telephone numbers which first screened for housing units and for units which were occupied by renters. The sample of managers was obtained by seeking information on how to contact the managers from the renters themselves.

A number of characteristics of the sample of renters should be noted when considering the data about restrictive policies and their impact on families with children. Over two-thirds of the sample (68 percent) have no children living in the household. Thus, restrictive policies are directed at about one-third of potential renters. Of those renters with children, four in ten (42 percent) have only one child living with them and an additional one-third (38 percent) have two children. Thus, over three-fourths of renters with children have no more than two children in the household.

Relative to their proportion in the total population, minority group members are overrepresented in the renter population. More than one-fourth of the respondents were nonwhite, and these minority group members were more likely than white renters to have children in the household. Female-headed households are also overrepresented. More than one-third (37 percent) of all the households with children in the sample are female-headed. It should also be noted that the income of renters is more concentrated in the lower ranges; over 50 percent of the respondents reported total household income below $14,000. Thus, their rental options are constrained by income.

One-fifth (22 percent) of the renters in this sample live in single-family dwellings, six in ten (60 percent) live in apartment buildings or flats containing two or more units, and the remainder live in duplexes, townhouses, condominiums, or rental units above garages or in commercial establishments.[2] Families with children are more likely than families without children to rent single-family homes.

Some of the data which follow are presented from the perspectives of both managers and renters; other parts of the data are based on reports from one group or another. Occasionally, there are discrepancies between the reports of managers and reports of renters. In part, the discrepancies are attributable to two factors. First, manager's data do not exist for every renter in the sample. Second, some renters are unaware of and thus tend to underreport the extent of policies which exclude or restrict children.

Nature and extent of policies and restrictions concerning children

There are numerous management policies and restrictions that limit the ability of families with children to find suitable rental housing. In addition to policies prohibiting the renting of units by families with children in what commonly has been referred to as "adult only" apartments and housing developments, there are restrictions or limitations on the ages of children allowed in units, the maximum number of children or family members, the sharing of a bedroom by children of the opposite sex, and the buildings in complexes or floors in buildings (i.e., the location) where children are permitted. For each of these restrictions, variations can be found. For example, age restrictions can limit children over a specified age, e.g., no children over two or no children over twelve years of age, or they can limit children under a specific age varying from two or three (no preschoolers) to seventeen or eighteen years of age (no school-aged children). Often, however, age restrictions are not clearly defined and are left to the discretion of the building managers or rental agents.

It should be noted parenthetically that a multiplicity of restrictions could exist and be reported by any single respondent. Nonetheless, the decision was made that for each respondent reporting more than one limitation, only one was recorded. The recorded limitation was based on severity. For example, restricting children under a certain age was viewed as more severe (and therefore recorded) than limiting the number of children allowed or where within a complex they could live.

In order to ascertain the extent to which these policies exist throughout the United States, the study initially focused on the issue from the perspective of the renters contacted in our national sample. About one in five (18 percent) said that there was a policy or restriction governing their rental unit or the rental units around them if they were in an apartment building or complex. Over half of the renters reporting restrictive policies said families with children were not allowed to live in their building or complex. This means that among our total sample of renters, one in nine (11 percent) said they lived in single-family homes, apartment buildings, or complexes which excluded children. Additionally, about 8 percent reported living in places that accepted children but with limitations on either their age, the number allowed, or where within the building or complex they could live. The remaining 82 percent of the renters said they lived in buildings or complexes which permit children without any restrictions on their age, number, or location.

Another way of considering the magnitude of restrictive practices in the rental housing market is to examine the number of rental units affected by policies or limitations on children. The total number of units represented by the 636 managers is nearly 79,000. About one-fourth (26 percent) of these units exclude families with children. Fully half of the units (50 percent) are places which accept children but impose at least one of the following limitations: limits on the number of children (46 percent of all units), limits on the ages of children (64 percent), forbidding the sharing of a bedroom by children of the opposite sex (21 percent), or limitations on where within the building or complex families with children can live (10 percent). Managers of the remainder of the units (25 percent) said they accept families with children without any special limitations. Thus, only one-fourth of rental housing units are available (with no restrictions) to families with children.

Factors affecting differences in policies

In order to target potential solutions to the problem, it is important to know what factors are associated with the likelihood that a rental unit will have restrictions concerning children. Specifically, the study addressed whether restrictive policies tend to vary with the type of dwelling (e.g., single-family home or apartment), size of the unit, racial composition of the neighborhood, urbanicity of the setting, rent of the unit, quality of the neighborhood, size of the building or complex in which the unit is situated, age of the building, and vacancy rate of the building. A summary of the policy differences for units which vary on these dimensions appears below.

Policy differences by type of dwelling. Predictably, single-family homes are much more likely than units in apartments to accept children without restrictions. While less than one-fifth (18 percent) of units in apartments accept children with no restrictions, over one-half (53 percent) of rented single-family homes are available with no restrictions on children.

Policy differences by size of unit. Efficiency and one-bedroom units in apartment buildings or complexes are more likely than units with more than one bedroom to be affected by no-children policies. As can be seen in table 3.1, 4 percent of all rental units with more than two bedrooms are situated in buildings or complexes which exclude families with children. Large units are also more likely to be situated in places which accept children with no restrictions.

It should be noted that, when we take into account the number of places which accept children but prohibit them in units of specific sizes, the percentages of units not accepting children will be greater than those shown in the first row of table 3.1. As a way of understanding the magnitude of these changes, we first asked managers who accepted families with children but with limitations on their number, "Does the number of children allowed depend on the number of bedrooms in the unit?" Virtually, all (96 percent) of the managers answered affirmatively. They were then asked, "How many children would you allow in your __-bedroom unit?" This question was asked

Table 3.1 Percentage of all rental units having policies/restrictions on children, by size of unit.

Policy	Efficiency	One-bedroom	Two-bedroom	Three-or-more bedroom	All
				Size of rental unit	
No children accepted	35%	41%	20%	4%	26%
Children accepted with limitations	45	41	54	58	50
Children accepted with no limitations	20	18	26	38	24
Estimated number of units	4,300	26,400	31,700	7,500	78,600
Number of managers	138	355	364	166	492

for each size unit in the building or complex. More than four in ten one-bedroom units in buildings/complexes where the number of children is limited are not available to families with children. At the same time, about 1 percent of the two-bedroom units and 5 percent of the three-bedroom units in places with number limitations are not available to families with children. When these units are added to units where children are not accepted as shown in table 3.1, the percentages increase. Among one-bedroom units, 59 percent rather than 42 percent are not available to families with children, while 24 percent rather than 20 percent of two-bedroom units are not available to families with children.

Policy differences by vacancy rates. There are no systematic relationships between the vacancy rates in apartment buildings and complexes and the extent to which restrictive policies on children exist. Buildings/complexes with vacancy rates of 10 percent or more are just as likely to prohibit children as buildings/complexes with no vacancies. There is also no consistent relationship between vacancy rate and the proportion of units permitting children but with limitations on their numbers, age, and location. This finding runs counter to claims that low vacancy rates allow landlords to impose restrictive policies.

Policy differences by size of community. Overall, the size of the community where rental units are located (large urban, small urban, or small town) does not significantly influence the proportion of units in places with restrictions concerning children. Similarly, there are no significant differences between cities and suburbs in the proportion of units where families with children are excluded or where limitations are imposed on them.

Policy differences by racial composition of neighborhoods and apartment building complex. The extent to which restrictive policies exist does vary, depending on the racial composition of neighborhoods as reported by renters. Units in predominantly white neighborhoods are more likely than rental units in predominantly black neighborhoods to restrict families with children (29 percent compared to 18 percent). In racially mixed neighborhoods, 25 percent of the units are not available to families with children.

Policy differences by housing and neighborhood quality. It has been suggested that policies/restrictions concerning children are most likely to be found in higher quality neighborhoods, and therefore prospective tenants with children are forced to seek housing in neighborhoods of lower quality. In order to test this supposition, the quality of neighborhoods within which rental units were located was assessed. Two indicators of neighborhood quality were used: one dealt with overall neighborhood satisfaction as reported by renters, and the second covered the extent to which selected neighborhood conditions were problematical for renters. At the same time the renters' housing satisfaction was used as an indicator of housing quality.

When each of these quality indicators was examined for rental units in buildings/complexes with and without restrictions, no relationships were found. The assessments of housing and neighborhood quality by people living in places which do not rent to families with children are comparable to assessments by people in places which accept children without limitations imposed on them.

When these same relationships were examined for rental units in large cities and in inner city locations, there were also no significant differences. The data do not support the contention made by many that rental units which allow children are of poorer quality and are located in low-quality neighborhoods.

Policy differences by age of building/complex. Another indicator of residential quality is the age of the building in which people live. No-children policies are most prevalent among newer (higher quality) units built during the 1970s. Whereas one in three units built since 1970 are in buildings/complexes not accepting families with children, about one in five units in places built earlier have restrictions. The oldest units (i.e., those built prior to 1960) are least likely to have any policy or restriction adversely affecting families with children. Thus residential quality, as reflected by the age of the building, tends to be associated with the presence of restrictive policies against children.

Policy differences by size of building/complex. When the percentage of rental units of two or more bedrooms having no-children policies is examined by size of the building, no systematic relationships are found between size of building and whether or not children are excluded. However, the size of the building or complex is related to the acceptance of children with limitations imposed on them. In particular, the proportion of units affected by number, sex, and location limitations increases as the size of the complex or building increases.

In sum, actual exclusion of children does vary by the type of dwelling, the size of the unit, the age of the unit, and the racial composition of the neighborhood. However, no-children policies do not vary by the vacancy rate of the building, the number of units in the building, the urban nature of the setting, or the perceived quality of the neighborhood.

Changes in exclusionary policies over time

One way of determining whether the prevalence of policies restricting children has been increasing is to compare current rates with estimates of rates at an earlier date. The data covering managers' reports as to when their buildings were constructed and when exclusionary policies went into effect enable us to make this comparison. From the responses of the managers in our sample, it is possible to determine what the policy situation was in 1974 for buildings/complexes which were built by that time. In 1974, children were not allowed in 17 percent of all units, while in 1980 they were excluded in 26 percent of all units. This substantial increase holds for units of all sizes. Since just under 15 percent of all units in our sample were constructed after 1974, policies associated with newly constructed buildings do not acount for the 50 percent increase in the proportion of all units where children are excluded.

Another way of exploring the extent to which policies excluding children have increased over time is to ask whether a policy was instituted after the building was constructed. In other words, was there a period during which a no-children building/complex did not have an exclusionary policy? About one-third (34 percent) of the exclusionary buildings/complexes constructed between 1970 and 1974 did not have no-children policies in effect until 1975 or later, while a similar proportion of buildings constructed before 1970 did not have no-children policies until 1975 or later.

Housing options for families with children

Estimates have been made of the proportion of all units that would be open (or, conversely, not available) to four prototypical families, given the combination of the variety of restrictions imposed by managers. The prototypical families are (a) a family with one child, (b) a family with two children of the same sex, (c) a family with two children not of the same sex, and (d) a family with three children.

A family with one child would be allowed to live in nearly two-thirds (64 percent) of all units. This figure decreases somewhat for families with two children—about half (55 percent) of the units would be open to them. If the two children are not of the same sex, this figure is reduced to 46 percent. Not surprisingly, a family with three children can select from only four in ten (41 percent) units in the rental housing market.

The ultimate consideration of an examination of rental policies regarding children is the impact of these exclusionary policies on the families themselves. It has been suggested that families with children bear the financial burden of exclusionary policies—that, on average, they pay higher rents in order to find a place to house themselves and their children. In fact, when we compare the mean rent paid by all families with children to that paid by all families without children, families with children do, on the average, pay significantly more. When the size of the unit is held constant, however, there is no significant difference between families with or without children in the average amount of rent paid. It is relevant that almost half (47 percent) of the renters without children are people who live alone and that almost nine-tenths (85 percent) of the renters with children have three or more persons in the household. When family size is held constant, there also is no significant difference in the mean rent paid by the two groups. Thus, the higher costs of rental housing for families with children are apparently attributable to the greater number of persons in the household and to their renting larger units rather than to the presence of children per se. It is important to note, however, that this analysis does not address the question of whether families with children occupy units of lower quality and thus, although they pay the same amount as families without children, are getting less for their money.

About half (49 percent) of the respondents with children in the household reported that when they last looked for a place to live, they found places where they wanted to live but were unable to rent because of policies about children. This did not vary according to number of children in the family, family income, sex of head of household, or race/ethnic background of the family. Thus, exclusionary policies concerning children limited the housing options and probably increased the housing hunting time and cost for nearly half of the respondents, regardless of their demographic characteristics or family composition.

The data do not directly support the often-repeated claim that female-headed households and minority groups are more likely to be victims of restrictive practices since, as renters, the groups encountered restrictions in roughly equal percentages. If one is a renter rather than a homeowner, majority group membership does not exempt one from the impact of exclusionary practices and, similarly, minority group membership does not appear to exacerbate the difficulty. However, female-headed households and minority households do experience the effects more often simply because they are more likely to be renters.

Over 40 percent of those who encountered frustration in hunting for a place to rent reported that they had to settle for a less desirable home because they have children. For these families, exclusionary practices affected not only the process of looking but also their ultimate living situation. As a consequence of exclusionary practices, almost one-fifth of all the families with children in the sample are living in homes they consider to be less desirable. The situation is even more extreme for families with three or more children in the household. Almost 30 percent of all the families with three or more children reported that they have had to settle for a less desirable home. Income, sex of head of household, and race/ethnic background do not appear to be related to whether the family has ended up in what they consider to be a less desirable home.

Nearly half of the respondents who encountered exclusionary practices, or 23 percent of *all* renters with children, reported feeling that they settled for a less desirable location as a consequence of restrictive practices against children. This effect is particularly strong for families with three or more children. Almost one-third (32 percent) of all families in the sample with three or more children reported having to live in a less desirable location. A less desirable location may mean a lower quality neighborhood or one which is less convenient for them, e.g., farther from work, family, and transportation. Regardless of the specifics of desirability, these respondents clearly indicated that they had been victims of exclusionary practices.

Similarly, low-income respondents were also more likely to report that they have had to settle for a less desirable location. However, sex of head of household and race/ethnic background do not appear to relate to reports of settling for a less desirable location as a result of exclusionary policies.

In sum, almost half of the families with children reported having encountered disappointment or difficulty in finding housing as a consequence of policies about children, and the situation has a particularly negative impact on families with three or more children and those in the lower income brackets. Families with three or more children have been forced to live in what they see as lower quality homes in less desirable neighborhoods; families with lower incomes have sacrificed neighborhood quality or preference more than housing quality. The policies, then, affect more families than the percent of places having restrictions would lead one to suspect initially. The data suggest that this impact is significant.

Renters' attitudes toward living near children

One of the justifications offered by managers for the promulgation of policies restricting children is that many tenants without children in their own households have a clear preference for living in places where children are excluded. It is often contended that persons without children select housing specifically to avoid children and that they would move if children were allowed to live in their buildings. So it is also an issue of pitting the rights and desires of households with children present against the rights and desires of those with no children. Nearly one-fourth (24 percent) of renters without children in the household did report that they have reasons why they prefer not to live near children. Of the reasons given, noise was by far the most frequently stated, with over half (55 percent) of the mentions falling into this category. Fewer than one-fifth (17 percent) of the responses had to do with destructiveness, property damage, or pranks. One out of ten responses focused on the lack of supervision by parents, while one out of twenty had to do with clutter of children's play paraphernalia. A small group (4 percent) mentioned that they like the amenities, e.g., social advantages, associated with an adults-only setting, while an equal number simply stated that they disliked children.

Contrary to expectations, older renters without children in the household were less likely to say they had reasons for not wanting to live near children. Whereas one-fourth (26 percent) of the renters under fifty-five years of age said they preferred not to live near families with children, fewer than one in five (18 percent) of the older renters responded in this manner. The differences are most acute among renters living in apartment complexes. An examination of the data indicates that younger renters without children are more likely than their older counterparts to live in places where children are allowed and present. Thus, they are cognizant of the presence of children and problems such as those being reported.

Of particular interest to policy makers and managers is whether people select apartments on the basis of whether or not children live there and what people who live in buildings with no children would do if children moved in. In order to address these issues, respondents living in buildings with no children were asked two questions: (a) "Did you choose to live in your building because children weren't living there?" and (b) "Would you move out if families with children were allowed to live in your building?"

One-fourth of the respondents with no children said they preferred not to live near children and one-fifth of those living in buildings which have no children in them chose their building because it had no children. However, 80 percent of the renters, regardless of their age, living in buildings with no children said they would *not* move if families with children were allowed to move in. Thus, while a substantial minority of respondents express preferences for or have selected living situations based upon the absence of children, the vast majority of renters in this sample, including those over fifty-five, would take no action if the policies or practices concerning children in their building were to change.

Managers' attitudes toward children

Those who make decisions about whether to exclude or limit children from rental housing do so on the basis of some rationale. The managers in this sample were presented with a list of possible problems associated with renting to children and asked if they thought each was a problem *in general*. Higher maintenance costs was seen as the most problematical, with four-fifths (81 percent) of managers reporting that it was a general problem in renting to families with children. Next most frequently seen as a problem was unsupervised children (73 percent), followed by noisy children (69 percent), neighbors who complain (61 percent), too much clutter (57 percent), and teenage parties (56 percent). Higher insurance costs was endorsed as a problem in renting to children by only 38 percent of the managers. Managers of buildings or complexes not accepting children are twice as likely as managers of buildings/complexes accepting children to view each item as problematical. Thus, those managers who presently deal with children in their buildings, whether or not by their own choice, do not perceive themselves as having experienced much difficulty.

More than one-half (54 percent) of managers think that families without children are bothered by children in the neighborhood, whereas fewer than one-fourth of such families actually report that they are or think they would be bothered by children. And the proportion of elderly persons who feel they might be bothered by the presence of children is even lower. Thus the belief that policies are needed to conform to the comforts of tenants far exceeds the desires of the tenants themselves.

Summary

Data from the national survey reveal that exclusionary policies concerning children are varied and extensive. More than one-fourth of rental units exclude children and half of the rental units are in places which accept children but impose restrictions on the number of children, ages of children, sharing of bedrooms of children not of the same sex, or location within a building or complex where children can live. There is a relationship between the extent of these practices and qualities of the units, such that smaller units, units in predominantly white neighborhoods, units in larger buildings or complexes, and newer units are more likely to be subject to exclusionary or limiting policies. These policies definitely have become more common in recent years.

According to community studies as well as the national survey, families with children report having confronted these restrictive practices, and many have had to settle for housing they consider to be less desirable or inconvenient. While female-headed and minority renter families are no more likely than other renter families to have encountered restrictions, the greatest burden appears to fall on low income families and families with three or more children.

Whereas one-fourth of renters without children would prefer not to live near children, only one-fifth of renters presently living in places with no children present would move if families with children were permitted to live there. By contrast, over one-half of managers believe that renters without children are bothered by the presence of children.

Thus, while no-children policies clearly limit the rental options of families with children, they do not currently appear to reflect the needs or demands of the majority of renters without children. Since these policies which affect many American families appear to be becoming increasingly pervasive, they warrant closer scrutiny. At the same time the expressed preferences and housing choices of older people and others without children need to be monitored. Specifically, efforts are needed in local housing markets to document the practices and places where subgroups of families with children are treated differentially. The burdens on all families with children who seek rental housing and the sentiments of property owners and families and individuals without children also need to be monitored. If, in fact, restrictive practices do not pose serious problems for families with children or discriminate against a particular subgroup (minorities, female-headed households), then legislation aimed at overcoming the burdens on a small number of families may infringe on the housing options and preferences of childless tenants and the property rights of landlords. For example, legislation aimed at opening up all rental housing to families with children may pose a threat to retirement communities and other planned housing arrangements attracting a predominantly elderly population. If, on the other hand, the burdens on families with children are excessive in any housing market and restrictive policies affect certain groups more than others, new and creative legislation is in order.

4 Housing the Extended Family in Sweden

Louise Gaunt

Abstract. Gaunt examines housing needs in Sweden in terms of two trends: the high proportion of one- and two-person households and the desire of related households to retain close contact. Data from questionnaires mailed to a random sample of married women aged forty-five to fifty-four in Gävleborg County in central Sweden are used to document the housing patterns of networks of extended families. Information was obtained on housing conditions, proximity to kin, frequency of contact, and mutual aid. Contact networks depend on private automobile transportation. It is concluded that geographic proximity would make symmetrical visiting between the generations easier, especially between grandchildren and grandparents. Housing communes and other housing schemes are reviewed as methods of achieving this goal.

Introduction

During the twentieth century households have become increasingly smaller. The large households of the nineteenth century have almost disappeared. Today almost two-thirds of the households in Sweden consist of one or two persons. The young move away from their parental home earlier, divorces increase, and the elderly seldom live together with their adult offspring.

The large number of small households has sometimes led to the false conclusion that people have become isolated from family and kin; on the contrary, what we see is an emerging pattern of networks of small but related households keeping in close contact with each other—in this chapter called the extended family.[1] This pattern calls for a different view of housing needs than we have been used to during the sixties and seventies, when the task was to accommodate the separate nuclear family.

Here I will briefly describe the living pattern of the Swedish extended family, based on my own study and other recent research. In the discussion I will suggest that the Swedish housing stock is such that generational social life is dependent on the automobile, which in turn creates asymmetrical relations between generations and prevents grandparents and grandchildren from being together. Elderly and children need to live within walking distance in order to be able to see each other on their own.

Generational social life. As part of the research project "Flergenerationsboende" (Housing the Extended Family) at the National Swedish Institute for Building Research, 388 middle-aged and married women answered a mailed questionnaire in a detailed survey of housing, proximity to kin, contacts and help between generations etc.[2] The survey shows that generations tend to live within reach of each other. It also shows the importance of proximity for contacts and help.

Proximity and contacts

Half of the women with living parents have them within fifteen kilometers (approx. ten miles), a third within five kilometers (three miles) and 14 percent within half a kilometer (0.3 miles). The proximity to adult children is a little closer (see figures 4.1 and 4.2). This may be because there are more households of them, sometimes even three or four, whereas the parents only consist of one household. As for the children's residence it can further be noted that it is quite common for many to live nearby, not, as sometimes believed, that only one child stays close when the others move far away.[3]

Contacts among parents and adult children are very frequent, especially for those who live near each other (telephone calls are not included in the survey). Within half a kilometer, most of the women saw their relatives the same day or the day before they answered the questionnaire. Within five kilometers, most of the women had seen their relatives at least once during the past week. At longer distances, more than fifty kilometers, most of the women had seen their children within the past month and their parents even less often. One of the

	<½	½–5	5–15	15–50	>50	km
Today, yesterday						35
Last week						25
Last month						18
Last 2–3 months						18
Longer ago						4
	14	23	12	13	38	100%

Figure 4.1 Distance and contacts between women and parents (every point marks one relation) (N = 245).

women commented: "If my parents lived closer, we would see each other more often."[4] Only 10 percent of the women-parents contacts and 3 percent of the women-children contacts had been made further back than three months. For grandchildren the pattern is the same as for adult children.

Although less detailed, a national survey shows the same pattern of proximity and contacts between generations.[5] Over the past twenty years, the number of elderly living together with their adult children has decreased by half. In 1976, only 1 percent of the total population lived in extended-family households which included three generatons, but 10 percent of retired men and 7 percent of retired women lived together with their children and their families. This is higher than the proportion of elderly who lived in nursing homes or other institutions.[6] Most of the elderly in the national survey had their own homes, and nearly half of all retired persons had at least one of their children within fifteen kilometers. Excluding those elderly with no children, there were actually as many as two-thirds who had a child within this distance. A small minority (6 percent) of the elderly lived alone and had few contacts with kin. Similar results have been found for Denmark.[7]

Distance seems to be the most crucial of the investigated factors for contacts. The number of extended family members outside her own

	<½	½–5	5–15	15–50	>50	km
Today, yesterday	●●●●	●●●●	●●●	●●	●●	43
Last week	●	●●●	●●	●	●●	25
Last month	●	●	●	●	●●●●	18
Last 2–3 months		●	●	●	●●●●	11
Longer ago			●	●	●	3
	16	26	16	28	34	100%

Figure 4.2 Distance and contacts between women and adult children (every point marks one relation) (N = 540).

household does not influence how often a woman meets any of them, nor does her employment situation. Old parents in institutions are visited as often as those who live in their own homes. ("I visit my mother twice a week in the nursing home. On Sundays she comes to stay with us.") Also, the sex or marital status of parents and children makes no difference. This contradicts earlier research, which found strong mother-daughter links (e.g., Young and Willmott).[8] The women in this study see their widowed fathers and their sons as often as they see their mothers and daughters. This may be a sign of disappearing sex differences in generational relations.

The national survey shows few regional differences, with only slightly more frequent generational contacts outside the metropolitan areas. For obvious reasons, recent immigrants have fewer kinship contacts than people who are born in Sweden. Few social class differences are found, with the exception of the professionals. While the average proportion who live farther away from their parents than fifty kilometers was around 40 percent in the Extended Family Survey, for the professionals and higher level government employees it was more than 80 percent. One reason may be that this group found it difficult to get jobs close to their place of birth, especially if this was outside the metropolitan areas. But they did compensate for the longer distances by more traveling; the differences in contact patterns was not dramatic. The same pattern, if not as pronounced, existed for distances and contacts with children.

A personal remark might be in place here regarding the professionals' common view of the isolation of the family. More than any other group, the professionals, at least researchers and journalists, are occupied with descriptions of society. In their work they may very well be influenced by their own experiences—in this case of having family far away. Their old mother back in the village becomes the symbol for all old people, their own isolation from close relatives is ascribed to all other families. Being privileged in most ways, it is difficult to imagine that one is unprivileged in any way at all and lacks the family contacts that most other Swedes have. If this is true, it might be the reason why kinship is a fairly unresearched area, at least in Scandinavian countries. Even housing policies, public care, support programs, and so on have very rarely, if at all, considered the importance of kinship in everyday life.

Although the general pattern is "the closer you live the more often you meet," there are exceptions. Some near neighbors had not visited each other lately. This may of course be because they do not like each other. The women, for instance, did not see their parents-in-law as often as they saw their parents, but there were also quite a few who had seen each other recently despite long distances.[9]

One point then is that many of the women and their relatives make great and time-consuming efforts to see each other. Had they been able to find closer housing, generational social life would have been easier. Time is limited for Swedish women today; most are gainfully employed and still have the major responsibilities for household and children. Middle-aged women may have four jobs: employment, household management, taking care of old parents, and looking after grandchildren.

Another point is that the majority of visits (roughly all visits beyond five kilometers—63 percent for women-parents visits and 43 percent for women-children visits) could not be made without a car. Some may very well use public transportation such as trains or buses, but some within five kilometers may also need a car, especially in bad weather.

The common pattern is that the younger go to see the older, except of course for the grandchildren. This pattern becomes more pronounced with increasing physical distance, but there are also exceptions to this rule when the visit includes an overnight stay. It is not uncommon that the parents stay overnight in the woman's house. One woman said, "My father is in hospital, but he comes to stay on weekends. He has his own room in the apartment." Overnight stays are highly correlated to long distances; 71 percent of the parents and 84 percent of the children living farther away than fifty kilometers have stayed overnight some time during the past half year in the woman's home. But overnight stays also depend on the size of the home, especially for the elderly. If the woman cannot offer a separate bedroom to her parents, they tend to stay overnight less frequently. For the children, the space consideration is less important for staying overnight in their mother's home, which of course quite often is where they lived before. The surveyed women have larger homes than average. One reason to hold on to their large unit when the children move away may be the need to have an extra room for overnight guests.

Mutual aid within the extended family

In Sweden it is a general policy that old people should be able to stay in their homes as long as possible, rather than taken into institutional care. Beside their pensions, many old people receive medical care and housekeeping help in their homes. This work is often carried out by middle-aged women other than their daughters and paid for by the community. The elderly have less need for aid from their own family than in many other countries, e.g., Britain and the United States. Recent research, however, has shown that the informal care of elderly is about as common as the formal.[6] Also, social service offices tend to reduce the home helper hours if the old person has a close relative in the city. One of the women in the survey commented, "My mother is totally dependent on having us nearby for company, visiting the doctor, household work. The home helper only comes once a week." However, most elderly manage household chores, shopping, and so on themselves. The need for generational social life is more a matter of emotional support than of practical help.

It is therefore not astonishing that helping the elderly with such things as everyday chores is much less frequent than visiting. About half of the elderly parents had not been helped with anything by the women during the past month. But widowed parents are helped more than couples, and older parents are helped more than younger. So the fact that little help is given does not indicate a lack of solidarity but rather indicates that help is given when it is needed. In a Gothenburg study the same was found. People saw their relatives mostly for company; when together they would have coffee, watch television, or just be around. For many adult children it was an obligation to keep in touch with their elders. It was common to visit for an hour on the way from work or from a weekend trip.[10]

A recent study by Swedish sociologists Liljeström and Dahlström shows that working class women first turn to their mothers for help with their preschool children and for advice about problems with their teenagers. They take responsibility for their elders, visit them often, and give them a hand. Few of the women mention workmates or public agencies when it comes to need for advice or financial or other kinds of help. Some say they turn to friends. The authors conclude, "Our data give no evidence for loosening kinship ties or that the family is disappearing."[11]

In the Extended Family Survey, the help mostly consists of household chores and errands. Personal or medical care is rare, and only 1 percent helped economically. To help the elderly seldom takes more than a few hours a week; only 7 percent of the women had spent more than ten hours during the past week helping a parent. The extent of help that the children get is about the same, with around half of the children receiving help during the past month. The younger children who have just left home are more often helped with household chores, and also economically, than the older. When the grandchildren arrive, many women get a new obligation as a baby sitter. But only in 9 percent of the grandchildren households is the woman a permanent child minder, as compared to 30 percent who have their children in public day care. A very high proportion of young mothers are employed in Sweden. The public day care system is generally considered of good quality, even if it is insufficient for the demand.

Even if the woman is the prime help giver in the extended family, there is at least some reciprocity. Ten percent of the women had had help with household chores from their close relatives during the past month, mostly from the children. But the mutual aid is definitely an extended family affair. Other relatives, such as brothers and aunts were only helped by 14 percent of the women.

Twelve percent had given a neighbor a hand during the past month, mostly with such things as watering the flowers or looking after the house when the neighbor was away. A common pattern in recent neighborhood studies is that people have fairly few and superficial contacts with neighbors. In small communities with a stable labor market, kin, friends, and neighbors are the same people and extensive help systems are developed. In such communities there is little need for institutional care such as child care. Parents, grandparents, sisters, and neighbors take turns in looking after the children, while mothers work. With some help from relatives, the elderly can stay outside institutional care much longer.[12] In larger communities and metropolitan areas with a faster population turnover, informal care systems do not develop so easily. Nonetheless, it is not uncommon that kin try to find housing close to each other. The vacancies in some housing areas in Stockholm have been used by relatives to solve the child care problem or to get granny living next door.[13]

Mutual aid within the extended family is dependent on proximity. Giving elderly parents a hand seems to be possible at distances up to fifteen kilometers, but farther away it becomes much less frequent. One woman says, "I would help my father more if I lived closer, but I can't get an apartment nearby." Looking after grandchildren is even more dependent on proximity. Babysitting occurred for 63 percent of the grandchildren within half a kilometer, compared to 31 percent of the grandchildren five to fifteen kilometers away and 11 percent of those living farther than fifty kilometers from the woman's home. Maybe this has to do with the grandchildren's mobility. At short distances they can go by themselves to visit granny. Another woman explains, "My grandchildren live in the next block. They come here after school for a snack and stay until their parents get home from work." If the children live farther away, they have to wait for their grandmother to come over or for their parents to take them. Housing location is important for helping each other. This will receive more attention in the concluding discussion, where also some suggestions for planning and future research will be made.

Discussion

Some major results of the Extended Family Survey are (a) Generations today do not share the same household, but often live within reach of each other. (b) Generations have frequent contact with each other, and the closer they live the more often they meet. (c) When they meet, it is mostly for company; help is exchanged when needed. (d) Contacts are highly dependent on proximity, even though there are many who will often travel long distances to see each other.

Planning for housing proximity between generations is an important task for the future. Extended families benefit from living close together. But how close is ideal? After discussion of this question some comments will be made concerning the housing situation.

Earlier it was stated that the majority of families need a car to see each other. For those who prefer not to meet very frequently, this may be a minor problem, but for the people who do want to meet their relatives often, frequent long distance driving is expensive and time consuming. One woman complained. "We don't like driving two hundred kilometers every second weekend, but my mother's garden needs looking after." There is also a large group who are not car drivers— elderly people and children. They need to wait for a visit or have somebody to take them.

Most elderly and children are not very good on bicycles either, at least not as far as five kilometers. Bicycling in traffic is not safe for children under twelve, and a recent medical report recommended that old persons avoid bicycling in city traffic. So elderly and children have to walk or take the bus if they want to go some place on their own. If they can't walk and if there are no buses, which certainly is sometimes the case, they must be taken by somebody with a car.

In Swedish neighborhood planning guidelines the recommended maximum walking distance to shops, schools, day care, bus stops, etc., is half a kilometer (0.3 miles). This distance is what most people are able to walk conveniently from their homes. For handicapped and very small children this may even be too far, especially after dark or in bad weather.

A convenient walking distance to visit relatives is of course not greater than that to shops or to school. This means that most visits beyond half a kilometer are difficult for the elderly and the grand-children to make on their own, and they will need to be made by the more mobile generations, the women, their husbands, and the adult children. When and how often to visit is up to them. This situation was commented on by one of the women: "I hate having my grand-children so far away; I do not drive, and their parents are too busy to bring them here every week."

Survey results show that the young-visit-old pattern becomes less pronounced with increasing proximity, and it disappears totally when generations live within half a kilometer. Only within this distance does everybody go to see each other, regardless of age. The conclusion is that, besides making it easier for generations to see each other often, close proximity also promotes symmetrical relations between generations. Within walking distance, no one is dependent upon another relative. The old parents can come and go as they want, and the grandchildren can visit their grandparents as they like, even without their parents being present.

Two Americans, focusing on the importance of grandparenthood, find that far too many grandparents are separated from their grandchildren in modern society.[14] From a large study they conclude that the bond between grandparents and grandchildren is second in emotional power and influence only to the relationship between parents and children.

Grandparents with strong relationships to their grandchildren have a richer and more meaningful life than elderly in general. To become a grandparent marks an important event in adult life. For the grandchildren, close grandparents mean family historians, caretakers, role models for older life, mediators between child and parents, etc. Children who have little contact with their grandparents still feel attached to them and are sad and puzzled by the separation. These feelings are shared by the grandparents.

The grandparent-grandchildren connection also becomes a bridge over the generation gap, since grandparents extend their interest to other children in the neighborhood ("Robert's playmates") and children feel warmth and interest in other elderly around them ("All old people are somebody's Granny").

The authors conclude that a necessary requirement for strong relationships between grandparents and grandchildren is that they live close to each other. However, they do not state how close is necessary. The Extended Family Survey suggests that walking distance is required unless of course the generation in between makes great efforts for grandparents and grandchildren to see each other often.

To answer the question "How close is ideal?" it is also necessary to answer the question "For what?" If the objective is to prevent the elderly's total isolation from family and kin, fifteen kilometers (ten miles) may be close enough. This distance enables the adult children to visit the elderly every week or so. If the objective is symmetrical generational relations and opportunities for grandparents and grandchildren to meet frequently, half a kilometer (0.3 miles) is the maximum distance.

Housing the extended family

What then are the possibilities for generations to find residences close to each other? Sharing a household is not a favored solution today, and it probably will not be in the future. In Sweden, granny annexes and other forms of combinations of small and large apartments under the same roof are uncommon. But there is one development which might very well benefit extended families, as well as other people: the housing communes that are now being built in several cities. These communes range from large staffed projects, combining special flats for elderly and handicapped with large family flats, to smaller un-staffed projects of between five and twenty units. Adjacent to the private flats are always communal areas such as a large kitchen, a dining room, and rooms for leisure activities; sometimes there is also a day care center. Many people feel that this form of commune is ideal, since it ensures a combination of privacy in the flats with com-pany in the shared parts of the building. Communal living can also make household chores easier. To cook for ten or twenty persons does not take much longer than to cook for two or three. By taking turns in preparing dinner, not every household in a commune has to cook every day and thus time can be saved for other activities, or residents can simply make ends meet in a limited time budget. Being part of such a commune might be a good solution for some extended fami-lies, especially with regards to their less mobile members, the grand-parents and the small children. The other commune members — young and old — may also benefit from having an extended family among them as a bridge between generations.[15]

Apart from rare cases, combinations of small apartments and larger homes are difficult to find in Sweden and most likely throughout all of the industrialized countries. The large multistory housing areas of the fifties and sixties were built with a variation of apartment sizes, rang-ing from studios to two-bedroom apartments. In these areas larger units do exist, but there are not enough of them for the number of families with two or more children. The child-rearing families move into new developments of row houses and single-family homes far away from areas with smaller apartments. The trend is also caused by the lower housing costs in owner-occupied homes than in rental apartments of the same size, and the environment in these develop-ments is considered better for children. Longer and more costly commuting is generally not thought to be a reason to stay in more central locations. This means a current segregation by age, which is fairly new to Sweden. The old and the very young households will increasingly find residence in the denser rental apartment areas closer to the city center, while the child-rearing families will live farther out from the center in owner-occupied single family homes.

Following are a few examples of how this trend may be counteracted. They will, of course, require further research. Can, for instance, larger homes be fitted into older areas or smaller units into single family and row house developments? Should extended families be supported so that people who wish to move close to relatives are given priority by housing agencies? Considering the high cost of formal care for children and the elderly, should families who want to move closer to relatives be granted extra homeowner loans or housing subsidies? When they give building permits and government loans, should social factors be considered by the authorities? Today the local authorities make their decision based on the long-term need for a new house. Thus, a young family who wants to build a home on their parents' farm may be refused a permit or a loan, because this house is of limited value to other people and may be difficult to sell later. The fact that the young family wishes to live close to the parents to be able to take care of them and/or to solve their own child care problem is not considered.

A final concluding problem might be the following: nuclear families today are small, with one or two children, and often with only one parent; but families do have more generations living in separate households. Divorced parents with joint responsibility for their children increase the number of small households with close relations to each other. The main part of the housing stock fits an obsolete view of family patterns: the isolated nuclear family with few relations and obligations to kin outside the family. How can this housing stock be accommodated to the family pattern that we see emerging: large extended family networks consisting of many small separate households? With harder times and maybe fewer social service supports, generations may have to depend on each other much more than they do today. In such a situation, this problem will become even more urgent.

5	Residential Fit and Mobility among Low-Income, Female-Headed Family Households in the United States
	Sherry Ahrentzen

Abstract. This chapter reports on a study of the housing of the large and increasing proportion of low-income female-headed families in the United States. Using longitudinal data, 1974–77, from the Experimental Housing Allowance Program in Pittsburgh and Phoenix, low-income female-headed families are compared with jointly headed families. Measures were devised for subjective and objective aspects of residential fit, adaptation, and adjustment. Findings indicate that female-headed families pay a higher proportion of their incomes for housing and that they search for different types of residences in different neighborhoods and apparently settle for less desirable housing than jointly-headed households. Implications for future research are reviewed.

Single parents, as a group, may have more than their share of difficulties. They are apt to be underfinanced and overburdened; they must meet a parent's responsibilities with a single person's resources. It would be good if their housing could be a source of sustenance for them rather than an additional set of problems. (Weiss, 1980, p. 76)

In 1980, approximately 25 percent of all households, an estimated 20.6 million, were headed by women (United States. Bureau of the Census—hereinafter usbc—1980). Of these, 8.5 million were family households with children headed by a female single parent. From 1970 to 1980, family households headed by women grew at a rate ten times faster than two-parent families (Shalala, 1980). A number of critics allege that the needs of these housing consumers differ from those of the traditional two-parent household and that these needs are neglected by a market attuned to the status quo (Leavitt, 1980; Lipman-Blumen, 1976; Schorr and Moen, 1979; Soper, 1980; Weiss, 1980). One characteristic that strongly distinguishes these households from others is their lack of economic and social resources. Female-headed families are likely to have less time and money than traditional two-parent families, simply because there is one less adult in the household (Masnick and Bane, 1980). Nearly 40 percent of families headed by women remain below poverty levels compared to 7 percent of families headed by men (Hapgood and Getzels, 1974). Since the majority of adults in single-parent families work (McEaddy, 1976), these women, in addition to their outside jobs, must assume all child care, household, and economic responsibilities and decisions.

While family life-stage is an important factor in studying housing patterns, few researchers have concentrated on families not composed of the traditional husband-wife-children. The little empirical work that does exist on housing for female heads of households suggests that they are less likely to be homeowners (Morris and Winter, 1976; USBC, 1973; United States. Department of Housing and Urban Development—hereinafter USDHUD—1978); more likely to live in housing with lower monthly rents or market values (USBC, 1973); more likely to live in multifamily units and older buildings (USDHUD, 1978); less likely to have their expectations of moving because of improved economic circumstances fulfilled (Duncan and Newman, 1975); move several times following marital separation, searching for homes that suit their new circumstances on a trial and error basis (Anderson-Khlief, 1981; Masnick and Bane, 1980; Weiss, 1980); and are less likely to prefer living in single-family homes (Winter and Morris, 1981). While the total population has an 80 percent probability of finding adequate housing for only one-fourth of their income, female heads of households have only a 53 percent probability (USDHUD, 1978).

Many of these findings derive from demographic studies of women in housing at one point in time, and they lack a theoretical basis. Often these studies fail to investigate possible reasons for housing differences—possibilities such as lower income, discrimination in the housing market, lack of information or time, or differing preferences and needs. Expanding upon these reports, this study explores the social and environmental context of housing patterns of female-headed families. The term "housing pattern" refers not only to the condition of a household's present home but also to the process of finding (or not finding) a home that meets one's needs and expectations in light of household and market resources and constraints.

The study

Two central components are examined here: (*a*) the fit between a household's needs and residential conditions and (*b*) efforts made to alleviate the undesirable situation. Elaboration on the conceptualization and measurement of these components follows.

Residential fit. Residential fit exists when a person's needs and desires are accommodated by the environment. Fit is generally assessed either by occupants' evaluations of their residences or by objective quality standards. Subjective indicators are often used because they frequently reflect the standards and qualities which tenants find most desirable. Yet, subjective assessments may be subject to multiple interpretations. Expressions of satisfaction may be a factor not only of existing conditions but also of perceived alternatives and future expectations. In addition, certain households may be less able to discriminate housing conditions as satisfying or dissatisfying because of limited experience with various living situations. This is particularly relevant for those in lower-income groups who may have prolonged experience with inferior or minimally sufficient housing conditions. A "learned helplessness" attitude may develop for those in inadequate environments, resulting in lowered aspiration levels. In addition to attitudinal or aspirational changes, individuals may adapt to inadequate situations by adjusting their behaviors and living patterns to better fit their environments. If such behavioral adaptation has occurred, adjustments to a new environment, even if superior to the present condition, would require learning new behaviors which may be difficult and discomforting (Lawton, 1980).

Another way of assessing fit is to concentrate solely on objective housing indicators and standards, such as structural quality, rent burden, and number of persons per room. Such measures often are indicative of health and safety hazards, especially for low-income households. For example, the incidence of home fires is related to poor heating equipment and wiring; home accidents are often the result of broken stairs and other structural defects; hazards to personal safety may be the consequence of poor lighting, inadequate locks, and other deficits (Hartman, 1975). Low-income households spending 30 percent to 40 percent of their income on housing may suffer deleterious effects on their health and well-being since a large expenditure of their meager income for housing may mean depriving them of or reducing the quality of other necessities such as food or medical care.

Nonetheless, use of objective indicators involves certain limitations. Objective housing standards are used extensively in assessing the quality of the nation's housing stock, and they are used by policy makers in determining various program allocations. However, such standards reflect relative rather than absolute deprivation and frequently they are not based on any scientific criteria or policy consensus (Baer, 1976), nor do they necessarily reflect the standards which consumers find acceptable and desirable (Grigsby and Rosenberg, 1975; Hartman, 1963; Struyk, 1981).

It is tempting to assume a strong positive relationship between subjective and objective types of indicators. However, a number of studies reveal a significant discrepancy between objective standards and tenants' attitudes and assessments (Hartman, 1963; Struyk, 1981; Grigsby and Rosenberg, 1975). Apparently these two types of indicators measure different facets of residential fit. Consequently, both types of indicators are needed for study in order to gain a complete understanding of housing patterns.

Adaptations and adjustments. Responses to housing conditions deemed undesirable include adjustments or actions directed towards the environment (e.g., searching, moving, making residential alterations) or adaptations made within the household, such as cognitive adaptation (i.e., change in expectations or evaluations of conditions). As Evans and Jacobs (1981) suggest, those attempting, but failing, to make an adjustment (such as moving) may respond thereafter by making a residential adaptation. In this chapter, only one type of adjustment is examined—search and mobility—because of its prominence among female-headed households.

Utilizing these concepts, a number of questions arise concerning the housing patterns of female-headed households in relation to those of joint-parent households. These questions are addressed with longitudinal data from lower income households. (*a*) Do female single-parent households experience less residential fit (objectively and subjectively defined) than joint-headed families? (b) Are female single-parent households less likely than joint-headed households to move, particularly as a means of adjusting to inadequate residential conditions? (c) Are female single-parent households more likely than others to search for a new home but not move (i.e., frustrated attempts at adjustment)? What differences exist in search efforts and what difficulties do they encounter?

Methodology

Description of data source. The source of data for studying these questions is information collected on participants of the Experimental Housing Allowance Program (EHAP). Authorized by Congress and directed by the Department of Housing and Urban Development between 1973 and 1980, this program involved more than 25,000 families in twelve metropolitan areas. EHAP was divided into three separate but interrelated experiments, each designed to address particular issues. The demand experiment focused on how recipients use housing allowances and on the types of housing and neighborhoods they prefer and choose. The data collected in the demand experiment pertain to the questions posed in this study. In the demand experiment housing allowances were offered between 1974 to 1977 at two sites: Alleghany County, Pennsylvania (Pittsburgh) and Maricopa County, Arizona (Phoenix).[2]

Information was derived from four sources. First, monthly household report forms (HRFS) were completed by each household, disclosing the previous month's income, rent, and demographic information such as age, number, and relationship of occupants, etc. Second, monthly administrative records on each household record the information of the household's allowance payment, whether or not the household was fulfilling program requirements, and whether or not the household was still participating in the program.

Third, periodic surveys of each household were administered at baseline (1974), six months after enrollment, twelve months after enrollment, and two years after enrollment. Information from these surveys include household expenditures; housing and neighborhood conditions, preferences, and satisfactions; search and moving behaviors; and residential alterations. These interviews were administered to the head of household and/or spouse.

Fourth, housing evaluation forms (HEFS), consisting of direct observation of each household's dwelling unit and neighborhood, were completed by trained housing evaluators. Each housing evaluation took approximately one hour. Quality control checks and strict guidelines for evaluating the dwelling unit were followed. Housing evaluations were performed at enrollment, annually thereafter, and whenever a household moved or an upgrade was reported. These evaluations contained information assessing the interior and exterior of the unit, the condition of basic housing systems (such as plumbing and heating), and the presence of health and safety standards. Standards on fifteen housing components (e.g., plumbing, heating, electrical wiring, roof structure, lighting, and ventilation) were developed from American Public Health Association-Public Health Service codes. A summary measure of housing standards was developed, utilizing the evaluations of these housing components.

Sampling. At each site samples were selected from the eligible population of low-income renter households. Block samples were drawn by cluster sampling of census tracts with median incomes of less than $10,000. Approximately 150,000 eligible dwelling units in selected block samples at each site were found. Of these a random sample of addresses was drawn for screening interviews. These interviews were designed to eliminate respondents who owned their homes or did not fulfill the income eligibility or household composition requirements. Income eligibility standards were such that net income could not be four times greater than the cost of modest existing standard housing for various household sizes in each site. All completed and eligible respondents from the baseline interview were offered enrollment in the demand experiment. More than 75 percent of the respondents in both sites accepted the enrollment offer. There was no consistent pattern of demographic differences between those accepting and declining the offer. In total, 3,601 households participated in the demand experiment.

Sites. Housing market and household demographic conditions varied between Pittsburgh and Phoenix during program implementation. Initial analyses were conducted separately by site. In most instances differences between sites did not exist, so data were combined. In the few instances where there are differences, the analyses are reported separately.

Housing allowances. The amount of housing allowance varied among households, and various requirements were tied to the receipt of these allowances for some households. Since this study is not intended to evaluate the effectiveness of the allowance program, these factors (i.e., amount of subsidy and treatment group requirements) are controlled in the analyses.

Constructed variables. Family household types: Households with children under eighteen years of age living at home were divided into two categories:[3] (*a*) female single parent (referred to as FSP), or those where the adult head of household was female and no spouse was present; and (*b*) joint-parent households (JP), or those households where both husband and wife were present.

At enrollment, there were 1,039 FSP and 1,238 JP households in the sample. There was a fairly large attrition rate in the sample. Two years after enrollment, 696 FSP and 730 JP households were still participating in the study. There were no significant differences between household types in reasons for leaving the program. Analyses of changes and adjustments over time use only those families who were in the program during the two years of the study.

JP and FSP households differed not only in household composition but also in employment status and mean gross income ($3,837 and $4,523 for Pittsburgh and Phoenix FSPs, respectively; $6,188 and $7,115 for Pittsburgh and Phoenix JPs). Racial composition also varied: 38 percent of FSPs compared to 25 percent of JPs were headed by a racial minority.

Objectively evaluated fit. This measure was composed of three factors: structural adequacy, as determined by APHS standards and the extent of repair needed (see Budding, 1980 for details); rent burden (i.e., ratio of monthly rent to gross income); and household crowding. A household was said to suffer a rent burden if it paid more than 35 percent of its gross income for rent and utilities. Although several standards of crowding exist, the one used in this study is "more than one person per room," the most conservative estimate in the sample.

These three standards are used extensively by researchers and policymakers. Yet, generally, they are considered exclusive of each other. The index of fit in this study allows for both separate and multiple housing deficiencies. The six nominal levels of this index include (*a*) rent burden only (i.e., no crowding or structural inadequacy); (*b*) structural inadequacy (i.e., no crowding or rent burden); (c) crowding only; (d) crowding and structural inadequacy occurring together, but no rent burden; (e) crowding and/or structural inadequacy while also suffering a rent burden; and (f) fit (i.e., none of the three housing deficiencies).

Subjectively evaluated fit. To assess residents' satisfaction with their homes if economic constraints were ignored, an item was used that asked respondents if they were given $50 more a month to spend on rent what they would like to do: move, remain in their present residence but have improvements made, or remain in their present residence with no improvements. Since the average rent paid by these households was $114 a month, $50 extra would allow them a number of alternatives to consider. This questionnaire item, referred to as residential change preference, is used as one measure of subjectively evaluated fit. The residential preference item was included only on the baseline survey. Two four-point scale items, assessing the degree of satisfaction with the dwelling unit and with the neighborhood, were included in all panel interviews. These two items are used in analyses examining changes in subjective fit over time.

Adjustments. On the periodic surveys, respondents reported whether or not they had searched for a home. Of these searchers, movers were classified as those who had searched and moved or were about to move at the time of the third periodic survey. Unsuccessful searchers were those who had at some time during enrollment searched and either stopped searching without moving or who were still searching at the time of the third periodic survey.

Findings

Do FSP households experience less residential fit (objectively and subjectively evaluated) than joint-parent households? Table 5.1 displays the proportion of different family household types experiencing objectively evaluated misfit conditions. A larger proportion of FSP households than JP spent over 35 percent of their income for rent for structurally adequate and structurally inadequate homes. JP households were more likely than FSPs to live in homes that were both structurally inadequate and crowded without suffering a rent burden. In addition, more than

Table 5.1 Proportion of family households experiencing objectively evaluated residential misfit, by household type and per capita income.

		Objectively evaluated misfit conditions					
		Rent burden only	Structural inadequacy only	Crowding only	Crowding & structural inadequacy	Structural inadequacy and/or crowding with rent burden	Fit
All income levels[1]	(n)						
FSP	(984)	32%	12%	2%	6%	36%	13%
JP	(1194)	16	16	7	15	13	33
Under $1000 per capita[2]							
FSP	(466)	26	7	1	9	54	2
JP	(265)	19	5	6	27	41	3
$1000–1999 per capita[3]							
FSP	(327)	40	14	4	4	29	9
JP	(566)	20	18	10	17	7	27
$2000+ per capita[4]							
FSP	(184)	34	15	0	1	5	46
JP	(357)	7	21	4	3	1	64

1 $X^2 = 363.22$, 5 df, $p < .0001$
2 $X^2 = 55.50$, 5 df, $p < .0001$
3 $X^2 = 167.73$, 5 df, $p < .0001$
4 $X^2 = 76.35$, 5 df, $p < .0001$

twice the proportion of JP than FSP households lived in objectively evaluated fit housing conditions.

A plausible explanation for these differences is the lower income of female-headed households. Having less income they are less likely to afford suitable homes. Displayed in table 5.1 are additional analyses, partitioned by per capita income. As income increases, the differences between household types also increases. For households of the lowest income group, gender of household head makes no difference in obtaining adequate housing conditions; these households are, across-the-board, in dire circumstances. As per capita income increases, however, discrepancies based on gender appear within the same economic status.

Differences also exist between household types for reported residential change preference or subjectively-evaluated fit ($x^2 = 26.67$, 4 df, $p<.0001$). Although a majority of all family household types wished to move, a statistically significant larger proportion of JP households preferred to move than did FSPS (69 percent of JPS, 60 percent of FSPS). FSP households were more likely to want to stay in their current residences and have improvements made (28 percent) than were JPS (18 percent). Twelve percent of both FSP and JP households wanted to stay with no improvements made.

Are FSP households less likely to move, particularly as a means of adjusting to inadequate residential conditions? One way for a household to increase its chances of fit is to move. FSPS were no less likely than JPS to move during their two-year participation in the program (approximately 50 percent of FSPS in Pittsburgh and 72 percent of FSPS in Phoenix moved).

Do these movers achieve the same quality of fit in their new homes? Mobility appears to be a better mechanism for achieving objectively evaluated fit for JP households than for FSPS who were in misfit conditions at baseline ($x^2 = 8.23$, 1 df, $p<.01$). Thirty-two percent of JP movers moved to better homes, compared to 20 percent of FSP movers. Moving JP households are much more likely to achieve residential fit than nonmovers (32 percent compared to 13 percent; this trend does not hold for FSP households (20 percent compared to 16 percent). No similar trends appear for subjectively evaluated fit.

Are FSP households more likely than others to search for a home but not move? What differences exist in search efforts and what difficulties do they encounter? Of households that search for a new home, there are no differences in success rates between FSP and JP searchers. In Pittsburgh, 70 percent of FSP searchers move; in Phoenix, 91 percent of FSP searchers move.

Even though FSP were as likely as JP households to move and to find a place to move to, they followed different search patterns. They were no more likely to look outside their present neighborhood nor did they differ on the number of neighborhoods searched in. However, FSP households focused their search efforts in neighborhoods with a larger proportion of low-income households and black households, with less Hispanic population and with a larger percentage of standard quality rental units (i.e., not dilapidated and with adequate bathroom plumbing). When controlling for income, household size, age, subsidy, and race of the households, FSPs still looked in neighborhoods with larger proportion of black households, $(F(1,680) = 5.62, p < .02$, more standard rental units, $F(1,687) = 5.95$, $p < .02$, and a smaller proportion of Hispanic households $F(1,680) = 9.74$, $p < .01$.

There are no differences between household types in the number of units visited or phoned about or the number of days of searching before selecting a new home. Although the effort expended, as measured by these items, does not differ between household types, FSPs are more likely to report search difficulties. A larger proportion of FSP than JP households reported search difficulties because of no ready access to transportation to homes they wanted to see (for Pittsburgh, $\chi^2 = 35.47$, 1 df, $p < .0001$ with 33 percent of FSPs, 10 percent of JPs; for Phoenix, $\chi^2 = 30.15$, 1 df, $p < .0001$ with 23 percent of FSPs, 6 percent of JPs). They also reported encountering more instances of discrimination in their search than JP households, $F(1,998) = 83.65$, $p < .0001$): 56 percent of FSP and 43 percent of JP searchers encountered at least one form of discrimination. Table 5.2 shows that a larger proportion of FSP households encountered discrimination because of children, unemployment, marital status, sex, and race. Besides children, FSPs differ from JPs on these characteristics. Some landlords may use no-children rental policies as a cover for other types of discrimination.

FSP movers and unsuccessful searchers were twice as likely as JPs to avoid searching in certain neighborhoods because they feared encountering discrimination ($\chi^2 = 14.53$, 1 df, $p < .001$ for movers; $\chi^2 = 9.64$, 1 df, $p < .01$). One-fourth of unsuccessful FSP searchers avoided searching in particular neighborhoods because of their expectations of being discriminated against.

FSPs also encountered difficulties because they did not know where to look for housing ($\chi^2 = 8.54$, 1 df, $p < .01$): 26 percent of FSPs, compared to 18 percent of JPs reported search difficulties because they did not know where to look.

Did the difficulty of the search affect households' subjectively evaluated fit with their residences? Figure 5.1 shows the percentage of JP and FSP searchers expressing satisfaction with both their home and neighborhood, broken down by whether the household moved or not, and the household's expressed difficulty of search. Difficulty of search does not have much impact on satisfaction for JP households.

Table 5.2 Proportion of searching households reporting discrimination encountered during housing search.

Housing discrimination because of:	FSPs (percentages)	JPs (percentages)
Children[1]	47	37
Source of income; unemployed[2]	34	11
Marital status[3]	27	3
Age	16	11
Gender[4]	11	0
Race (eliminating white[5] households)	9	4
EHAP participation	1	1
(N)	(489)	(510)

1 $X^2 = 8.71$, 1 df, $p<.01$
2 $X^2 = 80.45$, 1 df, $p<.0001$
3 $X^2 = 128.91$, 1 df, $p<.0001$
4 $X^2 = 28.00$, 1 df, $p<.001$
5 $X^2 = 12.73$, 1 df, $p<.01$

Both JP unsuccessful searchers and movers who reported a difficult search were no less likely than those JPS with easier search efforts to express complete satisfaction with their residence. However, for FSP households, significant trends appear. FSP movers with more difficult searches were less likely than other FSP movers to be satisfied with the residences they move to ($\chi^2 = 28.08$, 2 df, $p<.0001$). Perhaps the difficulty of the search affects their subjective evaluations or perhaps the difficult search leads FSPS to choose less-than-optimal residences. For FSP unsuccessful searchers, there is an opposite trend, but it is only marginally significant.

In addition, FSPS searched for different types of homes than JP searchers. Although the majority of all searching households seek a single-family dwelling, FSPS in both sites are less likely than JPS to search for a house and more likely to either look for an apartment or to have no preference ($\chi^2 = 15.69$, 2 df, $p<.001$ for Pittsburgh; $\chi^2 = 26.97$, 2 df, $p<.001$ for Phoenix). This tendency may reflect lowered aspirations of female single parents cognizant of their inadequate resources; however, this trend holds when partitioned by per capita income groups (table 5.3). Surprisingly, in the highest per capita income group, FSPS' desire for a house rapidly declines.

Table 5.3 Type of dwelling unit sought by family households, by household type and per capita income (in percentages).

Per capita income	Household type	Type of dwelling unit			
		House	Apartment	No preference	(N)
Under $1,000[1]	FSP	73	15	12	(240)
	JP	90	5	5	(111)
$1,000–$1,999[2]	FSP	68	16	16	(173)
	JP	85	9	6	(244)
$2,000 +[3]	FSP	46	35	19	(74)
	JP	77	15	7	(150)

1 $X^2 = 13.96$, 2 df, $p<.001$
2 $X^2 = 17.70$, 2 df, $p<.0001$
3 $X^2 = 22.13$, 2 df, $p<.0001$

Searchers were asked whether or not particular items were important in selecting a home. Differences between household types on selection criteria generally reflect differences in personal resources and the greater dependence of FSPs upon access to neighborhood services. FSPs' greater concern for rent payments and public transportation access and less concern for parking facilities and convenience to work reflects their smaller incomes, higher unemployment, and reduced car ownership. Their lower preference for a single-family home may reflect less fit of this structure type with household needs of single parents.

Conclusions and directions for future research

In examining housing patterns of female-headed families, this study addresses two major concerns: (*a*) compared to other families, are female-headed families more likely to live in inadequate and undesirable homes (that is, are they more likely to experience residential misfit?) and (*b*) is the search and moving process an effective means for FSPs to move toward better housing?

The use of the combinatory measure of objectively evaluated fit provides a more detailed picture of housing conditions of female-headed families than standard demographic and census reports (USBC, 1973; USDHUD, 1978). Although FSPs are no more likely than other families to live in homes that are crowded or structurally inadequate,

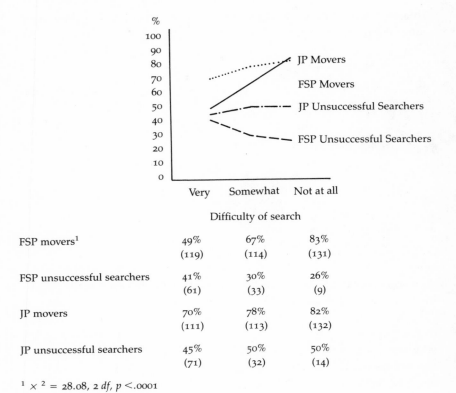

Figure 5.1 title region:

%
100
90
80
70
60
50
40
30
20
10
0

JP Movers
FSP Movers
JP Unsuccessful Searchers
FSP Unsuccessful Searchers

Very   Somewhat   Not at all

Difficulty of search

	Very	Somewhat	Not at all
FSP movers[1]	49%	67%	83%
	(119)	(114)	(131)
FSP unsuccessful searchers	41%	30%	26%
	(61)	(33)	(9)
JP movers	70%	78%	82%
	(111)	(113)	(132)
JP unsuccessful searchers	45%	50%	50%
	(71)	(32)	(14)

[1] $x^2 = 28.08$, 2 df, $p < .0001$

Figure 5.1 Percentage of family households reporting satisfaction with both home and neighborhood at fourth panel by expressed difficulty of search.

they are more likely to live in these conditions while paying a high proportion of their income for rent. And to live in the absence of these three conditions (rent burden, crowding, and structural inadequacy) is a feat that female-headed families are less likely to achieve, even considering income differences. Lack of income is not the only barrier these households face in improving their housing conditions; market discrimination and reduced expectations may play a role as well.

By addressing households' assessments of their residences given financial opportunities, the residential change preference item allows residents to evaluate their homes in a wider context of preferred changes and minimized constraints. Conventional subjective measures often constrain tenants in evaluating their residences in absence of other options. Although the differences in the residential change preference item are statistically significant, the distribution patterns are substantially the same, differing between family household types by approximately 10 percent. Thus, the differences between households in subjective fit seems relatively slight.

The higher rates of mobility reported for female single parents in other research (Masnick and Bane, 1980; Long, 1972) have not been substantiated here. This may be because only lower-income households are examined here, whereas other research studies include more income levels. In addition, previous research indicates that single-parent households are most mobile in the first few years following marital breakup. The households studied here, chosen for their stable family status during program participation, may have been in the single-parent stage for quite some time.

Initially, it seemed that low-income FSPs and JPS search and mobility patterns were equivalent: these households search and move with the same frequency. Yet, when considering efforts, methods, and results, search and mobility patterns are quite different between family households. FSPs search for different residences (e.g., type of structure and size) and they look in different neighborhoods; this is a reflection of their different household needs and resources. For fear of encountering discrimination, they limit their search to certain neighborhoods.

FSPs seem as likely as JPS to find a home within similar times periods. However, this does not mean that they find the same quality of home. FSPs are less likely to find homes that are suitably spacious, structurally sound, and with rents less than one-third of their income. This comparable search time for lower quality homes may reflect FSPS' lower expectations or less persistence in searching for an adequate and suitable home.

The search process is fraught with more difficulties for FSPs: discrimination, lack of transportation for searching, and lack of knowledge of where to search. But these difficulties do not seem to deter FSPS from finding a place. If this study focused exclusively on behavioral measures as indicators of fit, as Goodman (1978) suggests, it would appear that FSPS are as likely as JPS to achieve fit from moving, since they move with the same frequency to a home they presumably desire. But when both objective and subjective indicators are utilized, conclusions differ. Search difficulties frequently deter these single parents from finding a home they are satisfied with and that is suitable. Faced with search difficulties and compounded by their own lack of resources, these households may move with the same frequency as other households, but they may just settle for less.

Although female-headed households are less likely to live in homes that have no structural deficiencies, crowding, *or* high costs relative to their income, they are no less likely to be satisfied with these homes. These findings suggest that female-headed households may be satisfied with less because the constraints they encounter in trying to improve their housing situations are too difficult and stressful to make such an effort worthwhile.

Another possibility is that rent burden does not influence the extent to which a household is satisfied with its housing; rather, households may consider rent burden more a factor of their economic satisfaction. Since households headed by women are less likely to achieve objective fit because of rent burden, with or without other housing problems, their equivalent satisfaction may be the result of households not considering rent burden in their expression of housing satisfaction.

A final explanation may be that dwelling unit factors are not as important to female-headed households as are neighborhood factors, and that these neighborhood factors have a strong influence on their expressed satisfaction with their homes. Such an assumption is supported by the findings that female-headed households have different reasons for desiring a residential change (Ahrentzen, 1983). FSPs place more importance on perceived neighborhood conditions while JPs are more likely to consider rent burden and type of structure (i.e., housing attributes).

As questions about the housing patterns of female-headed households are addressed here, more questions arise. Are other forms of adaptations or adjustments such as residential alterations, more beneficial to FSP households than moving? Are there specific household characteristics of FSPs (e.g., extended family in the home) which alleviate or exacerbate residential misfit? Since single parenthood often is a temporary stage, is there a critical period, such as the time immediately following marital separation, when housing problems are most salient or critical? What are the short- and long-range expectations of female-headed families? What are the psychological costs of not meeting these expectations? Are other forms of housing, not examined here (such as collective housing and owner-occupied homes), desirable? Are housing patterns of male single-parent households or households headed by elderly women similar to those of FSPs? Are processes such as learned helplessness or cognitive dissonance occurring in FSPs' expressions of subjective fit?

A number of these questions are being addressed in a larger study (Ahrentzen, 1983). Although many questions remain unanswered, there appears to be little argument that the housing patterns of women are substantially different than those of the traditional family. Documenting and understanding these differences will aid future housing policy decisions. As Marcuse (1971) and Solomon (1974) maintain, policy that is not targeted toward the varied needs of the population's particular subgroups eventually becomes ineffective for the intended recipients. For example, financial relocation assistance alone may provide joint-parent families with greater benefit in improving housing quality than it provides single parents. For single parents, who suffer not only from minimal economic resources but also from time and geographic constraints and market discrimination, and who hold different residential expectations, financial assistance needs to be coupled with programs that assist families in the search process itself.

As the country's household population becomes more heterogeneous, as women continue to participate in the work force, as the mortality gap between men and women continues to widen, and as divorce rates steadily rise, the image of the "typical" household becomes harder to evoke. As housing resources diminish while the household population increases, both public and private sector planning policies will attempt to meet and satisfy the housing demands of the country's heterogeneous household population—of which over one-fourth is composed of households headed by women.

II | The Provision of Housing:
The Role of the State

Introduction
David Popenoe

At a time when the U.S. government has virtually withdrawn from the public support of housing, at least for low-income families, it is especially instructive to look at the role of the state in the provision of housing from a cross-national perspective. The chapters in this section examine selected housing policies in several key Western nations, and they point up some remarkable differences in political attitudes and government performance. Even if one assumes that some social and political convergence is occurring among advanced societies, widespread cross-national discrepancies among housing policies are still the rule. Yet one gets the feeling in reading these chapters (and others in this volume) that some common housing trends are emerging. Pushed by public opinion and by economic realities, these trends are tending to make the housing stocks and urban configurations of advanced societies more similar among cities than they have been up to now.

It has sometimes been noted that the world can be divided into three basic culture complexes, based on the type of eating utensil that is used: the fork, chopsticks, and fingers. The intellectual utility of pushing the implications of this distinction is questionable, however. More intellectually fruitful, at least in the field of urban studies, is the division of urban areas of advanced societies into two basic complexes: one based on the rental apartment in multifamily housing units, and the other based on the privately owned, detached single-family dwelling. The rental apartment culture complex, which is found in continental countries such as France, Germany, and The Netherlands, and the Scandinavian countries, consists of a number of urban features that are directly or indirectly related to this form of housing type and tenure. These features include relatively compact cities, with well-developed public transportation and public community services such as parks and playgrounds and a comparatively small "equity gap" between the best and worst housed. The private house culture complex, on the other hand, is associated with large, sprawling cities, private automobile transportation, weak community facilities, and a wider housing gap. This complex is found predominantly in the English-speaking countries: the United States and Canada, Australia, and, to a slightly lesser extent, the United Kingdom.

The dissimilarities between these two distinct housing and urban culture complexes have typically been attributed to a variety of historical and geographical factors. Not to be overlooked, however, is the role of the state. Ever since the Great Depression, or the end of World War II at the latest, the state has played an important role in the provision of housing in each of the advanced nations. This role has ranged from what could be called comprehensive housing planning outside of the normal housing markets by the governments of some countries, notably Sweden, to limited policies that merely seek to enhance the operation of the housing market, the prototypical example being the United States. For the most part, in each nation the state's role has served greatly to strengthen the preexisting housing and urban forms, although sometimes with consequences that were neither intended nor desired.

At the one extreme, the government of Sweden by and large has taken over from private capital the dominant position in the housing market. Since World War II, 45 percent of all new housing in Sweden has been erected by public authorities, with another 20 percent in the hands of consumer cooperatives, leaving only 35 percent for the private sector.[1] Moreover, the government also has carried out a massive housing allowance scheme wherein monetary assistance is provided based on both family size and economic necessity. With almost 65 percent of Swedish housing having been built since World War II, Sweden is now a world leader in the ratio of dwelling units per capita and in the high standard of amenities within those units. Sweden is also reputed to be the only Western nation where the middle class spends a higher percentage of its income on housing than does the working class.[2] In addition, Swedish government action has been instrumental in providing an urban environment in which there are relatively few class differences, the neighborhoods of the working class being very comparable to the neighborhoods of the middle and upper classes. Thus it can be said that the Swedish state's role in housing has led to some outstanding housing and urban achievements. Since virtually all the publicly provided housing has been in the form of rental apartment units, often in massive, high-rise buildings, this aspect of the Swedish urban scene has been heavily accentuated.

At the other extreme, the United States, a formal role for the state in housing could almost be said not to exist, with reliance put heavily instead on the private market. Only about 2 percent of U.S. housing is public, for example, the lowest percentage of any advanced industrial society. Yet the American government has in many ways continually been stimulating the housing market, mainly for the benefit of the middle class. The assumption has been that the poor would inherit the (hopefully still adequate) housing which the middle class vacates when it moves into new quarters, the so-called trickle-down effect. This policy has resulted in a society whose middle class has become quite elegantly housed in fine suburban neighborhoods, but whose lower classes, the trickle-down effect notwithstanding, inhabit housing and neighborhoods that are among the worst in developed countries. It has also resulted in strong reinforcement of the private house complex.

The articles in this section mainly deal with nations that fall between these two extremes. Postwar housing policies in Australia have been remarkably like those of the United States, although without quite such negative consequences. One notably different policy, as discussed in the chapter by Newton and Wulff, was the public construction for later sale of a large amount of single-family detached housing for moderate income families. At least from the consumer's point of view, as suggested in the chapter by Kilmartin, this policy has been quite successful. In America the direct building of public housing has almost always taken the form of multifamily rental housing, a type of housing that is often so out of keeping with surrounding areas that the families living there carry a certain stigma. This is one of the findings of a growing body of research which looks at the user perspective, summarized in the chapter by Anderson and Weideman.

Canada, too, from a cross-national perspective is not too different in its housing policies from the United States. But Montreal, the city examined in the chapter by Dansereau et al., is the exception that proves the rule—it is a city whose lines are more continental European than they are American. The chapter emphasizes the important role that public action in Montreal has played in maintaining this distinctiveness.

In Great Britain, which in a great many respects stands midway between the social and political extremes of Sweden and the United States, there has been a fairly long tradition of the public supply of low-cost housing, the so-called council housing that makes up over 30 percent of the British housing stock. Even in comparison with many European nations, Britain has been a little out of line in having such a high percentage of publicly owned housing. Yet today, as the chapter by Forrest and Murie makes clear, Britain seemingly is becoming more similar to the other English-speaking nations through selling off to private ownershp a large part of its public housing stock and at the same time cutting back on construction of new public housing. In times of economic decline, the authors note, housing is cut more than other services because there are fewer resistances to such cuts, as compared with such public services as education, health, and income maintenance.

Because the great period of economic growth of the past few decades is now all but over in most Western nations, the British housing experience has in fact become fairly typical of the other nations as well. There currently is underway a widespread retreat by governments from the direct provision of housing, not only in the United States but in most of the European countries, as pointed up in the review of European housing policies by Huttman. As she notes, the retreat is due not only to economic decline but also to the fact that in many of these nations the supply has largely caught up with the demand, and several of the nations even had housing surpluses during the middle seventies.

Often overlooked in this changing housing scene is what seems to be a widespread and even burgeoning trend toward privately owned and occupied single-family housing. Even in Sweden, as Genovese points out, there is currently a ground swell in favor of what one might call the U.S. (but it is also the Australian and Canadian) style of house type and tenure. At the same time there is a growing aversion on the part of consumers in countries such as Sweden for the massive multifamily units that so dominated the housing market after World War II. In part, this is because as countries grow in personal wealth (the current economic misfortunes notwithstanding) they can afford to build more of what is by most reckonings a more expensive form of housing. Also, there are those who argue that the owner-occupied single-family house is so intrinsically a part of capitalist systems that such systems find innumerable ways to make homeowning economically desirable, even in such Social Democratic-dominated nations as Sweden.[3] According to these observers, the consumer resistance to rental housing is in large part due to the comparatively (and unnecessarily) high economic costs associated with that form of housing.

Yet one still gets the impression that in Western nations, at least, there is a kind of natural yearning on the part of a large number of people for a home of their own—at least sometime during their life cycle—a home that provides privacy and that provides them the freedom to manage, maintain, and improve it. If this attitude proves really to be widespread, and if governments continue to cater to it, the convergence of urban forms in advanced societies will proceed much more rapidly than most analysts previously thought possible. Such convergence will not necessarily take place around the American detached house form, however. The last decade in America has shown a quite surprising shift to much higher-density attached housing. Whether public or private, the common new house type in the Western world is the low-rise, high-density unit, either what Americans call town houses or garden apartments. In this respect, the suburbs of Houston are coming increasingly to look like the suburbs of London and Stockholm. No western state, at the present time, seems willing or able to counter this significant housing shift in any real way. Indeed, most support it, either directly or indirectly.

Even though the trend toward homeownership is viewed with alacrity by much of the middle class, one reasonably can suppose that over the long run it will exacerbate the economic situation of housing for the poor, even with a moderate amount of trickle-down, and it also will promote the increased segregation of economic classes. Attempts to solve the problem of sociospatial segregation by public action have not often been successful, even when there is a strong will. In van Vliet—'s chapter on the new towns of Israel it is shown quite clearly that, despite the government's stated intentions, an unintended consequence of new-town building has been a perpetuation or increase of segregation. A similar example of an unintended consequence of government action has been the "white flight" in U.S. cities—the result, at least in part, of government-mandated busing policies.

Despite the current tendency toward state inaction in housing, it is not out of line to speculate that the cycle will turn back in a few more years, and that Western nations will again see their governments move into the housing business in more significant ways. For no society has yet been able to provide adequate housing for the lower classes through the private market, and the nation that has relied most heavily on this approach, the United States, has the sorriest record in this regard. It seems doubtful, however, that Western governments soon will become involved with housing in the massive way that some did during the past few decades. And it seems equally doubtful that we ever again will see the large-scale construction of high-rise, multifamily buildings that have dominated the state's role in so many countries during the recent period. If in form, the future seems to be focused on low-rise, high-density housing, in administrative policy we will probably see much more public action on the cost side of housing, enabling consumers to have a larger choice of house types and tenures than in the past.

6 | Restructuring the Welfare State:
Privatization of Public Housing
in Britain

Ray Forrest and Alan Murie

Abstract. Forrest and Murie review the widespread provision of public housing in Britain since 1919. Important changes since 1979 include the sale of council (public) housing and other steps leading to the privatization of housing. Residents of public housing are increasingly composed of the disadvantaged, powerless poor in marginal occupations or on welfare, in contrast to the earlier broader distribution of working-class households who could resort to union wage demands or political action. Key changes in British government housing policy are reviewed in detail. Implications of the changes go beyond public housing to include social mobility, the distribution of wealth, and political orientation and, most broadly, to reflect a restructuring of the welfare state in Britain.

Introduction

One of the major areas for academic debate in the advanced industrialized economies in the seventies concerned the structural limits to the expansion of the welfare state within contemporary capitalism. Some accounts regarded the maintenance and expansion of the state welfare provision as necessary for the maintenance of capitalism. Within the British context in housing, this involved discussion of how far direct state housing provision—which had expanded continuously since 1919—could continue to grow and with what consequences. In the eighties council housing is, for the first time since 1919, in decline. The debate has shifted to address the structural limits to its further contraction. While public housing remains a major component in welfare state provision, it has become a major part of policies of privatization. Writing in 1974 Pahl commented:

> To a large extent Britain has got a more humane and generous approach to housing than other, ostensibly richer societies. This is largely due to the size and quality of its local authority housing, which, despite what its critics would say, is probably the best-managed publicly owned housing stock in the world. It is an enormous asset to our society and should not lightly be allowed to diminish (Pahl, 1974, p. x).

Ten years later the privatization of public housing, along with other developments in policies toward housing investment, rents, subsidy, and encouragement of owner occupation, involves a significant restructuring of housing. It forms part of a wider process to reorientate state intervention away from direct provision and toward the facilitation of market processes. Occurring in a period of high unemployment and economic recession, this reorientation makes the relationship between income and direct social welfare provision more pronounced. In housing it is contributing to a situation in which council housing is becoming the marginal tenure. The increasing concentration of vulnerable, low-paid and economically marginalized households in public housing has major implications for that sector. The economic and political powerlessness of this group is a significant feature of this process and it indicates a need to revise earlier views of the welfare state and of public housing provision.

Background

The provision of public housing has been a major component in the development of Britain's welfare state. Since 1919 and particularly following the end of World War II, it has grown steadily, in parallel with owner occupation. By 1981 almost a third of all households occupied state-provided dwellings, which is a significantly high proportion in the context of contemporary capitalism. Comparative figures for 1970–71 show that in Britain public renting accounted for 30 percent of housing—considerably more than in Australia (6 percent), New Zealand (6 percent), or the United States (1 percent). (See Kemeny, 1981.)

While powers to transfer publicly owned dwellings to private ownership have existed for a long time, the decision over whether to use these powers has been at the discretion of local administrations, and the enabling legislation has not provided strong incentives for would-be tenant-purchasers. The election in 1979 of a highly market-oriented Conservative government, committed to monetarist economic policies and reductions in state expenditure and provision, resulted in major changes in housing legislation. Local administrations were statutorily obliged to sell dwellings to interested tenants and that interest was fueled by discounts which reduced sale prices by up to 50 percent on market valuation. The reduction in the size of the public housing sector has become part of a general strategy to restructure and reduce state provision across the whole range of welfare services, including education, health, housing management, and even refuse collection. The consensus on the role of the welfare state which has existed since 1945 is now at an end, and the nature and role of the welfare state are being fundamentally questioned and, perhaps, irretrievably under-mined. While the welfare state had been regarded as an inevitable product and necessary component of the British social formation, it can no longer be seen as such. In the context of a labor and trade union movement seriously weakened by electoral defeat, economic recession, and high unemployment, the frontiers of state welfare pro-vision have been rolled back with little evidence of popular resistance or a weakening in the structure of legitimation. As Szelenyi (1981b) has observed, these processes evident in Britain and elsewhere have created some confusion on the left, given the sustained critique of the form and function of welfare provision (see, for example, Le Grand, 1982, Ginsburg, 1979, Gough, 1979). The antiplanning, antiwelfare stance of the new right has adopted many elements of this critique. The realization that a reduction in the provision of the means of collective consumption is possible without the imminent collapse of capitalism has posed serious questions for those accounts of state intervention which have seen welfare provision as necessary for the maintenance of capitalism (see, for example, the contributions in Pickvance, 1976). The shift in the political initiative to the New Right in Britain and elsewhere combined with the recognition of the signifi-cance, for example, of the role of the family (Balbo, 1982) and the informal economy has resulted in a review of explanations and analy-ses of the welfare state and its role (see, for example, Szelenyi, 1981b).

Within this context the disposal of a large number of publicly owned dwellings takes on a new significance. It would, for example, be misleading to view the sale of council houses simply in the context of debates about national housing policy. Increasingly the sale of council houses has been linked to issues of social mobility, the distribution of wealth and the less tangible notion of property-owning democracy (Murie and Forrest, 1980, Forrest and Murie, 1983, Kemeny, 1981). Perhaps more directly than in other European countries, the privatization of publicly owned dwellings is linked to broader political debates concerning the impact of tenure on the social structure. It is also true that the identification of particular political parties with particular tenures is more prominent in Britain than elsewhere (Murie, 1975, Bassett, 1980). In this sense any suggestion that the sales issue can be depoliticized is to ignore the roots and context of the debate. Rightly or wrongly, the Conservative party believes that the dismantling of the public rental sector is one means of undermining socialism. Crudely, the equation is that more homeowners means more potential Conservative voters.

In the period between the election of a Conservative government to power in May 1979 and the general election of 1983, over half a million council houses were sold in Great Britain. Sales represented some 8 percent of the council stock in England, and twenty-four local authorities have sold more than 15 percent of their stock (Forrest and Murie, 1983c).

Council house sales represent the major element in the government's privatization strategy as measured by capital receipts, value of sales, or the number of households directly affected. At the same time the rate of new building and acquisition of council dwellings is at an all-time low. A reasonable forecast of the impact of trends in new building, demolition, sales and acquisition would indicate that by 1986 some 64 percent of households in England will be owner-occupiers. Council housing will cater to less than one-quarter of all households. While this is still a large public sector in comparison with some other countries, and especially those with larger privately rented sectors, the reduction in size involves a significant reduction in rental opportunities as it is accompanied by a continuing decline in private renting (table 6.1).

Toward a Poor Law service

Recent literature and commentaries on British council housing offer a considerable contrast between the present status of council housing

Table 6.1 Change and composition of the housing stock: England and Wales 1914–85.

Composition in	Owner-occupier (%)	Local authorities and new towns (%)	Private landlords & other (%)	Total (millions)
1914	10	–	90	7.9
1938	32	10	58	11.4
1960	44	25	32	14.6
1975	55	29	16	18.0
1981	57	29	13	19.1
1985[1]	63	25	12	19.4
Net Change (millions)				
1914–38	+2.9	+1.1	−0.5	+3.5
1938–60	+2.7	+2.5	−2.0	+3.2
1960–75	+3.5	+1.6	−1.7	+3.4
1975–81	+1.2	+0.3	−0.4	+1.1
1981–85[1]	+2.4	−0.4	−0.6	+1.6

1 Estimates based on projections from current rates of building, demolition and transfers between tenures. This table has been compiled from Great Britain. Department of Environment. *Housing and construction statistics*, Hansard Vol. 5, No. 108 (21.5.81) and Cmnd. 6851, *Housing policy*, T.V.I., p. 39, London: HMSO, 1977.

and the picture of council housing between the wars or in the postwar period when it provided a privileged or preferential housing status. In particular, discussion in recent years has become increasingly concerned with the disadvantaged position of council tenants in the large number of less-desirable properties—high rise flats, difficult-to-let dwellings, and unimproved dwellings, many of which have been acquired from the private sector. A broader historical perspective refers to changes in the aims of council housing away from those of providing for general needs and more affluent working-class households and toward special needs and those with low incomes. Increasing reference is made to welfare housing, to Poor Law housing and to the "proper" role of council housing (catering for the elderly and disabled). Much of this comment comes from politicians and policy makers who stress alternatively the efficiency of subsidy and selectivity if council housing is only for those who "need" it or the undesirable consequences of developing a second-class service for the poorest.

Among the evidence frequently quoted to demonstrate how council housing is changing is that which shows that an increasing proportion of semiskilled and unskilled workers, of those on low incomes and of those dependent on welfare benefit, are council tenants (Murie 1983; Forrest and Murie, 1983b). There has been a steady trend through the seventies for those dependent on supplementary benefit (public assistance) to be council tenants. For example, in 1971 just over a half of all recipients were council tenants. By 1981 this had risen to 61 percent. Nor is this trend mirrored in the owner-occupied sector where over the same period the proportion had risen by only 2 percent (from 17 percent to 19 percent) (Department of Health and Social Security, annual statistics).

Further evidence supports this general picture. Thus, while in 1963 26 percent of households in the bottom three income deciles were council tenants, in 1979 this had risen to 47 percent; in 1972, 57 percent of unskilled manual workers were council tenants compared with 65 percent in 1976; in 1974, 39 percent of those not in paid employment were council tenants and in 1980, 44 percent. Statistics of this type have been widely used to emphasize social polarization between tenures as well as residualization of council housing (Murie, 1983). Other analyses of data over time relating the distribution of households between tenures according to income (Robinson and O'Sullivan, 1983) and socioeconomic group (Hamnett, 1983, Forrest and Murie, 1983b) confirm a view of increasing social polarization between the two main tenures. Taken in conjunction with a long-established bipartisan approach to the encouragement of owner occupation they justify a wide acceptance that the role of council housing has changed and is changing. Harloe (1978), for example, has referred to "reducing the further development of the public sector to a residual role and hoping that owner-occupation will cater for the bulk of future housing needs," and he has stated: "public housing is implicitly seen as an ambulance service concentrating its efforts on the remaining areas of housing stress and dealing with the variety of "special" needs such as the poor, the homeless, one-parent families, battered wives and blacks [p. 17]."

Key elements in government housing policy

Against this general background of mass disposal of public sector dwellings and a shift toward a reduced role for public housing, we can point to four specific elements of government policy which form part of the overall privatization strategy.

The government's public expenditure plans published in February 1983 showed housing's share of total public expenditure as having fallen to 3 percent in 1980/81 from 7 percent in 1976/7. The planned share for 1985–86 is just over 2 percent (U.K. Department of Environment, Cmnd. 8789, 1983). Over the period of the present government, housing has declined from a major to a minor program, and the view that housing is a service which can in the main be provided by the private sector has made substantial impact. The impact of these changes was felt most immediately in local authority housing investment, although it has subsequently resulted in substantial cuts in subsidy to council housing.

Local authority allocations of loan sanction for housing investment were cut by 30 percent in real terms in 1980–81. A moratorium on all new housing contracts, grants and loans was introduced in England in October 1980. Housing investment allocations were reduced by a further 15 percent in 1981–82. These cuts have not been restored. Capital receipts—especially from the sale of council houses—have been used to maintain housing investment at broadly 1981–82 levels. But maintaining housing investment through this method is geographically arbitrary. Spending permission relates to where receipts accumulate rather than to aspects of housing stress or need. It is quite possible, for example, that council house sales will be highest in areas of relative affluence.

In Great Britain in 1981, 55,242 local authority dwellings were completed—the lowest number since 1926, with the exception of the war years. Houses started and under construction were both fewer than this, and the prospect is of yet lower completion rates. In the first six months of 1982, there were 16,665 completions. Nor has the private sector filled the gap. In Great Britain in 1981, private sector completions were 112,960—the lowest figure since 1954. Although improvement activity in both the public and private sectors has been maintained at a more steady level (but lower than in 1971–74) and has increased with policy changes in 1982, the total level of investment continues to be extremely low. By the mid-eighties the cumulative shortfall in new construction (of some half a million dwellings compared with previous forecasts) will be significant and will not be easily remedied in the short term.

Between 1979 and 1982, average rents paid by council tenants rose by 117 percent—more than twice the rate of inflation. It is right to recognize that rents in 1979 were in the government's analysis at their lowest real postwar level. Between 1975 and the second half of 1979, the real cost of council house rents in England and Wales fell by 10 percent. However, subsequent increases have raised unrebated rents to a level higher (in real terms) than at any time in the seventies.

The sharp increase in rents has occurred in a situation where households can undergo a means test to obtain assistance with rent through rent rebates or supplementary benefit. Rising rents and limited new capital investment have enabled a significant reduction in general (as opposed to household means-tested) subsidy to the local authority's housing revenue account. Such general subsidy had in the past been the basic mechanism for holding rents for all tenants down. General subsidy (from the Exchequer and local rates) for tenants as a class has been largely replaced by subsidy directed (through a means test) at those with the lowest incomes.

The general economic environment and rising rents have led to an increasing role for rebates, and the long tradition of general subsidy has ended. During a sample week in May 1982, some 1.3 million council tenants were in receipt of rent rebates—9 percent more than in the equivalent week in 1981 and 31 percent more than in 1980. The average value of rebates in these sample weeks rose by 64 percent between 1980 and 1982 (CIPFA, 1982).

Toward a self-financing/profit-making council sector

Changes in housing investment by local authorities and increases in rents have revolutionized council housing finance. The popular image of council housing is of a sector heavily supported by general subsidy from rate and taxpayer, and the reality is of a sector where in 1976–77 only some 43 percent of council housing costs were covered by rents. By 1983, however, this position had changed dramatically. Only some eighty local authorities in 1982–83 are in receipt of general (deficit) subsidy to their housing revenue account, and in 1983–84 this is likely to decline to fewer than fifty (with the national Housing Revenue Account in surplus). Rate fund contributions to local authority housing are also falling in real terms. In many areas rents and income-related subsidies are more than covering the costs of providing council housing. Rather than a generally subsidized service it could be argued that council housing is developing into a self-financing service with only the poorest tenants subsidized by means-tested benefits.

Other tenants with higher incomes can be payers of subsidy (through rent pooling), and they may be contributing as tenants to the costs of certain social and community services (for example, certain aspects of estate maintenance and social service aspects of housing including aid and advice on homelessness) and any cash transfers from the housing revenue account to nonhousing accounts.

Rewards for (some) homeowners

In contrast, the factors determining home owners "costs" remain unchanged. While continued high interest rates have a real impact on those with mortgages, tax relief subsidy automatically increases as mortgage payments rise. Comparisons between the levels of assistance received by owner occupiers through tax relief and the levels of subsidy received by council tenants are a matter of some controversy. Nevertheless, it is clear that, as general assistance subsidy for council tenants has declined and there has been no parallel change in tax relief arrangements, the balance of advantage in subsidy treatment has shifted further toward owner occupiers. The average subsidy per council dwelling has fallen substantially from £245 per dwelling per annum in 1978–79 to £142 in 1983–83. In parallel, for owner-occupier households in receipt of tax relief, subsidy has risen from £200 per annum to £370 over the same period. This growth in mortgage tax relief partly reflects the level of interest rates which rose sharply in the late seventies and early eighties (Hansard, 1983).

In addition, council tenants qualify for rent rebates on test of means, and in 1981–82 this represented an average annual subsidy of £58 per household (Goss and Lansley, 1981). This subsidy, along with supplementary benefit payments for housing costs, is regarded as income assistance rather than housing subsidy. In 1983–84 the estimated annual subsidy for council tenants from these income assistance sources reflected the high proportion of tenants on supplementary benefit, and it was £377. A smaller number of owner occupiers are in receipt of assistance with housing costs through supplementary benefit, but the estimated value of relief from capital gains tax in 1982–83 was £3,000. Affluent council tenants able to take advantage of the opportunity to buy their house benefit from a reduction in purchase price which averages some £7,000 per household. On the average, owner occupiers with a mortgage have household incomes which are about twice as high as those of council tenants. In economic or social terms, it is thus difficult to justify the higher levels of subsidy accruing to the owner-occupied sector.

Council housing as the marginal tenure

From these detailed considerations of what is happening within Britain's housing sector it is necessary to move the analysis beyond housing to appreciate the potential implications of these processes. Much of what has been stated earlier revolves around the position of the poor in relation to housing. But, in addition to looking at parts of the housing market and at features of services, it is essential to consider economic and occupational change. A focus on the marginal poor rather than special needs emphasizes the shift from manufacturing to service employment and changes which have marginalized some groups in relation to the labor market. Progressive deskilling, structural and cyclical unemployment do not affect all groups equally. Those in unskilled manual work and the personal service sector are most harshly affected (Showler and Sinfield, 1981).

Permanent nonemployment rather than temporary unemployment has the effect of politically and economically marginalizing substantial sections of the population. These groups are characterized by powerlessness as much as by any other characteristic. It is in relation to these considerations that strengthening the relationship between unemployment, low wages, supplementary benefit recipients, unskilled and semiskilled work and public housing is significant. The public sector is catering to a progressively higher proportion of those marginalized in the labor market, and it is this feature which is tangible and significant for discussion of change in the housing service. There is a movement from a position where owner occupation was a predominantly middle-class tenure, high-quality council housing was used by the affluent working class, and private landlordism catered to the poorest sections of the population toward one where council housing serves the vulnerable, low-paid, and marginalized population with a highly stratified and differentiated homeownership as the mass tenure. An approach which emphasizes economic and occupational change and powerlessness provides an opportunity to see changes in management style, size, quality of stock, and level of subsidy as symptoms or consequences of the powerlessness of those using the service to resist reductions in standards or to achieve high standards. The economic and political powerlessness of this group is both a factor in their becoming and remaining tenants and in the quality and terms of service they receive. It is important to recognize that the marginalized poor have always tended to be in the worst housing in each tenure and to have greatest difficulty in negotiating access to and through the housing market. What is new in the present situation is the increasing concentration of this marginalized group in the public housing sector. While parts of the privately rented sector continue to house the young and the transient, the single, and some immigrant groups, its continued decline has shifted the relationship of dependence onto the state sector. By and large, those dependent on state benefits in their various forms are increasingly dependent on state housing. This is particularly marked at a time when this marginal population is expanding as a consequence of economic recession and technological restructuring. At the same time public policy decisions, which are reducing new investment in the state housing sector, pushing up rents, reducing subsidies, and selling council houses, are reinforcing the residual nature of the services offered. Those unable to compete in the marketplace are offered progressively less.

There are other implications of focusing attention on power and marginalization. Perspectives which refer uncritically to the role of the state in the reproduction of labor power require some revision when the population involved is increasingly marginal to the productive process. Where services cater to the elderly and others not seen as a vital and productive economic resource, few interests are served by providing subsidy for more than a minimal level of service. The current direction of policy can be seen as one of enabling those able to prosper in the private market to do so (Forrest and Murie, 1983b). For those left in council housing, there is little economic pressure to maintain and improve services. The social costs of economic restructuring in terms of unemployment and interruption of earnings do not fall evenly and are concentrated on public sector housing. To minimize the financial implications of this, there is considerable logic in minimizing the costs associated with direct housing provision. Increased rents and means testing, council house sales, reductions in public expenditure, and subsidy in the council house sector are logical responses to a situation where those in or seeking council housing are unable to respond to increases in cost through wage demands or political action.

Furthermore the extent to which tenants have a common interest in opposing increasing rents and demanding improved quality of service is potentially undermined by opportunities for the more affluent to avoid or escape the impact of these developments through exercising their right to buy the council house they occupy. Government policy for the housing needs of the "productive" labor force is promoted through owner occupation rather than policies toward council housing. With continuing high unemployment and technological change, these differences will become more marked. Stigmatization associated with dependency is likely to be exacerbated by these developments and by any tendency for managers, policy makers, and a wider range of agencies to adopt authoritarian (Poor Law) policies for the undeserving underclass. In addition, the very status of tenant in an increasingly market-consumer and credit-oriented society is likely to add to the disadvantages of the marginalized poor. Access to credit and accumulation of wealth are significant attributes of homeownership. While not all homeowners benefit equally, there are advantages associated with individual homeownership which are denied to nonowners. This exacerbates the economic and political powerlessness which contributes to housing status.

Concluding comments

The privatization of public housing, expedited by the cuts in direct public expenditure on housing investment and subsidy, is an element in a wider restructuring of the welfare state in Britain. Other areas have been the subject of significant cuts in levels of service (Bull and Wilding, 1983). However, in a period of recession and high unemployment, the total budget for social security expenditure has grown. Health and social service expenditure has also grown in real terms, although not sufficiently to cope with increased need related to demographic changes (O'Higgins, 1983). In the general restructuring of the welfare state, it is housing that has involved the most marked cuts in total expenditure. Various explanations can be offered for this. "Technical" arguments may be put forward suggesting that it is easier to cut capital programs or that demographic or economic (unemployment) factors lead expenditure toward policy areas other than housing. However, political arguments are at least as worthy of consideration. Cuts in housing investment do not have an immediate or easily identifiable impact on a particular group. There are time lags before reduction in housing supply is felt, and there are turnover and other processes affecting who experiences changes and when. In addition, the development of a dual tenure system may have divided or confused political opposition to cuts in public expenditure. While privatization can be shown to put some tenants and potential tenants at a disadvantage, it is of considerable benefit to others. Attacks on health service expenditure or education or even unemployment benefits may be likely to draw a stronger and more united opposition—and not necessarily only from those who will immediately suffer a loss of service. If these "political" factors are significant, then the constraints on further privatization of public housing are more limited than the constraints on ways of restructuring in other service areas. In this situation the trends outlined in this paper are likely to continue, and the consequences in terms of the marginalization of council housing are likely to become more marked.

7 | State Intervention in Urban Housing
Markets: Melbourne, 1945–80

Peter Newton and Maryann Wulff

Abstract. This chapter reviews functions and causes of state intervention in the housing market. Against this background, statistical information is used in an examination of three major public housing programs in Melbourne during the 1945–80 period. It is concluded that extant theoretical perspectives of the role of the state provide only partial views of housing practice. Historical analyses of specific cases of state intervention within their broader context are seen as required for the development of a more comprehensive explanatory framework.[1]

Before World War II, public sector housing was virtually unknown in Australia. The private sector effectively dominated both the ownership and the rental sections of the housing market. By the mid-seventies, however, public sector involvement in housing had been firmly established, with more than 205,000 (or 5 percent) of all occupied dwellings in Australia rented from government housing authorities. A further 220,000 dwellings had been built by the public sector and sold to low-income households. In the state of Victoria, the Housing Commission had built or purchased 90,000 dwelling units by 1980; of these, 61 percent were located in the capital, Melbourne, a city of 2.75 million population.

Three major public housing programs have operated in Melbourne over the 35-year period of direct government involvement since 1945: large-scale villa estate construction (comprised entirely of single-family detached housing), high-rise redevelopment, and a housing rehabilitation and spot purchase program. Accordingly, this chapter aims to describe in some detail the various public housing programs operating in Melbourne since World War II and to explore the factors responsible for the diverse developments and programs that have occurred. In order to do so, this discussion is placed in the context of contemporary theories of the state. Merrett (1979, p. 275) argues, in fact, that "it is not possible . . . to theorize about housing policy without at the same time incorporating the contours of a theory of the state." State theory has been singularly important in alerting housing analysts to the links between housing and the wider social, economic, and political system in which it is embedded (Saunders, 1979; Merrett, 1979). In this chapter, the framework developed by Saunders (1979) concerning the functions and causes of state policies is adopted, and it forms the background for the discussion of Melbourne's public housing programs since 1945. Before proceeding to a discussion of these issues, it is necessary to consider some background to the public housing system in Australia in general and Melbourne in particular.

Public housing in Melbourne

The organization of public housing programs in Australia reflects the historical relationship between the federal government and the six states. Whereas public housing programs in Australia are managed by each of the six states, they are almost completely financed by the federal government. The varying pattern of federal allocation of housing funds in Victoria since 1949 is shown in figure 7.1. The scale of outlays reflects a number of influences, not the least of which mirrors changes in political power and philosophy.

In addition to financial constraints, each state housing authority is expected to operate within certain broad policy guidelines set by the federal government and laid down in agreements known as the Commonwealth State Housing Agreement (CSHA). The commonwealth state housing agreements, which are handed down, on average, every five years, provide an explicit statement of what the commonwealth considers its priorities to be with regard to public housing. Policy directives from the commonwealth, for example, have shifted over the years from an early emphasis on the construction of rental accommodation to a later requirement (under a newly elected conservative government) that a certain proportion of commission homes be sold to public clients at minimal deposit and on low-interest long-term loans. The most recent directive from the federal government, via the CSHA, concerns the setting of rents in commission flats to market levels (Burke et al., 1983).

Within the funding and policy constraints imposed by the federal government, each state in Australia administers its own public housing programs. The Victorian Housing Commission (HCV), the focus of this chapter, was established as a statutory authority in 1938 with wide-ranging powers to engage in site acquisition, new construction, and house purchase, as well as program administration. The early, prewar, objective of the HCV focused on slum reclamation, while later attention shifted to the rapid provision of low-cost housing to meet the shortage which followed World War II. Later, under a Liberal government in the fifties, attention focused upon increasing homeownership possibilities by selling commission properties to public housing clients. Most recently, the goal of social mix has attained priority, and systematic policies involving the spot purchase of new and existing dwellings throughout metropolitan Melbourne are under way.

The purpose of this chapter is to analyze, within the framework of the theory of the state, three major Melbourne public housing pro-

Figure 7.1 Victoria's allocation of federal housing funds, 1949–81 (in constant 1981 Australian dollars). *Source: State Intervention*, by Newton and Wulff (1983).

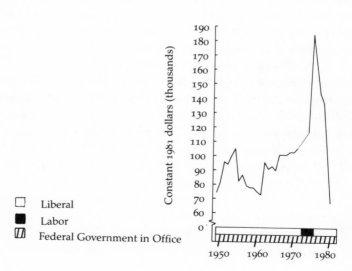

Constant 1981 dollars (thousands)

☐ Liberal
■ Labor
▱ Federal Government in Office

Table 7.1 Lagged correlation analysis between private sector and public sector residential construction activity in Melbourne, 1950–80.

Number of years lagged	Public sector lags private sector	Private sector lags public sector
0	−0.33	−0.33
1	−0.40 ($p<0.05$)	−0.31
2	−0.39 ($p<0.05$)	−0.25
3	−0.37	−0.23
4	−0.34	−0.23
5	−0.32	−0.22
6	−0.20	−0.22
7	−0.10	−0.24
8	−0.11	−0.25
9	−0.14	−0.22
10	−0.09	−0.18

Source: Australian Bureau of Statistics. *Victoria's building operations, 1950–1980.*

grams, namely: the construction and sale of houses on villa estates; high-rise redevelopment; rehabilitation, and spot purchase.

Functions of state intervention in housing

In examining the functions of state intervention in housing in Britain from a sociological perspective, Saunders (1979, pp. 147–48) argues that state expenditure in this sector may be considered important in three ways: (*a*) in directly sustaining production in the house-building industry, (*b*) in providing the material conditions of existence necessary for the reproduction of the labor force, and (*c*) in maintaining social cohesion of the society. Investigation of the functions performed by public housing in Melbourne suggests that all three functions have been represented in the state government's programs and policies over the past thirty-five years.

Stabilization and sustaining production

At the end of World War II, Australia was suffering from a housing shortage; homes were severely overcrowded, and many dwellings lacked basic amenities. Because of shortages of building materials and skilled labour, it took some years for the building industry to pick up (from 15,400 completed dwellings in 1945–46 to 57,000 by the end of the forties). Once the recovery was under way, however, it began a period of sustained production throughout the fifties and sixties which, according to Neutze (1977), not only made up for the backlog of construction and maintenance during the thirties and forties, but also raised housing standards to higher levels than ever before. Construction of houses by the state government contributed to this recovery. In the decade 1950–59, HCV completions comprised approximately 14 percent of Victoria's total. Subsequently, as the rate of growth in demand for housing began to parallel the rate of growth of supply, public intervention in house construction had declined to less than 4.5 percent of annual completions in 1980.

Further evidence of governments' use of the public housing sector to advance wider economic objectives is reflected in the countercyclical pattern of public investment in new construction in Melbourne between 1950 and 1980 (table 7.1).

In comparing the level of building activity by the state government with that by the private sector for the period 1950 to 1980, yearly data on new residential construction suggest that the public sector appeared to be consistently modifying its building program by increasing construction in periods when the private sector was in decline and, conversely, reducing the level of new public housing starts when the private sector was expanding. Such data illustrate the role of the public sector in stabilizing the building industry as a whole. Badcock has written similarly of the role of the South Australian Housing Trust (SAHT) as an instrument of economic stabilization in South Australia: "The fairly constant level of dwelling completions maintained by the SAHT between 1955 and 1968 coincides with a period of relative economic stability; but, thereafter, was deliberately countercyclical in an effort to compensate for fluctuations in private sector activity" (Badcock, 1982, p. 198).

In addition to the construction cycles of the HCV, another indication of the economic stabilization function of the state public housing authority can be discerned from its role in redeveloping the inner suburbs of Melbourne. The expressed objective of the redevelopment program, which is discussed more fully later in this chapter, was to sustain business activity in Melbourne's central business district. To do so, the HCV was actively encouraged during the fifties by Melbourne's regional planning authority to join with private enterprise in redeveloping, at higher population densities, large sections of the inner suburbs of the city (MMBW, 1954).

Reproduction of labor power through collective consumption

For private production to continue in an industrial society, it is necessary that the material conditions of existence, notably housing, be provided for its workers. Saunders (1979, p. 147) argues that, among other factors, the state must provide housing for the working class in order to ensure the continued reproduction of labor power required by industry. Merrett (1979, p. 279) has written similarly of the British public housing program: "the construction of dwellings is one of the major activities of reproductive production." And Pickvance states as well that state housing is most likely to be provided when "housing shortage is leading to labor shortage, or when wage levels lag behind housing costs. In each case the ability of labor to reproduce itself is threatened" (cited in Kirby, 1981, p. 1296).

The establishment of Victoria's public housing authority was due, in large part, to the need to reproduce a stable and productive work force. From the beginning, the activities of the HCV were closely associated with the general economic development of the state of Victoria. The HCV Annual Report of 1946 reflects this position when it states that housing and industry should be developed simultaneously in both the metropolitan area of Melbourne and in growing country towns (Victoria, Australia. Housing Commission—hereinafter HCV—n.d.).

During the fifties and sixties, the social reproduction function of the HCV was most apparent in its villa estate programs. This period was one of rapid social and economic change—industrialization was proceeding apace and the annual rate of population growth was more than double prewar rates, due largely to high levels of immigration. To attract labor and sustain economic development in the state of Victoria, provision of housing was a prime requisite. The construction of large estates of single-family detached houses, many of which were eventually sold to public clients, went hand in hand with the establishment of new manufacturing and automotive plants on the fringes of Melbourne (Wulff and Newton, 1983). Clearly, the material conditions necessary to attract and maintain a stable and productive workforce were established.

Maintenance of order and promoting social cohesion

Maintenance of economic and political stability is a principal function of government, and it can assume a number of forms (see Saunders, 1979, p. 148). The establishment of public housing in Melbourne can be seen as promoting social cohesion in two ways, first, as a welfare service to support the surplus long-term unemployed and low-income population of the city; second, as an ideological extension of the state's firm belief in homeownership. Direct government intervention in Melbourne's housing market in the late thirties can be viewed as reflecting the need to support the "surplus population" of the period, who were living in overcrowded and overpriced tenements in sections of the inner city. As Barnett states, "if slum reclamation by and through the state achieves no more than the physical and moral salvation of the children within these areas, it will have more than justified any financial sacrifice involved" (cited in Russell, 1972, p. 4). Thus, a combination of church-based "paternalistic altruism" and the fear of the slum environment hatching revolutionary communism (Russell, 1972, p. 12) provided an important stimulus to the formation of the HCV in 1938.

In subsequent decades the growth in material prosperity of the Australian population has meant the virtual elimination of slum conditions as they existed in the prewar period. As a result, during the fifties through the mid-seventies, the social cohesion function of the HCV assumed a new form: the legitimation of state activity by assisting low-income households into homeownership. The role of the state in legitimating the existing order in Australia is suggested in the sales policy of the HCV villa estates. Selling HCV homes to clients was a way of offering them a stake in Australian society and a reinforcement of the Australian value of homeownership which, according to Kemeny (1977, p. 47) "is undoubtedly the most powerful ideology in Australian social and political life" (p. 47). Moreover, Kemeny (1977, p. 48) argues that the belief in homeownership in Australia is seen to represent the "main bulwark against social, economic and political unrest, and that widespread home ownership (was) the antidote to threats to the capitalist system in Australia."

In the eighties, homeownership prospects for public clients are restricted almost completely. The increase in the cost of land and housing relative to wages (Bromilow, 1975), as well as the effect of rising mortgage interest rates on a household's ability to service loan repayments (Bromilow, 1977), have contributed to this problem. By 1980, unemployment had risen to its highest level since the thirties depression. With federal funding for public housing decreasing as well, the clientele of public housing is becoming increasingly welfare-oriented. In 1980, up to 50 percent of public housing tenants were relying on some form of income and rental support. Consequently, the social cohesion function of the HCV appears to be contracting and returning to its earlier welfare form, that of supporting a "surplus population."

Causes of state intervention in housing

Having outlined some of the major functions of state-provided housing, it is necessary to consider the explanations offered for state intervention in housing. A brief outline of contrasting theories illustrates the divergence of perspectives within the state intervention debate. The representational perspective argues that the pattern of public expenditure demonstrates a response by the state in advanced industrial society to newly emerging needs generated by rapid economic development. The structural changes which occur in national economies in response to world economic system pressures, as well as those pressures internal to a particular society, generate needs among various adversely affected segments of the population such as the poor, the unemployed, and the aged. The state, in turn, is seen to recognize the demands of these groups, and it responds for at least two reasons. First, societal capacity to respond has increased through increased economic growth and, second, there is a more or less built-in propensity for the state to further the public interest via redistribution and allocation in accordance with societal preferences (which the state is seen to reflect). The growth of resources accompanying industrialization are seen to either trickle down or be consciously directed to groups with perceived needs (Isaac and Kelly, 1981).

As Saunders notes, such representational perspectives adopt the view that the state is neutral in its functions and independent of any particular class interests. Instead, the state is called on by various interest groups to undertake a wide range of functions, with no single interest group being able to consistently dominate the state decision-making process (Saunders, 1979, pp. 150–57; also, refer to the pluralist-decision-maker theory described by Johnston, 1980).

In contrast, the instrumentalist perspective argues that state intervention in any sphere of society is caused by the very nature of capitalist society, particularly its class-based conflicts. While they do not discount a number of the processes that the representational perspective suggest are important in public sector activity, proponents of instrumentalist perspectives argue that these forces alone cannot explain the major direct causes of state actions. Rather, the basic processes guiding state expenditure in general and welfare expansion in particular are best explained by examining the class and institutional structures of advanced capitalist societies—in particular, the relations between classes, class conflict, and the interconnections between the state and private capital (Isaac and Kelly, 1981; Saunders, 1979). Proponents of this perspective argue that welfare-oriented public sector institutions and funding expand as a means of defusing threatening situations mounted against the state and the established socioeconomic order. Expansion of public expenditure is seen to take place on a major scale only when threat is sufficient and where the state must strive to maintain conditions favorable to capital accumulation and social harmony (Isaac and Kelly, 1981, p. 1357).

In many respects, the relative autonomy model is a variant of the instrumentalist approach. Whereas the developmental perspective argues that the state is neutral in its public housing function, and the instrumentalist model points out how state-provided housing is a reflection of the class structure of the society, this third perspective, the relative autonomy model, considers those situations under which the state remains neutral to capitalist interests and those situations where it does not. Merrett supports the utility of this last model when he argues that "This involves an exposition of the objective role the state plays in the maintenance of the social order and in underpinning the accumulation of capital whilst recognising that it constantly seems to appear to be above class interest and that it does not act at the beck and call of capital" (Merrett, 1979, p. 227).

While the instrumentalist model seems to imply that the dominant class in society is a homogenous, unitary formation which can and does manipulate the state to serve its own interests, the relative autonomy model argues that, given the internal divisions of the dominant class, the state is, in fact, relatively autonomous from them. Although the state still acts to protect the overall continuity of capitalist production, there is no one unitary class to which it is beholden. The entry into parliament of substantial numbers of working class representatives is seen to strengthen the state's autonomy relative to the dominant class (Merrett, 1979, p. 277). In addition, state bureaucracies are independent of industry and capital, while simultaneously dependent on the private sector for revenue. The often ambiguous connection between the Victorian Housing Commission and the building industry can be seen in this light, particularly through its high-rise construction program.

The housing programs of the HCV, 1945–80

The task now is to illustrate further how these theoretical ideas apply to specific housing programs of the Victorian Housing Commission. The overall program of the HCV since 1945 can be divided into three distinct types of activities: villa estate construction on broadacre sites; high-rise redevelopment (i.e., clearance and new construction); and housing purchase and rehabilitation. Some of these programs occurred simultaneously, but they are presented in chronological order of their emergence as significant programs in Melbourne.

Villa estate development

In the immediate postwar period, Victoria was faced with an acute housing shortage. This shortage became most evident to the HCV when "an advertisement for tenants for 31 homes in 1943 brought 1500 urgent claims" (HCV, n.d.). In recognition of this housing crisis, the HCV shifted its original emphasis on slum reclamation work to housing construction. According to an HCV report, "The Commission concentrated almost entirely on villa estates on broadacres, which represented few encumbrances to planning and building operations and gave the greatest return, in terms of dwellings produced, for the economic resources available." (HCV, n.d.)

The first villa estates were established on large tracts of land on the (then) outer fringes of Melbourne. The reasons stem from the effects of World War II. "The growing shortage of manpower and the essential building materials made it very hard to meet the enormous housing shortage . . . and . . . the commodity not in short supply was land on the outer fringes of the city, and the limited building materials and labour power available were concentrated into expanding outer residential areas" (Stevenson et al., 1967, p. 7). Nearly two hundred villa estates have been established in Melbourne since 1945, with a total of 39,000 houses constructed. Construction of these estates was undertaken for efficiency and cost purposes: to procure the greatest number of dwellings for the least cost. Villa estate development is generally believed to permit economies of scale in construction and administration although "the extent of these economies and how they vary with the size of estates have never been estimated" (Neutze, 1978, pp. 102–3). Nearly two-thirds of the very large estates of more than one thousand dwellings were built in the fifties, with most of the remaining large estates under way in the sixties. Contrary to the popular public image, however, not all villa estates are massive in scale. More than half of the estates in Melbourne comprise fewer than a hundred detached houses.

HCV construction activity on villa estates has reflected the prevailing ideology and preference in Australia for the detached house. The majority of stock built on villa estates since 1945 has been detached family homes. Indeed, 80 percent of all units erected on villa estates have been detached houses, while the remaining 20 percent of units have been in the form of one- to four-story blocks of walk-up flats. Another aspect of the villa estate program which reflects the legitimation role of the HCV is in the sales policy in operation on villa estates. Over the years the HCV has sold a majority of the stock on villa estates, so that by 1980 three-fourths of the 39,000 detached houses built by the HCV had been sold. The HCV sales policy clearly reflects the prevailing preference in Australia for homeownership, and the federal government, through the CSHA, had established the financial apparatus, incentives, and loans to make the sale of HCV dwellings possible. In fact, the fluctuating patterns of sales in Victoria illustrate the state's relationship with the federal government with regard to the commonwealth-state housing agreements.

In the initial years of its existence, the HCV was restricted, under the terms of the CSHA, in its sale of public housing unless full purchase price was forthcoming. The 1956 CSHA released the state housing authorities to sell public stock on their own terms. This policy continued, largely unchanged, for the next sixteen years. In 1973, the newly elected federal Labor government, through the CSHA of that year, restricted sales of state housing authority dwellings to no more than 30 percent of subsequent completions in an effort to stem this tendency. This federal policy initiative was ineffective, however, as the Victorian Liberal government, which was opposed to a limitation on sales in particular and to the federal government in general, was able to draw on existing stock for a record sales year in 1974. In subsequent CSHAS (1978 and 1981), the federal Liberal government has permitted each state to determine its own policy for the sale of dwellings, subject to transactions being on a cash basis and that sale price be at market value, the net proceeds being used to replace dwelling stock that has been sold. Under this scheme, sales more closely mirror completions, with the downward trend in both being a reflection of a reduction in federal funds for housing over the past five years or so.

That the state housing authorities be permitted or encouraged to sell their stock when there remains a formidable number of households on waiting lists for public housing (of the order of 20,000 households per annum in Victoria during the late seventies) is an issue which has received little attention until recently. Kemeny (1980, 1981) points out that the maturation of the public housing stock would have allowed the authorities an opportunity to give their tenants the benefits of historic costs in the form of lower rentals. The sale of public housing on low deposit and at low interest rates (characteristic of the period 1956–73) prevented the development of a larger and more efficient public rental sector. The size of the public rental sector has increased only marginally in Melbourne over the past twenty years, from 17,300 units in 1961 to 25,900 in 1980. In comparison, the total volume of public stock sold has risen from 7,300 to 28,000 units over the same period. Furthermore, and as Stretton (1978) points out, sales of early, well-located public housing left several of the state housing authorities with very little well-placed public housing for later generations of low-income tenants.

Redevelopment: Slum clearance and high-rise

The second main construction program of the HCV, the high-rise program, focused on the redevelopment of so-called slum sections of the inner areas of Melbourne. This program began in earnest in the mid-fifties, although the HCV had always viewed its fundamental mission as one of slum clearance. In fact, the creation of the Housing Commission in 1938 was largely in response to the report and recommendations of the Housing Investigation and Slum Abolition Board, published in the preceding year (HCV, 1967a). Priorities changed with the intervention of World War II, when overcoming an acute shortage of housing led instead to the villa estate program.

The resurgence of interest in slum clearance in 1956 has been linked to several events. In 1954, Melbourne's regional planning authority, the Melbourne and Metropolitan Board of Works (MMBW) issued its blueprint for the future development of the city. The section on housing concentrated on redevelopment, citing it as an urgent task and one to be undertaken by the HCV. Redevelopment of the inner city was to be undertaken in an attempt to arrest the trend of inner Melbourne population loss and the threat that this was thought to pose to the economic viability of the central business district (MMBW, 1954, p. 37; see also Merrett, 1979, p. 80 for a similar U.K. experience). The state, via the HCV, was expected to intervene in the economic stabilization of inner Melbourne. Redevelopment was to be undertaken at densities which reflected the historically determined concentration of people in slum dwellings: "the aim should be to re-house under proper living conditions at least the same number of people as are living there at present. There would be some advantage in housing a somewhat greater number . . . this cannot be accomplished with the detached or semi-detached single family dwelling alone. Row housing, walk-up flats and elevator flats must be used as well" (Melbourne and Metropolitan Board of Works, 1954, p. 38).

The ideological leaning of state officials was apparent in the establishment of this program. For example, slum clearance was a policy of the state Liberal party when it assumed government in 1955. In 1960 the then Minister of Housing, Sir Horace Petty, stated: "One of the major changes that must take place in metropolitan development in Victoria is that the sprawl of new suburbs must be arrested, and the inner suburban areas replanned and rebuilt to carry a reasonably increased population living in comfortable and up-to-date houses and flats" (cited in Kneebone, 1980, p. 3). Nor did the HCV lack its own advocates of slum clearance and urban renewal. Within the top management of the HCV, a senior architect, upon returning from a tour of European and North American cities undergoing redevelopment, extolled the virtues of block clearance and high-density redevelopment (Shaw, 1966). The parallels with international trends in high-rise redevelopment activity during the late sixties and early seventies indicate how prone the policies and programs of housing authorities are to influences, such as the sociotechnical philosophy of high rise construction prevailing in the sixties in western industrial societies, and forces beyond the bounds of a particular state.

A lack of finances for the redevelopment program plagued the state's activities from the beginning. As the federal government's financial contributions were restricted under the CSHA to loans for construction of new dwellings on broadacre sites, the Victorian state government was required to provide funding for all slum clearance and high-rise construction. Consequently, the redevelopment phase in Melbourne clearly reveals the links between the HCV and private capital. The financial backing of private capital was sought actively: "It is the opinion of the Commission that reclaimed areas require to be redeveloped in part by private enterprise and in part by the Commission" (HCV, 1965). Also, "private interest in the development of land reclaimed by the Commission is increasing, and it is proposed that some portion of the land required each year be set aside for redevelopment by private enterprise" (HCV, 1967b).

The attempt to encourage the participation of private enterprise in redevelopment had two objectives: (a) generation of revenue for state housing authority activities, and (b) creation of a mix of income groups within the inner area of Melbourne. The latter, it was hoped, would both stabilize the economic position of the central business district and promote a socially harmonious, socially mixed community.

These two objectives contain a number of contradictions. First, rather than generating a profit, the HCV suffered losses of at least 50 percent in the cost of assembling land sold to private enterprise (HCV, 1972); these transactions have subsequently undergone investigation by a Royal Commission of Inquiry. Also, the high-rise tower blocks proved costly to build, a factor which calls into question the economic rationale for public high-rise units. A study by Jones and Hartnett (1970), for example, costed elevator apartments some 50 percent higher than detached single-unit housing.

Second, the extent to which social cohesion in the community was fostered is questionable, as the high-rise program was seen to stigmatize public clients as well as contribute to organized community protest. Studies have indicated that the highly visible enclaves of high-rise development separated by ample open space from the nearby and better designed tracts of private medium-density housing served to increase the scope for external labelling of public tenants. Residence in the high-rise estates actually increased the social stigma of HCV clients rather than promoting an environment which would facilitate social interaction with the surrounding community (Gribbin and Instone, 1977). Gentrification of several inner Melbourne suburbs was also under way by the early seventies (Centre for Urban Research and Action, 1977). Rising real incomes and a relatively easier route to homeownership in the early sixties, combined with the postwar influx of migrants into inner city areas, provided the necessary ingredients for considerable private rehabilitation as well as growing resentment with commission activities. By the late sixties, a well-organized protest movement including residents, local government, the media, and the unions retarded the HCV's ability to undertake widespread clearance and precipitated the formulation of the Urban Renewal Act of 1970, which provided avenues for public involvement in HCV renewal schemes (Hargreaves, n.d.). The impact of the act was such that the HCV annual reports in both 1972 and 1973 reported a cessation in proclaiming new slum reclamation areas. The last residential tower block was completed in Melbourne in 1974. Notwithstanding the HCV's building activity in central city areas, the region's population has continued to decline through the seventies and early eighties, reflecting the increased per capita consumption of housing by households now resident in central Melbourne.

Rehabilitation and spot purchase

The third and most recent program of the HCV is in fact a set of small policy initiatives aimed at removing the stigma associated with either the large villa estates or the high-rise tower blocks. These programs reflect the state's continuing belief that both the public and private sectors need to cooperate in the revitalization of urban areas. Several motivating factors were advanced by the HCV for these new programs, among the more important being preservation of accommodation in the inner suburbs for low-income households. The Federal Department of Urban and Regional Development became actively involved in urban rehabilitation with the provision of tied grants to the HCV for the acquisition of a large high-rise estate in Melbourne (EHCD, 1978, p. viii). Soon afterward, the state government initiated a rehabilitation program that embraced the old slum reclamation areas in sections of Melbourne's inner suburbs. Within these areas, rehabilitation of individual properties proceeded where it was felt the original house was worth retention. In a very few instances, substandard houses were demolished and the sites used for individually designed "infill houses" which harmonized with the retained properties. The Urban Renewal Act of 1970 ensured a series of checks on unthinking clearance activities and ensured the opportunity for exhaustive public participation in the overall process.

To June 1978, only thirty-two properties had been rehabilitated in the specified areas, representing less than 1 percent of new stock added by the HCV in the period since 1974 (HCV, 1979). Despite increased activity in this area over the past few years, this program does not match either the villa estate or the high-rise programs in the generation of dwelling units for occupation by low-income households.

In reviewing the limited progress of most state housing authorities with regard to urban rehabilitation, the cost-effectiveness of the program has been questioned: "All the authorities have problems in justifying the added expense of acquisition and rehabilitation of inner-city housing. Compared with the cost of new construction on the outer fringe this form of housing is usually more expensive per unit. More-over, the effectiveness of housing policy is regarded by politicians in terms of the number of new dwellings constructed" (EHCD, 1978, p. 37).

A related program of the HCV, similar in objectives and scale, is the spot purchase program. "Spot purchase" refers to the systematic pur-chase by the public housing authority of existing dwellings in selected locations around Melbourne. As reported by the Ministry of Housing (1982), the spot purchase program "reflects a policy move away from the provision of new public rental housing in large estates in outer urban areas. Policy is now directed toward the integration of the min-istry's tenants into the existing urban fabric." The spot purchase pro-gram reflected an attempt to build up the rental stock, maximize locational choice for HCV clients, and reduce the stigma experienced by residency on easily identifiable commission estates. The economic stabilization function of this program was implied by the Minister of Housing when he argued that the program "provides a boost to pri-vate development, construction and building industries," which have experienced a slump in activity in recent years. There is now a com-plete reliance on the private sector for provision of stock for HCV spot purchase activities.

To date, both the scale of the spot purchase program and the loca-tion of houses purchased suggest the the HCV may well not meet its expressed policy objectives. In the first two years of program opera-tion, fewer than 250 dwellings had been purchased in Melbourne, far less than the average level of commission construction established in previous years. Moreover, the location of spot-purchased homes casts further doubt on its effectiveness, as large numbers of homes were purchased in a limited number of neighborhoods within Melbourne. This raises the question of whether the level of spatial segregation of spot purchase homes will, in some cases, be greater than that demon-strated by either the high-rise or villa estate programs (Wulff and Newton, 1983).

Summary and conclusions

This chapter has explored the influences on and of the state in the development and change of various housing programs in Melbourne over a thirty-five year period since 1945. During this time, the state, through the HCV, can be seen to have been undertaking, simultaneously, several functions, including: (*a*) stabilizing the economy, particularly through the building industry; (*b*) ensuring the reproduction of the labor force; and (*c*) ensuring social cohesion through the provision of welfare housing and promotion of homeownership. The particular housing programs employed by the state have been found to vary over time, however, in response to changing economic and political conditions. For instance, villa estate development continued at varying intensity until 1980, but it was most prominent in the fifties and sixties, when worker-housing policies were closely linked with federal immigration policy. Also federal funding of state housing was measurably higher under Labor than under Liberal administrations. It appears, therefore, that, despite their nominal constitutional state rights with regard to housing, the state housing authorities in Australia experience strong centrally imposed restraints on their autonomy through the commonwealth-state housing agreements. The phase of redevelopment and high-rise construction in inner Melbourne was a major exception, since it was funded solely by the Victorian government and motivated, in part, as a means of sustaining the economic viability of the central business district.

The usual lack of connection between abstract theories of the state and housing research has been observed by several authors (Saunders, 1979; Duncan, 1981). Saunders, for example, remarks on the "noticeable strain" (1979, p. 201), even a "hiatus" (1979, p. 207) between the two levels of understanding. This chapter represents an effort at merging state theory with a discussion of the nature and historical development of Melbourne's three major public housing programs. Upon completing this study, it seems fair to conclude that state theory, while particularly useful in highlighting the functions of the state with regard to various public housing programs, is not overwhelmingly helpful in explaining the causes or the underlying explanations for a particular program.

To illustrate, throughout the postwar period the construction of villa estates by the HCV suggests a dominant function of an advanced industrial state: providing housing to a burgeoning workforce. The sales policy operating on villa estates, that is, selling the homes on low-interest long-term loans to HCV residents, fulfills a commitment to homeownership, which some argue helps to maintain the social cohesion of the society. The extent to which villa estate construction helped to boost the building industry is less clear, although evidence has been presented which indicates that in periods of downswing in the private house building sector, government-funded housing activity tended to increase.

The analytical difficulty is that these state functions do not presuppose any particular theoretical explanations (Saunders, 1979, p. 148). For example, given the fairly steady growth in GNP in Australia during the heyday of villa estate development, the representational model might imply that the built-in mechanism of economic growth explains increased state expenditure in public housing. The state, it might be argued, was consistently representational in its stance on public housing, constructing and then selling single-family detached homes in response to the preferences of Australian households. Or does the instrumentalist model best explain this program, implying that the sale of villa estates reflected the interests of the ruling class in legitimating the capitalist ideology in Australia? The most productive explanatory model may well be the relative autonomy approach, in that this model encourages examination of the conditions under which the state remained neutral to capital and those under which it appeared to be beholden to capital interests. That task, however, requires exhaustive historical case study analysis.

Clearly, each perspective on the state offers a partial view of reality, and full understanding of the causes and explanations for state intervention in housing will emerge only after a detailed and multitheoretical consideration of the role of the state in a capitalist society; the ideologies and beliefs of the urban managers who design these state policies; and the economic, political, social, and technological conditions that exist beyond the boundaries of a particular state. Each state, as indicated by the various chapters in this volume, is part of a larger international sociotechnical and economic community, and, increasingly, state policies and programs with regard to housing will be seen to reflect this context.

8 | State Intervention and Alternative Tenure Patterns in Montreal

Francine Dansereau, Gerard Divay, and Jacques Godbout

Abstract. This chapter first reviews principal features which characterize the production and allocation of housing in North America. Outcomes are discussed as effected by visible policies (e.g., public housing) and the, in budgetary terms, much more important indirect policies (e.g., intervention in the mortgage market and fiscal measures to promote private homeownership). Criticism on these policies notwithstanding, housing conditions in Montreal, Canada, are shown as very satisfactory. Alternative tenure forms currently emerging within the same policy framework are discussed with an eye to future developments.

Introduction

The purpose of this chapter is twofold. First, to recall the main features of the housing production and allocation system which has prevailed in the United States and Canada over the last few decades, drawing attention to some of its peculiarities in the Quebec context, and emphasizing the role of public intervention in the general operation of the system and in the changes to which it is presently submitted. Second, to focus on emerging changes in the production of housing and its allocation to social groups, more specifically on the relative influence of *alternative modes of tenure*, such as condominiums, cooperative co-ownership, and tenant cooperatives, as compared to the more traditional forms of owner occupancy or tenancy.

Basic features of the postwar housing allocation system

In North America, the production of housing and its distribution to households is effected essentially through the private market. In 1980, as little as 2 percent of all dwellings in the province of Quebec were managed by public authorities or nonprofit organizations. As in the United States, the fundamental rationale for housing policy relies on the filtering process whereby the main target is the provision of a sufficient number of new dwellings for the middle or higher income strata. Because of a relative loss of attraction—hence, diminishing prices—the units vacated by these groups within the existing stock are supposed to filter to the next group down the income ladder, who in turn will relinquish their previous dwelling to the next lower stratum, and so on down the chain, until all income groups have "improved" their housing consumption—without incurring larger costs —and until the most deteriorated portions of the housing stock have been eliminated through abandonment or demolition (Grigsby, 1963). Direct provision of housing by the state is minimal and limited to the lowest strata: the poorest, the disabled, the retired, etc., when such action has not been restricted to replacing units eliminated through state intervention (urban renewal) simply because they did not seem to fall quickly enough into the abandoned or demolished category.

On a large aggregate level, this process, at least in the United States, is often cited as having led to the massive flight of the middle classes to the suburbs and to the consequent decline of the central city, of which neighborhood filtering is viewed as an integral part. This linkage with a specific form of urban development is not inherent in the filtering process per se; it is due to the fact that a large fraction of new housing consisted of privately owned single-family dwellings, which had to be developed outside existing built-up urban areas. If new construction had taken another form, e.g., higher-density rental apartments in central locations,[1] the ensuing consequences on urban form and on the socioeconomic differentiation of urban areas might have been vastly different.

We do not wish to enter here into a discussion as to whether these schematic views of the filtering process fit the actual operation of the housing market. The point which we wish to stress is that this system, and the particular housing form it has favored, have not evolved naturally, simply out of the objective advantages of single-family housing, out of some cultural ethos or out of the *preferences* of higher and, subsequently—through diffusion—of middle-income upwardly mobile family households.[2]

Equally, the observed patterns cannot be derived directly from the capitalist mode of production, i.e., from the laws of accumulation or circulation of capital largely responsible for the development of a consumption economy based on the automobile and the suburban home.[3] If this were the case, one would not observe, as we shall see later, significant differences in housing form and tenure, or in central city–suburban disparities between such economically integrated countries as the United States and Canada. Nor can the explanation rely solely on factors which are internal to the production of housing and residential space, be they the interests and actions of private economic agents[4] or sets of planning norms and prescriptions derived from larger ideological movements (e.g., the Garden City movement).

The provision of housing clearly brings into play all of these factors, but our focus here will be mainly on public intervention. We will try to illustrate how public intervention, dissected into its various and sometimes contradictory components, and visualized in interaction with private market forces set within a larger demographic, sociocultural, economic, and political-institutional context, has shaped the production and allocation of housing in certain directions and how, through changes in policy over time, it has come to foster or hamper newer developments, namely the "alternative" modes of tenure which will be examined further along in this paper.

Visible and disguised public steering

We stated earlier that in Canada, as in the United States, public intervention has essentially favored new construction by the private sector for consumption by households with the required ability to pay. The single most effective government measure designed to stimulate new construction has been the gradual setting up by the federal government of an easily accessible mortgage market, through the creation of the Central Mortgage and Housing Corporation and especially the extension, in 1954, of its activities to insure loans made by private financial institutions. With rising family incomes and the increased use of the automobile, this financing potential was progressively channeled toward the owner-occupier housing market. Until the early sixties, this market was divided about equally between single-family and two-family houses (including mixed-tenure duplexes typical of Montreal since the nineteenth century); later it became restricted more and more to the single family suburban home.[5] The net result has been a growing proportion of owner-occupied units in the total housing stock in the Montreal region (from 24 percent in 1951 to 42 percent in 1981), an evolution which has been most spectacular in the case of family households, among which the percentage of owners rose from 23 percent in 1951 to 52 percent in 1981.

The availability of cheap mortgages is not the only factor responsible for the rise in homeownership; many fiscal measures favor the owner-occupant. For example, the homeowner does not pay any tax on his capital gain when he sells his house; this privilege is exclusively reserved to this type of investment. Furthermore, paying a mortgage is a form of tax-free saving, whereas the income tax applies to all interest income above $1,000. Finally, there exists a registered home savings plan, which allows an income tax deduction of $1,000 per year up to $10,000 for first-time buyers.

Added to these fiscal measures are many temporary stimulative programs which provide subsidies to home buyers. Although those programs are the ones most publicized and with the greatest visibility, they are in fact far less important than the fiscal measures. So, in Quebec (Divay and Richard, 1981), as elsewhere in Canada or in the United States (Aaron, 1972), the homeowner has a considerable advantage over the renter, when we take all this into account. For Quebec, during the seventies, the advantages have been estimated to be in the order of nine to one in the homeowner's favor, excluding welfare payments to renters.

For renters the most important and lasting program has been that of public housing (Canadian $243 million), a shared responsibility of the federal and provincial governments. This program has provided close to 35,000 dwelling units in Quebec in the last decade, representing 6 percent of total construction and 14 percent of new apartments.[7] The federal government decided to freeze this program in 1979, although financial agreements already made involving construction programs were to be honored through 1984.

This withdrawal from public housing has been accompanied by the growth of the nonprofit and cooperatives sector, which the federal government clearly sees as a much more economical and less politically sensitive vehicle for federal aid. The federal government allows an important reduction of the mortgage interest rate, which can be as low as 2 percent. The federal and provincial governments also give subsidies for rehabilitation, and the provincial government gives $3,000 per housing unit in capital outlay. The essential difference with public housing is that there is no aid to cover operating deficits, except through rent supplements granted to a theoretical maximum of 15 percent of a project's tenants (the actual overall percentage is closer to 25 percent). Therefore, the emphasis is very strongly in favor of a balanced social composition in these projects, as opposed to the alleged ghetto nature of the housing projects of the previous decade. This official argument, which is partially in response to social criticism and to the demands of the sixties, also reflects a deliberate will on the part of the state to leave the housing field more and more to private initiative, as well as a global shift in official housing policy from emphasis on new construction and urban redevelopment schemes to gradual improvement and rehabilitation of the existing stock.

Other housing programs, various home ownership assistance programs, and tax shelter programs designed to stimulate private rental construction have been of a more short-lived and countercyclical nature. The aim of these other programs has been more to stimulate the economy, particularly the building industry, than to meet specific housing objectives.

At the provincial level, housing programs have served mainly as a relay for federal programs. The only really original intervention deserving mention here is that of the Rental Board. This agency is responsible for setting general rent increase rules, and, specifically, it fixes rents in cases of individual landlord-tenant disagreements.[8] The board's approval is also required before any rental unit is eliminated either through demolition, conversion to nonresidential use, conversion to condominiums, or repossession by the owner, etc. Many of these attributes of the Rental Board were added or reinforced in 1980 as part of a whole redefinition of its functions, reflecting a clear strengthening of tenants' rights. This has led the landlords' lobbies and private investors to turn the board into a scapegoat for all the present difficulties of the private rental sector.[9]

Similar to provincial intervention, municipal action has generally been reduced to a vehicle for policies developed at higher levels of government. One must note, however, the commitment of the Montreal administration to housing rehabilitation well before the provision of any federal-provincial financial support. In the past few years this has been shown by an especially aggressive revitalization policy, resulting in added pressure to gentrify inner city areas.

In short, state intervention has undergone many changes during the past few years. We will see how these changes are interacting with broader demographic, social, and economic forces to introduce new phenomena on the housing scene. Before we do so, however, a few words must be said about the evolution of general housing conditions.

Resulting housing conditions

As in most Western countries, the most obvious change in housing since the end of World War II has been a significant increase in housing consumption for the vast majority. This is shown by the classical housing indicators: the end of doubling up and of overcrowding and a number of housing starts much higher than net family formation, which has allowed and partly explains the spectacular rise in non-family households. During this period, incomes grew more rapidly than housing costs, allowing households to be better off without paying a larger proportion of their income for housing (median rent/income: 15 percent in 1978; Mathews, 1980).

This situation persisted in the Montreal area until the beginning of the eighties, in contrast with most Canadian and U.S. cities which have witnessed sharp rises in housing costs not followed by rises in family incomes, with a resulting decrease in access to homeownership during the seventies. The important out-migration from the Montreal metropolitan area during the second half of the seventies[10] might have alleviated the pressure somewhat, but we believe that the structure of the housing supply itself and that of the building industry are more important explanatory factors (Divay and Gaudreau, 1983).

The extremely fragmented and competitive character of the building industry and the large proportion of the housing stock represented by intermediate size structures have contributed in keeping housing costs down. The role of these particular Montreal structures, called duplexes or triplexes, consisting of two to five apartments (one of which is often occupied by the owner) is especially noteworthy here. Every apartment has direct outdoor access, so that common space and equipment are kept to a minimum and each occupant is responsible for maintenance. The proportion of this type of building has been estimated at 40 percent of the total Montreal area housing stock in 1977. If one adds to these "plexes" the other types of small apartment buildings (mainly four stories without elevator), such intermediate-size buildings make up 65 percent of the housing stock, compared to 6 percent for high-rise structures and 29 percent for single-family houses (mainly detached). In contrast, in the Toronto area in 1974 (according to the Central Mortgage and Housing Corporation study on housing conditions) 55 percent of all dwellings were single family houses and 21 percent were found in large apartment buildings containing more than fifty units, leaving only 24 percent for the intermediate level. Accordingly, only 29 percent of Toronto residents paid less than 15 percent of their income for housing expenses, as compared to 48 percent in Montreal.

This greater diversity or graduated character of the Montreal housing inventory might in part account for the fact that the filtering process has not created such wide central city-suburban discrepancies as commonly found elsewhere. The inner city, of course, is characterized by certain familiar trends: aging, a growing portion of nonfamily households (41 percent in 1976), an extremely high tenant majority (87 percent in 1976) and lower incomes (the latter associated essentially with nonfamily households since families in the same inner-city areas have seen their income rise at the same rate as that of the total Metropolitan area). More noteworthy, however, is the fact that the change in the balance between the inner city and the suburbs has not resulted in any greater concentration of older people in the inner city now than that observed in 1951. The same is true for nonfamily households. As for low-income families, the trend is even in the opposite direction, the degree of concentration in the inner city being lower than in 1951.

In addition, if we turn to the quality of the housing stock in the older areas, two main facts must be stressed. These neighborhoods exhibit physical conditions which are inferior to those in the rest of the metropolitan area, but there have been significant improvements. Data on sanitary facilities, heating systems, amount of green space per resident, etc., all indicate that the stock has been upgraded. More surprising still, this has been obtained by households at a relative rent-to-income ratio which is lower than in the fifties (Mathews 1983).

We may therefore conclude that the inner city in the Montreal metropolitan area has remained basically sound. Differing interpretations can of course be given to the available statistical data, but all observers would easily agree on the relative absence in Montreal of slums or areas of abandoned housing such as are found in many American cities, or of massive squatter movements as in Germany (Einem von, 1982). Immigrants, as in other Canadian cities, are generally well integrated into neighborhoods (Goldberg, 1980); there are no high vacancy rates for certain housing developments as in Sweden during the seventies; there are no acute social problems in the public housing sector comparable to that of many American cities.

However, this picture now seems to be changing. High interest rates, increasing concentration in the building industry, stricter governmental controls, and new requirements from financial institutions (e.g., higher down payments) are some of the reasons which may be mentioned to explain the deterioration of the situation, expressed through diminishing housing starts and higher pressure on the remainder of the housing stock. These changes also favor certain tenure changes in the old stock, which is now beginning to attract the middle class as in many other North American cities where gentrification is taking place.

Alternative tenure choices

The seventies witnessed the development of various new modes of occupancy and management on the Montreal housing scene. Tenants' cooperatives as well as condominiums made their entry at the turn of the decade and then grew very slowly until 1980, with very sharp rises since then. During the same period, undivided co-ownership (where property of the building is shared between partners who are all jointly responsible for financial and all legal aspects) spread through the old housing stock, as a substitute for condominium conversion, which has been prohibited since December 1975.

The usual interpretations given to these recent phenomena are numerous. Aside from rising costs due to energy prices, interest rates, and the like, some researchers emphasize demand factors (e.g., United States. Department of Housing and Urban Development—hereinafter HUD—1980) such as demographic trends (the aging of the population, the large baby boom cohorts, etc.) and new life-styles (more nonfamily and especially one-person households, more childless couples, two-earner and single-parent families, a higher divorce rate, and more flexible living arrangements). New values, such as the emphasis on conservation and rehabilitation, on urban social variety and stimulation also reinforce the attraction of central city locations. Finally, the economic advantage of homeownership as a shelter against inflation reaches childless or nonfamily households who typically until now would have remained rental apartment dwellers. These very broad explanations certainly refer to basic forces, but if one examines more closely the dynamics at work in the development of the various new housing alternatives, it becomes quite clear that supply factors, especially public intervention which is our main focus here, have also played a leading role.

Nonprofit tenant cooperatives

Tenant cooperatives (whose membership secures the right to occupancy of a dwelling belonging to the cooperative for the payment of a nominal "social share" which cannot be capitalized and resold on the market), as we have mentioned earlier, clearly have been a government creation on the Montreal scene, as part of the global shift in housing policies toward neighborhood preservation and housing rehabilitation. State-subsidized cooperatives—because of their obligation to comply with housing codes in order to obtain funds—have deliberately been conceived as channels for extensive housing rehabilitation in parts of the city where action by private landlords could not easily be expected without causing drastic resident displacement. Accordingly their target population is the income level between that of middle-income households reached by homeownership assistance programs (Dansereau and Godbout, 1981).

The artificiality of the program has been reflected in a very slow rate of implementation. The provincial government has had to set up a whole array of technical resources to stimulate the creation of cooperatives and to guide them all the way through the design and implementation of their projects. We have already mentioned the $3,000 capital subsidy per housing unit. The provincial government is also financing technical resources groups, the goal of which is to help with the development of nonprofit tenant co-ops. This effort has been quite successful, and cooperatives are now becoming increasingly popular, not only with lower-income but also with young middle-income tenant households[11] who find they can no longer afford to buy a home. However, the very substantial financial aid granted to co-ops, and their nonselectivity in terms of members' income, create an increasingly contradictory situation for the state. Costs are growing heavily and, as has happened previously with public housing, the federal government is contemplating means of withdrawal. A reassessment of the program is underway, and there is increasing talk of replacing all present measures with a universal shelter allowance.

New condominium construction

Unlike nonprofit tenant cooperatives, condominiums provide a means of building some equity, since the owner retains full title to his unit (exclusive use areas), as well as a share of the common property (the land, the structure of the building, the outside walls and openings, etc.), all of which can be freely resold at market value.

In the Montreal area, the initial impetus given to this type of tenure, and especially the dominant form it then took (i.e., low-cost suburban row housing, serving mostly young families who were first-time buyers), was strongly influenced by state intervention. In order to stimulate lower costs in housing construction, in 1970 the federal government launched a countercyclical program granting special subsidies to innovative low-cost projects, and condominiums were widely used in this respect. Many problems were encountered in those first projects, which were huge but poorly built. They soon acquired a poor reputation, and they literally killed the condominium concept in the Montreal area. Moreover, the price gap between standard single-family houses and the average condominium row house (less than 15 percent, as compared to 25–35 percent in British Columbia, for instance) was too narrow to offset the disadvantages of condominium life (Dansereau and L'Ecuyer, 1980).

When the condominium concept was reactivated a few years later, it took an entirely different shape: mainly luxurious high-rise apartments occupied by one- or two-person households, among whom were an important fraction of well-off empty-nesters and retired people. Although this change of orientation corresponded to demand characteristics, it was also dictated by supply factors. The depressed state of new rental construction, after a period of overproduction and very somber profit-making perspectives due to rising building and operating costs and tightened rent control, in addition to a thinning out of clientele with the necessary ability to pay, encouraged builders with large landholdings in high-density zoning areas to turn to the condominium market.

Conversions from rental to condominium units

The history of conversions from rental to condominium units in Quebec has been brief. As elsewhere in many North American cities, the process started in the first half of the seventies, but it was quickly halted by a moratorium in 1975, which in practice remains in effect. The projects involved were mostly of recent and relatively good-quality construction. Many benefited from accelerated depreciation tax rates or various subsidies. But, as these special conditions were coming to an end at the same time as the buildings became fully subjected to rent control (from which new construction is excluded in Quebec for the first five years), the profitability of the rental operations became extremely dubious compared to the quick profits made through condominium conversion. Most tenants could not afford or were not willing to buy their apartment. On the whole, 22 percent did so (exactly the same percentage as observed in the United States; see HUD 1980), thus entailing important changes in the socioeconomic character of the buildings. Changes were more dramatic in older buildings, especially within much sought-after inner-city areas inhabited by long-term residents.

These hardships met by some groups, added to preoccupations about a shrinking rental market supply, in addition to escalating and sometimes hidden costs incurred by ill-informed purchasers, led to the adoption of the 1975 freeze on conversions. In turn, one of the effects of this measure was to trigger underground conversion movements, from rental or mixed-tenure buildings to undivided co-ownership.

Undivided co-ownership

In contrast to condominiums, undivided co-ownership is a form of ownership where the owners are collectively responsible for the whole building and not simply for their own apartment. There is only one mortgage. This type of ownership is very distinct from the nonprofit tenant co-ops which we have previously described; it is similar to co-owner co-ops found in the rest of Canada and in the United States. There is an ideological debate in the Quebec co-op milieu about the compliance of owner co-ops with cooperative principles; indeed, in an owner co-op the housing unit can be sold on the market with profit, while it is taken out of the profit-making housing stock in the case of the tenant co-ops. This tenure form takes on a special importance in the Montreal context, due to the large fraction of mixed-tenure buildings ("plexes" referred to earlier) in the total housing stock. These buildings are the essential target of undivided co-ownership and therefore the main target area for gentrification.

In contrast to condominium conversion, the shift in occupancy from renter to owner requires no legal procedures and permits the displacement of a tenant by an owner when the unit is for his own use or for the use of legally specified relatives, as opposed to cases where the building is owned by a corporation or an official cooperative. This means of acquisition for multiple-owner occupancy was initially used by spontaneous partnerships of a few households linked by friendship ties. When, in a later stage (1981), the practice spread to professional realtors, who literally created groups of would-be co-owners for the acquisition of buildings containing as many as fifty units, protests rose from tenant organizations, and the provincial government moved to restrict the rights of an owner to repossession of a unit for his own use to properties which contain a maximum of four units. This partial prohibition has led simultaneously to a greater geographic dispersion and to a channeling of pressure to smaller buildings. Consequently, the portion of the housing stock which is presently the most seriously threatened by gentrification is precisely that which is inhabited by some of the most vulnerable population segments, i.e., an aging population, protected by long-term personal landlord-tenant relationships governed by the rules of the informal economy (Krohn et al., 1977).

Of course, state intervention is not the sole factor responsible in this gradual housing allocation change. The purely private market mechanisms also point in the same direction: when demand from the new "settlers" pushes rents and sales prices up in a certain area, the latecomers are forced to look elsewhere, and they thus create new points of settlement which make the whole process more and more difficult to predict and control. These developments, in addition to internal tensions created over time within undivided co-ownership projects, due to the lack of legal status, will undoubtedly spur the institution of new rules formalizing the shift from rental to owner occupancy while redefining traditional property rights in order to maintain some security of occupancy for tenants.

Summary and conclusions

The first part of this chapter reviewed the basic logic that governed the production and allocation of housing to social groups in Quebec since World War II. As for the rest of North America, the main feature of the housing system has been the production of new housing for middle-income households who could afford the costs of production and maintenance, on the assumption that the needs of the lower-income groups would be met through the filtering-down process. As we have seen, this system has been greatly influenced by two different types of governmental policy. The more visible ones, such as public housing, were aimed at low-income households, and were much less important in budgetary terms than the less visible policies (intervention on the mortgage market, low interest rate, fiscal measures, and incentives to homeownership). Indeed, we have estimated that the less visible policies were, during the seventies, approximately nine times greater than the more visible ones in financial terms.

Although the results of this system can be criticized in many ways, the examination of the Montreal housing scene revealed, to a certain extent, a satisfying record: good quality housing at a relatively low cost; a large proportion (65 percent) of small apartment buildings built by a small and competitive housing industry (especially duplexes and triplexes which are often occupied by their owners); a comparable progression of family incomes in both the suburbs and the central city; and the same proportion of elderly in the central city as thirty years ago. As shown in the second part of this chapter, the picture is now changing. New modes of occupancy, such as tenant co-ops and condominiums, have been examined. Once again, public intervention appeared important in shaping these alternative tenure forms. Such tendencies have led to a redefinition of traditional property and to the loosening of the traditional ties observed between tenure and housing type (houses being owned and apartments being rented). They also result in the blurring of the opposition found between owning and renting, as well as between private and public forms of housing (co-op housing being an intermediary formula).

How will these new forms of occupancy (co-op housing, condominium) affect the future of households, more specifically low-income households? Nothing is definite at this point. Some observers think that the low-cost rental housing stock will go out of the reach of medium- and low-income households, not only because of the gentrification process that is taking place but also because of the important part of the housing stock that is transferred to the ownership market, leading to inflationary pressures.

One can also predict that, with the actual diversification of housing occupancy types, a household will no longer have to buy a single-family house to be an owner. They may buy, instead, their own apartment, whatever the type. Since it is assumed that these households can afford the rent in the first place, they should also be capable of paying the related costs of ownership (mortgage, taxes, and maintenance). The only problem is the down payment; this could, however, be lent by the government. After all, the preservation of a large rental housing stock is not desirable in itself so long as households are able to obtain good housing at a reasonable cost and with a degree of choice.

9 | Housing Young People in Israel:
Public Policy and Private Preferences

Willem van Vliet—

Abstract. In Israel new towns have formed a strategic context in which to achieve broader national objectives, most notably a socially integrated and spatially balanced population. Within this framework, the government has formulated a housing policy offering young couples incentives to settle in new towns. Against this background, national survey data are used to compare the quality of the residential environment in new towns with that of other urban areas, according to standard housing measures and respondents' personal evaluations. Implications of the incentive program for population integration and dispersal are explored, and several public policy considerations are reviewed.

Background

There exists an extensive and diverse literature on new towns. Part of this literature is concerned with economic and physical criteria for planning new communities, and it focuses on issues of site selection, financing, the provision of jobs and housing, and the formulation of standards for services, utilities, and facilities (e.g., Golany, 1976; U.S. Department of Housing and Urban Development, 1981). New towns have also been studied within the context of urban development policies (e.g., Golany, 1978; Clapp, 1971), with some studies adopting an explicitly comparative perspective for the analysis of the processes and goals of new-town policies (e.g., Godschalk, 1967; Merlin, 1969).

Others have examined the ideological background of the new-town idea (e.g., Altman and Rosenbaum, 1973; Allen, 1977). Furthermore, residents' evaluations of new towns as places to live have been the subject of extensive research (e.g., Lansing, Marans, and Zehner, 1975; Weiss and Burby, 1976). A relatively small part of the literature concerns itself with the relationship between new-town policies and other national objectives. By and large, studies in this last category have strong economic overtones, often approaching new towns as growth centers within the framework of regional or national development strategies (e.g., McLaughlin, 1978; Neilson, 1978). However, a number of authors have considered new towns in relation to a broader set of goals. For example, Heraud (1968) has examined to what extent British new towns constituted socially balanced communities and achieved the integrated composition of the population, which was an aim of the new-town policy. Likewise, in a more wide-ranging assessment, Alonso (1970) has critically reviewed the contributions of U.S. new towns toward goals of social, economic, and demographic policies.

This chapter supplements the literature on new towns in two ways. First, using national survey data for Israel, it compares young couples who live in new towns with young couples who live in other urban settlements regarding levels of residential satisfaction, as well as more objective indicators of housing quality. Second, this paper examines the extent to which the Israeli government's housing assistance program for young couples, inducing them to locate in new towns, supports the national goals of social integration and geographical dispersal of the population.

The first sections describe the background of Israeli new-town development and its objectives, including particularly integration and dispersal of the population, and outline the nature of the young couples' housing assistance program. This is followed by (1) a comparison of the housing situation of young couples in new towns with that of those in other urban settlements, based on selected objective indicators of housing quality and couples' own evaluations, and (2) an examination of whether and to what extent young couples' housing decisions, made within the framework of the government's new-town incentive program, contribute to the goals of integration and dispersal of the population. The conclusion discusses implications for public policy.

Israeli new-town development

Since the establishment of the state in 1948, the Israeli government has founded some thirty new towns, which today house about 18 percent of the national population. These figures suggest that new towns have been an important concern of Israeli policy makers and planning officials. Various considerations have formed the basis of this concern; they are briefly discussed below.

In 1948, the large majority of the Israelis lived in urban areas. According to Spiegler (1966:13), 77.5 percent of the total population in that year lived in the narrow coastal plain between Haifa and Tel Aviv, occupying 11.1 percent of the national land area. Adding the Jerusalem district, Grunfeld (1978) arrives at the figure of 81.3 percent, with Tel Aviv alone accounting for 43.2 percent of the entire population and its share of industrial production, commercial enterprises, and cultural activities being even larger than its relative population (Shachar, 1971:363). The southern district, comprising 70 percent of the total land area, held only 1 percent of the national population. There were virtually no medium-sized towns, so that the settlement structure of the country was very much bipolar, made up of congested urban areas and small agricultural settlements (Berler, 1964). Establishing new towns was seen as a valuable remedial strategy to address this gap (Comay and Kirschenbaum, 1973).[2]

A more equal distribution of the national population was thought to be important for a number of reasons. To begin with, it was believed that settling sparsely populated regions would overcome imbalanced regional growth (Gradus and Stern, 1980). The aim was to build integrated regional networks by planting new towns as urban service centers in uninhabited areas, following principles of central place theory to create a complete, hierarchical urban system (Shachar, 1971). Furthermore, in some cases new towns were to provide the labor force needed to exploit undeveloped natural resources, particularly potash and phosphate deposits. Occupying frontier regions was important for defense purposes, too, as a means to strengthen the security of vulnerable border regions.

The most important stimulus for the establishment of new towns was, no doubt, the mass influx of new immigrants which, within the first four years, doubled the national population (Berler, 1970). In keeping with the antiurban, prorural bias of zionist ideology at that time (Cohen, 1970b; Altman and Rosenbaum, 1973), nearly 300 agricultural settlements were established during the initial three years (Shachar, 1976:83). However, these settlements could absorb only a fraction of the new immigrants, partly because of limits on infrastructure and accommodation and partly because of the reluctance and inability of immigrants who had been accustomed to urban life-styles to adopt a rural way of life (Cohen, 1970b). After the first few years, scarcity of water and land supplies also restricted further agricultural expansion and pointed in the direction of establishing new urban settlements (Shachar, 1971).

The national government took upon itself the task of founding and developing new towns; the implementation of this strategy was facilitated by its possession of 92 percent of the total land area (Pressman, 1980:50) and the dependence of the immigrants on the authorities for housing, employment, schooling, medical services, and so forth (Brutzkus, 1966). This situation also provided the government with a rare opportunity to exploit housing as a tool of social policy by directing immigrants to specific neighborhoods or housing developments in order to achieve an ethnically and demographically integrated population. (Carmon and Manheim, 1979; Shaham, 1974; Ginsburg and Marans, 1980). Indeed, this objective has been of foremost importance in the process of nation-building involving the absorption of large numbers of recent immigrants from many different countries.

Thus, the development of new towns was viewed as a potentially powerful instrument to accomplish two principal objectives, namely, dispersal and integration of the population. In this context, the Israel Government Yearbook still stated as recently as 1980 (p. 114) that the programs of the Ministry of Housing are based on national objectives, including a "redistribution of the population" and a "redirection of the affluent population to weak quarters in order to create a healthy social fabric." The ambitions and good intentions of policy makers and planners notwithstanding, some new towns have prospered and grown, while others have floundered and stagnated. Reasons for the problems which some towns experienced concerned the fragmented approach of the government, whose agencies failed to coordinate their tasks effectively (Kahane, 1963; Cohen, 1970a); the prior existence of a strong national network of rural settlements (Soen and Kipnis, 1972); tension between national and local governments (Aronoff, 1974); difficulties experienced by urban residents adjusting to life in new towns modeled in the early years after the English garden cities (Cohen 1970b); unwillingness of people to move to or stay in environments without a congenial composition of the population (Borukhov and Werczberger, 1981) and lacking jobs, schools, and recreational opportunities equal to those in the large cities (Kirschenbaum and Comay, 1973); and inability to attract private investment that would propel economic growth (Berler, 1972).

Studies of Israeli new towns have generally recognized the large differences between them and have attempted to group them into homogeneous types or clusters as a basis for alternative development strategies (Berler, 1970; Lichfield, 1971; Grunfeld, 1978; Handelman and Shamgar-Handelman, 1978). Among the policies adopted to stimulate new-town development is the current program of housing assistance for young couples. The following section briefly describes this program.

The young couples' housing assistance program

Over the years there have been a number of programs intended to help young Israelis in obtaining housing. These programs have been developed largely under pressure which came about as a result of inequities felt to exist with the situation of new immigrants who, in comparison, received generous housing privileges. A program specifically for the needs of young couples was initiated in 1970 and substantially revised several times afterwards.[3] At present the majority of young couples rely on this aid for housing. It is not necessary to describe here the details of this program and the changes that have been made in it. The purpose here is to point out a basic tenet of the program and of earlier schemes, namely the provision of extra benefits and more favorable terms of assistance to those who settle in new towns.

For example, in an early program an apartment in a new town required a down payment of only 10 percent to 15 percent of the purchase price; the remainder could be financed with mortgage loans over a twenty-five-year period. In comparison, the down payment in Tel Aviv was 50 percent, with loans to be repaid within ten years. In another program (Saving for Housing), apartments in new towns, selling for lower prices, could be financed up to 75 percent with loans carrying only 4.5 percent interest for twenty-five years; in big cities, loans could only cover up to a maximum of one-third of the (higher) purchase price, with 8 percent interest repayable in ten years (Spiegler 1966). Also, public housing built for young couples would be in areas selected by the government for development.

Currently, the government is no longer directly involved in construction. Instead, it makes land available to private and semipublic development firms with stipulations concerning, for example, a minimum proportion of rental dwellings. As implemented at present, many questions surround the effectiveness of this approach regarding the solution of young couples' housing needs. Some observers have noted that it is the cost of housing and not its availability which poses a problem (Newsview, 1981; Werczberger and Marcus, 1981). This is also the premise on which the Ministry of Housing now operates, as its principal form of aid to young couples is now in the form of direct subsidies, accounting for more than twenty-five percent of its budget for 1982 (Ministry of Housing, 1982).

In order to qualify for aid, young couples have to apply to the Ministry of Housing, whereupon, if approved, they receive an eligibility card which entitles them to a mortgage loan or rental subsidy. The amount of the loan or subsidy is determined according to a point system where the more needy couples receive more aid. Indicators of need include current living conditions, gross income, and size of family. The responsibility for finding suitable housing thus rests with the couple. In urban areas the apartment cannot be larger than eighty-five square meters; in new towns no such restriction applies. In earlier schemes, those settling in new towns would receive additional loans and more favorable repayment conditions. Such additional incentives are now more closely tied to specific locations. In the present system, couples who decide to settle in new towns will get relatively generous loans, regardless of the number of points they have. Benefits obtained from the Ministry of Housing are supplemented by other government incentives (e.g., regarding taxation).

To review, the types of assistance given to young couples and the specific terms of such assistance have been changed several times and are continuously being adjusted to reflect ongoing developments. However, throughout these changes a constant feature has remained the provision of relatively more generous aid to couples who settle in new towns. The remainder of this chapter examines implications of this policy.

Residential choices of young couples

The previous sections of this chapter provided background information on the new-town development and the housing assistance scheme for young couples in Israel. From this information, three goals can be distilled for the public policy directed at housing needs of young couples. In the first place, the program aims, of course, at helping young couples to obtain adequate housing. Beyond this, two important subsidiary goals are the social integration and geographic dispersal of the population. A comprehensive and detailed assessment of the merits of the assistance program in the light of these three goals is beyond the scope of this chapter. Instead, the objectives here are (*a*) to form a picture of the housing situation of young couples in new towns as compared to that of those in other urban areas, and (*b*) to examine whether the residential choices of young couples are in line with the goals of social integration and geographic dispersal of the population. To explore these issues, existing data are used from a national survey ($N = 2,591$) conducted in 1977 by the Central Bureau of Statistics for the Ministry of Construction and Housing. Supplemental information is taken from several earlier studies.

Housing conditions: Some objective indicators

In 1977, about 10 percent of the young couples still lived with their parents or with relatives (Central Bureau of Statistics—hereafter CBS—1978:21); among those who had married in the two years preceding the survey this proportion is much higher (22 percent), but it drops off sharply among those who had been married for more than two years. In accordance with the Israeli norm of homeownership, more than half of the couples (54 percent) had bought their apartments, although the proportion of owners is considerably lower in the new towns than it is in other urban areas; correspondingly, there are relatively more renters in the new towns (see table 9.1). New-town apartment owners were about evenly divided between those who had bought their apartment from a public building company (47 percent) and those who had bought their apartment from the existing stock (44 percent); in other urban areas, relatively few had bought from public building companies (19 percent) and more had bought from private construction firms (23 percent) or the existing stock (56 percent). The greater role of the central authorities in the provision of housing in new towns is also apparent among the renters. Almost 60 percent of the new-town renters lived in apartments managed on behalf of the government, whereas only one third had a private landlord; this contrasts sharply with the corresponding figures for other urban settlements (respectively, 17 percent and 76 percent).

In regard to the number of rooms, there is little difference between couples in the two locality types. On the average, new-town couples are slightly better off (2.65 compared to 2.54, including kitchen), but the advantage is offset by their larger household size which results in

Table 9.1 Housing conditions of young couples in new towns and other urban settlements.

Housing condition:	Location of residence	
	New towns (percentages)	Other urban settlements (percentages)
Tenure:		
live with parents or relatives	12	11
rent	36	24
self-owner	47	59
Owners bought from:		
public building company	47	19
private building company	3	23
stock of existing apartments	44	56
Rented apartments from:		
government	59	17
private landlord	32	76
Average size of apartment	69 m^2	72 m^2
Apartments larger than 75 sq. meters	22	34
Average number of rooms	2.65	2.54
Average number of persons per room	1.30	1.28
Exclusive use of		
kitchen (1971)	97	96
toilet (1971)	98	95
bath and shower	41	72
shower only	58	27
heating	84	83

Source: Central Bureau of Statistics 1978; pp. 20, 21, 26, 27. Central Bureau of Statistics 1972; pp. 8–9.

a 1.3 person-per-room ratio. New-town couples tend to live in smaller apartments (on the average 69 square meters compared to 72 square meters) and a smaller proportion of them live in apartments larger than 75 square meters (see table 9.1). There are virtually no differences in basic dwelling amenities, except that a higher percentage of those who live in other towns have a shower plus bath than those who live in new towns; a higher percentage of the latter have a shower only.

Summing up the main differences between young couples in new towns and those in other urban places: the former are more often renters and less frequently owners, they have more dealings with the government either as renters or as mortgage payers, and they tend to live in smaller apartments. It should be stressed that the information presented here represents only a single point in time; a fuller picture would emerge if the figures were viewed in a temporal perspective. Unfortunately, data which allow comparisons over time are very scarce.

The data indicate that a large majority of the couples had an apartment at the time of their wedding, and virtually all had one within a few years thereafter. However, it is not clear to what extent this should be attributed to the government's aid program; indeed, Lithwick (1980) has seriously questioned the adequacy of the program, which has since been revised but not reevaluated. Nor is it clear how much the housing decisions of the young couples are a result of choice and how much of constraint. The question of choice or constraint is important with a view to the level of residential satisfaction and the possibility of selective migration. These two issues are addressed below.

Housing conditions: Some subjective indicators

A survey conducted in the early sixties by the Ministry of Housing (1966:45) showed little preparedness among young couples to move to new towns. The proportion agreeing to move unconditionally ranged from 8 percent for one of the older new towns (Kiryat Shmona) to 22 percent for one of the more recent ones (Arad); the provision of housing did not radically alter the picture (a rise of respectively 6 percent and 8 percent), but the provision of housing *and* a job greatly increased the proportion willing to move to a new town (up to 81 percent). The notion that economic opportunities play a prime role in considerations of whether or not to stay in or move to a new town is also corroborated by results from more recent research (Kirschenbaum and Comay, 1973), and it ties in with studies conducted elsewhere (Rodwin, 1970).

However, social factors also exert considerable influence. Another survey in the mid-sixties among young couples in a variety of localities found that those living in a close-knit working-class neighborhood in Tel Aviv with a person-per-room ratio higher than the rest of the sample refused most strongly (82 percent) to move to a new town (Ministry of Housing, 1967:122). The importance of the population composition of new towns for attracting and retaining people has been noted by several authors (Berler, 1972; Borukhov and Werczberger,

1981) and is in keeping with the experiences of other countries (Sarkissian, 1976).

In the above-mentioned survey (Ministry of Housing, 1967:127), the percentage of new-town couples completely satisfied with their living conditions ranged from 8 percent to 14 percent. The most important determinant of satisfaction was housing; next was nearness to family and relatives. Another study conducted more than five years later among a large sample representing the national population of young couples found more than half to be quite satisfied or very satisfied with their dwelling conditions (CBS, 1972:22–3); however, couples in new towns were considerably less often satisfied than those in other urban areas (39 percent compared to 55 percent). Also, more than half of the new-town couples indicated plans for changing their apartment within two years.

The most recent national survey of young couples enables a comparison of satisfaction levels in new towns and other urban settlements with respect to more specific aspects of the housing environment (see table 9.2). The data show young couples in new towns to be less satisfied on each of the ten dimensions asked about. In some instances—such as satisfaction with medical services, number of rooms, and educational opportunities— the differences are minute; in other cases—as, for example, shopping, transportation, size of apartment, and especially building and neighborhood upkeep—the differences are sizable. The pattern which emerges suggests that new-town couples are consistently less satisfied with their housing and neighborhood conditions than their counterparts living in other urban areas. This indicates the possibility that the public policy of directing young couples to new towns runs counter to the preferences of young couples regarding the best place to live. If this is the case, one might assume that couples living in new towns are there, at least in part, because they cannot afford a preferred alternative; thus one might expect them to be of a lower socioeconomic class and more dependent on government aid. The following section confirms this.

Subsidiary goals: Integration and dispersal of the population

It has already been shown that new-town couples rent and buy public housing more often than couples in other urban areas. This greater dependency on the government is largely a function of the lower

Table 9.2 Young couples' satisfaction with living conditions, by location of residence.

	Location of residence	
Satisfied with:	New towns (percentages)	Other urban settlements (percentages)
Health care, medical services	75	77
Shopping for daily needs	68	77
Transportation	58	67
Layout of apartment	56	61
Number of rooms	54	58
Size of apartment	53	60
Social environment	50	56
Neighborhood maintenance	49	61
Building maintenance	44	62
Schools	28	31
N	24,000	34,600

Source: Central Bureau of Statistics 1978; p. 25, table 22.

socioeconomic status of the new-town couples. The differences existing in this regard are indicated by various measures of social class. While there is little difference in the proportion of employed husbands, fewer new-town husbands work in professional jobs (20 percent compared to 29 percent). Also, husbands in other towns have more often attained high levels of education and enjoy higher incomes (see table 9.3). Possession of and access to a car is twice as frequent in other towns. Furthermore, the ethnic composition of the population, which in Israel is correlated with social class, is different for new towns and other towns; in the former there are fewer native Israeli young couples and more from African and Asian origins.

Recapitulating, new-town couples tend to have lower incomes, own a car less often, have a lower education, and work in professional jobs less often; more of them are from African or Asian backgrounds and fewer of them are native Israelis. The differential composition of the young couples population along lines of social class and ethnic origin contradicts the goal of social integration. Thus, the government policy of providing extra aid to those who settle in new towns may help needy couples who depend on such assistance to afford an apartment, while at the same time it works as a selective mechanism in opposition to the goal of achieving a socially integrated population.

Let us now take a look at the second subsidiary objective, dispersal

Table 9.3 Household characteristics of young couples in new towns and other urban settlements.

Household characteristic:	Location of residence	
	New towns (percentages)	Other urban settlements (percentages)
Husband employed	90	93
in professional jobs	20	29
Husband's annual income (indexed)	88.4	100
Husband's education		
less than 10 years	41	33
more than 12 years	24	32
Own a car (1971)	8	16
Use a car (1971)	9	20
Husband's ethnic origin		
Asia/Africa	39	23
Europe/North America	16	18
Israel	45	59

Source: Central Bureau of Statistics 1972; pp. 13–14. Central Bureau of Statistics 1978; pp. 5, 8, 10–11.

of the population. Data from the 1978 national CBS survey show that, of the 15,700 couples who had moved since their marriage and were living in new towns at the time of the survey, 2,275 (14.5 percent) had come from other urban settlements.[4] While this movement was counterbalanced by 1,440 couples moving in the opposite direction from new towns to other towns, some 82 percent of the new-town couples stayed in the same settlement or moved to another new town (CBS, 1978:17), and it is likely that the then-prevailing housing program influenced them in the decision. These figures compare favourably with the high rate of out-migration which has been typical of many of the new towns (Ash, 1974; Berler, 1970; Borukhov and Werczberger, 1981).

There is some further evidence for the relative success of the dispersal policy regarding young couples. In 1971, 14 percent of the Jewish couples married between November 1, 1967, and October 31, 1970, were new-town residents (CBS, 1972); in 1977, the figure for those married between September 1, 1973, and August 31, 1976, had more than doubled to 32 percent (CBS, 1978). During these same periods, the corresponding figures for the proportion of the *total* population living in new towns was both times about 18 percent. Also, when considering the different age distribution of the population in new towns and other towns, it is hard to deny the dispersal policy a certain measure of success. However, the issue would not appear to be the number of people redistributed so much as who is being directed where and at what cost. Data presented earlier in this chapter have already pointed out that new-town couples have different ethnic and social class backgrounds and are consistently less satisfied with their living conditions.

Review of findings

This chapter has been concerned with the housing assistance program of the Israeli government for young couples, and particularly with possible implications of the provision of extra aid to those settling in new towns. In this connection, objective and subjective indicators of the housing situation of new-town couples were compared with those of their counterparts in other towns; furthermore, we examined the relation between the policy of giving differential incentives and the overall goals of a socially integrated and geographically balanced population.

The findings generally indicate only small differences in objective indicators of housing quality such as density conditions and basic amenities; the only noteworthy difference was the greater preponderance of renters among new-town couples. Nevertheless, couples in other towns were consistently more satisfied with each of a range of living conditions. Further, the housing program appears to contribute to the dispersal policy, primarily because of the dependence of low-income couples on government aid. Private preferences favor more centrally located towns. Thus, in the process of providing housing aid within the framework of a dispersal policy, the government seems to reinforce tendencies to sociospatial segregation.

At this point, a word of caution is appropriate. The new towns which have been grouped together in this chapter include places frequently offering very different living conditions. Any successful development strategy would have to take such differences into account. It should also be noted that the data have been taken from secondary sources; this is appropriate for a historical analysis as intended here, but a policy analysis aimed at making programmatic recommendations would need to utilize more up-to-date information. Some of the differences observed between new towns and other towns have decreased during the past decade, whereas others have increased. Noteworthy in connection with the latter is the average income of new-town husbands, which dropped from 92.9 percent of that of husbands in other towns in 1971 to 88.4 percent in 1977 (CBS, 1972:36–39; CBS, 1978:11).

Discussion

Considering these qualifications, some observations can still be made. To begin with, the public policy of directing young couples to housing in new towns runs counter to private preferences for other towns. The reluctance of young couples to settle in new towns is shared by various other segments of the population (see, e.g., CBS, 1981). Those who can afford it tend to choose other towns, whereas low-income couples who are more dependent on the government more often have to locate in new towns. This results in a paradoxical situation. Eliminating socioeconomic inequality as a barrier of access to the housing market has traditionally been an important rationale for government intervention in housing (True, 1979). However, the specific aid allocation system analyzed here acts to reinforce sociospatial segregation. It should be noted that this is not a peculiarity of the Israeli situation. Mechanisms with similar effects of sustaining social class divisions operate, for example, in Britain (Ineichen, 1981) and New Zealand (Smith and Thorns, 1980).

Another observation concerns the issue of housing tenure. Research in several countries has shown that ownership tends to be associated with higher residential satisfaction (e.g., Brouwer, 1981; Lane and Kinsey, 1980). This study found more of the new-town couples to be renters, presumably because they cannot afford to buy an apartment or because they do not want to commit themselves to a long-term stay in a new town. They are also less satisfied with their housing conditions, particularly regarding maintenance, which is a problem typically associated with rental housing (Ministerie van Volkshuisvesting, 1978). While a lack of attractive opportunities for home ownership may be a problem in the new towns, in older towns it is a lack of affordable rental housing. The government is keenly aware of the problem and has been taking some measures to correct the situation (e.g., Rubinstein, 1981), but as yet without much success. Also the lack of rental housing is a problem not only in Israel, but one that is now plaguing many industrialized countries, and Howenstine (1981) has suggested that a radical realignment of policies is needed in order to solve it.

Finally, it should be emphasized that the housing policy for young couples should be seen in a wider societal context. As elsewhere (e.g., Leather, 1981), there is a need to determine priorities between different policy areas. Currently, the government is increasing its budget for the establishment of new settlements (Ministry of Housing, 1982), and much effort and money are being spent on expanding the city of Jerusalem (CBS, 1981b). These are political decisions concerning the allocation of scarce resources, and they themselves are weighed against alternative priorities outside the field of housing.

The Users' Perspective on Government Housing

James R. Anderson and
Sue Weidemann, United States
Rosalie Genovese, Sweden
Leslie Kilmartin, Australia

Abstract. The user perspective of government-provided housing is represented by three articles dealing with the United States, Sweden, and Australia. Anderson and Weidemann describe the evolution of user perspectives in the United States, beginning in the last half of the nineteenth century with the concern of reformers and humanitarians for the plight of the poor and the immigrants. In the depression of the thirties, the emphasis shifted to the economic consequences of low-cost housing, especially as a stimulus for the economy. During this period, many large-scale programs to develop and maintain housing were established including, in 1937, the Public Housing Administration. Explicit concern with users did not emerge until after World War II. Recent studies on user satisfaction with low-cost housing are reviewed, indicating research possibilities and opportunities to develop better housing.

In Sweden, often viewed as a model of government housing, significant user dissatisfaction has developed, according to Genovese. Dissatisfaction centers on the issues of citizen participation in the planning for housing and neighborhoods, the number of housing units for sale compared to rental units, and inequities resulting from social and land-use segregation. These issues developed from the new high-density housing built around Stockholm to meet the housing shortage. In the seventies, neighborhood groups formed to express discontent with lack of citizen participation in the planning process and to press for construction of more single-family homes rather than rental apartments, a step which would reduce the segregation of the poor in high-rise rental units. The status of current efforts by the Swedish government and by citizen groups to deal with these issues is reviewed in detail.

Kilmartin comments on Newton and Wulff's article on public housing in Australia after World War II, adding the responses of low-income households. Kilmartin, using his 1976–77 study of Hampton Park, discusses one type of program Newton and Wulff describe in Chapter 7—villa estate housing. Located in the metropolitan fringe of Melbourne, it was built for low-income clients of the Housing Commission of Victoria (HCV) who were purchasing their homes from the HCV on favorable financial terms. Interviews with the residents indicated that homeownership was their main reason for moving to Hampton Park but that only 60 percent found the location convenient, suggesting a trade-off between price and location. Kilmartin raises questions for further research focusing on how low-income groups housed on the metropolitan fringe actually travel within their local sector of the metropolis, on whether employed women and ethnic minorities suffer special disadvantages, and on the need for social planning for community facilities and shopping.

The United States
James R. Anderson and Sue Weidemann

A history of concern for problem housing

No doubt societies have always had concern for their housing, but the focus has neither remained constant nor singular. Certainly one concern has been for the residents of poor quality housing and for the effect of that housing on society.

Humanitarian concern. During the last half of the nineteenth century this concern was certainly evident in the United States, as reformers and humanitarians became aware of the congestion and sanitation problems in the housing of immigrants and of labor-class individuals and families. In many cities, housing committees of civic leagues, chambers of commerce, and charitable organizations were involved in the investigation of housing conditions and the development of solutions to poor conditions, solutions which included local building codes and model tenement designs. These concerns continued during the early part of the twentieth century. Humanitarians seeking to deal with the squalor and misery found in sections of many cities called the first conference on city planning in 1909. There, and at a second conference a year later, the problems of inadequate housing were debated and the need for improved housing codes, zoning ordinances, and basic planning was stressed (McKelvey, 1963).

A primary concern for the resident of poor housing during these years was not a concern for the perspective of the user. Instead, it was a humanitarian concern for the plight of the user, as well as a concern that the social and health problems found in areas of poor housing should not be allowed to spread to areas of good housing.

Economic concern. These early concerns became secondary when the depression struck in the thirties. During this time the focus of concern was economic, and the first large-scale programs to assist in the development and maintenance of housing were created. The Home Owner's Loan Corporation, the Federal Housing Administration, the Resettlement Administration, and the Public Housing Administration were among the programs created as a means to economic recovery as much as a means to provide improved housing facilities (National Resources Committee, 1957).

It was not until after the establishment of the Public Housing Administration, in 1937, that there actually began to be a sizable group of residents in government housing in the United States. During this period the concern appears to have continued to be for the welfare of the residents of poor housing. However, there is little indication that any interest in learning about these residents' perspective about the government housing in which they lived had yet developed. There were obvious reasons for this lack of interest. In the first place, many viewed the public housing program simply as providing a means to stimulate the depressed economy. Second, the standards of construction for the government housing were higher than found in the existing slum housing; government housing was obviously better, so there was no need to obtain the users' perspective. Also there was the expectation that the duration of residency of an individual in government-supported public housing would be short. This housing was viewed often as a place to get back on one's feet, as a temporary aid to those suffering from the depression. Thus, because the users were obviously benefiting from the government housing, their perspective was not felt to be necessary.

After the depression and World War II, housing problems became acute. There was a call for "a decent home for every family in a suitable environment" in the 1949 Housing Act, and, as a result, in the late forties and fifties, extensive construction of government housing occurred. The associated clearance of slum housing with inadequate sanitation, deteriorating structure, and the like continued to be seen as a public purpose (Schneider vs District of Columbia, 1953, cited in Haar, 1971).

Emergence of concern for the users' perspective

An explicit concern for the perspective of the residents of government housing began to develop clearly after World War II. For example, Wirth (1947) pointed out that "we cannot proceed far in the analysis of housing as a social problem until we know more than we do about the nature and extent to which people's desires and expectations in respect to housing are realized or frustrated" (p. 138). Cooper (1977) points out that at least two large public housing authorities, in San Francisco and Chicago, began to express concern for the users' perspective when they addressed the issue of livability in 1948 and 1952, respectively.

By the end of the fifties, two significant events were occurring. First, residents were expressing discontent with some housing that, by conventional standards, was apparently good, as well as resisting removal from some housing that was apparently bad. Second, researchers were beginning to document the residents' perspective of their housing.

This documentation included a number of important studies. Among those, Rossi (1955) was perhaps one of the first to begin considering the housing residents and their perceptions and values. While Rossi's concern was with mobility, i.e., changing addresses within the same urban area, he raised questions about the potential causes of that mobility and their relation to slum conditions. Fried and Gleicher (1961) and Gans (1962) were among those describing the attachment and positive meaning that the slum had for its residents.

The work of Jacobs (1961) continued to emphasize the importance of the users' perspective by pointing out that planners and urban designers have "gone to great pains to learn what the sages and saints of modern orthodox planning have said about how cities *ought* to work and what *ought* to be good for people and businesses in them . . . when contradictory reality intrudes . . . they sling reality aside" (p. 8). One such reality is shown in the pronouncement of a housing project resident that "Nobody cared what we wanted when they built this place. They threw our houses down and pushed us here and pushed our friends somewhere else . . . Nobody cared what we needed" (Jacobs, 1961, p. 15). Thus, there were apparent issues, reflecting residents' satisfaction with their housing, that were not addressed simply by the removal of slums of bad housing and the construction of new.

By the mid-sixties there was substantial social disorder in the United States. Riots in cities were taken as a symptom of deeper problems in the society. One of those problems, defined by the National Commission on Urban Problems, was that housing assistance programs, i.e., those slum clearance and new construction programs sought by the humanitarians in the early part of the century, were being directed toward "patterns of life assumed appropriate or acceptable for people who can independently afford good housing . . . [but] do not apply to the variety of lifestyles, family types and conditions of lower and moderate income families" (1968, page 499). The commission identified a need for information related to "user needs" to correct this deficiency. Likewise, the President's Committee on Urban Housing (i.e., the Kaiser Commission) called for a dramatic increase in the research and development expenditures of the U.S. Department of Housing and Urban Development, partially to "identify the human needs which housing helps serve" (1968, p. 194). The need for the users' perspective of government housing was explicit.

An early model for making the users' perspective explicit to architects and planners, became available during the sixties, when a series of design bulletins and other publications from the United Kingdom began to appear. Publications such as *House planning: A guide to user needs with a check list*, Design Bulletin 14, outlined the British experience with examining residents' views of their housing environments and considered ways in which information from user perspectives could be useful for policy and planning. These bulletins heightened the designer's interest in the users' perspective.

By the end of the 1960s, it was certainly clear that a humanitarian concern for users was not sufficient. Research was beginning to demonstrate that housing experts and the users of government housing did not share a common viewpoint. For example, in a Detroit area study, Lansing and Marans (1969) showed substantial differences in the perceptions of planners and neighborhood residents concerning what constitutes a high-quality environment. Obviously, to the extent that perceptions and values held by designers and planners differed from those of the users, then the users should experience less satisfaction with the environments shaped by those designers and planners.

Focusing concern for the users' perspective. Concern for the users and understanding their perspective of their housing resulted in the development of several focuses. One focus has been on residents' satisfaction. For example, Michelson (1977) focused on satisfaction with housing as a function of urban, suburban, apartment, and detached house characteristics. Campbell, Converse, and Rodgers (1976) examined satisfaction with the residential environment as one of the "domains of life experience" related to overall life satisfaction. Following this approach, Marans and Rodgers (1975) developed a conceptual model of how the residential environment contributed to satisfaction with the neighborhood as well as with the house.

While Marans and Rodgers (1975) were interested in resident satisfaction because of its potential importance to the perception of quality of life, others began to examine residents' satisfaction as a variable important in its own right. Francescato et al. (1979) became interested in satisfaction primarily for its potential as a user-based criterion for housing evaluation. It was their view that examining satisfaction with the residential environment would provide information about specific attributes of the housing environment that contributed to satisfaction. With this knowledge, designers, planners, administrators, and others in the housing field would be able to focus more closely on issues that would have the greatest impact for residents, in terms of their satisfaction with their housing.

Opportunities resulting from knowledge about residents' satisfaction

It is now apparent that there are opportunities for the development of a better understanding of housing by considering the users' perspective. In addition, when that perspective has focused on residents' satisfaction it has been shown that specific information valuable in the design, planning, and management of housing can be obtained. This has been demonstrated in a series of studies conducted at the University of Illinois.

Francescato et al. (1979) clearly demonstrated in their comparison of thirty-seven subsidized government housing sites that residents' level of satisfaction with their housing varies from site to site. Some housing was judged more satisfactory than others. Further, the amount of variation in satisfaction that Francescato et al. found within various government programs was far greater than that found in comparisons made between those programs. This casts doubt upon the potential of macroscale analyses to determine the reasons for the success of any specific housing program. General beliefs such as "public housing is bad" or "high rise housing is bad" ought to be recognized as questionable at best, and it is not until sufficient evidence is obtained from the users' perspective that such assertions can be adequately tested.

There is also evidence that macroanalyses are inadequate to take into account the perspective of different user groups. For example, Francescato et al. (1975) and Weidemann et al. (1975) found that predictors of residential satisfaction, for a sample of residents at a number of sites, varied among different user groups—based on age, education, and sex. In addition, Weidemann et al. (1981) found differences among youth, adult, and elderly residents in their perceptions of a specific housing site.

While some objective characteristics of residents are useful as a way to examine differences among user groups, those characteristics have generally been found to be unrelated or only weakly related to satisfaction. Residents' age, sex, income, and the like were found by Francescato et al. (1974) to be unrelated to residents' evaluation of the multifamily housing as satisfactory. In addition, demographic characteristics were found by Lane and Kinsey (1980) to be unrelated to residents' evaluation of single-family dwellings and neighborhoods as satisfactory. Furthermore, residential mobility studies that have attempted to explain satisfaction on the basis of demographics and gross characteristics of the housing have not been especially successful (e.g., Varady, 1983). They have been able to account for only small portions of the total variance in reported satisfaction.

In contrast to the research examining objective characteristics of the residents as direct predictors of satisfaction, studies that have sought to account for satisfaction by examining subjective responses of the users (i.e., residents' beliefs and perceptions of the sociophysical environment) have been able to account for much higher percentages of the variance in satisfaction. This has been the case in the research of Francescato et al. (1979), Anderson and Weidemann (1981) and Weidemann et al. (1982).

As noted earlier, by taking the users' perspective into account it is possible to better understand why some housing is more successful than others. Thus, Francescato et al. not only demonstrated that residents' attitude towards their housing varied across sites, they also demonstrated that the various sources of that satisfaction are identifiable and measurable. They used path analysis to begin to define sources of satisfaction that hold across all sites, that is, to develop a general model indicating to what extent various physical, social, and managerial attributes of the residential environment are predictive of satisfaction. Such models can guide architects and planners by indicating important issues to confront in the design of new housing.

In contrast, Anderson and Weidemann (1980) and Weidemann et al. (1982) sought to learn from the users' perspective what their concerns were at specific sites. This information was then used to develop proposals for design and management changes. A structured process for including the users' perspective in the redesign of government housing has evolved from this work (Anderson, Weidemann, and Butterfield, 1983).

Sweden
Rosalie G. Genovese

Sweden is often seen as a model for other countries because of its advanced social planning and policies. Yet residents and policy makers have been grappling with various issues affecting user satisfaction: participation in the planning of housing and neighborhoods, the supply of housing units for sale compared to rental units, and inequities in living conditions resulting from aspects of social and land-use segregation. Questions also arise about whether existing housing meets the needs of diverse household types and life-styles. The recent reexamination of housing policy in part grew out of protests by neighborhood groups dissatisfied with housing and planning policies of the early 1970s. In recent years, the government has attempted to change or modify policies responsible for the most widespread user criticism.

Postwar housing policies and programs, devised to meet acute shortages, played an important role in creating some of these problems with user satisfaction. Long waiting lists for housing and overcrowded conditions led to the construction of these new suburbs, especially around Stockholm. Originally conceived as new towns where people could both live and work, an early one like Vällingby consisted largely of low-rise buildings and had a density of twenty-four persons per acre, low compared to later ones (Popenoe, 1977). The newer suburbs were dormitory communities in which high-rise buildings predominated, with row houses and single family homes located away from the centers, segregating higher-income residents. Families who left Stockholm for this new housing were often dissatisfied with the move.

The formation of neighborhood groups in Sweden and Denmark in the seventies followed the development of community action and advocacy planning groups in the United States during the sixties. Whether in city neighborhoods facing urban renewal or in the new suburbs, residents expressed their discontent. To a large extent, they were reacting to the lack of citizen participation in planning. Government agencies tended to work through established groups such as trade unions and political, professional, or other interest groups, in addition to property owners (Häggroth, 1976: 111–14; Romberg and Vitarello, 1971: 182). Small, informal, or ad hoc groups formed to pursue a specific neighborhood issue or goal were not consulted (IFHP, 1979: 34).

Established procedures required only one-way communication from the top down. Officials arranged public displays or circulated printed information on proposals, but did not expect feedback. Moreover, plans were made public late in the process, partly as a way of discouraging speculators (Romberg and Vitarello, 1971: 127–28). Ad hoc groups had little chance to influence planning since they learned about projects only in the last stages when modifications were difficult. A similar process prevailed in Denmark, and it was protested by informal groups.[1]

As in the United States, these neighborhood groups demonstrated that planners were not infallible and that "expertise" was not a sufficient reason why residents should accept plans as proposed. One classic example of a lapse by experts was that a new suburb, Skärholmen, opened without a fire station (Anton, 1975: 206–7).

Moreover, government values and users' preferences did not always coincide. Planners' egalitarian objectives were reflected in the design of new housing. Standardized units contributed to the values of equality and economic efficiency, but their layouts did not always meet users' needs or preferences. Moreover, the sameness of the living space had an alienating effect on some. It was difficult for residents to express their individuality in a flat or apartment just like their neighbors' (Genovese, 1975). The government's emphasis on rental accommodations served to further its egalitarian aims, as well as to meet housing shortages (ibid.), yet public opinion surveys and informal conversations with Swedes showed that a considerable majority preferred homeownership over renting (IFHP, 1979: 27; Popenoe, 1977: 222–23).

Residents' dissatisfaction with housing

Residents' dissatisfaction with housing was widespread enough for government to conduct research into the causes of and solutions to the problems. The authorities found significant differences in user satisfaction with the older suburbs which met residents' preferences for "variation, cosiness, well-being and human contact," and the newer housing estates which did not (Swedish Ministry of Housing and Physical Planning, 1975: 21). The newer suburbs like Skäholmen and Sollentuna might have made sense to the planners, but residents found them monotonous and characterless. They were criticized not only for their size, density, and lack of trees, but also for shortcomings related to the needs of dual-worker families (ibid.). The lack of job opportunities increased the isolation of women unwilling to commute long distances to work. Women who wanted to reenter the labor market found few employment opportunities close to home (Svennson, 1976: 10; Sandberg, 1975: 56).

Women with young children faced additional problems. The shortage of day nurseries on the new estates hampered their ability to remain in the labor force. Moreover, the environments offered little in the way of play space for children. Women and children often seemed trapped in their housing units. Liljeström (1977: 5) voiced the concerns of many: "Since the residential areas specialized in only one function, housing, they readily turn into event-poor milieus which make fertile soil for sadness and melancholy. As a rule geographically marked-off residential areas are equally impoverished of events. More than that: the selection of events is virtually identical. It is simply not worth the trouble to search for other surroundings." Adults and children tend to turn inward and family life becomes more privatized, since adults often focus on activities and interests outside the neighborhood and children may lack social networks there (ibid.).

The government response

The most frequently proposed solutions to these criticisms were that more single-family housing should be built and that a wide range of services should be provided close to blocks of flats (Swedish Ministry of Housing and Physical Planning, 1975: 21). These recommendations echo the preferences and orientations of the forties. More public transportation in planning both areas to be rehabilitated and new estates also was recommended. Large numbers of vacant flats in new estates must have added impetus to governmental decisions to institute policy changes. Between 1973 and 1974, 40,000 vacant flats caused serious financial problems for municipal and nonprofit housing companies. The state had to provide financial aid to avoid deterioration in many residential environments (Svennson, 1976: 11).

Other actions also were taken. Criticism by parents, women's organizations, and trade unions led to an increased emphasis on day nurseries and supervised afterschool centers (Svennson, 1976: 10). In 1973, a government resolution called for special efforts to meet children's need for play facilities and residents' interest in space for recreation, leisure, and social interaction (Swedish Ministry of Housing and Physical Planning, 1975: 22–23). Moreover, greater attention is being devoted to creating employment opportunities within the suburbs (IFHP, 1979: 28). Although the plan had been to have many residents live and work in Vällingby, by the time industry had located there most residents already were working elsewhere. Then, those hired for the jobs could not obtain housing in the same community (Genovese, 1975: 54). The later dormitory suburbs offered relatively few jobs for residents.

The new housing bill introduced in 1974 signaled significant policy changes, especially a commitment to building suburbs on a smaller, more human scale, with a diversity of housing types and more low-rise buildings. The orientation also changed to building more one- and two-family homes, in keeping with user demand. Finally, more emphasis was placed on resident participation, although formal channels continued to be favored (Swedish Ministry of Housing and Physical Planning, 1975).

Resident participation in the planning of new areas raised some problems. How could those who would ultimately live in an area be identified? Proposals tended to be circulated for comment to the same established organizations that had always been consulted. When a new development was small, however, future residents sometimes participated, from the design through the final stages. The result was a high degree of resident satisfaction both with their home and environment (IFHP, 1974: 34).

A new aspect of participation was included in the Housing Bill section "The Foundations for a System of User Democracy," with its provisions for giving tenants a say in plans to modernize or alter buildings and surrounding areas. This section outlines a system of codetermination for tenants and landlords (Swedish Ministry for Housing and Physical Planning, 1975: 23–24). Property owners had long been notified about planning decisions that affected them (Häggroth, 1976: 111). Now tenants were to be given the power to stop large-scale rehabilitation or plans that would drastically upgrade a building and place it beyond their means. However, there was always the danger that a landlord would prefer to demolish a building rather than meet tenant demands. On the other hand, tenants could not ensure that modernization would be carried out. All they could do was to apply to the authorities for a renovation order.

The bill tries to define who will speak for tenants. Tenants as a group are given influence over the entire building and surrounding area. In practice, this means that the local branch of the tenants' movement represents tenants (see *The tenants' movement in Sweden*, 1981). With regard to individual units, the tenant is given the right of codetermination if possible. Tenants in blocks of flats had already gained the right to redecorate their apartments without seeking landlord approval.

The title of a recent article, "Is codetermination a bluff?" (Lidmar, 1982a) indicates that tenants still may not have much influence in rehabilitation decisions. Although tenants have the right to see that building rehabilitation is modest or limited to repairs needed to bring it up to standard, Lidmar argues that landlords are encouraged by public finance regulations to make more sweeping changes. As a result, on average, only about one in six tenants move back after renovation. One tenant tells how she had to move out of her flat during the renovation period. She was about to move back into the modernized dwelling which, in her view, had lost most of its charm yet cost three times as much as the 450 kroner she had previously paid (ibid., 16). Although tenants have the right to move back to a renovated unit at the new rent, they do not have the right to compensation if they do not move back (ibid.).

Current and future housing issues

Both policy makers and critics continue to grapple with a number of issues. Some of these are attributable to the swing of the pendulum back toward an emphasis on ownership rather than rental housing. This concern is part of the larger problem of residential segregation, especially on the basis of income.

By the end of the seventies, about 40 percent of the population lived in owner-occupied single-or two-family homes, with 60 percent in rental units (IFHP, 1979: 25). The number of single- and two-family dwellings has increased in recent years, as the majority of new units constructed were of this type. For example, in 1960 only 25 percent of the new units built were one- or two-dwelling houses, compared to 72 percent in 1970, 69 percent in 1980, and 66 percent in 1981 (Swedish Association of Municipal Housing Companies, 1982).

Homeownership is opposed by some policy makers because it increases economic differentiation among population groups. In Sweden, as in many other countries, homeownership is indirectly subsidized. Households above certain income limits are much better off owning than renting housing. Moreover, inflation increases the value of their investments, further widening the gap between them and their lower-income neighbors who must pay constantly higher rents for their dwelling units.

Several proposals aim to minimize the economic gap between owners and renters by (a) limiting the amount of interest on mortgages that can be offset against income or by (b) improving the economic situation of renters. Twenty-five percent of the renters live in flats owned by cooperative housing associations like the National Association of Tenants Savings and Building Societies (HSB) and the Cooperative Housing Organization of the Swedish Trade Unions (Riksbyggen). Another 25 percent live in housing owned by public housing corporations (IFHP, 1979: 27). One proposal would increase the number of cooperative housing associations by allowing tenants to buy the property they have been renting. Another proposal gives tenants a say in the management of neighborhood services as well as building services. In experiments with neighborhood councils in four different housing estates with 2,000 dwellings, tenants decided issues relating to recreation, playgrounds, traffic, street cleaning, and refuse collection. Those in flats[2] owned by the cooperative housing associations already can assume a greater share of their costs themselves and thus limit rent increases. Similar arrangements are being made for privately owned and public corporations.

The argument about ownership compared to rental housing may be settled by economic factors rather than by consumer preferences or egalitarian values. The proportion of owner-occupied units is not likely to grow substantially in the future owing to rising costs of energy, roads, water, and sewers, as well as higher monthly costs and real estate taxes (IFHP, 1979: 28).

Social segregation also concerns policy makers. Swedish policy has been to provide housing allowances to low-income residents rather than to build subsidized units which would foster segregation and discrimination. However, various forms of social segregation still occur. Some areas with concentrations of households with low incomes and social handicaps are "characterized by strained social contacts, bad schools, limited service facilities, and worn out outdoor spaces" (Lidmar, 1982b: 2). Such conditions go against "official goals concerning a just distribution of resources to the inhabitants" (ibid.). There is also a growing trend toward age segregation.

Therefore, over the past five or ten years, the central housing authorities have adopted the goal of making all environments and areas attractive and accessible to diverse population groups. Much effort has centered on how to retrofit existing areas within towns to make them more equally attractive to all households. In some areas, segregation might be decreased by improved office and commercial services; in others, increased density might be needed (ibid.).

Swedish authorities also are likely to emphasize more diversity in housing to meet the preferences of different household types. Extended families or communal living groups need more space than is called for by uniform guidelines and standards (see Gaunt in Chapter 4 of this book and Vestbro, 1981). Some elderly and handicapped households may want less space, conveniently arranged for those with limited mobility. At the end of the 1970s, new guidelines were developed to ensure that the handicapped had access to new dwelling units. Moreover, multipurpose service houses are being built in some areas so that the elderly do not get segregated in their own buildings, away from those of other ages and life-cycle stages (Lidmar, 1982b: 4). In general, more attention is expected to be given to providing residents with an array of welfare and leisure facilities (IFHP, 1979: 28). This move is in line with resident dissatisfaction with suburbs that contained housing and a shopping center, but little else.

Another direction for the future may be more experimentation with flexible housing units. Some architects recommend such units to meet the needs of various household types or the same household at different life-cycle stages. Although systems for building multifamily houses with changeable components have been developed, they have been put into practice only on a very small scale.

It remains to be seen whether the changes that have been instituted by the housing authorities will serve to meet residents' demand for a greater say in the planning of their homes and neighborhoods. For tenants particularly, the actual influence they can exercise over their living conditions may be too little to make a difference in their lives. Furthermore, an increase in nontraditional households could lead to demands for housing units more in line with their life-styles and needs.

Summary. Paying heed to the users' perspective leads to two general benefits. First, this can provide information for a theroetical understanding of whole classes of housing environments (e.g., multifamily housing, housing for the elderly, etc.). This can directly benefit new housing. Better theoretical models of housing can lead to more correct decisions for choices in housing environments; they can reduce the likelihood of errors in planning and design.

Second, it can provide information regarding specific housing environments. This can directly benefit the management and redesign of existing housing. It can tell what is working well and what is not, so that changes may be made to improve the quality of any specific residential environment.

In short, attention to the users' perspective of government housing in the United States can result in better housing now and in the future.

Australia
Leslie Kilmartin

In Chapter 7, Newton and Wulff provide an analysis of the provision of public housing through three quite different programs in Melbourne in the period after World War II. They attempt to examine the usefulness of state theory in understanding the role and policies of the state housing authority, the Housing Commission of Victoria (HCV). Three views of the state are outlined: the representational, which holds that the state is independent of class interests; the instrumentalist, which holds that the state is the associate of the capitalist class; and the relative autonomy model, which holds that the state may serve the capitalist class but often reserves the right to act contrary to the wishes of that class.

While state theories provide some explanation and insight, I will argue that such approaches lead to rather partial findings and programs since they ignore consumer responses. Very little is known about the housing and tenure preferences and needs of low-income households. Such knowledge would provide the basis on which a successful and humane housing policy might be constructed. The preference structure of these households with respect to such matters as tenure type, dwelling type, relative housing quality, and ecological location within the metropolis are as yet uncharted. Only consumer-oriented housing research will provide researchers and policy makers with these fundamental data.

For purposes of this paper, discussion will be confined to one of the three programs of the HCV to which Newton and Wulff refer, namely the villa estate program. In particular, data are drawn from my study of the residents of an outer suburban estate which, from the outset, was occupied by commission clients who were purchasing their home from the commission.

Public housing and homeownership

A striking feature of the housing system in Australia is the high proportion of owner-occupiers. With around two-thirds of all dwellings being owner-occupied, Australian levels of homeownership are among the highest in the world (Kemeny, 1981: chap. 1). This relatively long-standing tradition, the financial benefits of homeownership, compared with renting and the stigma generally associated with renting have all combined to generate a now well-entrenched ideology of home-ownership: there is a widespread belief in the inherent superiority of homeownership over other forms of tenure.

This ideology is so pervasive that it has even penetrated the state-provided housing system. Thus state housing authorities, encouraged as Newton and Wulff show by the federal government, have actively pursued policies of sales of their stock to tenants and other low-income persons. Newton and Wulff point out that the HCV has gradually sold a majority of its stock on villa estates, so that, by 1980, three-fourths of all detached houses built by the commission have been sold. Set against the benefits which homeownership confers on public housing clients are the alleged costs of location. Elsewhere, Newton and Wulff (1983) show that the HCV has constructed its villa estates on the periphery of the metropolitan area. They argue that, although the Commission had no explicit location objective to its villa estate construction program, metropolitan fringe land was most frequently used because of its relatively low costs.

What follows provides a users' perspective of the Commission's peripherally located villa estates built for occupancy from the outset by purchasers rather than tenants. In particular, we shall examine the satisfaction of the residents and some of the implications of their residential location.

Background

The Hampton Park estate is some 35 kilometers from the central business district of Melbourne and approximately 6.5 kilometers from the regional industrial employment center of Dandenong. At the time of the study (1976–77), it was, together with some private residential development, a rather isolated development. The estate was completed for occupancy during 1973–74, and it comprises 259 detached houses on blocks of approximately one-fifth of an acre. Each house contains three bedrooms and was designed by the commission and built by a firm with an established record of home building for clients in the low- to middle-income categories in the private sector. To the observer, the estate was remarkably free of the usual stereotypical design features, and the quality of the housing was comparable to and compatible with that on the adjoining private estate.

The details of the contract between the occupants and the commission are of particular note. The occupants were required to pay a small deposit (87.4 percent paid Australian $500 or less), and the repayments on the "contract for sale" were also quite modest (the average being approximately $31 per week, or approximately 13 percent of average weekly family income). These conditions were clearly very favorable, and they illustrate the earlier point that the commission was enthusiastically promoting homeownership for this group of clients.

The occupants. All but 3.6 percent of the dwellings were occupied by married couples with their dependent children. The average age for the parents was 34 for males and 31.2 for females, and the modal number of children per family was two. In income terms, both males and employed females (33.7 percent of the females were employed full or part-time) were low-income earners, and the great majority were in unskilled or semi-skilled jobs. Educational attainment levels were correspondingly low.

Housing satisfaction

The average length of time on the commission's waiting list was slightly more than four years. A substantial majority of the households (85.2 percent) had been tenants in the private sector before moving to Hampton Park. The dominant motive among these residents for their move from their last address was the desire to become homeowners. In fact, 97.4 percent of the respondents rated this consideration as either very important or important in their decision to live on the estate.

In response to another question, 96.5 percent of the respondents indicated that being a homeowner was either important or very important to them. All but one respondent were of the view that it is better to be purchasing from the commission than to be a tenant of the commission. Indeed, these residents strongly opposed tenancy whether public or private. Many respondents throught that rent was "dead money," that tenants have no control over rents, and that homeownership confers economic advantage and enhances financial and occupancy security.

It is clear from the foregoing that the residents of Hampton Park were highly motivated to homeownership. It is not surprising, therefore, that they manifest high levels of satisfaction with their homes, especially since their homes are of objectively good quality. Just under 90 percent of the residents indicated that they were either attached or strongly attached to their homes. The proportion registering satisfaction is even higher in Hampton Park than it was in Canterbury,[1] a centrally located, more established, middle-class suburb. It is considerably higher than for the residents of Hopper's Crossing,[2] a private residential estate in the outer western suburbs. In Hopper's Crossing, only 68.3 percent of residents were attached or strongly attached to their homes, and yet these were comparable in both standard and age to those in Hampton Park.

While freehold tenure was considered desirable, the question must be raised as to whether it is occupancy of a house rather than an apartment or whether it is ownership of a dwelling which generates greater housing satisfaction. In their study of commission tenants in a (then) outer suburb, Bryson and Thompson (1972) report high levels of housing satisfaction. These findings suggest that, regardless of tenure type, dwelling type may be a major source of satisfaction. Only consumer-oriented research can help to disentangle preference for tenure and preference for dwelling type.

Locality satisfaction

Despite high levels of house satisfaction, residents of Hampton Park might well be expected to be rather less satisfied with their location on the metropolitan periphery. Perhaps this location imposes costs on them which a more central location would not. When asked to rate the general convenience of their residential location, only slightly more than 60 percent found it convenient, and only 13.3 percent found it very convenient. This compares quite unfavorably with the residents of the more central location of Canterbury, all of whom found their location convenient in some degree. Clearly then, for some Hampton Park residents there was a trade-off between the desirability of becoming a home purchaser and the inconvenience of having to move to an outer suburb to achieve that goal.

There is at least one qualifying consideration in the matter of convenience. While Hampton Park is not "generally convenient," it is quite well-located in terms of most work trips. A majority of employed persons rated their residence as convenient to their place of work, and 46 percent of the males and 61 percent of the employed females work within 5 kilometers of their homes. Even the well-located residents of Canterbury have only 25 percent of males and 48 percent of employed females living so near to their work. For the residents of Hopper's Crossing, the proportion of males and employed females working within 5 kilometers of their homes drops dramatically to 6 percent and 2.5 percent, respectively.

Of course, distance from place of employment is not the only or best indicator of convenience. The duration of the journey must also be taken into consideration. The Hampton Park males had a mean journey-to-work time of 24.5 minutes. On average, the male Hampton Park resident is therefore no worse off than his Canterbury counterpart, whose mean journey-to-work time was 24.1 minutes. The male workers of the outer western suburb of Hopper's Crossing have journey-to-work times that are almost identical with those for Hampton Park males: a mean travel time of 25.6 minutes, with a standard deviation of 16.1 minutes.

Thus, we see that outer suburban location, per se, may not be a major source of dissatisfaction. Indeed, it may be that the assumption that such locations impose costs and cause dissatisfaction is a result of a mononucleated model of the metropolis. In fact, Melbourne and many other large metropolises have developed in such a way that residents may now be able to meet most of their important needs, including employment, within the local region. Consumer-oriented behavioral research will assist in our understanding of how residents use and relate to whole metropolitan areas and local and other metropolitan regions.

There may also be important differences in urban behavior based on such attributes as gender and ethnicity. For example, it is probably the employed females of Hampton Park rather than the employed males who suffer the disadvantages of location. A number of studies have shown (e.g., in the United States, Madden and White, 1978: 1–2, and in Australia, Manning, 1978: 181) that women tend to have shorter journeys to work than men. This is certainly the case in both Hopper's Crossing and Canterbury, where the average differences between the sexes are nine minutes and five minutes, respectively. In Hampton Park, however, average female journey-to-work times are almost identical with those for males.

Females also have a much higher reliance on public transport than males (17.2 percent compared to 2.5 percent). When asked about the difficulties men and working wives encountered, the latter were three times as likely to be seen by male and female respondents as suffering from poor public transport provision. The absence of shops was seen to fall heavily on nonemployed females. The importance of consumer-oriented research in highlighting differential impacts of location on social groupings such as males and females is apparent.

Social planning

As private estate developers, the HCV has typically done little more for its clients than provide housing. While it coordinates the activities of some other agencies which provide physical infrastructure, it rarely ventures into comprehensive social planning. Residents, asked about services or facilities which were lacking, mentioned several different types. Most commonly, the absence of adequate public transport was criticized. The estate has no fixed rail services and is therefore totally reliant on one privately-operated bus service to provide access for adults to the regional shopping center and, for children, to the nearest high school. The service does not operate after noon on Saturdays or at all on Sundays. At the time of the study, students in high school had to cut their last class in order to catch the last bus home.

Another commonly mentioned absence was in local shopping facilities. Nor was there a full-time local doctor or dentist. A very frequent complaint was made about the absence of a local pharmacist, a much-needed service for families with young children. Finally, the absence of community facilities and facilities for children's and teenagers' recreation was also frequently noted. It must be noted that this low level of social planning is typical for both public and private estates on the periphery of Australian cities (Brennan, 1973; Bryson and Thompson, 1972; Faulkner, 1978).

Conclusions

Newton and Wulff argue that a consideration of some HCV policies and programs indicates that the commission has sometimes acted in conformity with the instrumental model of the state. Thus, following Saunders (1978: 148–49), the commission can be seen to have engaged in activities which have sustained private production and capital accumulation, reproduced labor power through collective consumption, and maintained order and social cohesion.

Let us now examine these functions of the state as represented by its housing commission's actions in the case of the development of Hampton Park. First, the system of private ownership of land has meant that the commission has had to purchase outer metropolitan land from private landowners, including, possibly, land speculators. Indeed, the commission has been shown in a recent public inquiry to have paid vastly inflated prices for land on the metropolitan periphery (Victoria: 1981). Since in Victoria the state does not embark upon such schemes as land banking or land leasing using its powers of eminent domain, it permits private landholders to accumulate wealth by assembling large parcels of land in the path of suburban development. Second, it is clear that, in providing low cost, good quality housing, the commission has provided some of "the natural conditions of existence" (Saunders, 1979: 147) which the clients might otherwise not have enjoyed. However, it has failed to provide much in the way of extrahousing facilities, or what Saunders (p. 147) refers to as "the means of the cultural conditions of existence," at least in the form of local social planning. Finally, it seems likely that the policy of sales to clients—on such attractive terms—is likely to promote social cohesion and order through satisfying the aspiration for homeownership, but, also and more importantly, by binding clients into a system of long-term mortgage indebtedness. This requires of the beneficiaries a commitment to employment stability, saving, and respect for the rights of private property.

It is also worth noting that the commission may have bestowed its benefits on a section of the "deserving poor" rather than those in more severe housing crises. Thus, Neutze (1978: 102) reports that the commission of inquiry into poverty found that only 26 percent of Australian adult income units classified as poor were housing authority tenants and that only 28 percent of housing authority tenants were classified as poor. State-assisted entry into homeownership launches certain fortunate households on a new housing security and life-chance trajectory which they otherwise could not have enjoyed. At the same time, the commission diminishes its total housing stock and thereby deprives others in poverty of good quality shelter.

Despite these interpretations of the function of state intervention in housing, it should be borne in mind that, in the case of the clients who purchase public housing, the commission may be seen to be pursuing a very humane policy. While such clients may be described pejoratively as the "deserving poor," the fact remains that they *are* low-income families in need of housing. Left to their own devices, they may never have been able to save enough money for a deposit and might never, therefore, have enjoyed those economic and psychological benefits that freehold tenure bestows.

11 | Policy Approaches to Social
Housing Problems in Northern and
Western Europe
Elizabeth D. Huttman

Abstract. Huttman presents an overview of the evolvement of post-World War II housing policies in Europe, particularly Western Europe and Scandinavia. Detailed descriptions of program focuses and trends reveal the influence of changing economic conditions. Current and prospective developments are discussed, and special consideration is given to disenfranchised groups affected by recent policy measures.

Introduction

A housing crisis exists both in the industrialized northern and western European countries and in the United States. New trends in housing subsidies and in types of housing provision are evolving in all these countries. These housing trends are the result of a variety of factors typical of the industrial and post-industrial stage of development, as described in the first chapter of this book. For northern and western Europe, this stage of economic development should be subdivided into three phases. First is the early postwar period with a continuation of war shortages and economic deprivations, a period that over time saw continual improvement. The second phase is a period of economic affluence, started in the mid-seventies or even earlier, where citizens had a second home and long holidays and bought their primary living unit. The third phase, starting in 1981, is where the "Wirtschaftswunder" (economic wonder) bubble burst, and northern and western European countries (hereafter referred to as "northern") suffer from an economic recession and then from economic stagnation, which decreases the number of jobs and government revenues and is accompanied by high interest rates.

In each period the economic situation has affected the type of housing the government has subsidized, as well as the users' preference and ability to pay for certain types of housing. In each period the type and degree of urbanization and suburbanization has affected government policy in supplying housing and improving the total environment.

The demographic factors, such as degree of population growth and extent of household formation related to number married, divorced, and single (both young and old), also have their effect on what type and how much housing is built (see introduction to housing need section). In addition to these factors, the historical situation, such as in the early postwar period, has had an influence on housing policy. The political philosophy of the government, including the degree of enthusiasm for the welfare state orientation, also determines whether the state takes a major role in providing housing, either social housing or the more comprehensive variety mentioned in the overall introduction (and found in Sweden).

The two sections below describe the early postwar housing conditions and policies and then the second period of changed trends due to economic affluence, with references made to the third or present period, that of economic recession and economic stagnation.

The early postwar period was one of housing shortages due to lack of building during the war, to the depression before the war, and, in many countries, to wartime bombing. Countries that had an early industrial revolution, such as Britain, suffered from another problem: they had old tenement units such as the back-to-back dwellings in the midlands cities that needed to be demolished or upgraded. In some countries however, because of bombing, much of the urban housing stock, such as that in West Germany and in Rotterdam, was erected after World War II (Raes, Economic Commission for Europe, 1981).

Major urbanization trends existed after the war. Mass postwar migration to the cities from rural areas occurred in all of these countries and contributed further to a need for housing. In some countries, e.g., France, there were abandoned units in rural areas and a shortage of units in the cities. Postwar demographic factors also shaped housing needs and policies. There was increased household formation as the men came home from the war and started families. The need was for family housing, and subsidized housing was built in terms of family-size apartments with three or four bedrooms.

Because of the economic limitations of the governments and of the population in the early postwar years, the housing was also built in massive cheap projects of small rental units. Both this economic situation and the postwar political orientation of a welfare state nature dictated that the state build the housing. Harloe (1982) called it the "socialization of housing." Housing was a major political issue in northern and western Europe.

Postwar government intervention

Mass housing production programs were introduced in most northern European countries under a variety of subsidy systems. These programs were mainly oriented to families of the solid working class and even to the middle class. The main focus was on provision of subsidized rental apartments, in or on the fringe of central cities, either directly owned by the local authorities or government-subsidized through nonprofit housing associations.

New towns, the most innovative type of subsidy program, carried the subsidization and planning further. Often surrounded by a greenbelt of agricultural areas and parklands, whole new towns of mainly government-subsidized rental units were built with national funds.

The underlining goal, especially in Britain, was to build in a way that stemmed the production of massive housing estates that extended the city's boundaries, and instead produced whole new infrastructures with town centers, industrial parks, office buildings, and, above all, residential housing. In Britain and The Netherlands, new towns were purposely located a considerable distance from the current urban boundary. The intention was that a greenbelt would contain development. In the Stockholm area and the Paris area, the new town, while having some boundary between it and the central city, was seen mainly as a residential satellite community feeding workers in to the central city. In some cases, new-town development was seen as a way to revitalize poorer regions of the country and stop outward migration from these areas; that was an aim of the Scottish new towns.

Land use policy also reflected a socialization of housing. New towns were built on land either already owned by the local authority (Stockholm) or the country, sometimes because of a landbanking policy, such as Toronto has. In Sweden and Norway—and much earlier in West Germany too—it was assumed that municipal governments had a duty to acquire land in advance of development in order to shape, rather than merely regulate, the growth of cities.

In Britain the land both for new towns and local authority-subsidized housing programs was compulsorily purchased. The land for the new town was produced by drainage and fill in Holland's reclamation of the Zuider Zee to use for new towns such as Lelystad and for agricultural activities. The local authority rental complex type of subsidy program was prevalent in Britain as well as new town building. In other countries, such as Sweden and Switzerland, municipalities built some social housing.

In Britain, local authorities, using national subsidies, built huge housing estates of rental units, with the Greater London Council leading the way. In many inner-city areas in Britain the authorities also engaged in massive slum clearance (demolition) programs and built council housing on the site. By the seventies, a third of British housing units were council housing units or new town development corporation units (a very small proportion of the whole); there were also some voluntary association units.

In other countries, the subsidies mainly went to various housing associations that built massive amounts of housing. "In France, Austria, Germany, Scandinavia and The Netherlands, industrial, political, and religious movements developed various patterns of voluntary and cooperative associations, which were later adopted by governments as their principal instruments for the provision of housing" (Donnison, 1982). In The Netherlands, the housing associations were the main recipients of government funds; usually there were three associations in a town, representing religious and other affiliations. In Amsterdam in the seventies, there were about seventeen, some representing occupational or political groups. As the funding source, the national government set the annual allowable rent increase and set housing standards.

Thirty-two percent of the Dutch housing completed in 1978 was still housing-association housing, about the same proportion as in 1970. In The Netherlands, the percentage of municipal-built units was low, only 16.3 percent (1970) to 2.6 percent (1978) of units completed. In 1970 Denmark also was building a considerable amount of housing-association housing (27.3 percent of units completed), but this had decreased by 1978.

The West German subsidy assistance to housing, though very major, has not focused housing associations as much (18 percent of units completed in 1970 and only 8 percent in 1978), even though, as Muhlich (1978) reports, nonprofit businesses have been encouraged by receiving public loans and aid in acquiring land to build upon. The legal status of the nonprofit builders has improved, and they have, Muhlich (1978) says, rendered a great contribution in widening the range of housing for low-income groups. Nor has the West German subsidy program ever been prominent in terms of supplying public housing (only 2 percent of units completed in both 1970 and 1978). The West German government has been reluctant to allocate a large role to social housing. The Germans have had indirect subsidies to private investors which, by 1978, built 90.5 percent of the housing. However, some social housing in West Germany has been produced by and for trade unionists.

In Italy and in France, industries such as the automobile companies have built a considerable amount of social housing for their workers (Harloe).

In many countries, housing allowances, rent subsidies, rent rebates, or some similar type of subsidy that covers the difference between a certain proportion of a person's income and the rent, play a part in the total subsidy program. Sweden and West Germany have had major housing allowance programs. In the late sixties, 40 percent of the households in Sweden were covered by a housing allowance, and the percentage was still high in 1978.

Some countries have means-tested housing allowances for the poorest households in a *certain* housing. Britain and The Netherlands, for example, have brought in individual rent subsidy programs for their poorer renters in council housing and association housing units respectively. These means-tested programs are used to allow them to raise the rent in their council housing or housing association units (The Netherlands), with the assumption that most tenants can afford the higher rent and those who cannot will take the rent allowance. In Amsterdam, the rationale behind a means-tested individual rent subsidy system was to raise rents in the older housing association units, since many of these units were occupied by middle-income households; this has not fully been realized. Second, individual rent subsidies were intended to make newer housing association units more affordable to young couples; however, the subsidies were not high enough to accomplish this with full success since new housing was fairly expensive.

Rent regulations have also been a part of the European housing picture. In Britain in the mid-sixties the rent controls after the Milner-Holland committee and the 1965 Rent Act expanded security to tenants. The rent control system changed to include a fair rents tribunal (which turned out to be used more by landlords than by tenants). Rent control existed for private housing in The Netherlands and in a number of other Northern and Western European countries. It was supported as a measure in these countries to keep private rents down, but it also had another result, the low allowable rent increases and the various regulations discouraged the landlord from staying in the housing market. This is a point to which we will return later.

Housing for special groups: Housing for the elderly

The main housing for special groups in the sixties and seventies was subsidized housing for the elderly. Many countries, such as Holland and Britain, built numerous complexes or other special housing for the elderly. By 1976, "in The Netherlands sufficient places in residential homes for the elderly were available practically everywhere" (Vogelaar, 1976). One year later, when the author studied these residential homes for the elderly with meals service, light housekeeping, infirmaries, recreation facilities, and such, the government was starting to cut back on admissions by using medical criteria for admittance. At that time 10 percent of The Netherlands' elderly were in such homes; 15 percent were in specially designed apartment complexes, and that number was to increase. Britain, too, developed "sheltered" housing early. This specially designed housing has a lounge room, used for lunch clubs and social activities, and a common garden. It usually has full apartments, generally in the form of bungalows or low flats. The projects have a warden overseeing the aged. The project has an alarm system or intercom connected to a warden's dwelling or to a central office if the warden is off duty. Ash (1982) reports that "the warden sees that the residents get the services they need and promotes mutual support and social activity among the residents." In the ones the author has visited, a dedicated social work system exists. Ash reports that the number of sheltered housing units increased rapidly, from 35,000 in 1963 to more than 300,000 in 1979. While most were provided by the local housing authorities, the housing associations supplied about one-fifth of these sheltered units (half the housing association tenants are elderly).

Denmark has provided accommodations for its elderly in a number of ways. These include sheltered housing units, with a common dining room, nursing service, recreation programs, and some housekeeping. These sheltered housing units are usually attached to nursing homes that are the pride of every Danish municipality, as the author found in her study there. The author, reporting in *Housing and Society* (1982) on the 1977 situation, states: "Because the number of Danes in the 75-and-over category is increasing and these nursing homes are expensive and short in number, with waiting lists, an attempt has begun in the last decade to provide a cheaper and more independent living alternative for elderly who do not require extensive nursing care but need some help; that is, the addition of service apartments to the nursing home. A number of nursing homes built in the last five to ten years also have such service apartments. In fact, for many such projects the number of service apartments outnumber the nursing wing units and this is considered desirable" (p. 241). These service apartments have a full kitchen. In addition, the Danes have ordinary nonprofit housing projects for the elderly, mixed with family apartments. A Danish Ministry of Housing report (1974) stated that "in recent years in nonprofit housing schemes permission has been granted to build up to one-third of the total number of dwellings as one-room apartments, which are let separately. . . . A total of 500 to 600 of these one room dwellings are being built annually" (p. 16).

Owner-occupied households also receive an indirect subsidy in most northern European countries, as in the United States; that is, they can write off certain housing costs such as mortgage interest and property tax on their income tax. In Britain, there is tax relief on mortgage interest. In addition, in the late sixties an option mortgage system was brought in which extended benefits equivalent to tax relief to house buyers who had incomes too low to pay the standard taxes; rate rebates were introduced. Subsidies for the house buyer are regressive, giving more aid to those in expensive houses (Bigsworth, 1981; Nevitt, 1966). Muhlich (1978) reports the same situation for West Germany: in 1971, the upper half of the taxpayers received three-fourths of this indirect subsidy to homeowners (*Statistics year book*, 1975).

New trends in the mid-1970s

Economic prosperity in Northern Europe was evident by the mid-1970s. In this "Wirtschaftswunder" (economic wonder) period in northern Europe, governments were able to fund a large number of units, both private and public sector housing, peaking in the early 1970s—for some countries peaking in 1973–74 and for others, such as Sweden and Britain, in 1970—and dropping each year after that (ECE, 1980). Per capita income was high, in some countries equal or nearly equal to that in the United States. Many citizens could afford improved housing; an increasing number of them improved their quality of housing by buying private units, causing private investors to be a larger percentage of the total builders. Quality of housing and the total environment, including improved amenities, replaced quantity of housing as the interest of the population.

Urban migration from rural areas decreased in this period, but there was increased movement of the middle class to the suburbs. Even new subsidized housing for the working class was put up in the suburbs.

Demographic factors changed in this period to decrease the emphasis on supplying family housing. Lower birth rates meant fewer large families. Later marriages, such as in Sweden, produced a large singles population of young people who wanted their own residence, as Van Vliet— reports in his chapter on Israeli young people. Gaunt reports in her chapter that, in Sweden by 1983, two-thirds of the households consisted of only one or two persons. Ash reports for Britain that half the increase in households from 1961 to 1971 was in one-person households. Some were migrants from rural areas, many were university students or new job aspirants. In addition, longer life expectancy meant an increased number of older frail singles who required special housing. Due to increased divorce rates, there were also more female-headed households.

Immigrant workers swelled the urban population in this period. In some countries they made up more than one-fourth of the work force. Some were ex-colonials who were permanently in their new countries, while others, as in Sweden and West Germany, held temporary work permits. Some were single men, but many had large families. They all needed housing and they found it in inner-city slum areas, to a large degree abandoned by the stable working-class families who had moved into subsidized units or even bought private housing, often cooperative or condominium apartment units. This was because the housing shortage was over for the stable working-class families.

In 1983, three decades after the beginning of these postwar housing intervention programs, the European situation, and with it the housing needs and programs, has changed considerably. First of all, as mentioned above, the great scarcity of housing for the working class has disappeared, although special, often marginal workers in certain inner-city areas were in greater housing need than ever, and the increase in housing costs may cause many to have problems. The U.N. data show that the number of dwelling units per 1,000 inhabitants increased greatly from 1960 to 1978, for example, by 37 percent in The Netherlands, 40 percent in West Germany, 42 percent in Switzerland, and 26 percent in Denmark, although by only 20 percent in the United Kingdom. While it was a housing stock growing old, it was greater in number than household formation in some countries. In 1982, Donnison reports that, for the year 1980, an "apparent surplus of housing is now emerging in most of the more affluent European countries" and states that some new housing problems have emerged that would not be possible without a surplus of units. These problems include those of hard-to-let flats, including rejection of high-rise units.

This surplus of housing, even though it does not always consist of cheap or desirable units, means that political support for a massive government house-building program has dwindled in most countries. With this recent economic recession and the government need for budget cuts, support for a large program is also lessened. McKay (1982) summarizes studies of the present European housing situation: "Certainly the *political* demand for cheap family housing for a broad segment of the employed population has decreased in most countries." For years housing was a major political issue in most of these countries, but this seems to have ended (Donnison, 1982). In West Germany, Muhlich (1978) reports: "Housing policy is seen at present as a peripheral policy area, especially with the presently abundant provision of housing." The emphasis has moved above all from building *new* units, often in poor locations, to quality *improvements* of existing units and neighborhoods, as the ECE Committee on Housing reports. In some countries the number of units being rehabilitated exceeds the number of new units being built. As far as new building, data indicate that the private investor was gaining and the local authority or housing association, as investor, was decreasing (Eurostat, for 1970 to 1977–78). This was especially true for The Netherlands and Britain.

The economic recession of 1981–82, followed by a period of economic stagnation, increased the number of homeless. At the same time, it decreased political support for a subsidized housing program. It intensified some of the housing policy trends mentioned, such as the need to house the homeless and the desire to sell council housing.

The economic crisis, with its high unemployment rates and lower government revenues, meant a cry for fiscal austerity by the governments, a pulling back from welfare state programs, especially housing. Populations were increasingly more concerned about high taxes than about keeping welfare state benefits. There was a changeover from socialist party-run governments to conservative party governments in Britain, West Germany, and some other countries.

Economic factors, such as high interest rates and high building costs, cut back on both the construction of new owner-occupancy units, which few could afford to buy, and on rental units where high costs and low-rent potential made investment unprofitable. Even by 1979, the ECE statistics (1980) showed that building was sharply down from 1973, with the monthly average of dwelling units constructed down one-fourth on average for the United Kingdom, almost one-half for The Netherlands, and around two-thirds for West Germany.

With the increased number of newly unemployed joining the increased number of singles in the need for private rentals, competition was sharp for the decreasing number of such units, as a result of rehabilitation and demolition activities, as well as conversion to owner occupancy. Homelessness was increasing.

While a number of immigrants had returned to their own country if on a temporary work permit, many were still legally or illegally in the host country, and in many cases their children were reaching marriage age where they would form a separate household.

The housing trends and policies discussed in the following pages span the two periods of the mid-seventies and early eighties, with attempts to distinguish between the two.

The new trends in European housing policies

Greater interest in owner occupancy. The "socialization of housing" has ended, Harloe (1982) feels, and housing has moved back to being a market commodity. This is partly due to increased owner-occupancy, a movement that has occurred among the lower middle class and even the better-off working class, who in the early postwar period considered renting the acceptable state. This new interest turned them away from political support of subsidized public or nonprofit rental housing (Harloe, 1982).

The affluence that had come to northern Europe in the late seventies was partly responsible for this change. This new affluence allowed them in the late seventies to realize their preference for a unit they owned, often a detached house surrounded by a green plot in a suburban area (Ungerson and Karn, 1980). These groups had now come to a point where they could demand *quality*, a certain amount of private space meeting certain desired housing standards (see the Ash chapter). Governments too supported the idea of quality, for they no longer needed to build a *quantity* of housing (Donnison, 1982).

Britain's Thatcher government has especially promoted homeownership. Thatcherites speak of the pride of homeownership and the virtues of the homeowning class. They claim that their mission is to enable households able to prosper in the private housing market to do so and to give the incentive to all Britons to invest in land and a home (see the chapter by Forrest and Murie in this book). The Thatcherites kept various types of subsidies to homeowners high, though they cut council housing subsidies in the eighties.

Tax relief for homeowners. Tax relief, as well as below-interest mortgages, is the main way the Thatcher government has done this. In their chapter, Forrest and Murie report that for 1982–83 the average mortgage tax relief was more than one-third higher than the average per council housing unit subsidy in Britain. In Sweden, where tax relief has also been given to owners, Lindberg (1978) attributes the great increase in homeownership in the seventies (from 30 percent of all units built 1961–65 to 71 percent built in 1978) partially to "the fact that all interest on loans is tax deductible so that it is very favorable for many families to invest in their own homes." He also attributes the increase in homeownership to the lack of private rentals.

Loan variations. Not only the indirect subsidies of tax deductions, but special loan arrangements also have helped people with moderate income to acquire mortgages. "In some countries interest rates (have) compelled governments to envisage a new system of financing," the ECE Committee on Housing (1981) reports. For example, in Sweden there has been a variety of loan periods, there are "first loans, at a rate of interest slightly below the market level, calling for no repayment until other loans have been repaid; and second and third loans at similar privileged rates of interest, repaid over 30 to 40 years." All three types of loans are available to all the principal types of investors, but percentage of the capital cost of the building covered varied by type of borrower, with owner-occupiers getting less than public groups.

Increase in homeownership. This increase was the result of the measures listed above. Not only in Sweden, but in the United Kingdom also by 1984, there was a considerable increase in homeownership to an estimated 57 percent, from 42 percent of all dwellings in 1960 (Forrest and Murie chapter). In other countries, private investors in 1977–78 were building a larger proportion of the total new units than they did in 1970; for example, in The Netherlands from 52 percent (1970) to 65 percent (1977–78), with public and nonprofit group building the rest; from 79 percent to 90.5 percent in West Germany; and from 70.5 percent to 82 percent in Denmark.

New house purchases down. The situation has changed. Continued economic stagnation in Northern Europe in the early eighties has decreased the ability of many households to buy a house. The economic crisis has caused unemployment. The fluctuating high interest rates have also effected the building industry's ability to sell houses, as have the high costs of building houses. Housing costs have risen faster than the consumer price index (CPI). The difference was large in The Netherlands, where, on average, 1970–77 new housing costs rose to 10.4 percent average increase a year, and the United Kingdom, where new housing costs increased on average 17.1 percent a year. In other countries, the housing cost and the CPI each rose around 10.5 percent a year for Denmark, France, and Sweden. Only in West Germany, with its 6.1 percent annual housing cost increase, were things better for 1970–77; however, Meuter (1982) says that, for 1981, private housebuilding costs were twice as high as in 1977, and interest rates on mortgages in 1981 double those in 1979 so that "only high income households . . . can afford a private home today." This inability to pay the high costs of new housing has now caused houses to remain unsold and the building industry (1981–82) to cut back on building. Harloe (1982) sees a possible future situation that leaves many potential home buyers with no place to go, a situation worse than the present U.S. home-buying one, where it takes a two-earner family to afford a home purchase. The young couples will not be able to afford to purchase a unit because of its price; they will not find affordable private rentals as these are decreasing rapidly (see below), and they do not qualify for whatever social housing there is or do not want it because it is in an undesirable area. For some of them, rehabilitated housing (gentrification) will be the only way to go, as is true for some American households.

Rehabilitation. Today in Europe, the focus is not on new building but on renovation of inner-city obsolete housing. The Europeans have come to rehabilitation late. In some countries, such as Holland, there was early historic preservation of dense inner-city housing and in some countries some early private gentrification (middle class return and upgrading of slum areas) such as Islington, United Kingdom, but it was minor. In Britain, with its old housing stock, in the early post-war period, slum clearance was stressed. In others, little demolition was done, but new housing was built on the fringe of the towns. However, in 1982, the ECE Committee on Housing reported that improvement and modernization of housing was becoming increasingly the main focus of government efforts. They state that in Sweden the activity of maintenance, improvement, and modernization of housing is nowadays greater than investment in new house building. The ECE also reports that in the Federal Republic of Germany maintenance, modernization, and improvement work account for 37 percent of total investment in the residential sector in 1981. Their reasons for doing this primarily are to restore the inner-city area in order to keep the city vital. They also see that people in these areas want improved quality and that they must provide amenities, neighborhood improvements, and the like. This is especially true as the middle class move back in because they prefer the inner city to the suburbs or find it cheaper than buying new houses.

These governments' present concern is to determine what should be rehabilitated and what torn down. They are interested in standards of rehabilitation, and of course they are worried about the costs. They are beginning to realize it is not a cheap business and that by improving the inner-city deterioration problems one causes other problems. Meuter (1982) illustrates this from his research in Cologne. He suggests that the rehabilitation policy, based on the theory that the inner city should be revitalized, suburban sprawl halted, and inner-city populations provided with more class mix, turned out to be a policy that decreased units for the poor and pushed them to outer estates or squatter housing. He states that, in the seventies, the Cologne government had a policy of promoting homeownership and rehabilitation of inner-city units in working class areas. However, with rehabilitation, the inner-city rents rose dramatically. The demand for these old houses kept growing so that estate agents speculated on them, modernized them with government subsidies, converted them to condominiums, and put them on the market. The prices jumped almost 100 percent in five years, according to Meuter (1982). In some districts, more than 10 percent of the stock was sold between 1976 and 1980.

Poor tenants moved out, with a number going to new social housing of 4,000 units built in the mid-seventies on the outskirts of Cologne. This housing had not been popular because of its bleak high-rise appearance, its high rent and its distance from town. However, due partly to the housing shortage caused by this inner-city rehabilitation, the project was filled, with 70 to 80 percent of the residents being foreign workers.

This rehabilitation, due to demand for the inner-city area and home-ownership and the consequent subsidization of the housing needs of displaced underprivileged tenants in social housing, was expensive, as Meuter states (1982). These poor people, unable to pay the higher rents in the outer-area units, although subsidized, were unable to keep up payments, and then the state had the added cost of evicting them. All this was caused by the shortage of inner-city private inexpensive rentals. The demand was so great, according to Meuter (1982), that there were about 10,000 urgent cases of waiting households, and government policy on rehabilitation had only made things worse. Meuter concludes that "the government made a housing policy that sounded reasonably possible to rationally carry out . . . inner city rehabilitation." But, as he adds, "because of the housing shortage, it meant private capital was draining the city of cheap rentals to meet middle class demand." The additional problem, he states, is that the high housing costs were making it impossible to provide cheap-rent social housing.

Loss of private rental housing. A major trend in a number of Northern European countries was loss of private rental housing. In 1947, about three-fourths of the housing units in Denmark, France, and West Germany were private rentals. In The Netherlands and Britain, rental housing was also high. However, by the mid-seventies in The Netherlands, only around 10 to 15 percent of the units were rental units, and in Britain private rentals had decreased from 58 percent of the housing stock (in England and Wales) in 1938 to 13 percent in 1981. And it is estimated that in France and Denmark rental units are now one-third of all units.

New rental construction is at a very low level. The reason is because rents are not high enough to pay for high building costs, high interest rates, and housing maintenance costs. In West Germany, for the new privately financed rental units to be profitable there must be a much higher rent than West Germans, who expect a low rent (no more than 15 to 25 percent of their income) are willing to pay (Wienen, 1982). Even in 1978, Muhlich concluded that: "investment activity in private rented housing building (in West Germany) can only be expected again when obtainable initial rents approach once more running expenses."

Data giving overall increases in rent in all types of housing show rent increases much lower in most European countries than incrases in disposable income (OECD, 1978), and thus investors are not likely to get a high return on their money. Meuter (1982) gives only 3 percent for newer units in West Germany. Increase of rents, for public and private together, 1970–77, were around 9 to 10 percent per year in The Netherlands and Denmark, while average increase in disposable income was 11 percent and 12 percent, respectively. In West Germany it was 5.5 percent for rent increases and 8 percent for disposable income increases.

Rent regulations

This low increase in private housing rents is to a large degree due to rent controls. In Britain, low rents under their rental control policies were in addition considered a major contribution to loss of private rentals. Donnison, giving reasons why the loss of private rentals has been more severe in Britain than in other countries, states that, while in most of "western Europe, the private landlord has generally been regulated and subsidized, restrictions on his rents have been repeatedly modified and relaxed, and have been concentrated most heavily upon selected areas of shortage." In contrast, in Britain landlords, he says, "have been treated sometimes as parasites to be ruthlessly suppressed, and sometimes as paragons of free enterprise to be unleashed in haphazard and unselective fashion." These landlords have suffered from an increasing number of controls the government has introduced that did not exist in owner-occupancy housing, Harloe (1982) reports.

As a consequence, British landlords have sold off their rental property for owner-occupancy and thus decreased the number of private rents. Harloe (1982) gives costly management as another reason the supply of property shifted from rental to ownership. With most stable working class and middle class in either British council housing or, more likely nowadays, owner-occupancy housing, private renters are often the types of persons small landlords, especially those living in the building, consider management problems or not the preferred type but transient singles or large families, including immigrants; this makes these small landlords want to sell out (Paley, 1978).

In 1980, in Britain, a new act was designed to give landlords more freedom to raise their rents. It also increased their ability to evict their tenants, decreasing the legal rights of tenants.

Immigrants in private rentals. Many of those in the worst of private rentals are recent immigrants. In Britain most of the immigrants are permanent resident ex-colonials such as Indians, Pakistanis and West Indians, as well as Irish. The Surinams in The Netherlands and many ex-colonials in France are also permanent residents, and thus their housing problems are long-term ones. In other countries, immigrants are for the most part there on a temporary basis, under limited time work permits; this is true in West Germany and Sweden, for example. Their presence also causes a serious housing problem, although with the recession their number had decreased. In all these countries, there is now a second generation of immigrants, often born in the host country. Many stay on, as do their parents, illegally, under some sub-terfuge, or legally, depending on the country. All these immigrants need housing.

In Britain immigrants rent private units or buy old houses in slum areas. The West Indians, of all residents in the United Kingdom, are the ones most likely to live in the worst housing, that is the 12.2 percent needing essential repairs or the 8 percent missing a basic amenity. The old houses awaiting slum clearance are, as far as owner-ship, in some areas most likely to be owned by Pakistanis. Rex (1965), in his early study of Birmingham immigrants, found this group buying large old houses in slum areas and converting them to multioccupancy housing for themselves, their kinsmen, and other immigrants. Rex (1965) also reports that, once multioccupancy housing started on a street, whole streets changed quickly from owner occupancy to lodging houses. A ghetto was born.

Birmingham authorities failed to recognize the positive function of these boarding houses and responded to the situation by first requiring permission for starting a new lodging house and then planning demolition of the housing by making part of the area a redevelopment project. At first the accompanying responsibility of rehousing immigrant families held them back, but in the seventies, Henderson reports, slum clearance did occur. Many Asians were applying for council housing because their houses had been purchased by compulsory means (Henderson, 1983).

In West Germany, immigrants also live in old inner-city units. Ipsen (1978), from his careful study of immigrant housing conditions in three working-class areas of Mannheim, reports that in general the immigrants had poorer housing conditions than the German population in the same areas. Ipsen (1978) reports that these foreign workers lived in housing lacking adequate sanitary arrangements and electrical fixtures with overcrowded rooms and exorbitant rents. He adds that "not only results from our research in Mannheim but also numerous results of research already published verify this description quantitatively."

Government provision of housing for immigrants. In Northern European countries, the housing authorities now house some immigrants in subsidized housing. This housing is often the least desirable of the stock. In 1978, in the newer outer-area new towns around Stockholm, the larger units that were unpopular with Swedes were occupied by "guest arbeiter" families. In Malmö many outer-housing estates had large populations of Yugoslav and Turkish workers. In The Netherlands, Bijlmermeer, the very large estate outside of Amsterdam, was unpopular and therefore many apartments were rented to the Surinam population, as well as to other immigrant groups. Donnison (1982) reports, for Sweden and The Netherlands, that "small but expensive flats intended for single persons have been taken by immigrant families who overcrowd them in order to pay the rent."

In Britain by the mid-seventies, a number of immigrant families qualified for council housing, although Henderson (1983) reports that they were still less likely to be admitted than white families with the same qualifications. They were usually put on an estate with a bad reputation. Henderson found, in his Birmingham study, that Asians and especially West Indians were given older units. West Indians with children were more likely to be offered high-rise apartments than were whites with the same number of children. They are offered a limited number of estate choices. Henderson (1983) feels that their treatment is a combination of racism and their being a stigmatized disadvantaged group which is poor, female-headed, new to the neighborhood, etc.

Dispersal of immigrants has been recommended at various times. In Birmingham for a short time, Henderson (1983) reports, the housing authority tried a dispersal policy by placing six white neighbors on each side of a black tenant. The policy was withdrawn. In 1984 the Department of Environment is again trying to encourage choice of estates for immigrants.

In Britain the dilemma of the policy of trying for a mix of groups on the estates is that the better-off tenants will opt out of public housing entirely or will wait for a better placement.

Homeless persons

While there may be a surplus of housing and even empty council housing in Britain, as well as in other European countries, this housing is usually for the permanent residents, the stable working-class and middle-class families. It does not usually take care of the inner-city transient marginal group such as young singles, unemployed, alcoholics, and even large immigrant families; private rental housing of a transient and/or undesirable nature shelters this group, with many single people in hotel accommodations or furnished rooms. In places such as London, however, the demand for furnished accommodation is much higher than the number of furnished units available (Ash chapter). Thus there is a dual housing market with most of the population fairly affluent and comfortably housed, with a surplus of their type of housing available, while a transient poor, inner-city population is inadequately housed and, with the decrease of cheap private rentals, even homeless.

Because of the high unemployment in the eighties and because of increased cost of standard housing, the number of homeless has increased. The large student population and other separate young-person households, which have resulted from an increased desire to live away from parents, also causes the increase. Many families also cannot find units because they are unacceptable to public and private landlords, although they are the victims of family breakup, that is female-headed households; they follow the cultural pattern of female-headed households (West Indies); or the family is considered unsuitable because it is an extended family (Indians). These homeless are expected to move in with relatives, and in her chapter Ash points out that many do share units, especially the young married sharing with parents.

A number are homeless. Kearns (1979) estimated the number of homeless in London to be higher than 150,000. The numbers in The Netherlands are also considered high, since in Amsterdam alone there are 58,000 on the waiting list for housing (1982). In Cologne more than 10,000 were on waiting lists (Meuter, 1983). Some have become squatters, that is, they live in unoccupied government-owned and privately owned buildings. They are usually young and male (Kearns, 1979). In Amsterdam in 1982 it was estimated there were more than 10,000 living in abandoned buildings, and even in small Dutch towns there are squatters. In both London and Amsterdam they are now given semilegal status.

In Britain, homeless in general are covered under the 1977 Homeless Persons Act, which demands that local housing authorities find housing for such persons. The main means that local authorities use to improve the plight of transient singles and marginal family groups is to put them in shelters supplied by welfare departments. In the past few years they have also put them in the older council housing units that have a bad reputation.

Hard-to-let subsidized housing

Housing with a bad reputation has been a problem in Britain in many areas for a number of years. Ash in her chapter and Forrest and Murie in theirs mention the problem. Ash estimates that about 5 percent of the units are hard-to-let. The original causes in Britain were location and architectural design, especially high rise. Mothers were very unhappy about high rise. Another reason that followed was that the local housing authorities concentrated their bad tenants on these estates and then did little maintenance. These estates then developed a stigmatized reputation that was hard to rectify. Considerable vandalism occurred on these estates. It got to the point where there were many empty units; Donnison (1982) reports there were more than 100,000 units or 2.2 percent of the stock actually vacant in 1979. This stock has now been filled with the homeless and immigrants and other so-called marginal tenants.

In northern Europe, some subsidized housing also has been unpopular; it is usually outer-area housing, that is, long slabs of six to eight stories high and a block long. In the outer new towns around Stockholm, this housing was built in the late sixties; these high-density developments had little landscaping and poor external appearance. As many as 20 percent to 30 percent of the units were occupied by foreign workers. Lindberg (1978) felt that the demand for owner-occupancy might have been a reaction against this environment of high-rise housing.

The most notorious subsidized housing in The Netherlands is in the new town of Bijlmermeer, twelve miles from Amsterdam. Its 12,000 units of high density are in machine-built high rise, again long slabs. Newman (1983) reports that this development was emptying out at the rate of 100 units per month in 1982. There was considerable vandalism. Part of the housing was being converted into a residential center for youth. In Britain some were converted for use by singles, including the elderly.

Another trend in Britain is the sale of council housing. This involves the best units, not the worst. Because it takes the best out of the rental pool, it is considered a threat to the reputation of all subsidized housing. Some feel it is the Conservatives' way of breaking up a major element of the welfare state, the 30 percent of the housing that is council housing. About 8 percent of the council housing stock had been sold by 1983 (Forrest and Murie chapter). This policy of selling subsidized housing to tenants has also spread to The Netherlands, where van Vliet— (1983) reports that municipal governments had sold a portion of the "social" housing to buyers who qualified.

Future trends

There is likely to be more emphasis on finding innovative ways to allow people to buy their own homes. With conservative governments coming in in many countries and with the present economic stagnation, it is unlikely that more subsidized housing will be built. These governments instead might give landlords more incentives to build private rental units. There is likely to be some more emphasis on the housing of special groups, but for some of these groups (the homeless and the singles) we doubt that it will be of high quality; the opposite is likely to be true for housing for the elderly.

III | The Provision of Housing:
Self-Help Arrangements in
Less-Industrialized Countries

Introduction
Padmini Gulati

The extraordinary pace of urban growth in developing nations has exacerbated old problems and given rise to new dilemmas for national and local policy makers. One of the more serious problems is the growing inequality that has characterized rapid urbanization and modernization in all but a few developing nations. Nowhere is this growing disparity more evident than in the settlements of the poor, in the vast tracts of "informal" self-constructed housing that surround almost every major city. The squalor and abysmal living conditions that exist are reflected in the health and morbidity statistics, which are significantly worse than in the rest of the city.

The articles in this section discuss several aspects of this phenomenon. Gulati's article presents an overview and examines self-help housing in its several manifestations in various Third World societies. Valladares summarizes the themes of the very extensive research that has been carried out in Brazil on the topic. The articles by Sandhu and Herlianto study selected issues related to low-income housing; the former focusing on planning that is oblivious to the housing needs of the poor and the latter discussing some of the difficulties in implementing self-help housing programs. El-Messiri's exquisite case study of an Egyptian squatter family presents a sharp contrast to the pathological or pathetic squatter families described in the early "marginality" literature on squatter settlements.

While the housing problem is the most visible manifestation of the pain that accompanies economic and social transformation, it cannot be considered in isolation from the prevailing social, economic, and political climate. Neither are the solutions purely technical. Quite clearly, the underlying assumptions regarding the nature of the phenomenon have shaped decision makers' responses to it. The squatter settlements that the poor have constructed in response to the housing crisis they faced have traditionally been viewed in a negative light, as Gulati points out in her chapter.

Oscar Lewis, whose writing on the "culture of poverty" was influential in shaping poverty policy in the United States in the early sixties, did much of his early research on the subject in the barrios or squatter settlements of Mexico. Lewis' central thesis, that the poor are "different" and have created a variant subculture that is dysfunctional in terms of their economic, social, and political integration into their societies, is echoed by various writers, who explore the marginality theme in their work on squatter settlements. Valladares touches on the literature of this early period that focuses on the so-called theory of marginality. Gulati highlights some of the policy decisions that were based on assumptions regarding the marginality of squatters. Many of the, at best, clumsy attempts to eradicate squatter settlements appeared to be based on the notion that squatters are somehow responsible for their own predicament. Their innate characteristics made it difficult, if not impossible, to live otherwise. These convictions about the nature of squatters made it all the easier to destroy their settlements, which were visually offensive to the more affluent segments of the population. Systematic attempts to undermine the economic base of squatter settlements have also been detected. Such economic activities as were carried out by squatters were termed "unproductive," "superfluous," or "undesirable." Regulations to restrict activities common to squatters such as street vending, shoe shining, scavenging, and repair shops set up on street corners must be viewed in this light, although other factors are not to be discounted.

That urban planners and architects are not immune to this perspective is evident in Sandhu's paper on Chandigarh. Chandigarh was to have been one of the urban showpieces of postindependent India and the capital of the flourishing Punjab region, which had lost its former capital to Pakistan. It was mainly designed by the French architect, Le Corbusier, who had won international acclaim for his creative and innovative urban designs. Chandigarh is visually pleasing to those who have a partiality for modern architecture. Sandhu's paper highlights the irony that, while the poor constitute a majority of the population of Chandigarh, as in all Indian cities, the master plan only makes minimal provision for their housing. The poor who are provided with housing are in fact a very elite group who work for the government. The rest of the poor, who are overlooked by the planners, must fend for themselves. Their solution is the proliferation of the self-built housing that rings the periphery of Chandigarh, in contravention of the master plan.

Since the seventies, alternative and more sophisticated explanations for the existence of squatter settlements have become more prevalent. The characteristics of the squatter himself or of his subculture are now seen as not all that different from the rest of the population, as Gulati points out in her article. He is an integral part of the urban proletariat of newly industrializing societies; his job and activities are closely linked to the activities of the "modern" sector, although at low wages and low levels of productivity.

The squatter described in El-Messiri's case study, in fact, emerges as a thrifty, hard-working individual, embodying some of the virtues commonly associated with the Protestant ethic. Ahmed and his second son work in the nearby munitions factory, but their wages are barely sufficient for their daily living expenses, which do not include rent. Despite this, Ahmed and his family sacrifice and save for a distant future. Eventually they build themselves a two-story home of brick and cement, with some minor assistance from the government, but mainly relying upon their own efforts. In contrast to the marginal individuals portrayed by Lewis and his imitators, Ahmed turns out not only to be an educated man, but also to have enlightened views on female education, even rejecting an appropriate match for his only daughter so she can complete her education and become a teacher. Egypt, despite its modernizing tendencies, still has a very large education gap between males and females.

Especially interesting is El-Messiri's description of the savings institutions (gamciyas) formed spontaneously by groups of squatters linked by friendship and blood. Ahmed and his family are, over time, able to save fairly substantial sums of money, much of which is channeled into housing improvements. If Izbet Zein, the squatter community described by El Messiri, is representative of such communities, it has important implications for public policy. One must look for explanations of the phenomenon of squatting outside the subculture or characteristics of the squatter.

An increasingly influential school of thought has come to view the proliferation of squatter housing as a result of mistaken public policies, which have reflected the preferences of affluent segments of the population rather than the public interest. The supply constraints in low-income housing have been caused by actions or inactions on the part of public authorities, which have resulted in inefficient and/or inequitable resource allocation.

The theme of the exploitation of labor which came into vogue in the seventies is touched on by the authors surveyed by Valladares and Gulati. Leeds, one of this group, contends that true squatter settlements appear only in capitalist societies in the throes of transformation into industrial economies. The major financial and social institutions are structured to benefit the affluent at the expense of the lowest-income groups. At the same time demographic trends, together with social and economic policies pursued by ruling groups, depress the wages earned by residents of squatter settlements and limit their access to credit. Valladares discusses the role of the National Bank of Housing (BNH) in structuring the flow of housing credit towards the affluent segments of the population at the expense of the low-income groups they were ostensibly set up to serve; thus self-constructed housing becomes one of the few housing options open to the poor.

Eventually the ideas of these "revisionist" thinkers permeated the upper reaches of government although, as Valladares points out, elitist or militarist regimes continued to follow their traditional, repressive policies. Another factor was the rising concern in international circles about the growing polarization in Third World countries and the resulting political instability, which led to a new interest in urban poverty and measures to alleviate it to a degree. Politicians came under pressure from their own impoverished workers, as well as international lending institutions, to change policies that impacted adversely on the ability of the poor to earn a living and live in a safe, sanitary environment.

Conventional public housing came increasingly to be viewed as inappropriate and expensive. Solutions urged by Turner and some of his followers were seized upon by decision makers as a way out of a dilemma of scarce resources and a seemingly inexhaustible demand for low-cost housing. The poor were now to be aided and not hindered in their attempts to solve their own housing problems, through self-help or mutual aid. The key was to provide them with increased access to credit, building materials, security of tenure, and public services. Public policy objectives were served by improving existing squatter settlements or by providing serviced sites where squatters would build their own housing, either through mutual aid or through the employment of local residents for specialized tasks.

Over the past ten years, programs to upgrade squatter settlements and set up sites-and-services projects have become widespread. The World Bank alone has provided more than $2.5 billion to finance settlements that have sheltered more than ten million persons.[1] Some of these efforts have been examined by Gulati. The implementation of these programs have not been without difficulties. Herlianto focuses on some of these in his article on the kampung improvement programs in Indonesia.

The Indonesian experience in squatter settlement improvement is of particular interest because of its massive scale. It represents the first nationwide attempt to provide improved housing for the urban poor, through the upgrading of squatter settlements and the provision of serviced plots. On balance, it appears to have been a notable achievement, given the very large number of households involved. Especially impressive is the return on the initial investment to local government which, according to World Bank estimates, ranged from 67 percent to 100 percent—a neat convergence of equity and efficiency objectives.[2]

Herlianto's paper makes it clear, however, that the achievement could be even more impressive if some of the interorganizational difficulties that plagued the program could be ironed out. Various agencies, for reasons that related to their organizational missions and the availability of financing for squatter settlement improvements, began programs that targeted their efforts at either the residents or the environment of the squatter settlements. These programs appear to have operated independently of each other, responding only to what their sponsors perceived to be a critical need which related to their own mission. Inevitably, over time there was a wasteful duplication of effort, delays in program implementation, and gaps in critical areas, occasioned by a singular lack of communication among the agencies involved. The Indonesian government finally came to terms with the situation and set up an agency to coordinate the efforts of the multiple agencies and levels of government involved in improving the kampungs (squatter settlements).

Current evaluations of programs in several very different countries show, on balance, positive results. Self-help housing, with controls and supports, can seemingly provide some answers to the acute housing shortage Third World countries face in the immediate future. It may however only be a partial and inadequate response to the grinding poverty that low-income urban populations in developing countries face in their struggle to survive in an increasingly difficult environment.

12

The Rise of Squatter Settlements: Roots, Responses, and Current Solutions

Padmini Gulati

Abstract. Gulati assesses the self-help approach developed by John Turner to upgrade squatter housing in the Third World. The Turner model includes the government's giving legal tenure to squatters and providing some infrastructure and services; squatters themselves provide materials and labor on an exchange basis or for the cost of meals. The Turner model has been criticized because it results in low-density housing at the urban periphery, unlike high-rises constructed by the government. Consequently, squatters have high transportation costs, and there are problems in providing water and electricity to outlying locations. The implementation of the Turner approach is described in Brazil, Zambia, Peru, Kenya, Chile, India, Indonesia, El Salvador, The Philippines, and Senegal. The basic causes of squatter settlements are structural: the increasing concentration of land ownership; the limited supply of urban housing in the face of rising demand as rural people migrate to cities; segmented labor markets with many low-income people; and changes in official policy on investments and regulation. The Turner approach is seen as increasing the supply of low-cost housing within those constraints.

The housing crisis experienced by many Third World cities has resulted in the emergence of squatter settlements, which house in many instances the majority of the residents of their cities. These settlements can pose a hazard to the safety and health of their inhabitants and the surrounding community. This literature survey will document how a fundamental ignorance of the structural causes of squatter settlement formation has led to solutions that are both inhumane and counterproductive. The approach that is endorsed by the United Nations and several international organizations contains variations of what is known as the "Turner" model. Turner advocated the "directed development" of squatter settlements. His model relies on the squatters' own capacity for self-improvement, with minimal public intervention. The role of government is usually to be limited to the form of some form of legal status and access to credit by the squatter. Public provision of infrastructure and services can also be an ingredient of this model. An assessment is made of programs that appear to have implemented this approach.

The explosive growth of squatter settlements

If recent population trends continue, approximately 64 percent of the urban residents of cities with populations of more than five million will, by the year 2000, be living in the Third World. In Asia and South America alone, the urban population is projected to double from the current 929.9 million (1980) to approximately 1880 million by the year 2000 (Hauser, 1982, tables 1.1 and 1.2). The swiftness with which this urbanization has occurred and the enormous problems that this poses are scarcely recognized. Most developing countries report rural-to-urban migration rates of 4 percent to 8 percent each year. Lima's population has grown 100 percent in the lifetime of its middle-aged residents. Calcutta's current population of 9.6 million is projected to reach 19.7 million by the year 2000, while Cairo and Casablanca will double in size during the same period (Hauser, 1980, table 3.2).

This remarkable growth is caused in part by diminishing job opportunities in rural areas, following the switch to cash crops from subsistence farming and the resulting displacement of large numbers of peasants. This process is accelerated in some instances, as in Mexico and the Philippines, by the movement of giant agri-businesses into the rural communities of the Third World (Tabb, 1978). The growth of population in the cities of the Third World, in contrast to what happened in the industrialized west, is not based on an increased industrial demand for labor but is a result of tendencies within rural areas (McGee, 1971). Few Third World cities have the industrial base to absorb this enormous influx of people. Even in the richest Third World countries, opportunities for productive employment have not kept pace with population growth.

One direct result of this process has been a housing crisis. Almost three-fourths of the new urbanites are now living in densely packed slums, or what are known euphemistically as "spontaneous settlements." These vast stretches of makeshift structures that circle virtually every major city in the developing world are a visual expression of the breakdown of conventional mechanisms for the provision of housing when confronted with problems of such awesome proportions. These squalid settlements, often without such basic amenities as water, sewage disposal, or electricity, house in some instances the majority of the population of their cities. Fire and flood are not uncommon facts of existence.

Today, spontaneous settlement has become one of the major forms of shelter in the Third World and all the indicators point to its continued importance in the future. By 1961, approximately 25 percent of the populations of Djakarta, Kuala Lumpur, Manila, and Singapore were housed in this manner. So were half the populations of Tunis, Algeria, Casablanca, Dakar, Abidjan, Kinshasa, Nairobi, Mombasa, Dar es Salaam, and Durban (IBRD, 1972). More recent statistics, while not strictly comparable, since they group squatter settlements and slums together, indicate that the problem has been aggravated in these cities, with the exception of Singapore, which has embarked on a massive housing program (Grimes, 1976). Today more than 60 percent of the populations of Casablanca, Kinshasa, Ankara, and Calcutta are living in slums or squatter settlements. Lima, Bombay, Buenos Aires, Istanbul, and Mexico City have more than 40 percent of their residents living in similar housing (Hauser, 1982, table 2.2).

Defining characteristics of squatter settlements

Definitions of squatter settlements vary, but a common theme is that they are areas where people build homes in violation of formal rules about property rights, zoning, and types and quality of construction (Epstein, 1972). The defining characteristic is the illegality of tenure. The squatter occupies land legally owned by another without his consent. A second attribute is that their existence is not formally approved by the appropriate local authority and it infringes on existing land use regulations and building standards (Seymour, 1976).

Although squatter settlements are occupied, by and large, by very poor people, this is not necessarily true for all settlements, especially the older settlements, where the head of the household is usually a wage earner. In appearance some of them may be indistinguishable from working-class subdivisions.

Squatter settlements go by various names. They are known as villas miserias (Argentina), barong-barong (Philippines), bidonvilles (Morocco), favelas (Brazil), ranchos (Panama), colonias proletariat (Mexico), or bustees and jhugis (India and Pakistan). Much of the early literature on squatter settlements focused on their marginal character. They were viewed as marginal both to the socioeconomic system of production and to the system of consumption of goods and services. Marginality was extended to cover their formal and informal participation in political parties, unions, and decision making both at the community level and at the city and national levels (Germanii, 1972). Squatters were viewed as individuals who were not integrated socially or politically into the life of the city and possessed of a variant subculture which was dysfunctional in many respects (Lewis, 1968). Empirical evidence indicates that, in some countries at least, squatter settlements are not marginal in being a transitional stage between the rural countryside and the cities. On the contrary, they appear to be formed by persons who already have a foothold in the local economy, which enables them to build themselves a house (Turner, 1967).

Sources of squatter settlement formation

An emergent view is that these squatters do not lack ties to the rest of urban society. It is the nature of these ties that has led to sharp contrasts between them and their affluent neighbors (Epstein, 1972, p. 265). According to this perspective, the reason for the housing crisis lies in the disparity between supply and demand in the low-cost housing market. Demand is only partly caused by the rapidity of rural-to-urban migration. The more influential factor is the high rents in relation to the incomes of the urban poor. Because of their depressed standing in the labor market, squatters are unable to purchase housing in the quantities and at costs that have any relation to their incomes (Turner, 1966). A World Bank study of six cities indicates that the percentage of households unable to afford the cheapest complete shelter unit ranged from 68 percent in Nairobi to 35 percent in Hong Kong (World Bank, 1975). The study assumed that households would devote 15 percent of their incomes to housing. This fraction seems too low to Westerners accustomed to paying higher proportions of their incomes for housing. It would be well to bear in mind that many of these same households suffer from calorie deficits that would preclude them from spending any higher proportion of their income for shelter (Berg, 1981).

Under such circumstances the tendency is to avoid the housing market altogether and squat on land that is not in active use, either for speculative or other reasons. A conflict derives from the potential use of the land both for profit making and for basic living needs (Turner, 1966, p. 61). Leeds suggests that squatter settlements will be most concentrated in those societies where intense competition exists between different classes for the same land and where land use is dictated by speculation and profit. The empirical evidence is not as unequivocal, but it does point to the fact that the incidence of slums and squatter settlements is not simply a function of GNP, per capita income, or rates of migration. The high proportion of slums and squatter housing in relatively affluent societies such as those of Malaysia, Brazil, Mexico, Chile, and Venezuela, which also have a highly inegalitarian distribution of wealth, lends some support to this view. Seemingly, societies that rely on market solutions to their housing problems have yet to resolve the issue of providing enough housing for their low-income members. Under these circumstances, the only feasible solution is the creation of housing which involves only the cost of materials and a minimum of labor paid for by meals or the exchange of labor. Labor costs become minimal and the costs of capital, administration, and builder profits are eliminated (Leeds, 1969).

The low income of the squatter is ascribed to the dual economy that prevails in most Third World cities. The first economy consists of the capital-intensive, remunerative modern sector and the second of the labor-intensive traditional or informal sector. The latter includes petty trading, domestic service, and small home-based manufactures. One view is that only the informal sector has the capacity to absorb a sizable number of the urban labor force, although at high levels of underemployment and low levels of income. The cause of this is traced to external factors such as the spread of capital-intensive technologies to the Third World. By this means, the system of industrial production can turn out more goods with fewer workers. The net result will be that an ever-increasing segment of the work force in Third World economies will find itself outside the primary sector of the economy; they will, however, support the primary sector in a wide range of occupations (Jacobs, 1980).

An alternate view is that the squatters provide an abundant supply of cheap labor which spans both the industrial sector and the labor-intensive service sector (Epstein, 1972, p. 270). They help keep the cost of labor down through their abysmally low standard of living; at the same time their purchasing power helps finance the industrial system from which they are largely excluded. However this direct transfer of capital is not the only means by which they support the market economy. Since they build their own homes, go without minimal municipal services, and make few demands on the educational system, they have internalized certain public costs. Industry is thus permitted to channel capital that might otherwise go to finance these services into industrial investment (Roberts, 1978). The housing itself is a major input into the local economy (Jacobs, 1980, p. 235). Estimates of the investment that these squatter settlements represent vary. In 1972, the investment in squatter homes was valued at $100,000 in Caracas, and at $3,000,000 in Bogota (Bamberger, 1974). World Bank-financed squatter upgrading and sites-and-services projects in El Salvador, The Philippines, Senegal, and Zambia generated substantial amounts of employment and income. The less tangible impacts on commercial and manufacturing enterprises within the projects, while visible, were difficult to estimate (Keere and Parris, 1983).

Unemployment statistics in Latin American squatter settlements ranged from 8 percent to 27 percent and suggest that the great majority of the inhabitants are regularly working in the formal economic system. Recent studies of World Bank-financed projects for former squatters confirms this hypothesis (Keere and Parris, 1983, pp. 38–39). Such statistics though tend to disguise the substantial underemployment that is so pervasive in Third World countries and the fact that so many of the tasks performed by squatters in the service sector could be carried out with less time and effort in a more industrialized economy.

In addition to the jobs located in the general urban economy, many persons are also employed within the squatter settlements. Construction workers are said to be in demand for the tasks that require skills beyond those that the average squatter possesses. Small businesses of all types appear to flourish within squatter settlements. Buying and selling from each other is an occupation that begins almost from the inception of the settlement. Bars, restaurants, repair shops, barber shops, grocery stalls, and vegetable stalls have been reported in most settlements. Hundreds of peddlers have been observed to go back and forth from central markets to the settlements by bicycle, by bus, or by taxi, carrying goods for resale. A vigorous underground economy flourishes in many settlements. The potential for self-employment may be a major reason why squatters prefer their settlements to public housing.

The issue of marginality

It would appear from the foregoing discussion that squatter communities, despite their negative stereotypes, are, on the whole, well-integrated communities, with a strong associational life based on cohesive kinship groups and friends from the same place of origin. As in other low-income communities, networks of kinship and informal neighborhood relations develop, along with a range of more formal organizations. These tend to be centered on the goal of obtaining some important service for the community or maintaining its existence in the face of external threat. Associational activity around these goals tends to be stronger at the inception of the settlement than later, when many of the initial problems have been demonstrated to be insoluble (Mangin, 1965).

Existing research refutes the popular view that squatters are marginal to the political system. Ray's studies of the barrios underscores the fact that squatter settlements, perhaps from their very inception, are plugged into the political structure (Ray, 1966). The leadership may indeed have obtained the tacit support of one of the governing political parties in the city, without which the settlement could not have continued its fragile existence. In Asia and Africa, squatter settlements swelled in numbers in the former colonial territories after World War II, when national governments based on popular support came into power. For example, in Zambia, despite the under-utilization of land, squatting barely existed prior to independence. After independence, the reluctance of the various levels of government to intervene was a major factor in the genesis of squatting on both private and public land. Because of internal circumstances, the political support of squatters became important to the rival political parties between 1963 and 1973. The "shanty towns" vote was also important in municipal politics (*Zambia mail*, 8/29/70). Thus, squatter settlements were able to forge links of mutual aid with politicians, which were a major factor in their survival.

Where official attitudes are hostile, advanced planning, community cohesion, and a formal organization are crucial to the success of a squatting operation. Technical help of a sort that individual members cannot commandeer on their own may be required. Even after a successful squatting operation, a formal organization is needed to prevent eviction, adjudicate disputes, and make demands on the system for needed public services (Mangin, 1967, pp. 70–71).

In Brasilia, there existed among the migrants, the entrepreneurs who were to build the city, and the local politicians an unwritten tacit compact which had some benefits for all the parties. The entrepreneurs building Brasilia in the relatively unpopulated interior were assured of a ready supply of cheap labor. The municipal authorities, by pronouncing squatter settlements illegal, did not have to provide critical urban services such as electricity, sewage, and a permanent water system for a crucial component of the city's work force. The squatters were able to help themselves to the debris on the construction sites to build their homes, although this arrangement was never formalized (Epstein, 1972). Squatter settlements could be viewed as one of those regular irregularities through which societies engage in needed tasks while denying the existence of or at least any support for the phenomenon (Peattie, 1974).

Although viewed as repositories of social pathology, squatter settlements in many parts of the world have fewer crimes, delinquencies, unstable homes, and promiscuity than other low-income residential areas (Goldrich, 1966). On the contrary, family cohesion is strong and kinship ties are important and a source of mutual aid in times of crisis (Rotundo, 1965). Squatters, especially rural transplants, may retain some of the traditions of neighborliness and mutual aid which are a feature of village life. Aid may be extended to newcomers from the same village of origin.

Social control of individual behavior is extended through kinship and other groups (Pearse). With few exceptions, the nuclear family plays an important part in the settlements studied. Although some instances of social disorganization, such as job instability, criminal violence, and irregular sexual unions, have been noted by some researchers, these appear to be no higher than in the slums of the cities where these studies took place (Mangin, 1967, p. 72). The core of the problem may lie not within the squatter settlements themselves, but in the structure of society.

Research validates the thesis that the migrants maintain an extensive network of personal relationships in the city and are not socially or psychologically isolated from the rest of the city. One-third of Kazemi's sample reported loans from friends and relatives, who were desperately poor themselves (Kazemi, 1980). The weight of the evidence would suggest that squatter settlements are in no way fundamentally divorced from the cities they surround. They are neither rural in character nor marginal socially, economically, or politically. Janice Perlman sums up this particular perspective: "Faveladas are not marginal to Brazilian society but integrated in a manner detrimental to their interests. They are not socially marginal but rejected, not economically marginal but exploited, and not politically marginal but repressed" (Perlman, 1976).

Official attitudes

Official attitudes toward squatters throughout the world ranged from benign neglect to outright hostility. Sometimes the needs of the economy or of politics may dictate a policy of looking the other way, as in Brasilia. Although the official view appears conditioned on the premise that squatter settlements are breeding grounds for social pathology and need to be eradicated, practical politics determine otherwise. Legal violence against squatters is not infrequent, however, especially in authoritarian regimes not based on popular support. Instances are recorded in diverse parts of the world of extreme callousness toward the human rights of squatters. In Manila, after years of neglect, a new administration decided to enforce public nuisance laws and thus eradicate squatter settlements. Squatters were forcibly evicted, and their settlements were demolished in the core city. They were moved to a distant site, which was devoid of public transportation, employment, or any services. They were simply dumped on the site and expected to build their barong-barongs in an area which did not have materials that could be used for such construction (Dwyer, 1974). Forcible eviction and violence toward squatters appears not to have been infrequent under the Shah's regime in Iran (Kazemi, 1980). Reports from Chile indicate that violence toward squatters and clashes between squatters and police are a feature of life under the Pinochet regime (*Washington post*, 11/20/83).

The official view of squatter settlements as breeding grounds for social pathology has led to attempts to engage in massive slum clearance and public housing or community development projects designed to integrate the squatter settlements into the rest of the city.

These attempts were at best failures (Epstein, 1972). They reveal a fundamental ignorance of the genesis of squatter settlements.

Current attitudes and policies

In recent times, a greater awareness of the structural factors underlying squatter settlement formation, such as the increasing concentration of the ownership of land, the constrained supply of urban housing in relation to mounting demand, segmented labor markets which create a large aggregate of persons with relatively small incomes, and official policies with regard to investment and regulation, has led to some modification of the original hostile attitudes.

Increasingly, decision makers appear to subscribe to the view that, where possible, squatters should be given some security of tenure and the settlements should be provided with basic amenities such as a water supply, electricity, and sewage. Some planning bodies have succumbed to the inevitable and favor setting aside land for squatters, provided it does not conflict with other necessary land uses. This stands in marked contrast to the earlier attitudes of planners who either ignored the existence of the lowest-income groups or at best thought in terms of providing for them at some distant future time. This usually meant low-income housing which, while meeting certain minimum standards for the most part based on Western standards, reached only a fraction of the target population. Squatter settlements were thus either condemned or not included in their planning models.

The Turner model

A planner who was strongly critical of this approach was John Turner. Turner recognized the initiative and creativity of the poor. In his view, they had created their own solutions to their housing problems. His prescription is the directed development of spontaneous settlements which are to be linked to a security-of-tenure policy. Turner's central thesis is that the housing standards set by the authorities are out of touch with economic reality and incongruent with the needs and demands of low-income urbanites. The cumbersome red tape and expense of developing conventional "instant" housing must be contrasted with the spontaneous mobilization of group effort found in squatter settlements. Housing built by the squatters is much more functional in terms of their own needs and the capital investment required. In "self-help" housing, not only is there much more living space available, but the dwelling can be enlarged as the need arises. The need for credit is either reduced or eliminated. Credit is scarce in Third World societies, and the cost of an "instantly built" or semifinished structure can be quite high. Even if interest rates are subsidized, it might entail an unacceptably high level of debt for the squatter household. A major advantage of building a house in stages, as the squatter does, is that it permits the investment of nonmonetary sources. The owner-builder and his household provide initiative, skills, and labor. Building a squatter house in stages facilitates bonds among the household members, the squatters, and the community they all live in. Social stratification, which is a feature of public housing, is less prevalent in squatter communities, especially in established settlements (Turner, 1967). Turner's biting criticism is reflected in his statement that "the most striking thing about this type of development is that it has taken place independently and even in spite of public institutions. If governments could induce the same initiative, efforts and sacrifice for their own housing and urban development, both living conditions and the rate of economic growth would be immensely improved" (Turner, 1967, p. 10).

Grudgingly and at long last, public authorities are coming to the conclusion that squatters can provide solutions to their own housing needs, with some help from planners influenced by Turner. High rises, except in high-density cities such as Hong Kong, are rarely socially or economically feasible (Turner and Goetze, 1967). In relation to income and the amortization capacity of beneficiaries, high-rise, high-density developments require a large capital outlay. They do not compensate for the financial and social economies of progressive development. Finally, the priorities of squatters, such as easy access to work sites and public services, homes that can be expanded to meet fluctuating family needs, and the income-generating possibilities of their dwellings, are in marked contrast to official norms, which stress the physical size and appearance of the dwelling.

The Turner approach has not escaped criticism. Poor design and layout have been observed in many squatter settlements. The building patterns do not allow for rationalization. A major problem in fostering squatter settlement is that it would imply relatively low population densities, with squatter settlements being located on the periphery of cities. This is in direct contradiction to the economic inability of squatters to pay the transportation costs involved in traveling long distances to work (Dwyer, p. 214). This solution to the housing problems of the urban poor could also pose some intractable problems for municipal authorities, who would have to provide water, lighting, and other municipal services over long distances.

The concept of planned "spontaneous" settlements, however, is one that has been endorsed by several international agencies, such as the United Nations and the World Bank, and by some national planning agencies. Sites-and-services and squatter settlement upgrading are some of the manifestations of this approach, which are being replicated in several countries in the Third World.

Implementation

The literature provides several examples of the successful implementation of variations on the "Turner Model." During a liberal episode in Brazil's political history, the administration authorized an official agency to help squatters reconstruct their favelas, leaving them as much choice as feasible in the construction of their housing. Technical aid was made available as desired. Self-help labor was to be used not only in construction, but also in terms of infrastructure. Existing community and social networks were left undisturbed, as the planners at CODESCO, the housing agency, recognized the important role they played in community cohesion and mutual aid. Much of the necessary management functions were delegated to these community organizations, with CODESCO only providing some guidelines. Housing plans, although developed by COEDSCO architects, were submitted to the residents for criticism. They were then drastically altered to conform to the practical requirements as well as the aesthetic values of residents. The assurance of a decent dwelling and the promise of basic amenities had an electrifying impact on the morale of the squatters and resulted in the physical transformation of the settlement. Cheap credits, provided by CODESCO for materials, and specialized labor aided this process. The final price was about 40 percent of what similar housing built through conventional methods would have cost (Leeds, 1969).

Similar programs are reported from Zambia. The thrust of the effort was to provide social and physical services to the major squatter settlements in Lusaka, the capital. Squatters were provided with a thirty-year occupancy license and given some modest financial and technical assistance in building a new home or improving the old one. The services provided included new roads, lighting, communal water taps, and community services such as primary schools and urban health centers. Hardware stores to sell building supplies for credit were also established. The total cost to the household was somewhat less than it would cost to rent a single room in the city. User control of the settlement was a built-in feature of the plan (Martin, 1978).

Other attempts to implement this approach appear to have produced mixed results. A housing law passed in 1961 in Peru was designed to improve the barriadas. Provision was made for families to obtain legal title to their land on the payment of a nominal fee and to renovate and sanitize the barriadas. The implementation of the law was somewhat slow and ineffectual. It also involved a successful attempt by the government to co-opt voluntary organizations within the barriadas and control their operations. There was also a controversial attempt to relocate squatters to designated areas some distance from the city. These strategies appear to be a direct violation of the Turner model. One might state, however, that, despite the many weaknesses in conception and execution, this intervention by the state did in fact change the face of many squatter settlements. Physical amenities were obtained by thousands of families, although these families represented only a fraction of the need. Many of the heads of households in the barriadas have with time become wage earners, and some have converted their original shacks into two-story concrete houses. They could now focus their efforts on community concerns such as paved roads and adequate water supplies. By sponsoring self-help, the state was able to satisfy important needs at small cost to itself (Michel, 1973).

The housing crisis in Nairobi forced the government to consider and adopt a modified version of the Turner model. A sites-and-services project was promoted in Kariabangi (Ross, 1973). Although houses were built on the plots assigned to the erstwhile squatters of Nairobi, the program could not be claimed as an unqualified success. The distance from the city and the lack of employment opportunities led to a mass exodus of the original squatters. Although their places were quickly filled by other homeless people, the project was a failure in terms of its original objective. As a result of this experience, the city changed its plans and simply concentrated on providing public services to existing squatter settlements.

Chile is also said to have attempted an ambitious housing program for squatters during the ill-fated Allende regime. Operation Sitio was to have provided a choice among three types of dwellings for squatters and quite generous community services (Lozano, 1967). It is not clear whether the program has been continued under the present junta.

India has experimented with bustee improvement in several of its largest cities. One version provides for certain community improvements in the bustees. The other provides, in addition, schools, dispensaries, and play spaces. Self-management does not seem to be a feature of this program, and it is hardly coincidental that management and rent collection are major problems in the Indian experiment (Herbert and Hayck, 1968).

In Indonesia, attempts to deal with squatters were originally restricted to moving them to new and unimproved sites in distant locations. Some projects were built on improved sites in Grogol, Supi, and Padjamapen, but these were open only to government employees or members of the armed forces (Milone, 1971).

Some promising results are emerging from World Bank-sponsored projects on three continents. The World Bank has been active in this field since the early seventies. Forty such projects are in different stages of completion, and four of them were selected from their inception for extensive monitoring and evaluation and were designed to test what the Bank termed the "progressive development" model in implementing urban shelter projects. The four sample projects were in El Salvador, The Philippines, Senegal, and Zambia. While the results fall short of their sponsors' expectations in several important areas, they do provide a confirmation of the validity of the concepts embodied in the Turner model.

The projects studied were able to increase the national production of low-income housing by up to 50 percent. The quality of the housing produced by the participants was better than expected. Families continued to invest time and money not only in their own homes, but in community amenities such as sidewalks, parks, and community centers. The sites-and-services projects were able to reach families in the twentieth income percentile, while upgrading projects were able to reach even lower. Both types of projects have led to significant improvements in the provision of water, sanitation, and other basic services to a large number of the urban poor. The results have been so satisfying in The Philippines and Indonesia that these programs have been replicated on a national scale. The projects themselves have generated substantial employment possibilities for their residents. In

El Salvador, the findings indicate that a project of 7,000 units can generate US$412 million (1978–79) wage income. Family participation in the construction and upgrading of their homes, in El Salvador, for example, reduced costs by as much as 30 percent per house.

However, the findings also identified some serious problems in implementation. The large number of different government and private organizations involved in the provision of basic services presented a severe coordination problem, which resulted in increased costs and delays. The goal of stimulating small businesses within the projects offered a support package to small businesses, and the Zambia project included the provision of plots of land for markets and other business enterprises. Cost recovery proved a problem in three of the four projects, although the causes and severity of the problems varied significantly (Keere and Parris, 1983, pp. v–xv).

Assessment

These programs, varied in content and execution though they may be, have some common elements. The failures ignore the structural elements already described, the formation of squatter settlements. The market is unable to supply housing at costs that are affordable to the bulk of the working-class population in cities. They also overlook the squatters' innate capacity to solve their own housing problems. Police action is used to control and direct the growth of squatter settlements, while the needs and wishes of squatters for proximity to work and to family and for friendship networks and access to community services are disregarded. Legislation to inhibit profiteering and land speculation is omitted. The net social costs and financial burdens to the community are far greater than are entailed in the Turner model or the variations it has spawned.

It is not possible to generalize from the few descriptions of cases where squatter settlement programs were successfully implemented. We may, though, discern some common elements. The programs all appear to have harnessed squatter initiative, and their participation in decision making could be an important element in their success. The role of the government sector is limited to enacting security of tenure legislation and providing the support services that are important to an undertaking of this nature. As one might expect, the Turner model is more acceptable to those regimes that are dependent on some measure of public acceptance.

Squatter settlements will continue to be an important element of housing in many Third World cities for the foreseeable future; there appears to be no alternative in sight. Improving them while regulating their growth is both the humanitarian and the pragmatic solution to the housing problem.

13

Popular Housing in Brazil:
A Review

Licia Valladares

Abstract. This chapter provides a guide to the literature on housing for low-income groups in Brazil, especially in São Paulo and Rio de Janeiro. During the 1960s, a rapid increase in urban population was accompanied by an increase in squatter settlements (favelas), which were studied under the then prevalent "theory of marginality." Later, in the sixties and seventies, favela studies were guided by theories on the exploitation of labor and by Marxist theory on capitalist accumulation. The housing policies of the National Housing Bank (BNH), created in 1964, are another major focus of the literature on low-income housing. The many studies critical of the BNH center on its shift from social emphases to profit-making models which make it impossible to build for the urban poor. The most recent emphasis in the literature is on peripherally located squatter settlements, which differ from favelas in that the residents often have legal occupancy and the housing occupies large tracts which have an overall plan.

Introduction

In the recent past, much has been written about low-income housing in Brazil. However, there has been no systematic review of the more than 200 relevant research reports. The purpose of this chapter is to provide a selective guide to the extant literature.[1] After a brief sketch of the historical background of housing studies in Brazil, we focus on three main areas: (1) the favelas (squatter settlements), (2) the housing policies of the National Housing Bank, and (3) housing in peripheral areas.

In the sixties, the rapid increase in urban population highlighted the issue of housing, including the vigorous expansion of favelas in the country's large cities. Major pioneer studies on the favela came out during this period (e.g., Leeds, 1969). Later, with the creation of the National Housing Bank (BNH) and its thorough involvement in housing affairs, many studies came to deal critically with this bank's activities and programs. More recently, attention has been focused on the low-income outskirts, or peripheral areas, of the metropolitan regions, where self-built housing is the most common form of construction. In the past few years many authors have pinpointed the issues of land rent and urban land use as fundamental to the understanding and formulation of urban policies in general and housing policies in particular (Vetter, 1975). Another general theme concerns the urban struggles and conflicts over housing issues out of which social movements have grown.

The above thematic evolution followed changes in Brazilian political and urban arenas; a decisive influence of prevalent Latin American sociological thinking of the sixties and seventies on housing studies is also evident. Favela studies, for example, developed when the so-called "theory of marginality" was in vogue throughout Latin America; this theory focused on discussions of the integration or nonintegration of lower-income urban populations in relation to urban unemployment and favelas. While more evident in the work of some authors than others, the theory of marginality appears in all social science studies on housing in the early seventies.

Later, when the theory of marginality was replaced by a focus on the exploitation of labor, the theory of capitalist accumulation began to gain influence and contribute to a new field of research on low-income housing tracts and self-built housing in the urban periphery. Another significant theoretical contribution to housing studies in Brazil stems from Europe, where new developments in Marxist theory, within the theory of accumulation, have fueled the debate on the relationships among the state, capitalist urbanization, housing, and the conditions of reproduction of the labor force.

A complete review of the aforementioned issues and approaches is beyond the scope of this chapter. Instead, we will concentrate on favelas, housing policy, and peripheral housing. The first studies in this regard date back to the fifties and sixties, but the bulk of the literature has come out during the past decade, when housing was established as a field of studies in Brazil. The impetus for many studies has come from new postgraduate programs in the social sciences and planning. Also, government agencies finance an increasing number of studies. In addition, there are contributions from foreign researchers, particularly on the favela (squatter settlements).

Although all Brazilian cities have housing problems, most studies have focused on Rio de Janeiro and São Paulo, where research facilities are found, where the crisis is most visible, and where research results can be used politically.

Favelas

Among the various housing alternatives for the urban poor in Brazil, the squatter settlement, best known as favela[2] (or mocambo, invasão, or baixada) is the most common and most important. Research on housing started in Brazil in the sixties, when the favela was seen as the "natural" habitat of the urban poor and the theory of social marginality was in vogue throughout Latin America. Originally associated with precarious housing conditions, the marginal population came to be identified with traits such as low income and educational levels, underemployment and unemployment, disorganization of families, anomy, and lack of social participation. Marginality was seen as something to be physically eradicated, a manifestation that had a simple cure: remove favela dwellings and provide for the public construction and financing of "adequate" low-cost housing.

The first favelas appeared in the urban landscape in the 1890s. By 1950 favelas housed 6.7 percent of the total population of Rio de Janeiro; 9.3 percent in 1960, and 13 percent in 1970. More recent municipal estimates point to the existence in 1981 of 377 favelas with a population of 1.5 million, which is 25 percent of Rio de Janeiro's population.

Favelas in São Paulo are more recent than in Rio, and they house fewer residents, especially when compared to the percentage of the population living in other types of low-income housing. In 1958, no more than 1.3 percent of the city of São Paulo lived in favelas, a figure which grew to 1.6 percent in 1975 when 117,000 people lived in favelas, as compared to 615,000 in tenements and 1.8 million inhabitants of "precarious" housing on the periphery. According to more recent estimates, in 1978 São Paulo's favela population had reached 4.1 percent of the city's population.

Given the makeup of the favela itself—its clear geographical limits and the fact that it houses a significant portion of low income, urban sectors—it has been used by many researchers as a social and spatial point of reference for the study of many issues, e.g., working-class ideology and symbols, nutritional patterns and habits, labor markets and small independent production, political behavior of the inhabitants, women in the favela, etc. This discussion deals strictly with housing, specifically: (a) the process of occupation, (b) characteristics and significance of favela living, and (c) alternatives for government policies.

The process of occupation

A distinguishing feature of the favela is the way in which the land became occupied. Through appropriation of empty urban spaces, the favela comes into being as an illegal form of land tenure, since it is generally "based neither on property nor on rent paid to the legal proprietors" (Leeds, 1969: 151–52). The data on ownership of lands occupied by favelas in Rio are revealing. According to the 1964 survey, 23 percent of favela areas belonged to the federal government, 27 percent belonged to state governments, 44 percent belonged to private proprietors, and 6 percent was of doubtful or unknown ownership (Valladares, 1978: 31). In 1974, 55.9 percent of favelas in São Paulo were located on private property, 37.1 percent on city government land, and 6.6 percent on state or federal lands.

A pertinent question concerning the origin of the favelas is whether or not they were occupied through organized invasions. How was the land taken over by the invaders? Studies in different cities suggest that, in Brazil, occupation takes various forms. In Rio de Janeiro, for example, the pattern has been one of gradual takeover; in some cases, occupation has been encouraged by the proprietors themselves or by canvassers and politicians (Valladares, 1978: 14). In Salvador, the takeover pattern, beginning in the forties, has been based on collective movements which mobilize hundreds of people. As for São Paulo, there have been several types of processes. There are two forms of land invasions in Belem: direct takeovers, without the participation of third parties; and indirect takeovers, when the new occupant does not actually invade, but rather purchases or rents a shack that already exists.

"Squatters' rights," the legal recourses that actually or potentially accrue to the possessor of land without title, are barely touched on in the literature. An exception is the study by Conn (1968), who discusses the favelados ability to obtain and to retain land and points to the Brazilian Civil Code, which grants possible defenses against possessory actions.

Characteristics and significance of favela living

The significance of favela living is one of the most emphasized aspects of the literature. Under the clear influence of Turner (1969) and Mangin (1967), some authors have characterized the favela as a solution rather than a problem, pointing to its functionality, which involves aspects such as locale, nonpayment of rent, low-cost transportation, architectural creativity, etc. Moreover, other authors perceive the favela as just one of the several housing alternatives open to the low-income population. According to these authors, there is a range of choices for housing which are equivalent analytically, but not as real possibilities, since choices depend not only on changes in family units but also on external conditions (e.g., labor market fluctuations and changes in government policies affecting favelas). In this sense, the favela is a solution only at a certain moment in the life strategy of family groups.

Recent studies in São Paulo and Rio have examined the role of the favela in the housing history of low-income families. Contrary to the common view that the favela is one stage in the progression of the migrant—a sort of trampoline—it was found that in São Paulo the favela can enter into a family's housing history after the family has lived in better conditions. Data show that 41 percent of the migrant favela inhabitants who had lived for some time in different conditions moved to the favela by a process of descending filtration. In Rio it was found that the favela may occur at either the beginning or at the end of a family's housing history. Sometimes this is the outcome of relocation programs. Valladares (1978) found that favela residents, expelled to a public housing development, often either move back to a favela or settle on the periphery of Greater Rio in low-cost housing tracts. This often means they have passed the house on by selling their rights to third parties.

Alternatives for government policies

Much of the literature on favelas seeks to analyze the history and evolution of government policies toward these settlements, e.g., Valladares (1978). Nearly all studies deal with Rio de Janeiro where, more than anywhere else in the country, favelas have been the subject of a series of policy measures. There are two basic policy approaches which have developed: (*a*) removal of the favelas (remocão), implying resettlement of the inhabitants to other areas and the eradication of the favelas from their original site and (*b*) upgrading of the favelas (urbanizacão), which involves substantial improvements to physical infrastructure and assumes that the residents will remain in the area. Urbanizacão also implies the division of the favela into lots and some type of resolution to its land-tenure status.

In Rio de Janeiro, government intervention in the favelas has been widespread. The expulsion of squatters first occurred in the early forties, when 8,000 residents were transferred to provisional housing. From 1960 on, these programs intensified, and squatters were offered participation in a governmental house purchase plan. Within fifteen years, a total of 137,774 people were evicted from Rio de Janeiro favelas. No other Brazilian city has undergone such massive removal programs, although in Salvador in the late sixties, measures were taken to end the invasões particularly along the city's seashore and tourist areas. In São Paulo, residents were transferred to provisional housing villages in 1971. Direct evictions, executed by the proprietors themselves, seem to be more the rule in São Paulo, since 55.9 percent of the favelas are located on private property, 62.3 percent have no more than ten shacks, and 94.9 percent have no more than a hundred housing units.

The adverse effects of removals have been widely emphasized. Primarily concerned with the disintegrative effects of removals on the lives of favela dwellers, studies have documented the rise in housing costs and the drop in family income due to the increase of expenses, transportation, and unemployment caused by the distance from labor markets. Others have pointed to the disintegration caused by the destruction of the social ties of solidarity present in the favela (Salmen, 1969).

Along with removals, favelas have been upgraded, especially in Rio de Janeiro, although on a small scale. The church has promoted upgrading. Its outlook has evolved from advocating the cleaning up of the favela with the "sweat and work" of the inhabitants themselves (during the fifties) to present support for favela residents in their struggle for land tenure and upgrading measures.

Generally caused by changing political situations, there have been variations in government policies also regarding favelas. Thus military or elitist regimes have swayed toward more repressive policies (remocão), while a more populist regime is more committed to social and humane solutions (urbanizacão). Another issue is the political and electoral significance of favela constituencies. It is argued that extensive removal policies can only occur when favela populations lose the bargaining power represented by their vote (Valladares, 1978: 26–27).

Less has been written on the favela upgrading experiences. The classic research case is that of Bras de Pina (Rio de Janeiro) where, after eight years of upgrading measures, 75 percent of the dwellings had been transformed into brick houses. On the other hand, the upgrading project also meant that many favela residents were displaced by outsiders. It has also been suggested that population turnover through market mechanisms shows that, in the long run, removal and upgrading of favelas can have similar effects.

In recent years, a greater vitality of partisan politics has meant that the political and electoral role of the favelas has regained some of its former weight in housing policy decisions. Thus, the National Housing Bank (BNH) has launched a program to create a nationwide orientation toward upgrading favelas, taking account of the residents' associations. The first experience of this participatory planning has already run into difficulties over the residents' demand to acquire ownership of the land.

Housing policies and programs of the National Housing Bank (BNH) and their impact on the urban poor

Most of the literature concerning government housing policy in Brazil follows the creation of the BNH in 1964. The BNH was created in the midst of the political and economic crisis facing the new regime which took power in the 1964 revolution. That crisis and the measures taken by the emerging government in attempting to overcome it are the starting point for most studies.

While some authors have presented a broad analysis of the new political and economic model, here those aspects most closely tied to the creation of the BNH will be examined. All interpretations recognize the crisis of the real estate sector, from 1960 to 1964, which resulted in an increasing housing shortage. The root cause of this crisis was the inflation, which discouraged investments and promoted a boom in speculation in the large cities as well as a breakdown of the real estate sector. During this period, the construction materials industry cut

back production to the bare minimum, and construction of new housing units was also reduced. This situation was aggravated by the
various rent laws passed between 1946 and 1964, which also discouraged investments in the housing sector.

On the political side of the crisis was the discontent of the urban
poor, demanding attenuation of the effects of a prolonged depression
which had its origins in the anti-inflationary policies. Favelas were
recognized as potential tension points which could lead to conflict.
Thus, the government perceived the need to appease the masses; one
way was to offer private ownership of housing to the people. To own a
house was presented as a symbol of security, status, and income.

The BNH has now been in existence for more than twenty years. It
has gone through different phases and has been severely criticized by
social scientists and urban planners. It has been claimed that, following its initial emphasis on social policies, the BNH has taken on ever
greater economic functions to the benefit of private enterprise. Moreover, it has been transformed into one of the most efficient elements
in the new economic strategy implemented after 1964. It introduced
indexing for housing loans and benefited directly from the Seniority
Security Fund (FGTS)[3] and the Brazilian Savings and Loan System
(SBPE). Nevertheless, the BNH has not been able to keep its promises,
i.e., to provide low-cost housing for the Brazilian urban poor. This
failure occurred because of the profit-oriented model it adopted, indexing, and greater priority which was given, in the long run, to middle-
and upper-class housing projects.

Many studies have analyzed specific BNH programs, especially those
aimed at low-income families. Recently, the BNH itself began financing
research institutes to evaluate its programs. All the studies give detailed
attention to the operation of the programs, the performance of the
various housing agencies, the quality of dwellings, the relations between borrowers and the agencies responsible for executing housing
policy, and projected and actual clientele. They discuss the successes
and shortcomings of the whole range of programs for the low-income
sector in terms of stated housing policy objectives.

It is stressed that the housing programs and projects are not serving
the sectors for whom they were originally intended. Even among
those served within the priority income sectors, borrowers are concentrated at the upper limits of the target income range. Market forces
cause a high turnover rate among residents. Another important aspect
is the presence of a much higher demand for low-income housing

than the system can supply. Also, studies dealing with bureaucratic procedures in the access to housing have shown that, outside the official norms, favoritism and clientelism have made it possible for many people to get unfair priority. All research emphasizes the construction aspects of housing developments, whether in terms of shortage of infrastructure or in relation to building deficiencies concerning the quality of building materials and architectural limitations. Finally, there are constant criticisms of the location of these projects which generally are very far from the city centers and cause an excessive burden on the labor force in its day-to-day commuting.

Periphery: Low-income housing tracts and self-built housing

Studies on housing in Brazil have recently become concerned with a fairly new phenomenon: the fringes of major cities have expanded to such a degree that they have become important working-class residential areas. These areas differ from favelas mainly in terms of the land-use pattern and the land tenure. Residents commonly have legal occupancy, and the housing tracts follow a preestablished plan. Peripheral growth began to occur in the thirties and it has intensified since the fifties, yet only during the seventies, when the scale of the phenomenon made it hard to ignore, has a body of empirical information and theoretical interpretations emerged.

The recent literature represents a break with the theory of social marginality due to the influence of Francisco de Oliveira, who has argued that working-class homes, built by the owners themselves using days off, weekends, and different forms of mutual aid, should be seen as a principal item in the reproduction and dilapidation of the work force. Housing, as a good produced by this operation, is paid for by nonremunerated labor. While this good is not apparently appropriated by the private sector of production, it does contribute to increasing the rate of exploitation of the labor force, since its result, the house, is reflected in an apparent lowering of the cost of reproduction of the labor force—of which housing expenses are an important component. It also contributes to depressing real wages. Therefore, this practice fits in admirably with the process of capitalist expansion, which is based on the exploitation of the labor force.

Studies from this perspective were first carried out in São Paulo and later in Rio. They were concrete field studies of outlying housing tracts. Three basic, complementary approaches distinguish the various studies. The first uses a historical perspective to analyze the origins of land distribution in Brazil from colonial times to the present; it emphasizes peripheral settlements as one of cities' main mechanisms of expansion, bringing together considerable segments of the working population. The second approach emphasizes comparative analysis, showing tendencies in the self-built housing process over the past three decades in terms of the determinant social, economic, and technical aspects. Finally, the great majority of the studies approach the matter through a description of self-building and a discussion of its significance for the reproduction of the labor force.

Peripheral segregation of the working class

Brazilian authors use the word *periferizacão* to refer to the pattern of urban expansion which concentrates the urban poor in the outskirts of the major Brazilian cities. Periferizacão can be seen as a spatial projection of the process of capital accumulation and its consequences for the working-class habitat. Its physical segregation is dictated by the growing distance between its location and the nuclei of the urban-industrial centers. In addition, authors point to the precarious housing conditions, the nearly complete lack of infrastructure and urban services, the deterioration of health conditions, and the dubious legal status of some tracts.

The main factors which have contributed to the process of periferizacão are the salaries of the working class, direct expulsion from inner cities due to favela removal programs and urban renewal, indirect expulsion due to urban legislation and taxes, and real estate speculation. On the other hand, the periphery has the attraction of informal social relations among the settlers, real estate agents, and buyers, allowing the working class to get into and out of contracts and solve problems through face-to-face relations. Peripheral growth expands through the movement of groups from one periphery to a poorer one.

Low-income peripheral housing tracts

Working-class residential settlements on the periphery have generally occurred in three phases: division of land, first settlements, and later developments. Studies on these low-cost housing tracts have defined the roles of those involved in the transactions: the landowner, the tract manager, the real estate agent, the state (represented through local power structures), and the resident.

Most tracts are located in former farm areas incorporated into the urban space through the development of transportation systems and thus targets for real estate speculation. A piece of land becomes a tract through a concession agreement between the landowner and an agent, or through a partnership agreement between the two. The capital involved is sometimes only sufficient to divide the tract into small plots; at other times it is substantial, coming from big investors who use small real estate companies as a front.

Commercialization of the tracts follows fairly similar procedures. For the residents, some of the important purchase conditions are: installments are based on what the purchasers can actually pay; a down payment is not always required, and the total price of a lot plays a small role in the purchase decision, since the amortization period (which varies from five years to ten years) is a major factor.

Sales are promoted through procedures that reveal a strategy oriented towards popularizing the tract: leaflets and brochures distributed in areas of heavy traffic, advertising at work places, and stands set up at strategic locations. The contract of purchase and sale stipulates that the lot will be forfeited after three months delay of payment, although there are indications that this recourse is little used, because of high costs and delays in court suits. Negotiation is a frequent practice, implying resale of the lot either to the same purchaser or to a third party. The viability of lot sales is based above all on the virtual absence of infrastructure and urban services in the tracts; it is precisely the lack of these conditions that is sold to the purchasers.

Another central point is the legal status of the tracts, many of which are actually "clandestine" because of noncompliance with infrastructure and urban service requirements. Since tract approval is controlled by city law, there are many forms of illegality, varying with each city and from tract to tract. The proliferation of these low-income tracts is provoking irreversible consequences for the general conditions of the urbanization of large cities, yet positions differ in relation to the state's responsibility.

Studies on peripheral tracts have also examined the role of the residents. Settlement of the area itself increases property values, since it lays the base for its later development. It is important that in many tracts, because of government inaction, the local population itself provided the introduction of minimal infrastructure. Improvements become a determinant factor in the very process of growth of the peripheries; there are residents who take immediate advantage of whatever improvements are obtained: they sell the lot or building or subdivide it to sell or rent.

Self-built housing

All authors who write on self-built housing consider this practice as one of the main aspects of the reproduction of the labor force. They call attention to the significance of self-construction as a housing solution promoted by the working-class itself in the absence of government housing policies or of a formal market compatible with the wage levels of this majority of the population.

Self-construction has been defined as "the process by which the owner builds his house by himself or with the help of friends and relatives . . . during the hours in which he is not performing remunerated labor." The definition is valid for work whether collective or not and for construction work done on one's own home or another's. Thus, the term self-building also means the production of urban space (churches, schools, streets, etc.).

The self-building process has commonly been characterized as a survival strategy. The labor pool normally consists of family members, but may include friends and neighbors. Paid labor may also be contracted, especially for specialized tasks. The work is done on weekends, holidays, or at night. Some authors have identified the existence of labor networks based on reciprocal labor commitments among several homebuilders. Such arrangements may go on for an extended period of time. The significance of the term mutirão has become important in the debates. While it has been defined as "enforced solidarity," others claim that it is not an example of "class solidarity." They argue that it is a service-bartering arrangement, that the neighbor relationship is not the determining factor in such cooperation, and that the arrangement contributes indirectly to maintaining low wages and extending the work day.

Availability of financial resources is crucial in self-building. There are two obstacles to the first stage of house building. First, a financial commitment to the purchase of a lot precedes the decision to begin construction. Second, those building their own houses generally live in rented housing, which limits their capacity for handling initial expenses. Taking the cost of initial building material into consideration, it is clear that the period between purchase of the lot and completion of the first room—the point at which the family can move into their own house—is the crucial phase of the self-building process.

There are various ways of gaining access to the necessary resources: working overtime at one's job; taking second and odd jobs; exchanging vacation time for pay; obtaining loans on company savings plans; year end bonuses; entrance of more family members into the labor market; home budget cutbacks, especially in food; sale of household and personal goods; and falling behind on payments for the lot. Materials and building techniques are essential to building one's own house. Material purchase will be conditioned by the uncertainty of resource availability and will have to be effected little by little to meet the minimum needs of each construction phase. With few alternatives for low-cost financing, most of these homebuilders buy the cheapest material available. Selection generally is limited to the supply available in the small building materials stores which proliferate around these low-income tracts. Building techniques are simple, and the construction will be periodically discontinued; this often means deterioration of unfinished sections.

A final concern is the relation between the self-constructed house's use and its exchange value. While its use value is the initial impetus for self-building, the house also has a potential exchange value which means that it will be seen as a commodity to be traded under certain conditions. Some authors also see the option as a security factor in the face of job instability and the life crises to which this segment of the population is frequently subjected.

Self-building, the solution of the working class to its housing problems, has been seen as the only alternative left to the worker. It is a solution that arises in a context of deterioration and urban dispossession of the labor force and under a state which does not provide a housing policy in line with the needs of the working class. On the other hand, this housing solution is a very advantageous one for the prevailing political and economic system. The latter view is based on an interpretation of self-building as a means for lowering wage rates. The argument is also directed at the political and ideological implications of owning one's own house. The expansion of the number of private owners reinforces the belief that the legal right to private property is an unquestionable right and reinforces its value as an unconditional aspiration.

Conclusion

Much has been written regarding popular housing. Nevertheless, there are still important issues yet to be studied. There are, for example, few studies on the history of housing in Brazil. Work is now being done on factory-worker villages which were prominent in Brazil from the end of the nineteenth century to the first decades of the twentieth century. Only a few studies have focused on the history of urban renewal programs and their impact on the urban poor in inner-city slums (corticos) and on the contrast between the living and housing conditions of the rich and of the poor. Other important gaps are the lack of studies on favelas that deal with land tenure and squatter rights. Also, little has been written on conflicts involving landowners, the state, the Catholic Church, and squatters themselves in their struggle for land and housing. A final point to be made concerns the research design and data-gathering methods used. There has been a clear preference for case studies and qualitative methodology. Future studies might benefit from a comparative approach and the use of available census data.

14 | Integrated Kampung Improvement Programs and Mutual Aid in Indonesia

Herlianto, Wilhelmus Hofsteede, and Padmini Gulati

Abstract. Programs to improve the kampungs (squatter settlements) in which three-fourths of low-income urban Indonesians live, are described and analyzed. A range of kampung improvement programs have been developed by local and national governmental agencies often in collaboration with international agencies and the Dutch government. Concentration on improving physical infrastructure alone has come to be recognized as costly and short-term and is being replaced by integrated approaches combining social and economic changes for long-term improvement. However, the integrated approach raises issues of subverting grassroots efforts into bureaucratic regulations and the problems of coordinating bureaucracies that have conflicting agendas. To expedite coordination, the Ministry of Land Use and Environment has been designated as the national coordinating body and the mayors as coordinating entities at the local level. Indonesia has the enduring tradition of gotung royang, the practice among villagers of mutual aid on projects of benefit to all, such as building schools, irrigation systems, and roads. A variant of gotung royang is voluntary assistance with the expectation of assistance in return. A 1981 case study of the rural village of Cilenkrang illustrates how voluntary assistance operated effectively in implementing a housing and water supply improvement program of the Ministry of Public Works. Elements of gotung royang carry over into urban kampungs and may provide a useful basis for action. Coordination was not a problem in Cilenkrang, since only one government agency was involved.

Background

Indonesia is an archipelago in southeast Asia, consisting of thousands of islands. It has a total population of 147 million (1980 census figures), and it is the fifth most populous country on earth. One-fifth of Indonesia's population now lives in urban areas.

In recent times, an increasing number of national and international agencies have attempted to respond to the growing crisis in the provision of shelter to low-income urbanites by fostering programs to improve the kampungs (the informal housing sector). While these programs have the same broad objective of improving the quality of life in the kampungs, they also reflect major differences in the missions and means of the sponsoring organizations.

This chapter takes a closer look at these programs and tries to identify some of the problems that relate to deficiencies in services, as well as program overlaps, occasioned by the gaps in communication among the agencies involved and the lack of input from the residents of the kampungs.

The shortage of housing for the low-income urban population of Indonesia has now reached crisis proportions. It is estimated that three-fourths of Indonesia's urban residents live in kampungs (slums and squatter settlements). The flow of migrants from rural areas continues with no end in sight. In Indonesia, the physical environment of most of the kampungs is worsening. Efforts are being made by numerous national and international organizations to remedy this situation. Government bodies, local and central, and organizations such as the IBRD (International Bank for Reconstruction and Development), UNEP (U.N. Environmental Programs), UNICEF (U.N. Children's Fund), USAID (U.S. Agency for International Development), ADB (Asian Development Bank), the Dutch government, and others, have demonstrated an interest in funding kampung improvement programs for the urban low-income population.

Although some physical improvements have been carried out over the years in the kampungs, the evidence suggests that the changes have been short-term and limited in their impact. The high costs entailed have curtailed replication. The improvements have reached only a fraction of the needy population. There has also been a perception that merely focusing on physical conditions will not bring about the hoped-for improvements in the living conditions of the kampung dwellers. The emerging philosophy is that only a comparative integrated approach that combines social and economic elements with physical improvements can make any significant long-term changes in the kampung environment.

Several ministries and international organizations have moved forcefully to fill the void. The role of the ministries of public works, education, health, social affairs, and others is quite important in promoting and initiating a range of improvement programs within the kampungs. UNICEF and UNEP have initiated community development programs and research efforts. Training programs for motivators and social workers have also been developed alongside the major physical improvements that have been carried out with the World Bank loan. Since the kampungs occupy almost three-fourths of the urban residential areas, successful kampung improvement will have a marked impact on the urban environment of Indonesia.

The range of kampung improvement programs

The primary goal of the kampung improvement programs is to raise the quality of the living environment of very large numbers of low-income persons to at least a minimally acceptable level. The major programs that are targeted at the kampungs can be subdivided into (a) programs that focus mainly on improvements to the physical infrastructure of the squatter settlements, and (b) programs that are primarily concerned with the health and social and economic well-being of the squatters themselves and target their efforts at the provision of services and income-enhancing measures. There is naturally some overlap between the two types of programs, since the different elements contained in them cannot always be separated.

Physical improvement system

The Subharatnam Program in Surabaya and the Muhamed Husani Thamarin Program in Jakatra were two of the earliest kampung improvement programs and were originally an intrinsic part of Indonesia's first five-year development plan. Through subsidies, they attempted to prod municipalities and the kampungs themselves to initiate projects and improve the physical amenities and services available in the settlements. These programs were first implemented in the cities of Jakatra and Surabaya, but they have since been widely emulated in other cities.

These programs have since evolved in several new directions. There is a good deal more municipal and central government intervention than in the past. The impetus for the programs now comes from the two levels of government rather than from the kampungs themselves. Changes have also occurred in relation to the funding source, the scope of the projects, and the complexity of the projects.

The World Bank Program, while emphasizing physical improvements, did not overlook the need for social amenities and income generation. The World Bank has invested heavily in squatter upgrading programs since the early seventies. Upgrading schemes endorsed by the Bank attempt to provide security of tenure to squatters, as well as the essential infrastructure that the settlements need. Another feature of the Bank program is that it also extends credit, materials, and technical assistance to squatters for the improvement of their own dwellings. A broad range of services can be financed under this program. They include neighborhood improvements that center around such physical amenities as improved water supplies, sewage, electricity, and roadway services, as well as community facilities such as schools, clinics, and health centers and the needed equipment for them. The program is initiated by the central and local governments, with the central government providing the subsidy, which is financed by the World Bank loan.

The Kampung Improvement Pioneering Project is much larger in scope than any of the previous programs. Originally part of the third Five-Year Plan which began in 1979, its scope was greatly enlarged and extended to cover two hundred towns of varying sizes. The goal is to complete this program by the end of the five-year period.

The aim of the program is to stimulate local municipalities to improve the kampungs. A beginning subsidy of about $5,000 per ha (hectare) is provided, and it is hoped that the municipalities will eventually continue the program with their own resources. Large towns receive approximately $1,000,000; medium sized towns about $500,000; and small towns around $300,000. This project is fully financed by the central government, and some selected towns get additional subsidies from the IBRD, ABD, USAID, UNICEF, and the Dutch government, among others.

The main emphasis of this program is on improving the physical infrastructure of the kampungs through the provision or improvement of roads, bridges, sewage facilities, potable water, sanitation, etc. However, health and educational facilities are also included as components of this program.

Social and economic programs

The UNICEF Program emphasizes the social as well as the physical well-being of the kampung dwellers. While improved sanitation and garbage collection are recognized as important, the main focus is on the social and economic factors that contribute to the well-being of kampung residents. Many of the educational, health, and nutrition programs promoted by UNICEF attempt to reach mothers and children, groups that are often overlooked by planners. While some elements of the UNICEF program concentrate on aspects of the physical environment, such as garbage collection and communal water supply, the main thrust of the program is on training personnel in education, nutrition, credit, housing improvement, and health care practices to manage the service programs offered within the kampungs. The program is fairly limited in scope and primarily intended as a support to the major kampung improvement projects. The program is currently being implemented in two cities, but it is expected that it will be extended to several others.

The U.N. Environment Program favors an integrated approach to kampung improvement. While the array of measures initiated by the program touches on such conventional environmental concerns as garbage collection, human waste disposal, water management, and energy conservation, the program sets its sights on affecting the quality of social existence within the squatter settlements. The program attempts to improve the earnings potential of the kampung dwellers through skills training and the establishment of small businesses, cooperative ventures, and savings and loan arrangements. It provides sites for small-scale industrial ventures and recreational, cultural, and educational facilities. It includes health and community development components.

This sudden spate of interest in the kampungs, after years of neglect, is welcome from one perspective, but it also raises a number of disturbing issues. A major issue is whether the best use is being made of available resources. Will this be another case of bureaucratic ineptitude and mismanagement ruining an excellent idea? Has what is essentially a grass-roots effort been subverted into a bureaucratic nightmare overweighted with red tape and a myriad of regulations which have in the past wrecked many worthy projects and public enterprises in developing countries? Although Turner, one of the principal proponents of squatter improvement projects, advocated the "directed" development of squatter settlements, it was the initiative and creativity of squatters that he lauded. It is now accepted that the priorities of the residents of these settlements are not necessarily identical with those of the public agencies that sponsor these improvement programs.

Another inherent problem suggested by this proliferation of agencies and programs is that these bureaucracies may have conflicting agendas and are essentially not accountable to the supposed beneficiaries of the programs. Lack of coordination, duplication, and waste are major problems with which decision makers must cope.

Popular participation and mutual aid

The remainder of this paper will focus on another important issue, namely, popular participation. Numerous studies have documented the need for group cohesion and solidarity during the early phases of settlement. Others have pointed out that squatter settlements tend to be self-integrated communities with strong associational life. Many of the migrants retain the village traditions ingrained in them prior to their arrival in the city.

One of the most enduring traditions of Indonesian village life is that of gotung royang, a practice which has survived generations of colonial rule and decades of disruptive modernization. Gotung royang, or mutual aid, is an ancient institution, which is characterized by strong obligations between people who are mutually dependent upon one another. The two principles governing it are reciprocity and equality. Most common tasks are carried out through teamwork, one expression of the strong bonds that unite small communities in agricultural societies where face-to-face interaction among the total membership is the norm.

Under this form of gotung royang, residents of a village engage in tasks that are of benefit to the entire community. These may range from the construction of new roads and irrigation works to the building of schools. Labor on these projects is a common obligation and a responsibility of the male head of household. Similar practices have existed in precolonial times in other parts of Asia. This type of gotung royang is not entirely voluntary, as it is an obligation that cannot be rejected with impunity. However, only a decision by the community can make such an activity obligatory.

What follows is a case study of another form of gotung royang, characterized by voluntary assistance rendered without the intervention of village leaders. Here the help is given by neighbors, kinsmen, and friends, with the expectation that it will be returned when needed. This assistance could take the form of physical labor, the lending of equipment, or both. The discussion illustrates the effective use of gotung royang to carry out housing and environmental improvements. Although this case study is set in a rural village, some of the same elements are present in the urban kampungs, though perhaps not to the same degree, as mutual aid still remains a strong tradition in Indonesia and elsewhere in nonindustrialized Asia.

Case study of the village of Cilenkrang

The village of Cilenkrang is situated in the province of West Java, about ten miles from the city of Bandung. It is a densely populated village, with a somewhat diverse economic base. Although traditional occupations such as agriculture, fishing, and cattle raising still predominate, a substantial number of persons are employed in the nearby textile mills. In 1981 it had a population of 11,746.

This case study is based on information supplied by a number of persons who were directly involved in a housing and environmental improvement project sponsored by the Ministry of Public Works. Interviews were carried out in 1981 by three students from the Social Research Institute at the Catholic University in Bandung, under the supervision of two instructors.

When leaders in the village of Cilenkrang were informed that public funds were available to the village for housing improvement, they called a meeting in the village hall. A total amount of Rp4,300,000 for environmental and housing improvement would be made available, if it were matched by a sum of Rp2,425,000 by the village. The government subsidy for improving thirty houses was Rp1,200,000, or Rp40,000 (about US$400) for each home. Each homeowner who qualified for the subsidy would need an additional Rp50,000 (almost US$500) to make the required improvements.

The meeting was attended by all the village officials, the members of the community council, and some of the villagers. At the suggestion of the village headman, it was decided that the hamlet Cigagak would be the site of the proposed new project. It was lacking in basic amenities such as clean water, and several homes were badly dilapidated.

When he learned of this decision, a retired soldier who lived in the hamlet took the initiative of organizing a meeting of the residents of the hamlet. The meeting was chaired by the leader of the subdivision. Initially the residents were ambivalent. They were afraid the project was beyond their very limited resources. However, they gradually became convinced it was in their self-interest to improve their housing environment and participate in the project. At this meeting thirty homes were selected for improvement. It was also decided that the project would be a cooperative venture. The homeowners would make a monetary contribution, but all the neighbors would participate in the physical labor.

At the next meeting called by the headman, a committee was set up to implement the work. The eight-member committee consisted of several of the formal and informal leaders of the village. The homeowners whose homes were to be improved met with the committee to discuss what needed to be done, but they also wanted further information about the project. They decided to set up a subcommittee to organize the training course. During these meetings, the villagers learned what materials would be made available to them and what they would have to acquire on their own. It emerged during the course of their discussions that the villagers' first priority was safe drinking water. However, they were willing to go along with the housing improvement if the provision of clean water were part of the total package.

Training

The focus of the training was on giving the villagers technical help in building construction. Practical instruction in roof construction and bricklaying was an integral part of the training. During the course of their training, the villagers visited the nearby village of Ciburu, which had just completed a housing and environmental improvement project. There were also some group discussions on the concepts of mutual aid and self-help led by two officials, one from the Office of Social Affairs and the other from the Office of Village Development. Three working groups of ten persons each were formed. The group leaders were selected by the headman. Technical competence, especially in carpentry, appeared to be a prerequisite for being a group leader. Both the formal and informal leaders were involved in different phases of the training, some taking a more active role and clarifying some of the points made by the government officials who conducted the training. They also elaborated on the issues discussed in which they had some expertise. For example, one of the leaders, a woman who had been instrumental in forming a savings association and active in housing improvement in the past, talked about some of her experiences. She and a primary school teacher also discussed the suggested improvements in terms of the advantages to the physical health of the villagers.

The work begins

In March 1980, the actual construction on the homes began. The two government officials who were primarily responsible for implementing the project kept in close touch throughout. The actual purchasing and transporting of the needed building materials was done by the village administration, although the finances of the project were controlled by the Office of Public Works and the Office of Village Development. Some of the village officials also directly participated in the actual construction work. One of the women's groups (the welfare section) took an active role in the project, providing light refreshments for the working men and making suggestions about the layout of the vegetable plots.

The homeowners met regularly with their leaders, trying to decide what materials they would purchase with the government subsidy of Rp40,000 that each of them had received. They also got some new ideas on how they would obtain the additional resources they would need for upgrading their homes. The extended family was a resource some of them used, while others sold animals or produce to raise the additional money.

Once a list of the needed materials was compiled, the group leader handed it to the village community council, which was able to obtain a discount on the bulk purchases. Most of the work was done through the traditional Indonesian practice of mutual aid known as gotung royang. Tasks such as laying the roof tiles, erecting the bamboo walls, and fixing the doors and ceilings, which require the cooperation of several persons, were carried out by the task groups. The painting of walls and the building of fences were done by individual homeowners. Some of the tasks were carried out by the small groups but others involved the entire group.

After the homes were completed, the group turned its attention to the physical infrastructure of the hamlet. They constructed a water reservoir, a communal washing and toilet facility, and a community hall. Even the women and children participated in these phases of the work, as did the adult male population of the village.

The marked improvement in the hamlet stimulated the villagers living nearby to emulate their neighbors in improving their homes, although they were to receive no subsidies. It was reported, and later verified by the researchers, that an additional forty-five homes were improved, as were some of the communal facilities such as footpaths. Several facilities for storing water for drinking and washing were also constructed. Some additional toilets were also built at this time.

Implications

What becomes very clear in this study is that the public officials who administered the subsidies were content to stay in the background and allow the village leadership, together with the rank and file residents, to reach consensus on priorities and set up their own procedures to reach these goals. The government officials played an enabling role, providing information and technical assistance when needed. By building upon the existing traditions of mutual aid and cooperation, responding to the felt needs of the village, and using the existing leadership channels, the project was a resounding success. The use of small groups in carrying out needed tasks appears to have provided the participants with social satisfaction as well. The villagers expressed a desire for more of this form of activity for future projects.

Another feature of the project was the two-way communication observed by all levels of government and the village residents. Frequent and regular feedback was reported during all phases of the project.

The major factor in this success story was that the project corresponded to a felt need, and the villagers were able to structure the project to fit in with their priorities. The use of existing traditions, the two-way flow of communication, and access to credit and building materials were also features that were important to this project's achievements. Another point was that only one ministry had a major role in the implementation of the project, i.e., the Ministry of Public Works, although other agencies played a supportive role. The lack of friction between the key officials may have played a part.

While this case study indicates what constitute some of the necessary ingredients for a successful project, it is by no means clear that all these conditions exist elsewhere, especially in the urban squatter settlements that have been targeted for upgrading. The numerous programs that have been set up by the different levels of government and by numerous departments and ministries, because the funding was available, have overlapping jurisdictions. Competition for the same source of funds could result in diminished cooperation among the different agencies. The involvement and interest of so many bureaucratic organizations presents the danger that the spontaneity and creativity of the residents will be crushed as bureaucratic heavyhandedness overwhelms the programs.

The greatest danger is that priorities will be set by the agencies involved and not by the supposed project beneficiaries. Overzealous officials, in an effort to show measurable results, may neglect or override the traditional mechanisms for decision making in the community. The unfortunate result could well be that the necessary ingredients for successful project implementation, the community's own capacity for problem solving and enthusiasm to improve their lot, could be smothered under bureaucratic inertia.

The lack of interagency coordination and cooperation and its resulting problems could be solved in one of two ways: (*a*) communication among the upper echelons of the departments and ministries involved and (*b*) communication between the departments and ministries involved and the project beneficiaries. Both processes would go a long way toward prevention of duplication of services and gaps in service provision, both arising from the lack of coordination.

Because of the considerable sums of money and individuals involved, Indonesia appears to have moved in the second direction. The Ministry of Land Use and Environment has been designated as the coordinating entity, which would seem appropriate. The minister has high visibility and influence and was instrumental in setting up the successful Integrated Kampung Improvement Program. However the necessary organizational framework in which coordination can occur is presently lacking.

The mayor has emerged as the coordinating entity at the local level. In most communities, the mayor is assisted by a KIP (Kampung Improvement Project) Implementing Unit, headed by a project manager. This arrangement could lead to variable results among communities. A strong mayor with a commitment to kampung improvement could produce results in one community dramatically different from those in another headed by a weak mayor with a lukewarm, if not negative, attitude toward squatter settlements.

The fostering of existing traditions, even in urban environments, of mutual aid and community participation, could go a long way toward resolving some of the problems in coordination that are beginning to emerge. One factor that project designers would do well to keep in mind is that projects planned and implemented without the participation of the beneficiaries may not survive the departure of the planners. The continued maintenance and improvement of the environment is ultimately up to the residents of the kampungs themselves. It is they who need to set up a structural mechanism to ensure that the improvements continue to be maintained. Projects that ignore the participation and input of the residents of the community they serve do so at their own peril. The potency of gotung royang (community self-help) should be considered a valuable resource and a necessary ingredient of any kampung improvement program.[1]

| 15 | Housing the Poor in a Planned City: The Chandigarh Experience |
| | Ranvinder Singh Sandhu |

Abstract. This chapter is a case study of how the poor are housed in the planned city of Chandigarh in the Punjab region of northwest India. Developed on the neighborhood unit plan in the early 1950s, Chandigarh had 380,000 inhabitants in 1981. Only 13.5 percent of the poor are accommodated in government units built for the lowest status public employees. The remainder of the poor (public workers and others) are housed in informal housing built by the poor on the out-skirts of Chandigarh. Interviews in 1976 indicate that a majority of the poor in both public and informal housing are in the scheduled castes (formerly untouchables). However, the poor in public housing are much more likely to be natives of Punjab, long-time Chandigarh resi-dents, and members of large-family households and to have monthly incomes of more than \$36. Residents of informal housing are grossly overcrowded and they lack sanitary facilities, medical services, trans-portation, parks, post offices, and firehouses. In sum, the situation of the poor in the informal housing sector in Chandigarh is no better than in older, traditional cities.

Background[1]

Chandigarh is the first planned city constructed in the northwestern region of India after independence. The planning of this city was entrusted to Albert Mayer, who prepared the first layout. When one of Mayer's partners died in an air crash, Le Corbusier took charge. In 1951, he developed a new layout in collaboration with others. He conceived the city as a living organism. The basic concept underlying the plan is that of the neighborhood unit, which is self-sufficient for its day-to-day requirements (Perry, 1939). The layout of the city follows the well-known gridiron pattern. The entire city is divided into forty-six sectors. These are rectangular in shape and are arranged in six rows.

Chandigarh was declared a town in 1961, when its population was 89,321 persons. During 1961–71, it had a growth rate of 166 percent, but in 1971–81 this rate dropped to 70 percent. In the last two decades (1961–81), Chandigarh's population has increased four times, and its population in 1981 census was 371,992 persons. According to the 1971 census, the major portion of the city work force (76 percent) was in the tertiary sector, followed by the secondary sector (19 percent), and the primary sector (5 percent). At present, Chandigarh serves as an administrative center for two states (Punjab and Haryana) and a union territory.

The poor are found in the most squalid and dilapidated sections of older cities. Is this unfortunate fact of life modified to any degree in a planned city? This chapter will examine the evidence from Chandigarh — India's model planned city — and assess if planning has made any significant improvements in the environment of the poor.

Housing

Housing in Chandigarh can be divided into two categories: (a) public/semi-public: provided by government or semi-government organizations for their employees; and (b) private: occupied by the owners themselves or rented to tenants.

Public housing varies according to income. Of the fourteen categories of housing, the two least expensive categories are reserved for the lowest status workers in the public and service sectors of the economy. These types of housing are scattered over most of the city. In the master plan of Chandigarh, a cluster of these houses is known as a peon village. The most striking fact is that only 13.5 percent of the poor can be accommodated in the housing designed for them within the city (Sandhu, 1983). Private housing is not within the reach of the poor. As a result, unplanned slum communities have proliferated on the outskirts of the city to meet the need for low-income housing. This paper will examine in some detail the actual living conditions of the poor in Chandigarh, India's planned model community.

Research background

Two types of housing are examined in this chapter: (*a*) public housing designed for the poor by the planners and (*b*) self-help or informal housing constructed by the poor themselves on the periphery of the city, in contravention of the actual master plan for Chandigarh. A purposive sample of 248 households was drawn from both public housing and informal housing. Interviews were conducted with the head of each household during the period of January–March 1976. Of the total number of households interviewed, ninety-eight lived in public housing, while 150 dwelled in slums or informal housing on the periphery of the city. The response rate was 100 percent. The first part of this chapter focuses on the inhabitants of the two types of housing described in this paper. The second section concentrates on their housing environment.

Socioeconomic characteristics of households

Caste and occupation. A majority of both groups (64 percent in each category) belongs to the scheduled castes.[2] The major difference in the two groups relates to the nature of their employment. The respondents in public housing are all employed by government or quasi-governmental organizations. Only 25 percent of the respondents in informal housing are similarly employed. The majority of respondents in informal housing work in the service sector of the economy as laborers, rickshaw pullers, cobblers, and the like.

State of origin. Some 75 percent of the household heads in public housing are natives of the undivided Punjab state. Only 19 percent of the household heads in informal housing came from there. The rest were from neighboring states.

Length of residence in Chandigarh. Another difference in the two groups is their length of stay in Chandigarh. Of the public housing households, 81 percent had been residents of Chandigarh for more than ten years. Only 28 percent of the informal housing heads had lived in Chandigarh for the same period of time.

Size of the household. Informal housing households were somewhat smaller in size than public housing households (3.9 persons as compared to 6.2 persons). Another difference related to single-person households. Only 3 percent of this household type were found in public housing compared to 37 percent in informal housing.

Monthly household income. Variations between the two groups also exist in terms of household income. While 79 percent of the households in public housing in 1982 had incomes that ranged between US$20 and US$36 per month and 21 percent had incomes of more than US$36 per month, half of the informal housing dwellers earned less than US$20 per month, and only 2.5 percent earned more than US$36 per month.

Clearly, there are differences between the two groups studied, some of which can be ascribed to occupational differences. The master plan for Chandigarh, while providing some housing for the lowest class of government and semi-government employees, appears to have overlooked the poor employed outside the public sector. This will become more evident as next we examine their housing conditions.

The housing environment

Below, we shall discuss dwelling types in public and informal housing. In addition, we will examine various facilities, services, and utilities provided for them.

Public housing. Public housing consists of so-called 13-J type and economy houses. These are two-room houses with a plot size of 62.5 square yards to 125 square yards. They are arranged in long rows (see photograph 15.1). A 13-J house consists of two rooms of 80 to 90 square feet with kitchen and veranda. Latrine and bathroom are at the other end of the plot. The economy house also consists of two rooms, but its size varies from 60 to 80 square feet. There is no kitchen; a veranda is used instead. A latrine and bathroom are located at the other end and are open to the sky.

The 13-J houses have a plinth area of 225 to 440 square feet and are inhabited by the poor, usually large families. In the present sample, the average household size is 6.2 persons, which means 3.1 persons per room, or 20 to 25 square feet per person. Because of lack of space, some of their activities spill over into the street. They also use open spaces for activities such as sleeping, parking, etc.

In Punjab University Chandigarh, employees are entitled to type "A" houses which are similar to type 13-J. Often, the university has allotted one house to two families in two-story flats. In cases where these houses are occupied by washermen, conditions are worse still, because they have to keep one room for storing and ironing clothes; therefore, they actually can use only one room. No doubt these people enjoy some conveniences, but they face many difficulties because space for their families is inadequate, the rooms are very small, they can maintain no privacy in these small units, there is no kitchen, the boundary walls of the rear court are too low to maintain privacy and they also give rise to a feeling of insecurity, and bathrooms and latrines cannot be used during inclement weather because they are open to the sky.

Informal housing. With the enforcement of the Punjab Capital (Development and Regulation) Building Rules in 1952,[3] all those persons who were living in katcha (mud) or pucca (brick) huts within the city were shifted to the fringe sectors of Chandigarh. Some of them got plots of 15 feet by 20 feet from the administration for a small monthly rent, but a majority (there are only 1,648 authorized huts out of a total of 7,004) built their katcha huts without permission at the newly authorized sites and in sectors that were lying vacant.

The informal housing has two types of huts, i.e., pucca[4] and katcha.[5] Most of the huts at authorized sites are pucca, but at the unauthorized and squatted places all the huts are katcha. These are arranged in rows and are constructed wall-to-wall. Usually two rooms are adjoined to each other, having their backwalls in common and facing in opposite directions. A majority are single-room huts, 10 by 6 feet to 12 by 8 feet. If they have more than one room, the size of the rooms is smaller, from 8 by 6 feet to 10 by 8 feet. Pucca huts are made of kiln-baked bricks; their roofs are flat and are supported by horizontal pieces of wood covered with earth. The pucca huts have small ventilators on the side walls and also have bigger doors than the katcha huts. The height of the roof from the ground is usually 8 to 10 feet. The walls of the katcha huts are made of sun-dried bricks. The roofs are sloping, with maximum and minimum heights of 6 and 4 feet, respectively, and thatched with grass and other waste material. They have one door. The height of the thatched roof from the center of the hut varies between 5 and 8 feet. In the middle it is supported by a wooden log, usually from a eucalyptus tree. All the houses have mud floors.

The single-room hut is the house of poor slum dwellers. It lacks all of the following facilities: kitchen, bath, latrine, and storage facilities.

It nevertheless provides for all the functions except latrine. Sometimes an open kitchen is made by extending the hut by a low wall into the street. A corner of the hut is used as a bathing place by females.

In our study, we found cattle-shed-type rooms, constructed by a public agency, about 15 by 15 feet in size. These rooms are shared by about twenty-five persons. In addition, some households even prepare their meals in these rooms, which are roofed with cement sheets that become hot in summer and cold in winter and that leak during the rainy season. Therefore, throughout the year, these people have to face problems in an overcrowded environment where the person-per-room ratio is 25 to 1.

As noted above, the single room hut is multifunctional, i.e., it is used as a drawing room, bedroom, guest room, kitchen, storage place, and bathroom. Sometimes when it is used as a kitchen the whole hut is filled with smoke because there is no outlet. This has an adverse impact on the residents' eyesight, and it further worsens the living conditions within the hut. Also, in many cases, cattle and human beings live under the same roof.

Facilities and services

Until 1970, there were no schools in the slums of Chandigarh. Subsequently, through the efforts and contributions of some of the residents and money made available through the city administration, a few primary schools were established. The schools were housed in temporary structures such as cattle sheds, with roofs made of cement (corrugated asbestos) sheets. The space provided is inadequate, and extreme overcrowding has resulted. Also, during rainy days schools remain closed because of inadequate accommodation. Medical facilities are equally inadequate; one dispensary serves the entire industrial slum. In the absence of sufficient public health facilities, medical quacks ply their trade at will, to the detriment of the health of the poor, whose credulity they exploit. There is no park or playground in the slum or near it. Areas surrounding the slum are open, but they have foul smells from garbage and stagnating water. All the slums are on the periphery of the city and are on no local bus route. Access to the city is thus poor. Furthermore, not a single post office exists in the slums, and there is no fire station around. In some slums, fire breaks out quite often. As a result, huts, clothes, beddings, etc., burn up every year.

Utilities

As far as public utilities are concerned, some are provided. In three authorized slums, there is partial provision for electricity and water. In one slum there are only eleven public taps at three places for 1,200 households. Similarly, only half of the huts have electricity. There is no sewage system in the slums, but in a few slums there are dry public latrines. In one slum, there are forty public latrines in one corner, but these have no doors and are not cleaned regularly.

The width of the streets in slums varies from 8 to 20 feet, they are unpaved and uneven, and they have open drainage, which functions poorly. Water stagnates at various places, especially during the rainy season (photograph 15.3). It is difficult to pass through these streets, as they are full of mud and water. In some cases, water also enters into the dwelling units, which may get flooded during the rainy season.

Some people own small dairies which are part and parcel of their houses. They usually tie their cattle in the street, and cattle dung is collected in the street or open area near the house. This creates a foul smell, especially during the rainy season, and it pollutes the surrounding environment.

From this description, it becomes clear that the areas populated by the poor lack basic services and facilities. Despite their location in a newly planned city, their housing environment is not demonstrably superior to that found in older, traditional cities. Due to the strict enforcement of the Punjab Capital Building Rules of 1952, the fate of the poor is more precarious and tenuous than in the older unplanned cities. It is a direct contradiction of the vision projected by Chandigarh's planner of "a city offering all amenities to the poorest of the poor of its citizens to enable them to lead a dignified life." (Sarin, 1975: 29).

Summary and conclusions

In this chapter we have attempted to draw a picture of the environment of the poor in Chandigarh. Most of these poor come from scheduled castes. Respondents in public housing are permanent employees, come from the neighboring states, and have large families. They get subsidized housing and other service benefits because of their employment. They are considered privileged among the poor. On the other hand, most of the slum dwellers who live in informal housing do not have permanent employment and subsidized houses. They come to the city from distant places. Their residential areas are situated on the periphery and are not considered a part of the city. Their slums have sprung up on the periphery because the planners could not accommodate them in the master plan. They live in one-room huts which lack all the facilities and utilities of a minimum house. These temporary houses cannot protect them from fire and inclement weather. As any typical slum of an old city, the slums of Chandigarh also have practically no community facilities, services, and utilities; if present at all, these are inadequate to fulfill the needs of the residents. Therefore, the environment of the poor, leaving aside the subsidized government workers in the peon villages of a new and planned city, is in no way better than the slums of an old unplanned city. On the contrary, these slum dwellers are always afraid of the estate officer's office, which often sends bulldozers to evict them in order to maintain the beauty and ordered development of the city. This shows that planners have failed to plan for a growing number of people, even though the chief planner promised to provide all the amenities of life to the poorest of the poor. The lesson to be drawn from the Chandigarh experience is that any plan should make provision for the poor who, after all, constitute the vast majority of the population in Third World cities.

16 The Squatters' Perspective of
Housing: An Egyptian View

Sawson El-Messiri

Abstract. The growth of squatter settlements in and around Cairo,
Egypt, after World War II is described and analyzed. Under the socialist policies of the 1960s, much public housing for the poor was constructed in walk-up apartments in large projects but, by the mid-
seventies, less housing was built for the poor. Now squatter settlements make up most of the poor's housing. Three types of Cairo
squatter communities are described: the east central cemetery area;
the hillsides, especially the Mokatam Hills; and those on goverment
land in the desert near the Helwan industrial complex. The squatters
near Helwan are industrial workers and have a strong social structure.
Here the underlying systemic process in "spontaneous settlements"
consists of collective action led by "pioneers," the claiming and defend-
ing of plots, and a social organization accompanying the physical
growth of the settlements. The case study of Ahmed, a squatter in
Izbet Zein in the Helwan area and head of a household of eleven,
illustrates these processes, as well as the government's Home Improvement Loan Program (1981). It is concluded that the squatter
settlements of Cairo are not transitional settlements for rural migrants.

Egyptian squatter settlements are a recent but rapidly growing phenomenon. Squatter communities are the ultimate form of illegal settlement and as such are completely ignored in official records. Some
officials even deny their existence. How and why did these settlements evolve, and what are the characteristics of the settlements that
exist in Cairo? The answers are to be found in the urbanization process as it occurred in Cairo and in the socioeconomic context in which
it took place.

It was not until after World War I that land shortage became an important factor in pushing peasants from the land and toward the cities. This movement, which began in the late thirties, gained momentum in subsequent decades. Between 1937 and 1947, Cairo gained three-fourths of a million new inhabitants. This growth was exacerbated by a rise in the birthrate, with three-fifths of the post-1947 population growth attributable to the excess of births over deaths. Between 1950 and 1980, the population of Cairo grew from 2.4 to 8.4 million.

The first squatter settlements sprang up after World War II in the cemetery area on the eastern fringe of the city. Between 1947 and 1960, the older quarters of the city had somehow to accommodate an additional 130,000 people. This increase was partially accounted for by the policy of the revolutionary regime, but a large number of these migrants could find accommodation only in the cemetery area.

The sixties witnessed the espousal of socialist policies and concern for equity in income distribution. Great strides were made in public sector housing during this period. In the period 1962–63, 21,000 units of public housing were built. The average for the decade 1960–70 was 11,000 public housing units per year, a record which has not been equalled since. The average number of housing units built annually, by both the private and the public sectors, declined from 52,000 during the period 1952–60 to 31,000 during 1961–72.[1]

The socialist regime's approach toward solving the housing problem in the sixties was to construct traditional walk-up apartments in large estates which are rented to low- and middle-income families. While these schemes have benefited thousands, there was not enough money available to provide shelter for all those in need. This shortage of housing units was further compounded by rural-to-urban migration and the 1967 war with Israel, and it led to an increase in squatter settlement in the cemetery area. It was estimated that, by 1973, the squatter population in the city's labyrinthine cemeteries had reached one million.[2]

The second wave of squatter settlement started in the sixties and spread south fifteen miles from Basatin to Helwan, an industrial suburb of Cairo about thirty kilometers from the central city. The location of the industrial complex in Helwan brought a new influx of middle- and low-income industrial workers.

During the first half of the sixties, more than 50 percent of the new industrial investment was concentrated in Cairo and Alexandria.

Helwan has now become the major industrial area of Cairo. Its population tripled from 177,000 in 1960 to 483,000 in 1976. As factories were built, work was started on housing for the workers, but the rate of housing construction lagged far behind the industrial expansion that had occurred. Despite the 50,000 public housing units that were built, fewer than 50 percent of the new workers were housed in these units. Although the large complexes of walk-up units had serious shortcomings and did not meet all the shelter needs of low-income groups, they did contain to some extent the problem of housing for the poor.

By the mid-seventies, socialist slogans had faded and with them many of the major projects that were designed to meet the basic needs of the poor. The amount of public housing being constructed declined at the same time that the prevailing ideology shifted the responsibility for providing for one's shelter needs from the state to the individual. Consequently, informal housing, which is also referred to as illegal, uncontrolled, unplanned, and unauthorized housing, was increasing. The bulk of housing currently being supplied in Egypt is informal housing. Of units built between 1970 and 1981, 84 percent in Cairo were estimated to have been informal.[3]

Statistics differ concerning the quantity and quality of informal housing, but it is widely believed that informal housing accounts for a significant if not the dominant share of housing at the present time. Squatter settlements are but one type of informal housing. Informal housing can also be legal or semi-legal in character. In the absence of official records, we cannot estimate the volume of squatting in Egypt with any accuracy. The general perception is that it is increasing rapidly.

The present situation is characterized by rapid population growth, a critical housing shortage, the emergence of a highly inegalitarian socioeconomic structure, the result of the return to free-market policies, the overprovision of urban land for higher-income groups, and the distortion of the housing market by the provision of heavily subsidized public housing for the few while help is denied to many. These factors lead inevitably to the exclusion of families at the bottom of the income pyramid from the housing market, overcrowding of existing accommodations, and the extension of the practice of squatting.

Types of squatter communities

Squatting in Cairo takes many forms, ranging from the construction and erection of makeshift roofs on existing buildings to the construction of two- and three-story walk-up structures on government-owned land. Individual squatters are found in numerous areas in Cairo, but squatter communities are limited to areas where they can occupy government land or very cheap land, such as cemeteries and outlying areas without utilities. This restricts the land options to three main areas: the cemetery area in east central Cairo; hillsides, especially the slopes of the Mokatam Hills; and the government land in the desert, mainly to the south of the city. These three areas have become centers for numerous squatter communities, which began with a relatively few individuals and have expanded over time. Their populations now range from 10,000 to more than 50,000.

These three main areas of squatter settlement have attracted quite different types of settlers. In the Mokatam Hills close to the old business center of Cairo, the majority of the squatters are employed in the numerous economic activities of the old quarter, i.e., street vending, shoe repair, and "cottage industries." Settlements here are not only residential, but are used for commercial purposes and small industries by both the settlers themselves and some of the residents of the old city.

A different type of settlement is to be found in the cemetery area on the eastern fringe of the city, which provides a more hospitable environment than the nearby hills while sharing the advantage of being close to the old city. This is why squatting in the cemetery area began in the late forties, while settlement did not begin in the hills until the sixties. Residents in this area are a mixture of low-income occupational groups who work in the nearby central areas of the city. Over a period of time, a series of subcommunities have developed in the area, some employed in tasks specifically related to the cemetery and funerary practices, and they may have come to regard the area as a normal residential neighborhood. It is clear that there has been steady and rapid growth in settlement in this area, but lack of adequate study makes it impossible to state whether the new settlers are primarily recent rural migrants or former residents of urban quarters. In the absence of statistical evidence, however, it seems reasonable to assume that the majority of settlers were formerly residents in nearby areas, though they may originally have come in from the countryside. The pattern of squatting, to which we shall refer later, makes it almost inevitable that squatters should formerly have been resident near the site of the settlement.

The third type of squatter community is in the desert areas around the industrial complexes that have been established since the forties. Rapid industrialization and urbanization in the Helwan area and the accompanying demand for housing for low-income groups created the pressures that led to squatter settlement, and, from the sixties on, the small isolated groups of squatters that had existed since the forties expanded rapidly and began to develop into identifiable communities with a solid social structure and close links with the urban center. The majority of working residents in these communities (socioeconomic surveys of these areas indicate from 50 percent to 70 percent)[4] are industrial workers in Helwan factories. Some come from an urban background and others from a rural background though they are not necessarily recent migrants. The rural migrants among the settlers have retained some features of the rural life-style, but the overall demography and economics of the communities exhibit mostly urban features. The communities depend economically upon work in the industrial complexes, and the settlers, as industrial laborers, enjoy the workers' benefits which were introduced by the government of the fifties and sixties. They are also more conscious of their rights than many other social groups and they try to maximize the advantages available to them in the urban context. The social structure in the communities in this third area is stronger than that in the other two.

Squatting on government land takes place in most cases by collective action, since the difficulties encountered in these situations require group support and protection. The group is usually formed by a number of persons who are either neighbors, friends who work together in the same factory, relatives, or rural migrants who migrated from the same village or province. In choosing a site, certain criteria are taken into account, these being proximity to the places of employment of the working members of the group and proximity to public services and utilities, such as exist in government housing areas for the industrial sites which abound in outlying districts. Since the areas potentially available to squatters are not included in any main services systems, competition for land becomes fiercer with closer proximity of the site to public utilities. Residential and industrial development toward the Helwan area has thus given rise to pockets of squatter housing in the desert areas close to the government housing projects and factories, facilities which the squatters need. The better the location the squatters move into, the more forcefully the authorities attempt to evict them.

The first squatters to move in are pioneers, acting almost as scouts for those who are to follow. They use various tactics in their confrontation with the authorities, keeping their children with them to convince the police that they are homeless and generally refusing to move. They accept the fact that they face a long struggle, and they may continue for months to reerect the shelters demolished by the authorities until they become an embarrassment. The authorities, for their part, are reluctant to use much force, unless the land is urgently needed for some project, and they prefer other means of persuasion.

Another tactic sometimes employed in the early stages of squatting is bribing those responsible for the eviction of the settlers. In this way they buy time, and the longer a squatter stays on a site the more difficult it is to remove him and the more secure he becomes. Concentrated attempts at eviction therefore normally take place only in the early phase, which may last for a year. This is the least secure period for the squatters and it is the time when the collective support of the group is important in order to protect the settlement both from the authorities and from other potential squatters who seek to make inroads.

The squatters usually come from nearby areas, where they may be tenants or living temporarily with friends or relatives, though in some cases they are literally without shelter because of some crisis such as the collapse of their home or eviction by their landlord. The squatters build temporary shelters or simply fence off a piece of the land where they settle. If they are evicted they can return to their original homes for a while before embarking on a new attempt.

When the authorities become weary of attempts to evict them, the settlers begin to wall off their plots of land, using large rocks. This phase also requires collective action, not only to provide mutual support against the authorities, but also to establish squatting rights recognized by the group of squatters and individuals involved. During this phase, when plots are being divided up, assigned, and walled off, the squatters need to be close to the site to ascertain their rights and resolve any conflicts over land. This stage may take several months, depending on the extent to which the squatters are still being harrassed by the police, the speed with which agreement between the squatter settlers is reached concerning the assignment of land, and economic ability of the squatters to reinforce their claim by erecting some form of shelter. The longer the first-built shelters remain intact, the more shelters are erected in the fenced-off plots, the more secure the settlers become, and the more the settlers invest in the improvement of their houses.

With the physical growth of the community, social organization develops. The settlers must rely on their own resources to meet their basic needs. In communities where a homogenous group of pioneer settlers exists with a strong social structure, such as the bedouin of the southern desert who form the community of Arab Kafr El-Elw, we find that the process of squatting is regulated. The consensus of all the pioneer settlers governs the use of vacant land within their own community. Thus, although squatter communities are identified as spontaneous, this spontaneity has an underlying systematic process that conforms to certain procedural strategies employed by squatters.

Case study of a squatter[5]

Ahmed is one squatter in a squatter community in the Helwan area, Izbet Zein, which is a small community of about 12,000 inhabitants and one of the closest squatter settlements to the urban center of Helwan. The fact that it was formerly swampland prevented it from being occupied by squatters until the sixties. This settlement is one of the six squatter communities in Helwan selected for an upgrading project, and in 1981 a home improvement loan program was also implemented there.[6]

Ahmed is the head of a household of eleven: his wife, a married son with his wife and two children, four other sons, and a daughter. As most of the residents of Izbet Zein, Ahmed originally came to Cairo from an overpopulated rural village to seek work. He was not a farmer by training, since he held a diploma and had found a temporary job as government employee in a town in upper Egypt. When he was dismissed, however, he was forced to work on the land for his wife's family, distant relatives of his own. His father, the Sheik of a Muslim religious association, had several relatives who worked in Cairo, and they persuaded him to join them. One was employed in a munitions factory in Helwan and through his contacts got him a job there.

When Ahmed moved to Cairo in 1950, he and his wife already had two children. His new living conditions were worse than those in the village, for they now lived in a rented room in a squatter community with no community services and minimal furniture (a bed and a sofa), whereas in the village they had a home with several rooms and more furniture. His wages as a factory laborer were also very low. Nevertheless, he welcomed the opportunity of the job in Helwan. His work on the land had been simply to help his father-in-law, so his own income had been very low, and he had always cherished the hope that he might one day migrate to the capital and work there.

The cost of living in the city was much higher than in the country. His costs included rent as well as food items such as grain, milk, and vegetables which in the past had been supplied by the family farm. More children were born, and Ahmed found himself with a family of seven persons to support. In order to provide for their basic needs he relied heavily on his wife. She learned from one of their neighbors how to make traditional braided headscarves and was able to earn about LE8 per month, while her husband's salary amounted to only LE5. (One LE = US$1.42 according to the 1983 exchange rate.)

Transfer to Izbet Zein

As a villager, Ahmed had the aspiration of all village people to own his own house, but with his limited economic resources it seemed he would never be able to realize his ambition. This was why he was interested to hear of the plan of some of his friends to move and settle in Izbet Zein. Its proximity to the industrial area made it attractive to the factory laborers who lived in outlying hamlets (Ahmed used to walk long distances to work to save the cost of transportation), and if they could acquire a plot of land and build a home it would save the cost of the rent they could scarcely afford. It was also conveniently close to the marketing and administrative center of Helwan. Ahmed and other Helwan factory workers planned to squat this area, and they began to squat on the land in 1964. They claim that the first settlement was established in only fifteen days. Families from all the neighboring areas began to move in.

As Ahmed and others tell the story, it seems that the squatters moved to Izbet Zein in groups, laid claim to plots of land, built walls of debris around them, and encouraged their relatives and friends to do the same. The original settlers claim that the problems they faced in taking possession of the land went on for several months. The police attacked the families constantly and tried to destroy the huts and shelters they built for themselves from September to December of 1964, but they failed to evacuate the land. On the contrary, the fact that the squatters had to struggle so hard to take the land generated strong feelings toward it and a sense that their fight earned them the right of ownership.

Ahmed had to defend the plot of land he had walled around on two fronts. He had to prevent its being taken over by other squatters and also to resist the numerous attempts of the police to remove the shelter. He describes the first days after moving to Izbet Zein as follows: "People came from everywhere and it was like outright war. They would attack each other with hoes (fas), each one saying, 'This is my land!' as if he had inherited from his father, and I would be standing among them with my hoe, shouting, 'Get back, this is my land!'" But after awhile each man settled on a plot of land recognized as his by the others. Then the fight with the authorities began.

Ahmed's wife relates that "The police used to come every day with a van. Wherever they found a hut they would call the bulldozer and knock it down. But the next morning they would come and find it rebuilt just as it was with people living in it!" The police were acting on the orders of the factory management because they wanted the land for industrial development, but in carrying out their orders the police were careful not to harm the families and children.

Ahmed's wife recalls: "When they came to knock down the houses, the policeman would say, 'What are you doing here?' and I would answer, 'I'm building a home for the children,' and he would leave me and walk away. Whenever any passer by asked 'What are you doing here? This is government land.' I would answer, 'We're the children of the government and we can't afford to pay rent.' After many attempts to knock down the houses, they realized that it was useless. The people were united against the authorities because they could no longer cope with the housing shortage. After four months the police stopped chasing us and destroying our houses."

Building the first home

After Ahmed's settlement on his plot of land was accepted by both the other squatters and the authorities, he and his family began to build their house. Being a laborer with limited economic resources, he adopted many strategies to make it possible to construct a reasonable shelter. His wife and children would come to Izbet Zein every day. He would go to work in the factory, while she would gather broken bricks and rocks from nearby to build a room for the family. He would help her when he returned from work. While the room was being built his wife would bring the children to the site.

She took twenty days to build the room, and during that period whenever a police officer passed by and threatened to demolish it she would answer him, "Knock it down on top of the children! I'm raising them for you. I raise them and you take them off to the army. That means we are the children of the government. Would you throw your own son out of your house?"

Living conditions were harder at Izbet Zein than in their former lodging. Ahmed's family, made up of seven people, ate, cooked, bathed, and slept in one room with no main services. The roof was of straw and sugar cane leaves. His wife would go every day to bring water from the public garden in Helwan. The sanitary facility was simply a barrel over a hole in the ground.

Strategies for home improvement

After six years, the family demolished the room and began to build in its place two rooms with brick and cement. Ahmed recalls: "I used to cut down the money spent on food piastre by piastre and gave up smoking to save a few piastres more so I could build." In spite of this, he was forced to sell his house in the village for LE100 to buy building materials. He and his wife, with the help of a neighbor who was a builder, built two rooms using reinforced concrete supports, and then built two more rooms beside them without reinforced concrete. They made the roof of reeds. In 1972 he joined a gamciya (savings club) and saved LE200, with which he built two more rooms on top of the first two.[7]

The family well remembers the difficulties they faced in getting together these small sums of money and how they lived in constant debt. Ahmed's wife recalls: "When my husband was paid at the end of the month we would settle our debts and live on what was left. I used to economize on food. Instead of buying meat four times a month I would buy it once and use the money we saved to buy three cart loads of bricks to build with." Apart from making economies in daily household expenditure, Ahmed's family set aside to provide for their children's marriages, as well as for building and improvement to the house. All members of the family are involved in different gamciyas.

The sacrifices made by the whole family in order that they should have a proper home make them feel that they have earned the right of ownership of the land. They do not see themselves as squatters but as owners ready to fight for their property. As Ahmed puts it: "If anyone dares to come near the house to demolish it, I'll bury him beside the door! I've built it with my blood. My children wore old clothes on feast days and went to bed hungry for the sake of this house. We have been through a lot."

Apart from their own self-reliance and perseverance, Ahmed's family were helped to build their home by the fact that the price of building materials in the early seventies put the project within their reach. After the initial erection and vertical expansion of the house to meet their growing shelter needs, Ahmed was unable to make further improvements. Half of the roof is still of reeds, the walls are bare brick, and the floor is earth, which leads to considerable suffering and discomfort in the winter. The family income is of course much higher than it was in the sixties, but Ahmed's commitments and expenses have also increased, as has the cost of living.

Source of income

Ahmed's household includes the eldest son and his wife and two children, but this son makes no contribution to the expenses of the rest of the household. Ahmed says, "I need help from my eldest son because I have small children, but since the day he began to work he has never had enough to give me any, even before he got married. The only help we have is God! My son has two children and his wife. They are quite enough for him to support!"

The second son is twenty-one years old and unmarried. He works as a lather in the munitions factory and earns LE60 per month, which he gives to his father. The son's income constitutes the bulk of the total family income, since the father is now a pensioner receiving only LE28 per month from the pension fund accumulated after his years as a worker in the munitions factory. His wife is in bad health (she has borne twelve children, of whom four have died, and is now once again pregnant) and she can no longer work to supplement her husband's income as in the past. The oldest daughter is now married and has left home.

The other members of the family do not work because they are still at school. The second daughter has the preparatory school certificate and is about to begin a course for the diploma of commerce. The next child is a son who has failed his primary school certificate examination and left school. His father is looking for a job or trade for him. The other two sons are six and four years old and too young to go to school.

Although the family comes originally from upper Egypt, the fact that Ahmed lives in Cairo and has received secondary education (his wife also reads and writes well) has led to his views being different from those of the traditional upper Egyptian. He is, for example, enthusiastic about the education of girls as much as of boys, and he is prepared to help any of his children, whether boys or girls, as long as they work hard at school, to continue their education as far as possible. When a suitor came to propose marriage to his daughter Ragaa, she refused because she wants to study for the diploma of commerce and become a teacher, and her father supported her. He is even prepared to economize on food in order to help her attain her ambition. On the other hand, after his son Muhammed failed his primary school certificate examinations he set about looking for a job for him.

In order to supply his family's daily needs, Ahmed works hard to supplement his income. He does casual jobs such as that of watchman. He also rents part of his home for LE15 per month. As a result, the average monthly income of the family is LE100, with extras amounting to an average of a further LE10.

Expenditures

When we examine the family budget, we find that there is no surplus from this income, and that there are on the contrary certain items for which no provision is made. These are paid for with the help of gamciya. Food and drink for Ahmed's family of seven persons consumes about 70 percent (LE71) of the family's monthly income, as table 16.1 shows. We also find that a total of LE6.40 is spent on fuel and electricity and LE3.60 per month on the children's pocket money and soap. There are also items of expenditure calculated on an annual basis as shown in table 16.2.

Since Ahmed's income barely covers his basic needs, he is unable to make basic improvements on his home, such as on roofing or decoration. He has no surplus capital, and at the same time labor costs and the price of building materials have risen steeply. It has also become impossible to form a savings club to accumulate the money needed for these improvements as Ahmed did when he was first building the house because: (*a*) a gamciya is based on a group of friends and neighbors whose standard of living is very similar. In Ahmed's area, there would not be a group with sufficient surplus income to pay regular contributions large enough to realize the amount needed; and (*b*) the amounts usually collected in these sav-

Table 16.1 Monthly expenditures of Egyptian squatter family.

Item	LE
Food	71.00
Fuel	3.40
Electricity[1]	3.00
Soap	.60
Children's pocket money	3.00
Total	81.00

1 This item is rather high, but Ahmed explains it by the fact that he has a TV, a fan, and a recorder; in addition it includes the married son's share as well as that of the tenant. (1 LE = US $1.42 according to the 1983 exchange rate.)

ings clubs are very limited, and they rarely exceed LE200 or LE300 in these communities.

The loan scheme

The improvement Ahmed has in mind could cost about LE3000, so it is inconceivable that he could save enough through a gamciya. The project remained an unattainable dream until the establishment of the loan program in Izbet Zein. Ahmed was one of the first to apply for a loan to pay for these urgent improvements, or, to be more precise, it was his wife who applied and then informed her husband. After she found out the regulations for repaying the debt, she persuaded her husband that, by living more economically and renting part of the house, they would be able to pay the installments. After discussion with his wife, Ahmed accepted the idea of applying for a loan.

After he agreed to apply for a loan Ahmed found out that his age (about sixty years) would be an obstacle to obtaining a loan, and he was advised that his married son should apply for another loan so that they would be granted enough money to make the necessary improvements. The son was granted LE1,200, which was enough to lay a concrete roof, face the bricks, have electricity installed in two rooms, and buy tiles for the floor. The money was not sufficient to pay for the cement and labor needed to lay the floor, and the tiles have been set aside temporarily.

Ahmed was awarded LE290 and was unsure what to do. He had hoped to build two rooms and a hall on top of his son's rooms with the reinforced concrete roof, but his loan was inadequate even though all the members of the family would have cooperated in the construction. As Ahmed says, "I'm against paying money to workmen for things we can do ourselves." Therefore, he hired workmen only for laying the roof (two carpenters and two iron-rod workers experienced in reinforced concrete) because this requires special skills. He provided food for the workmen and encouraged them to work more hours and finish quickly. The work was over in about a month, but he remained unsatisfied because only part of his dream had been realized. His son now lived in a room with a proper roof, and he himself had moved to an upper room "where they could feel the air and sun." He had lived all his life at ground level where it was damp, and he believes this is why he now suffers from rheumatism. Nevertheless, the small loan was only sufficient to build the walls of the upper floor, and again he was forced to make do with a roof of reeds.

Once again he had to submit to his original strategy of incremental improvement. It has taken Ahmed about thirty years to build a proper house, and now, even with the provision of a loan, he will have to improve it over a period of time.

Conclusion

On considering the various types of squatter communities in Cairo, we find that they were begun by a strong nucleus made up of a

Table **16.2** Annual expenditures of Egyptian squatter family.[1]

Item	LE
Clothing	62.00
Shoes	26.00
School expenses	39.00
School uniform for daughter	24.00
Social obligations	12.00
Medical Treatment	36.00
Household (recorder)	50.00
Renovations (installing a toilet)	85.00
Annual Total	334.00
Monthly Total	27.80
Average monthly expenditure (LE81 + LE27.80) = LE108.80	

1 1 LE = US $1.42 according to the 1983 exchange rate.

homogeneous group of individuals, who might be of either urban or rural origin. These groups became squatters either because this was the only means available to them of finding shelter or because acquiring their own home by squatting was a more attractive way of meeting their housing needs than remaining as tenants, often in accommodations built by other squatters.

Squatter communities in Cairo are not isolated from the life of the city; they have strong ties with urban systems such as education, health, economics, and politics. Nor are squatter communities transitional in the sense that they are part of the process of entry and assimilation into the urban life, as Janet Abu-Lughod's study of Cairo suggests.[8] She indicates that squatter communities have arisen to provide a first home for rural migrants, but this assumption is not necessarily true of all the settlements. Squatter communities are not, moreover, a transitional stage in a process of social and geographical mobility, as implied by Turner's typology of South America. This assumes a degree of social mobility of the lower classes from the city-center slum "bridgeheads" to land acquired by force. The resulting squatter communities are identified by Turner as "slums of hope" and a step along the way by which middle-class status seekers become owner-occupiers. The central areas of the city of Cairo from which the squatters emerge to lay claim to nearby land are not necessarily slums, although they are overcrowded and characterized by a deterioration in the standard of amenities. These areas cannot accommodate the new generation of the low-income groups who are in need of housing. The limited amount of land accessible to low-income groups, coupled with an increasing demand for housing, places considerable constraints on social mobility, and squatter communities are indeed characterized by the presence of a variety of occupational groups with a wide range of incomes. We cannot base a typology of Cairene squatter communities on a theory of social mobility.

In conclusion, we may briefly say that squatter communities in Cairo have not arisen as a stepping-stone into the city or as a rung on the social ladder. They are rather the product of an acute housing shortage, brought about by the disparity between supply and demand in the low-cost housing market.

IV | The Housing Environment:
Societal Organization and
Spatial Structure

Introduction
William Michelson

The chapters which form this section illustrate how complex a subject housing is recognized to be. Not one of the papers is concerned with the size, features, or design of housing. No one would seriously dispute that such traditional preoccupations of architects and builders are as relevant as ever to housing; yet public concern over how people live takes in a much wider set of considerations.

Den Draak's chapter, for example, traces locationally relevant consequences of broad policies implemented during the past twenty years in The Netherlands. First, the situation was ripe for a decentralization of the population away from the centers of existing large cities and into more remote, less settled areas, a movement not unknown at the same time in other European and American contexts. The consequences for both existing cities and for individual residents were duly noted, and certain incentives to reestablishing the growth of housing units in the central cities led to several forms of so-called gentrification, with minor but documented redirection of populations to these central cities. As part of his emphasis on high level response to the qualitative situations of different settlement patterns, Den Draak urges an urban social impact analysis. This is in recognition that both production and use of housing depends on considerations at higher levels of scale than individual market decisions for vital aspects of livability. Government actions can be instrumental in influencing the nature of housing and land use, even without government participation as an active developer, for example. Similarly, many aspects of livability reflect the situation of housing units with respect to other land uses, well beyond intrinsic components of dwelling units.

Grunfeld develops much the same theme in an examination of various aspects of segregation. He also uses materials from The Netherlands. The Dutch experience in this regard again is representative of developments in other nations. While no exact formula on the optimal degree and mode of integration or segregation of population subgroups and land uses is found or proposed, the importance of sensitive consideration of these patterns as they bear on both social and civic participation and on the efficiency of everyday functioning is stressed.

The emphasis of papers in this section on how planning in governmental and quasi-governmental levels of society can influence the qualitative aspects of housing and its provision continues in Pugh's description of Norwegian practices. He outlines how governmentally directed lending practices by banks have led in the direction of equity in the distribution of new housing units throughout the Norwegian population. He goes on to discuss other policies which affect the cost of housing and, in consequence, the feasibility of people buying or renting the housing they need or want. Such policies include governmental land banking and housing allowances. His chapter concludes with a look at the resultant place of housing in the perspective of people's total assets.

The implicit message of the first three chapters is made more explicit in Ylonen's more macroscopic analysis of housing in Finland. Explaining the national emphasis on decentralization of both population and authority within Finland, Ylonen shows how housing follows the societal trend. It is not treated as a problem area subject to unitary national policy, but reflects local wishes and decisions, which in turn are a function of desires to strengthen rural areas. Thus, while outsiders are familiar with notable housing experiments in the Helsinki region, very much more emphasis with Finland has been on modest, low-density housing on the outskirts of developing cities in relatively rural regions.

Thus, the chapters in this section illustrate not only the interpenetration of housing with broad and pervasive aspects of the societal structure but also the potentially strong influence of government. Simple arguments are often made about how governments should or should not become participants in the processes by which housing units are located, built, and allocated. Such arguments seem to imply that when governments are involved they have an influence which supersedes that of the social structure at large. When governments are not involved, the private sector is assumed by its advocates to provide for the public what is required as a consequence of demand and market mechanisms, under the premise that all aspects of demand are reflected by what people have to spend.

Reality is somewhere between these two simple arguments. Government activity takes place on a stage which includes varieties of actors, interests, and practices. These include stratification mechanisms, real estate and construction enterprises, demographic considerations, and, not least, practical aspects of how housing and location make everyday life easier or harder. Government is hence one force among many.

What governments typically offer to the mosaic of factors concerning housing are regulations and incentives geared to criteria less likely to be served by the market mechanism alone. National settlement patterns, geared to rational development of remaining land, conservation of energy, and rational distribution of the population, for example, are not likely to form a major focus among interests concerned primarily with land speculation or easy packaging of dwelling units. By virtue of promoting national or universal goals, often of a qualitative nature, governments may interject additional interests in the picture, but they do not thereby eliminate strong and pervasive forces which pertain to housing and its degree of success or failure on other grounds. For example, government practices which require high minimum standards for housing and which make new housing available to nearly all segments of the population do not necessarily thereby eliminate cultural and social factors which bring about segregation by socioeconomic status or country of origin.

On the other hand, because governments so seldom produce the panacea expected hardly appears a justification for eliminating their influence on behalf of selected considerations and population sectors. The needs of poor or unusual segments of the population are seldom catered to by profitmaking enterprises. They are relegated to the public sector after all, expected to make an entrance into the arena only to provide noncompetitively for society's low bidders.

The ultimate question is whether government is conceived as a positive moral force or a low-quality fallback institution. What the chapters in this section indicate is that governments can take proactive roles which serve noble purposes in the housing market and which do not find their counterpart in the private sector. The papers suggest also roles not as yet satisfactorily undertaken in such areas as segregation and discrimination, and they make clear as well the limitations of government action in view of the complexity and durability of social structure.

17	Segregation Trends in The Netherlands
	Frans Grunfeld

Abstract. This chapter is concerned with the quality of life in modern and post-industrial society. Relying on census data, results from his own research, and findings from other studies, Grunfeld identifies dimensions of segregation in the Netherlands and discusses implications of prevailing trends. The conclusion raises questions regarding ways in which planners can counteract or mitigate negative ramifications of ongoing developments.

Most available literature deals with spatial segregation exclusively in relation to ethnic or other cultural minorities. In The Netherlands the media usually focus on the substandard dwellings and on poverty and the often anomic situation of segregated minorities—mostly laborers from Mediterranean countries, immigrants from Surinam, and Molukkan people. It is clear that poor housing conditions, poverty in general, and cultural alienation are serious social problems, but is there such a clear relation between these phenomena and spatial segregation? If this relation exists, is it a causal one? Does it apply to ethnic minorities only? And, finally, is segregation a clear-cut concept, can we easily measure it?

If it is true that spatial segregation is the cause of serious social problems, then we have to focus on the question of whether we can measure it easily. In this chapter—written with the present-day situation in The Netherlands as a frame of reference—we shall deal with segregation in a broad context.

If segregation means physical and social isolation and if segregation is not limited to residential functions, it truly implies serious dangers for disintegration. And if, as we fear, segregation is rising while the welfare state is in crisis, there is double need to study segregational processes and their causes and effects and to search for effective counteraction. This chapter focuses on sociospatial planning. We realize that segregation has other, perhaps even more important, dimensions, but problems of society always need multidisciplinary approaches. We look at it from one of many angles.

Clarifying the concept

A leading Dutch dictionary (Winkler Prins, 1973) defines segregation as "A form of isolation which enlarges the social distance between two or more groups by increasing the physical separation between them." This is a very general definition; in this sense, nearly all Dutchmen live segregated from each other, purposely, in order to have a certain degree of privacy. Since individualization is a characteristic trait of modern Western civilization and since privacy is an acknowledged value, both for the individual and for primary groups, this kind of segregation, if that term may be used here, cannot be seen as a social problem.

However, the same source continues as follows, "We differentiate between *voluntary* segregation (self-segregation) and segregation that is forced upon us. A case of voluntary segregation is the situation of immigrants who live in the same neighborhood; forced segregation is the outcome of a policy of discrimination by a ruling group, for instance against a certain race or religion." Vance (1977) also makes a distinction between voluntary segregation which he calls congregation and "real" segregation, which always results from discrimination.

In reality, such a dichotomy is only found in extreme cases. Usually elements of force and elements of free choice form an inextricable mixture. For instance, in regard to the housing situation of ethnic minorities in The Netherlands, a number of questions may be asked. Do migrants from Mediterranean countries live in each other's proximity (*a*) because they can only in a very restricted number of places find a low priced dwelling whose owner (and neighbors) would tolerate them, or (*b*) because they prefer to live among their own kind from whom they can expect help, advice, and understanding since they are not fully assimilated into the dominant Dutch culture, and/or (*c*) because a certain concentration of households with a similar cultural background is needed to maintain certain conveniences for the supply of specific cultural goods and services?

These questions illustrate that, at least in The Netherlands, a mixture of preference and powerlessness plays a role in the formation of such segregated "natural areas." Therefore, we agree with the definition by Friedrichs (1977) that segregation is "a neutral indication of an unequal distribution of characteristics (of social groups) over the components of an entity." Blauw and Pastor (1980) rightly added that segregation is not synonymous with a social inequality (which we will discuss later) and also that the concept of segregation implies dimensions of space and time.

Concerning the spatial dimension, Van Engelsdorp, Gastelaars, and Cortie (in Blauw and Pastor, 1980) pointed out the necessity of differentiating between levels when studying segregation on a world, national, regional, neighborhood, or block level. But spatial segregation has also a temporal dimension: students, for instance, live often segregated on campuses, but only for certain periods. In the same way, there are typical class patterns in the choice of holiday resorts.

Some residential areas keep their specific status characteristics notwithstanding a steady flow of mobile individual households, while others change their character by means of processes of "invasion" and "succession." A further point is that segregation is a relative concept: on one hand there can be a greater or smaller concentration of homogeneous households within a given area; on the other hand there can be a greater or smaller degree of "community segregation" in the sense that not only is the residential population homogeneous but all their activities—residential, educational, employment, shopping, and other services—are concentrated in a restricted area. In the last (extreme) case we have the typical situation of the ghetto (Coing, 1966).

A step toward a more precise conceptualization is made by Van Hoorn and De Smidt (1981), who distinguish the concepts of mixture, dispersion, and segregation. An increasing mixture means more heterogeneity of categories and/or elements within one area. Dispersion relates to decreasing concentration (if the mean distance between elements of the same species becomes greater) or to decreasing clustering (if the division of categories over the area becomes more regular). The distinction between these concepts opens possibilities for more concise measures of segregation, which in turn is the concept covering both mixture and dispersion.

Aspects of segregation

In addition to such distinctions within the concept of segregation, it is important to look at the different fields of activity in which segregational tendencies may occur. Foremost among these are: housing, labor, social communication networks, and leisure.

Usually these fields are interconnected; certainly for the individual they form an entity. But segregation may or may not occur in one, some, none, or all of these fields. It is a one-sided view to see only residential segregation as a relevant matter for sociophysical planners. The segregation of industrial activities, for instance, also creates serious problems, though those problems are of another kind.

So far we have focused on what may become segregated. Other questions relate to who may become segregated and where. Segregation may cover one or more of the following categories of characteristics of social groupings: demographic (age groups, types of households, sex, etc.), socioeconomic status, and/or cultural (e.g., ethnicity, religion, and political affiliation).

Many surveys have corroborated the well-known American picture (see, e.g., Guest, 1977): concentration of family-households including children in newer, more or less suburban residential districts; singles and older couples closer to the central parts of the city. But these concentrations are generally rather weak. The process may be illustrated by the transformations in the city of Maastricht. There the proportion of singles living in the CBD (central business district) rose from 7 percent of the total CBD population in 1960 to 14 percent in 1971, while the proportion of singles in the entire city rose from 3 percent to only 5 percent during the same period. Furthermore, in 1960–81 we see in Maastricht's inner city a notable decline of the age group 0–14 and a strong increase of the group aged 65 and older (see tables 17.1 and 17.2). The concentration of elderly people in the inner city grew stronger during this period.

In contrast to some other countries, The Netherlands have no special suburbs for retired people, but large institutions housing old people were constructed everywhere only after World War II. Here we find forms of segregation on the microlevel which sometimes are socially problematic. The same situation pertains to students and, recently, for younger singles. Under the current subsidy rules, these categories become concentrated in houses specifically designed and constructed for them.

Table 17.1 Age distribution in the inner city of Maastricht: 1960–81.

	1960		1970		1981	
	Inner city	City total	Inner city	City total	Inner city	City total
0–14	21.6	29.9	16.8	25.9	10.5	18.0
15–24	15.2	15.4	17.8	17.2	19.4	18.0
25–49	29.9	32.3	26.3	31.5	33.6	34.3
50–64	19.5	14.7	19.2	15.1	15.2	16.8
65>	13.8	7.7	19.9	19.3	21.3	12.9
	100.0	100.0	100.0	100.0	100.0	100.0

Whether or not there is real segregation in these cases depends on the degree of dispersion and clustering of dwellings designed—or at least very suitable—for groupings with similar demographic characteristics and related special needs.

The dependence of such identifiable categories of households on the availability of specific subsidized housing types, and thus on certain areas where such dwellings are clustered, pertains to families with below-average incomes. Those who can pay high prices seem to have different preferences concerning the situation of their homes: luxurious apartments in central parts of cities and cottages and country houses attract households with high incomes.

The way in which the housing market operates in The Netherlands leads to a concentration of low-paid ethnic minorities, not in the highly subsidized low-rent corporation dwellings, but in privately owned old houses. By sublet, double occupancy, or other forms which result in higher than average densities, these households can afford the rela-

Table 17.2 Children aged 4–11 in Utrecht (per 1,000 dwellings).

District	1971	1981
Inner city	26.8	13.2
New neighbourhoods[1] Overvecht	49.5	23.7
Hoograven[1]	81.1	35.1
Kanaleneiland[1]	48.1	17.5
Total city	41.1	22.3

1   built after World War II.
Source: Statistical Yearbook, Utrecht.

Table 17.3 Utrecht: Ethnic minorities per 1000 inhabitants in the city's neighbourhoods.

Neighborhood	1974	1979
0. Inner city	79.7	89.4
1. Overvecht	17.4	22.2
2. Amsterd.straatweg tot spoorlijn	143.9	248.3
3. Amsterd.straatweg spoorlijn/Marnixlaan	48.3	87.0
4. Nieuw Zuilen	18.2	34.6
5. Vogelenbuurt cs	78.1	94.1
6. Tuindorp	12.6	13.7
7. Oost	39.6	41.0
8. Sterrenbuurt	38.6	46.8
9. Tolsteeg, Hoograven	14.7	31.7
10. Stationsbuurt A.Z.U.	79.4	85.4
11. Rivierenwijk, Croeselaan	18.7	40.5
12. Kanaleneiland	12.2	29.4
13. Kanaalstraat, Vleutenseweg	90.5	167.2
14. Oog in Al, den Hommel	6.7	13.4
Average	40.8	63.1

tively high costs of such dwellings. The distribution of ethnic minorities in the city of Utrecht is shown in table 17.3.

From this table, it can be seen that, while the proportion of ethnic minorities is rising in every part of the town, the largest increase is found in the old neighborhoods (02 and 13), where by 1974 this category was already overrepresented. The only exception is neighborhood 03, where the increase is also much larger than the city's average. In this case, however, there is an overflow from the adjoining neighborhood 02. From what has been said so far, it is clear that the residential concentration of specific categories of the population is in large part the outcome of the market mechanism.

However, as we have already indicated, concentration and, eventually, segregation refers not only to residence but also to activities. During the European Middle Ages there was practically no separation of activities or functions in space: home and workshop were located in the same building, etc. (Grunfeld, 1980). The rise of industrial production introduced and stimulated an ongoing process of specialization, both of activities and of land use. Long before the Chartre International d'Architects Modernes (CIAM) made it a basic principle for town planning, separation of functions was developing spontaneously as a result of specialized land use. Under the influence of economic forces—large-scale production—this separation of activity spaces became a serious force working toward segregation of land use, mainly by the increasing scale of the specialized activity space.

The beloved corner shops of Jane Jacobs (1961) are no more. Dispersed shops and workshops have disappeared. By now, even smaller towns have their concentrated shopping area and their supermarkets with parking lots. Industrial activity has left the built-up area of settlements and moved to "industrial parks" in the periphery. The small office in residential neighborhoods or above a shop has become rare, but the number of huge office buildings, concentrated in parts of the inner city alongside urban beltways has mushroomed. Small hospitals have been replaced by modern colossi on the edge of towns. Urban recreational life too is concentrated in one or a few specialized areas in the inner city. The neighborhood cinema is an unknown phenomenon to the younger generation. Some Dutch cities even try to concentrate prostitution in what are called Eros centers.

The same development can be seen in sports; there is hardly a solitary field for playing football, hockey, or tennis left. In most cities, towns, and even villages, there are municipal accommodations which house all kinds of sporting facilities: open air facilities as well as a gymnasium, indoor swimming pool, etc. Similarly, schools for higher education become smaller in number but much larger in size. Many municipalities have even planned large areas for different kinds of specialized formal education.

Many renowned old hotels in the vicinity of the central railway station and the city center are closing, while clusters of modern big hotels nestle near the places where the main freeways reach the town and where sufficient parking accommodation can be offered. Table 17.4 shows some of this transition for the region of The Hague.

The foregoing makes clear that all kinds of human activities, even within one urban system, are becoming segregated from other activities. So, when changing activities one must move each time to a new location.

Factors promoting segregation

There is an interdependent development in technology, division of labor, and specialization (Friedrichs, 1977). Division of labor and spe-

Table 17.4 Distribution of employment in The Hague central city, Zoetermeer-satellite city and The Hague suburban region (percentages).

	The Hague Central city		Zoeter-meer-satellite		Suburban region		The Hague region total = 100%	
	1972	1982	1972	1982	1972	1982	1972	1982
Agriculture	53.2	47.3	6.2	7.6	40.7	45.1	3,414	3,182
Industry	75.4	65.8	5.2	9.1	19.4	25.2	35,339	23,783
Construction	75.4	63.6	2.6	9.0	22.0	27.3	23,032	17,986
Transport and communication	88.9	81.2	0.8	1.9	10.3	16.9	16,673	17,689
Commercial services	90.4	76.0	0.6	5.6	9.0	18.5	41,827	48,373
Other services	84.2	75.1	0.7	4.7	15.1	20.2	86,885	109,256

cialization result in social differentiation. Both social differentiation and technological specialization foster spatial differentiation. Spatial differentiation, in turn, is a factor promoting the maintenance of social distance between groupings. Guest (1977) has categorized the different factors that influence the dispersion and segregation of urban residents. The supply of dwellings and types of residential environments are determined mainly by institutional activities. Personal preferences are more connected with individual needs and symbolic and sentimental factors.

Completely free choice of location and type of house does not exist. Even those happy few who can afford a privately designed house are bound to a complex set of rules and regulations (building permit, town planning regulations, license of a committee controlling environmental and aesthetic criteria, etc.), to accessibility of work and other sites which are important to the individual concerned, and to the always limited information about opportunities. Although nobody is completely free in deciding where and how to settle, there are great differences in the degree of freedom.

The complex of social forces governing the allocation of habitats does not have exclusively negative effects on the weakest actors. Many empirical investigations have shown that migrants have fewer adjustment problems if they can keep primary contacts with people of their own (sub)culture who are already more integrated into the local community. But their contacts should not remain completely restricted to these familiar contacts (Abu Lughod, 1969; Albrecht, 1972; Migranten in Slotermeer, 1960). In his classic study of the slum, Seeley (1971) observed that, although the concentration of poverty-stricken people increases the misery of these people, it also gives them opportunities for finding understanding and solidarity from others with similar experiences. The positive effects of the proximity of people in similar situations, with similar value systems, has also been observed by many other researchers (Coing, 1966; Gans, 1962; Grunfeld, 1957; Young and Willmott, 1957).

The processes of change resulting in a more homogeneous composition of the neighborhood population were shown clearly in the case of a postwar Rotterdam residential district (Grunfeld, 1958). In that period, shortly after World War II, town planners wanted to realize a greater "mix" of people and houses in new neighborhoods. One way to attain this objective was to plan different kinds of houses in one area: large and small, high rise and terraced, bungalows and cottages, dwellings for sale and dwellings for rent, and dwellings subsidized or for the free market. A good example is the neighborhood of Pendrecht in Rotterdam. The planner's stated aim was to create a "microcosmic reflection" of the whole urban community. The neighborhood was subdivided into a number of identical subareas, each with dwellings for normal families, for singles, and for the aged population. However, the planner's ideal to create a new local community in this way was not realized. In an investigation, a sample of the population was asked with whom and at which addresses they had social contacts. The aim of the question was to measure the extent to which the subarea functioned as a "unit of interaction." The majority of the respondents (sixteen of the twenty living in multistory houses and nineteen of the twenty-two who lived in one-family houses) had no contact with persons living in a different housing type. Of those who did have social contacts with people living in a type of housing different from their own, more than 50 percent said that those contacts originated from their membership in a voluntary association, such as a church. In other words, the subarea was not experienced as a unit of interaction (DeJonge, 1962).

The plans for Pendrecht, as well as many other plans from the 1950–70 period, were largely based on the idea of the "balanced neighborhood unit" imported from Britain. The underlying assumptions are summarized by Collison (1956, 1966): (a) The experience of living in a socially heterogeneous neighborhood is an enriching one and leads to better mutual understanding. (b) The working-class population will benefit from middle-class leadership. (c) There are important financial benefits for the municipality (which owns all the building sites and sells them after the completion of the infrastructure), when expensive buildings sites yield a profit with which the cheap dwellings for lower-income groups can get an extra subsidy. This is only possible in the case of a plan containing houses on all price levels. (d) Such a mixed plan can make for a more interesting total architectural image than the monotonous designs of middle-class suburbs.

Much criticism has been directed against the first two assumptions (Beshers, 1962; Blauw and Pastor, 1980; Grunfeld, 1976; Mann, 1958). Meanwhile, practical experience has taught that neither a very heterogeneous nor a homogeneous, often segregated neighborhood forms a satisfactory residential environment. Claude Fischer (1976) has summarized the situation: "What consequences can follow from life in the presence of very different others? They are consequences of very different social worlds, or subcultures, touching each other. For one, urbanites systematically avoid and ignore their odd fellow-citizens. Residential segregation encourages that outcome, and, even in mixed neighborhoods, people usually go their own separate ways. Beyond that, contrasts, competition, and conflicts between 'us' and 'them' can be expected." This observation applies to the findings of Dutch research also.

While it is true that a rather homogeneous composition of the population, certainly within a single block agrees with the residents' preferences, we should remember that such wishes are not uniform. Shuval (1962) has given a striking insight in a real situation: People possessing high status generally preferred to be neighbors of people with a similar status. However, people with a low social status preferred to be the neighbors of higher-status residents. This whole matter of the "optimal" population mix on different levels of scale is much too complicated to be resolved by an inventory of people's wishes and preferences.

Gans (1972) does not see many possibilities for planners to influence the patterns and kinds of social relationships in built environments. It is true that a certain distribution and location of dwellings may influence accessibility, proximity, potential for visual contacts, etc., but the content and intensity of such relationships is fully dependent on what individuals wish and do. Without the possibility of either evading or initiating social contact, the atmosphere of the residential environment would be full of tensions and conflicts. It is important, according to Gans, that the local population be sufficiently homogeneous for institutions to work and also that there is sufficient mix in the population to guarantee an economic base for conveniences and amenities serving many population strata.

Danz (1981) compared contacts among triads of neighbors and feelings of well-being in a number of identical apartment houses in The Netherlands; some triads had a homogeneous composition (similar demographic characteristics and socioeconomic status) and others had a more heterogeneous composition. He failed to find marked differences in patterns of relationships or feelings of well-being. In this case, however, the differences in income and in cultural background were quite small, since there were no members of an ethnic minority in the sample.

Effects of segregation of activities

A society built on division of labor and specialized functions where, as a consequence, land uses also become specialized and concentrated, has to give much attention to access to positions and locations. Such easy access is a condition for mobility. Specialization leads to social stratification. In the absence of mobility, social stratification can become rigid. Since, in our present society, all kinds of activities become more and more spatially separated, and since increase of scale has also increased physical and social distances[1] mobility has become a vital element in the system's function. Without a high amount of mobility there is opportunity for only a restricted range of activities and experiences. An increasing part of the population would become narrow minded and would feel alienated from society as a whole. Actions and decisions would be prompted by partial interests only and the incidence of conflicting partial interests would increase. Social inequality would become greater, again as a result of spatial inequality —the unequal chances for mobility and access to vital resources and powerful positions.

The postwar welfare state has tried to decrease such unequal opportunities and to coordinate partial interests into common well-being. To an amazingly large degree, it has succeeded as long as inequality could be diminished by upgrading the position of the weakest with some of the proceeds of economic growth. At the very moment that our economic growth stops and even begins to decline, the structure of the welfare state-society is shaken. In fighting the ensuing crisis of our society, sociospatial planning can play a role—not as the only and all-powerful remedy, but still as an important instrument for reform and innovation.

Of course, there are other aspects which are perhaps still more powerful than the realm of spatial planning: ethics, religion, politics, mass communication, etc. However, here we concentrate on the allocation and organization of space. The kinds of processes we have in mind may be illustrated by a well-known example: the increasing scale of specialized facilities results in larger physical distances. As Harvey (1971) observed, the lack of elasticity and the spatial inflexibility in the supply of cheap housing is the cause of concentration of low-income households in parts of the older inner cities. An unfavorable climate for certain facilities is the result. Many move to locations, often peripheral, with better access by the residential areas of middle- and higher-income groups. The departure of these facilities promotes further decay of older neighborhoods.

The decay of houses and of the environment goes together with a drop in value. It pays to demolish outdated structures, especially since the location in the vicinity of the city center makes it attractive to use the site for other purposes, so we see that worn out factories close down and decayed buildings are destroyed. The vacant site often becomes attractive for the construction of office buildings, the more so since employment in the tertiary sector is expanding.

For reasons of environmental nuisance, economic advantages, and so on, industrial activity became concentrated on a few industrial areas in outlying districts. The large-scale construction of dwellings after 1945 took place nearly exclusively in newly expanded residential districts, adjoining the existing urban districts, or in suburbs and satellites. Those modern and often well-equipped new houses attracted people with above-average incomes because they were more expensive than the older dwellings. This population was in large part employed in centrally located offices, while the remaining population of the inner city—the majority with low incomes and little education—had to find jobs in the industrial areas outside of the town (see table 17.5).

A few consequences of this development were increasing traffic congestion; relatively higher transportation costs for the lowest paid; relatively higher housing expenses in the inner city as a result of the diminishing stock of old (cheap) dwellings and an increasing competi-

Table 17.5   Employed population of three large cities according to educational level.

	Inner city		Total city	
	1960	1971	1960	1971
Amsterdam				
Lowest level	65.7(= 100)	65.9(= 100)	51.7(= 100)	52.6(= 100)
Lower middle	25.9	21.3(= 82)	35.5	31.5(= 89)
High school and more	8.4	12.8(= 152)	12.7	15.9(= 125)
The Hague				
Lowest level	57.7	61.8(= 107)	46.9	46.5(= 99)
Lower middle	30.7	24.5(= 80)	36.3	33.4(= 95)
High school and more	11.6	13.7(= 118)	17.8	20.1(= 113)
Utrecht				
Lowest level	58.7	58.7(= 100)	51.9	49.4(= 95)
Lower middle	28.0	21.6(= 77)	33.9	31.0(= 91)
High school and more	13.3	19.7(= 148)	14.2	19.6(= 138)

Source: J. den Draak. *De binnenstad als woonmilieu.* Amsterdam/Meppel: Boom, 1979. Computed from table IV-1, p. 78.

tion for such houses; and relatively high concentrations of unemployment in inner cities, caused by automation in industry and by insufficient information about opportunities among the least educated.

The decreasing mix (heterogeneity) of population in residential areas limits personal experiences and information, because there is not much differentiation in activities and interests among people with similar backgrounds. This is even more true for people with low levels of education and skill than for others who have a greater diversity of occupations and a higher degree of specialization. A higher degree of specialization often implies more contacts with other specialists, more mutual interdependence, and therefore a social network which is determined less by proximity and more by mutual interests (Grunfeld, 1970). For people with a low socioeconomic status, it becomes increasingly difficult to break through this geographically limited network of relationships, and therefore chances increase that their deprivation becomes permanent and that the already weak bonds with the greater community will disappear altogether.

What can spatial planning do about this unwanted development? In the first place it should be concerned with restricting the size of single-function areas and with securing the easy accessibility of all the locations in the area: for work, residence, recreation, shopping, etc. If specialized land use is on a small scale, if homogeneous clusters of population and activity spaces are of small size, accessibility becomes much easier. One way to attain this is to plan for increased density. The garden city ideal of low-density residential neighborhoods, which dominated town planning for a long time, has proven to have its shortcomings. Nevertheless, vast areas with such low densities have been created. Here are opportunities for modernization and real renewal by increasing the density (Burgers, 1980). This can be done either by building more and different dwellings in open spaces or by adding amenities (functions) that were until now absent. That density —if it leads to more differentiation—can enrich human experiences is shown by Van Vliet— (1981). His comparative study of children living in urban and suburban environments showed, for example, that city children had more friends and found more different land uses in their neighborhood than did suburban children.

Recently, some municipalities in The Netherlands have tried to counteract segregation by direct action, e.g., the assignment of dwellings to low-income ethnic minorities in such a way that a certain dispersion of this group would ensue. However, such actions met with opposition from two sides: the ethnic minorities resisted what seemed, in their eyes, a kind of deportation, while the neighborhood population was afraid of a devaluation of their property and the prestigious image of their neighborhood. Therefore, they do not welcome the newcomers who may then be threatened with social isolation (Gans, 1967). Such actions, aimed at preventing the stigmatization of neighborhoods, may result in the stigmatization of individual households; it certainly does not promote integration. Much better, therefore, are actions which create favorable conditions for interaction and mobility by diminishing physical distances.

Instead of a policy directed at restricting mobility, one would plead for the contrary. The confrontation of people with a variety of aspects and the promotion of personal involvement are vital conditions for the preservation or restoration of societal bonds. In addition to a focus on accessibility, the careful creation or preservation of artifacts that act as symbols with emotional meanings may help to restore feelings of belonging to a greater community.

We cannot return to preindustrial situations of small-scale institutions and a complete mix of land uses. Nobody would be prepared to pay the price: a strong decline in wealth. Nor can we cancel our technological attainments. Jane Jacobs' view of the metropolis (1961) is an anachronism. However, we can renew our urban structures in such a way that each settlement becomes an integrated mosaic of rather small clusters of specialized land use (Timms, 1971). This, however, requires a new orientation towards urban renewal and the courage to defend it.

18 Societal Factors Shaping the Internal Structure of Finnish Cities

Ari Ylönen

Abstract. Ylönen first describes the historical development of Tampere, Finland, with special reference to population and land use patterns. The present structure is then described as having resulted from a mixed economy and a decision-making system with significant inputs from public and private sectors. It is argued that the city of Tampere is not an isolated case but a manifestation of broader trends. Statistical information is used to document these trends.

Observations of differences in the ecological patterns of urban growth between the United States and Finland and other Scandinavian cities suggest that, among the latter, public policies have a greater impact upon city structures. In their comparative study of Boston and Helsinki, Sweetser and Sweetser (1968) concluded that the construction of new residential areas in Helsinki is planned in a more comprehensive way than in the United States. Other cross-national enquiries have stated that in Europe the governments have stronger control over land and greater capacity to plan. "The lack of public planning and control of land in the USA is just one part of a general pattern of weak government activity in almost every area of life, from welfare and health through national economic planning," says Popenoe in describing the range of differences. The Sweetsers also emphasize that "In the ecology of cities, as in many other aspects of societies, some ways of doing things are inseparable from ways of doing other things; if you accept one you must accept others."[1]

This chapter, a detailed analysis of government policy as part of the established decision-making system between public and private sectors, shows that, in a mixed economy, there is a double decision-making system in housing policy, with each sector having its own impact on the local community structure.

The analysis first describes the social development of the city of Tampere. The description draws on two spatially relevant variables: the integration/differentiation of population structure and of functional structure (degree of segregation in land use patterns). The observed trends are then interpreted as parts of societal urban and regional policy.

The changing city of Tampere

The connections between changes that have taken place in the internal city structure and societal changes is obvious when studying how the functions of a city have changed during the past two centuries.[2] In the following section, the three phases of Tampere's history are discussed in conjunction with changes in the city structure.[3]

Tampere was founded in 1779, primarily as a marketplace for the farmers of the province, as stated in the charter for the founding of the city.[4] The first phase lasted one hundred years. The second phase was the era of industrialization. The main task was the maximization of industrial activities, and, during this phase, the interaction between the city and surrounding province was based on the supply of work places in the city area. Population increased noticeably during these years. The first functionally specialized areas and segregated areas, the residential areas for working-class families, were founded. Originally, the working-class areas were inside the existing city boundaries; later a few areas were founded on the outskirts just outside the city limits. The third phase is characterized by productive activities and especially by consumption and traffic. Until the past few years, the increase in population was still fairly rapid. The abundance of places for consumption, public institutions, and other services is typical of this phase of development.

Characteristic of the present city is that it is a physical organization of consumption and public services. The city still offers job opportunities for people from outside the city, but the present trend seems to show an increase in the supply of opportunities for consumption and services.

When considering the postwar years, government policy is of overriding importance, but only in conjunction with the private sector. The character of the Finnish housing policy system has been affected in the following way: measures taken by the public sector have resulted in the desegregation of the population, but, because of the considerable interests of the private sector, the functional structure of cities has still been determined by separate private interests, by market forces.

This dual character of the housing sector can also be illustrated through individual residential area projects: at the initial stage of a project, the influence of the public sector is maximal concerning determination of both the population structure and the functional structure, but, after ten to twenty years, market forces and the residents' economic resources and preferences are more decisive.

The historical data in figure 18.1 concern the city of Tampere only, but research points to a similar trend in the functional structure of all middle-sized Finnish cities.[5] The renovation, i.e., desegregation, of working-class subareas started in Finnish cities mainly after 1950.

In describing Finland's cities of today, certain comments must be made. First, there are no areas in the Finnish city that are typically occupied by special linguistic or ethnic minorities. In this respect, the Finnish cities differ from many West European cities. As in Sweden, Finnish urban areas are rather compact, with most residents living in small apartments. Urban areas have a definite boundary; city and noncity are two quite separate landscapes. In most cities, the down-

Figure 18.1 The phases of development of the city of Tampere.

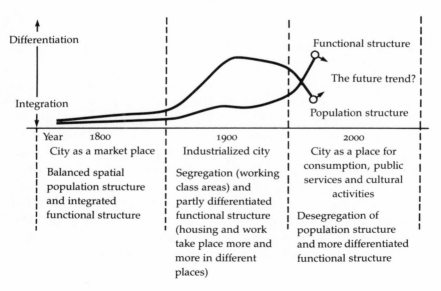

town areas have been well maintained, and many families are willing to live there. And, exactly as in urban Sweden, social classes are comparatively intermixed in Finnish urban residential areas. To the degree that residential differentiation does exist, it tends to follow the preindustrial residential pattern, with higher classes living close to the city center and poorer classes inhabiting the suburbs.[6]

Questions for consideration

Is it possible to find an explanation of the phenomenon described above—an explanation that covers the changes from industrialization to the modern city? What explains the interrelation of the trends of desegregation and the separation of the functional structure? Is city structure, described by these concepts, a reflection of nonspatial social processes in space? Can one find a manifest urban policy, or is the contemporary Finnish city a product of forces changing the entire society?

Population structure and functional structure have been chosen as concepts to describe the city; they are regarded causally as dependent variables, as they are in some studies independent factors of the urban way of life. In order to throw light on the relationship between city structure and social planning, urbanization in Finland will be studied as a result of decision making in Finnish housing policy and especially in economic and regional policies that dominate it.

The main factors in Finnish housing policy: 1950–75

Urbanization has been a somewhat sudden and late process in Finland, which evidently has created difficulties for local communities in terms of economic and planning resources required to cope with the extensive need for new housing.[7] Industrialization rapidly altered the industrial structure of Finnish society, but the major city building era, starting in the late fifties, was preceded in 1940–50 by a plan to conserve Finland as a semi-agricultural society.

The point here is that urbanization immediately after World War II was not keeping pace with the changing industrial structure. This could be called a deliberate attempt to conserve Finland as long as possible as an agricultural society. About 75 percent of the houses built during the years 1945–49 were located in the countryside.[8]

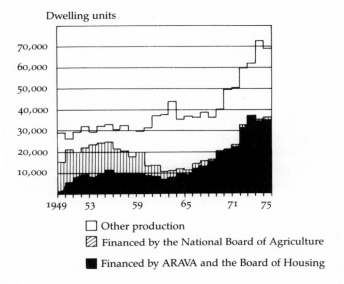

Figure 18.2 Regional development and housing production in 1949–75: The allocation of state subsidies for different types of production in Finland.

Later, in the fifties, a noticeable proportion of government subsidies was channeled through the National Board of Agriculture for construction in the rural areas (see figure 18.2). A great amount of the subsidies thus has been directed outside the urban areas. Indeed, it has been stated that the development of Finnish agriculture in the forties and fifties bears no resemblance to the development in east European or capitalist west European countries. In Finland, the number of small farms continued to increase. Nearly 100,000 new farms were established on the basis of the 1945 Land Acquisition Act for the evacuated population, disabled war veterans, widows, and ex-servicemen. As late as the fifties, attempts were made to stimulate small-scale farming. Finland was one of the few OECD countries where the number of farms grew during that period.

One reason for channeling public resources into rural areas was the necessity to obtain conditions for internally peaceful development after the war.[10] An alternative explanation is that the disagreements about urban policy between urban and rural parties made it possible to use small farmers, even into the late fifties, as a part-time labor force for the wood industry. This era was ended by a very sudden pressure in 1960–70 to allow a rapid change in industrial structure.[11]

The following statistics describe changes that have taken place in postwar Finnish society.[12]

(*a*) The industrial structure: In 1950, the percentage of active population working in the primary sector was 46 percent; in 1960, 35 percent; in 1970, 20 percent; and in 1975 15 percent.

(*b*) Urbanization: In 1950, the percentage of population living in urban areas was approximately 30 percent, in 1960, approximately 40 percent, in 1970, approximately 50 percent, and, in 1980, approximately 60 percent.

(*c*) The large volume of construction: In 1950, there were one million dwellings; in 1980, the number was 1.8 million. Neither the population nor the number of families has increased at the same rate.

(*d*) In 1980, there were 252,000 summer cottages; every fifth family had one.

(*e*) The tenure status changed as follows: in 1950, 55.9 percent and, in 1980, 61.0 percent owned their dwellings; in 1950, 31.1 percent and, in 1980, 20.9 percent were renters; and, in 1950, 11.5 percent and, in 1980, 8.3 percent lived in a dwelling provided by their employers.

Since World War II, housing policy thus has become a general tool

Figure 18.3 Housing investments in national economy: The proportion of industrial, housing, and other fundamental investments of the GNP at market price in 1954–75.[13]

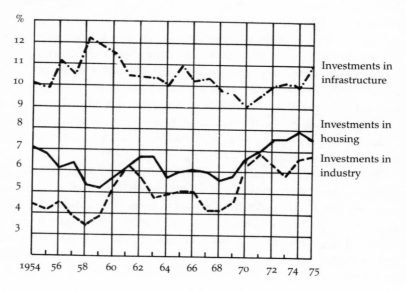

of social policy, with goals for internally peaceful development and regional decentralization of economic resources.

Housing policy also has been a means of national economic policy. Housing investments, of which state subsidies make up a considerable proportion, have been very sensitive to market conditions.

Market fluctuations have usually lasted from three to five years, and investments in housing production tend to follow the general development in market conditions somewhat belatedly (figure 18.3).

It seems justified to say that the housing sector has held an instrumental position in Finnish social policy; it has been a part of the larger economic system. The favorable effects of construction on employment are noticeable, and the housing sector has served especially as a means to balance regional differences and market conditions. Compared with other nations, the public sector is a rather powerful social force in Finland. The regulative power is exercised, however, in societal rather than in urban policy. Finnish housing policy has been subordinated to a position where it is a means for realizing public intervention into the regional development and national economy.

The dual character of Finnish housing policy: International comparisons

The relationship between the government and the private sector is historically different in Europe and the United States. The role of banks and builders in the housing market in the United States is an example of market forces exerting their influence rather freely. Since World War II, a central feature of the American housing policy has been its capability to provide land at a low price for most of those in need of their own dwelling. This has resulted in a vast number of privately owned one-family houses. It has been claimed that the argument for this kind of a housing policy is to draw a population into the system large enough that the market system as a whole is regarded as a legitimate way of arranging the national economic policy system.[14]

Housing policy is organized by the private sector in most European countries, also, but under strong state control. In many cases the state also acts as the initiator and coordinator in the projects. In effect, European housing policy and the American market solution have drifted apart. Public transportation absorbed a great proportion of the resources available in Europe, and a principle was adopted according to which the public sector was given a strong role in the housing sector. Vance has noted that, immediately after World War II, the European countries adopted a housing policy that rejected the idea of cheap sites and small privately owned houses as a possible solution for providing housing for most of the population.[15]

A more developed system of concepts is in order, to take a closer look at the differences in housing policy. The concept "dual character of the housing sector" has been adopted from Wallace F. Smith.[16] According to Smith, the housing sector, as a part of the larger economic system, is in most countries a combination of private enterprise and the actions of the public sector. The roles and power of both vary from country to country. As a rule, the private and the public sectors are highly dependent on each other as far as construction is concerned, and this is why there exists a dual decision-making system combining private enterprise and government intervention in the housing sector.

Three ideal types of housing policy decision making systems are relevant here: (*a*) the market system, (*b*) the planned economy, and (*c*) the welfare state system. These three types have been modified from Smith's typology.

The market system

To simplify the matter somewhat, it can be said that the housing market is determined in the market system on the basis of the law of supply and demand. The duty of the public sector is to provide an opportunity for those in need of a dwelling to evaluate, as voters, the success of the system in the political arena.

The planned economy

In a planned economy, the market forces are minimal. The public sector controls both housing production and the supply of dwellings. It also organizes how the needs of those in need of a dwelling are communicated to the decision makers. Moreover, the government organizes the evaluation of the sufficiency and quality of housing production and facilities.

The welfare system

The welfare system is the most complicated. All three components, i.e., the public sector, the market, and those in need of dwellings, influence the system in their own specific ways. The supply of dwellings is partially determined by the market forces, according to the law of supply and demand. Nonetheless, the public sector controls the market and the supply of dwellings to a noticeable extent. In the so-called modern welfare states, attempts have been made to evaluate the quality of living and housing conditions—in other words, to evaluate how well the demand observed by the market meets the actual needs of the residents. In the last decade—and in Finland only during the past few years—the residents have begun to realize their rights and to be more active in matters concerning their residential area and housing.

The Finnish housing policy decision making system comes close to the welfare system, which Wallace F. Smith has described as "public governorship" or "mixed entrepreneurship." As mentioned earlier, the state's influence in the housing sector has been significant in all countries. Indeed, the dissimilarities between housing policy systems in various countries are most obvious in the extent and form of influence that the market forces exert. The dual system refers to countries where both the market and the public sector, especially the government, have a strong influence on housing issues. The influence of the market forces varies also, according to the commodity marketed—whether it is primarily the location or the dwelling itself. In a pure market system, the site and location are important commodities. On the contrary, in Finnish housing policy, supported financially by the government, the price and the distribution of dwellings to different population groups have been the main objectives of state interventions. The local community infrastructure has also been molded in accordance with the conditions of landownership and land available at a low price (state supported suburbs for middle- and low-income groups).

The Finnish housing policy decision-making system

The need for a state-level view in a model explaining the development of the internal city structure becomes justified, since the public sector, especially the state, has a great deal of potential regulative power in Finland and in Scandinavian countries. This is not brought about by a hierarchical administrative system. On the contrary, so-called Scandinavian democracy is based on bipolar administration. Both the state and the local community have a strong authority. In Finland, state control is brought about by parliament and the government that, for years, in the state of political consensus, have had extensive power in controlling economic processes; in other words, they have guided Finland's economy to minimal losses in international market fluctuations. In addition, the state has a strong influence on the everyday life of the people, which has been called the negative syndrome of a welfare state.

The potential power described above has not been used, however, in Finnish urban policy, because political consensus is a precondition for the use of potential power. Since the center-left coalition came into power in Finland there has not been such political consensus in the field of urban policy as there is in matters concerning the national economy or foreign policy. Thus, the potential power of the state has not been used in urban development programs in Finland. The center party has traditionally been an agrarian party.

On the community level, the power of the public sector is based on the traditionally strong status of the local self-government that is guaranteed in the constitution, e.g., by the right of municipalities to levy taxes and by its monopoly in site planning. Consistent decision making has been hampered by the competition between local communities for taxpayers and, in addition, by the poor position of the public sector in local-level negotiations with banks, landowners, and builders about the construction to be carried out in cities. The weak position is based on the law, especially the Planning and Construction Act.

The residents are not included in the description above as persons with political influence, as members of a pressure group, or as persons in need of a dwelling and motivated by their preferences. The apparent improvement in housing conditions (in terms of conveniences) obviously has made the average newly migrated townsman satisfied and, accordingly, more passive during his first years in the city. This view is compatible with the general image of the role of residents in city building during the mass migration to cities towards the end of the seventies.

The organization of Finnish housing policy

As the volume of construction in cities has grown, the decision-making organization of construction has become rigid and insensitive to external pressures. Although architects and some residents have expressed demands for more traditional Finnish ways of building, the organization has stayed with standard solutions.

The most important components of the Finnish housing policy decision-making system, namely the state, the municipalities, banks, and builders, have partially overlapping goals. These include a steady rate of construction, or the goal that housing shortages must not be an obstacle for economic development. However, their decision making is based also on their own specific motives. In terms of concepts used in city planning aimed at certain objectives, it is difficult to describe such a network of connections among the groups mentioned that would make it possible to coordinate housing policy decisions at a local level. The study of explicit aims and motives of each component in the decision-making system makes the dual system a more accurate description.

The state. Capital for construction comes primarily from the state budget and from those banks which collect money from individuals and families who are saving for their own dwelling. Insurance companies also were interested in financing construction during the period in question. The objective of the government in construction is to redistribute incomes by supporting housing for certain regions and groups of population. The influence of the government in the decision-making arena where the public and private sectors meet is realized in the following way: the government controls a large proportion of construction, especially the production of rental units; it controls the price and quality of housing through norms and loan provisions; and it controls the regional distribution of housing production. To ensure that the volume of construction meets the demands set by the major city building era, the government has provided reasonable loans for builders to make construction a profitable business.

Builders often claim that state-supported housing production is unprofitable and has to be compensated by unsubsidized housing. However, it seems that construction of housing supported by the state has been very profitable. The increase in the number of enterprises was more rapid than the growth of housing production in 1965–73. This assumption of cheap money is also supported by the number of bankruptcies of the largest builders. The builders who went bankrupt constructed more buildings without government subsidies than builders on the average. Such facts do not verify the statement about the unprofitability of production supported by the state.[17]

The municipalities. Activity in construction is an important objective for all cities, as it enhances employment and the amount of population and, accordingly, incomes received through taxation. This has resulted in competition between cities for taxpayers and enterprises. Thus, economic factors continuously affect decisions concerning the city structure.[18]

The shared interests of banks and local communities are based on the common attempt of communities to promote commercial and industrial life within their area. High-ranking officials sit on bank boards, safeguarding local community interests.

From the viewpoint of town planning and housing policy decision making, the situation is, however, paradoxical. The bank boards make decisions that are not public. In community planning offices, housing programs and site plans are partly based on data obtained from banks and builders. Planners do not, however, reveal their real plans, as the price of land is sensitive to speculation. The planning apparatus of a community may prepare empty plans, which are not in accordance with agreements made by bank directors and the leaders of communities.

The banks. Banks exert great influence on enterprises. They finance housing production, and, especially in the sixties and seventies, they had a strong influence on business site construction. Banks have been very active in establishing decoy companies, which deliver dwellings for the customers who bring savings into the bank.

The role of banks in the field of construction is rather complicated in Finland. When construction is vigorous and there is a lack of capital, builders become dependent on short-term credit funding by banks. For the builders, the most effective means to maximize their profits has been building permits obtained on the basis of landowning; the banks have been in an advantageous position compared to builders, who must get a bank to finance their land deals. Banks have been able to control the financing of construction and even the bankruptcies of builders. But banks also have reasons to cooperate with builders. According to the banking act, banks are not allowed to act as agents for dwellings. Therefore, there are decoy companies, owned by the banks, which take care of the mutual interests of banks and builders; they deliver the dwellings.

Actually banks have financed the land deals and construction in order to get the right to act as agents for completed dwellings. In this way, banks can win clients and stimulate them to save for a dwelling; in other words, they can promote their own profitability.[19]

The builders. Builders act according to the principles of profitable business. Construction is made profitable through competition for "the right to build," i.e., for the size of buildings and cheap sites. As landowners, the builders determined to a great extent the prices of dwellings during the major city building era, 1960–75. Continuous construction without seasonal fluctuations and with standard building types is a prerequisite for amortizing the investments necessary in construction.

Decisions made by this system of conflicting motives among banks, the state, municipalities, and builders may appear irrational to citizens and citizen organizations. They often base their judgments about the legitimacy of the system on legislation concerning decision making in the city council. Indeed, if only the local level of the construction system is studied, it would seem to be irrational. Widening the perspective enables one to understand the objectives of some actions in site planning and construction. Even within the public sector there are conflicts, however, because the state and the municipalities also have different objectives and use different methods to realize them. There are conflicting views as to the provision of state subsidies for housing and in other decisions related to regional policy. Typically, cities are less willing to adopt new planning principles or to give their share of investments to conserve historically valuable areas or buildings.

Conclusions and a perspective
for the future

We may conclude that in a mixed economy there is a dual decision-making system in housing policy, in which both private and public sectors have their own kind of impact on the local community structure. The two main trends of this system during the last twenty to thirty years in Finland have been the desegregation of the population structure and the differentiation in the functional structure. The former is a result of the government's intervention into the use of capital in construction; the latter is a result of the private sector's strong role in the local decision-making arena.

The coexistence of the public and private sectors is expressed with the concept "the dual character of the housing sector," according to Smith. It is simply a combination of government regulation and free competition. The result has been a more equal city in terms of availability of public utilities and facilities for a large number of new and old city dwellers, and a higher quality of dwellings in terms of amenities. There are, however, doubts about the quality of city life and about the new consumption-minded way of life which is promoted by the modern city structure.

Our analysis suggests that the influence of the two sectors in the dual decision-making system will be quite different in the future. After the major city building era, the possibility of the public sector's intervention into building activities has diminished, along with the shrinking volume of construction. Therefore, it is probable that the housing market, because of its increasing sensitivity to residents' preferences, will again bring about segregational tendencies in the Finnish city structure. Elements of population resegregation can already be identified in Helsinki.[20] On the other hand, it can be assumed that the interests of the public sector to integrate the infrastructure of the city will increase. Principally, this would be a consequence of the growth in transport expenses, of the common understanding of the effects of air pollution, and of attempts to develop urban culture by promoting the return to functional integration.

19 Dutch Inner-City Housing in the Context of Revitalization Policies

Jan den Draak

Abstract. Den Draak situates housing policy within a broader context of urban development and inner-city revitalization. Census data illustrate changes in size, composition, and density of population in major Dutch cities. Inner-city policies contributing to these changes are discussed, and a plea is made to base urban residential plans on regional assessments of impacts at various levels and along different dimensions.

In the larger Dutch cities, striking developments in urban housing in the sixties and in the first half of the seventies occurred at the microlevel, at the neighborhood level, and at the regional level. At the microlevel, there was a decrease in average dwelling occupancy (for instance in Amsterdam this figure decreased from 3.3 in 1960 to 2.4 in 1980) and an increase in size of newly constructed dwellings. At the neighborhood level, there was a reduction in the number of dwellings per hectare in buildings under construction and a decline of the housing stock in the central parts of most cities, due to demolition, conversion to other uses, etc. At the regional level, there occurred a high degree of suburbanization along with increased individualization, a preference for living in single family houses in quiet environment, and motorization of the population.

All in all, the proportion of land use for housing increased substantially, and the growth of the urban area proceeded much faster than was expected on the basis of urban population growth. In addition, urban sprawl affected the central open area in the western part of The

Table 19.1 Percentage changes in population of four Dutch towns and The Netherlands, 1951–80.

Period	Amsterdam	Rotterdam	The Hague	Utrecht	Netherlands
1951–55	+2.8	+4.9	+5.6	+3.9	+6.1
1956–60	−0.3	+1.6	+0.3	+4.2	+6.8
1961–65	−0.4	−0.2	−2.2	+5.8	+7.1
1966–70	−4.9	−6.8	−9.3	+2.7	+6.0
1971–75	−8.4	−9.5	−10.8	−9.9	+4.7
1976–80	−5.2	−6.3	−4.7	−5.8	+3.4

Source: Data of Central Bureau of Statistics, The Hague.

Netherlands, and the extension of other forms of land use (such as the necessary infrastructural amenities) also led to enlarged space consumption. As a consequence, the population of the largest towns diminished in the sixties and, particularly, in the first half of the seventies. Table 19.1 illustrates this process.

Population decline started in Amsterdam and The Hague in 1958, in Rotterdam in 1964, and in Utrecht, the smallest of these four towns, in 1969.[1] In spite of additions to the housing stock which were still being made, this process continued into the seventies. However, the population decrease was smaller in the second half of the seventies than in the first half. This was not due to the building of more dwellings in the last-mentioned period but to a smaller out-migration from the cities as a consequence of the economic recession (less ability to buy a house in suburban areas) and some influence of effective policy measures to diminish suburbanization.

Together with the population decline and a related process of selective migration came out-migration of families with children, for the greater part belonging to the middle and upper income brackets, and in-migration of single persons, for example, young workers, students, and foreign workers. Thus, the proportion of the financially weak in the urban population was growing. The cumulative influence of decreasing purchasing power per capita, population decline, and selective migration led to an accelerated impoverishment of the larger Dutch cities. To illustrate, a recent article foresees that the decrease in the average income in the period 1976–86 will be 4 percent in The Netherlands, but 21 percent in Amsterdam (Kruijt, 1983: 859).

Changes in policy

The above-mentioned developments alarmed the municipal governments and led to changes in national government policy. On the whole, the importance of measures to produce or preserve a sound physical, economic, and social structure of towns is seen as a necessity. Nowadays, urban policy is, among other things, intended to maintain or increase population densities in selected urban areas such as the inner cities. Policies to increase population densities, in combination with other measures, can contribute to the revitalization of the larger cities. They also involve advantages for the public transportation system and the use of commercial and noncommercial services and facilities. Some measures mentioned in the Urbanization Report (1976) are (*a*) restriction of overspill and concentration of new building locations within the urban zones as close as possible to urban centers; (*b*) revitalization and recovery of existing urban areas, particularly by strengthening the residential function of the inner cities and by improving the residential environment; and (*c*) promotion of the economical use of space while preserving differentiation by limiting the decrease of urban housing density and by promoting space-intensive neighborhood plans.

In what follows, our primary focus will be on the Dutch housing policy for the inner city, corresponding with the policy measure mentioned under (*b*). Besides policies aimed at slowing down the cities' population decline, measures aimed at halting the departure of younger and financially better off families and furthering the social upgrading of decaying urban areas are also desirable. In this respect, we will also concentrate on the inner city and adjacent renewal areas.

Housing policies for the inner city

Dutch government policy is oriented toward revitalization and recovery of existing urban areas. In the sixties, inner-city policy at the local level attached much importance to traffic plans, expansion of central functions such as big offices, and a like approach with respect to land value. A marked policy changeover in inner-city policy became manifest in the beginning of the seventies. An increasing, partly organized opposition to the demolition of dwellings for traffic purposes or the construction of offices and to the neglect of the residential function for other more lucrative functions led to different policy goals.

A recent analysis of municipal policy intentions in the 1970s (Den Draak and Den Adel, 1981) found that enhancing the residential function is a generally accepted goal. The underlying rationales concern: (*a*) reasons intrinsically related to local residence, such as the demands and interests of potential residents, the existence of a specific supply of dwellings and the maintenance of a specific residential environment; and (*b*) reasons which point to the contribution of the residential function to other inner-city functions or to the significance and functioning of the inner city as a whole, such as the reduction of traffic problems, the strengthening of social control and feelings of security, the support of various facilities, the increase of liveliness, etc.

Reasons of the first type outweigh those of the second. However, in most cases, there is a mix of arguments. Besides, one must realize that reasons in category (*b*) have weak empirical support, particularly when compared with those in category (*a*); therefore, it is relatively "easy" to advance such arguments.

Another important item concerns the relation between policy objectives for the residential function of the inner city and for other functions in the same area, as well as residential objectives for the surrounding region. Our analysis reveals a growing tendency to posit the objectives regarding inner-city residence for their own sake, isolated from other objectives with regard to urban structure and other functions. On the one hand this means that objectives for the residential function of the inner city are either insufficiently or not at all related to residential objectives for other parts of the city or urban region (for example, adjacent old districts or suburbs); on the other hand a one-sided emphasis on the residential function of the inner city as a whole threatens the multifunctional character of this part of cities. In our view, maintenance of a mix of functions (housing, small business, offices, department stores, restaurants, etc.) is essential for the attractiveness and liveliness of Dutch inner cities.

Recent inner-city developments

Nowadays, additions to the housing stock of Dutch inner cities occur in three ways: (*a*) the construction of new dwellings in lieu of old dilapidated dwellings; (*b*) "urban infill" plans for open spaces in existing urban areas, where other types of land use prevailed in the past or on vacant land. A marked example is the proposal to construct new

Table 19.2 Changes in the housing stock and population of the inner cities of Amsterdam, The Hague and Utrecht, 1960–80.

Inner city	Housing stock				Population			
	1960–64	1965–69	1970–74	1975–79	1960–64	1965–69	1970–74	1975–79
Amsterdam	−9.6%	−5.8%	−6.2%	+0.8%	−14.4%	−18.3%	−18.9%	−6.8%
The Hague	−7.4	−15.3	−11.2	+3.2	−24.6	−21.9	−25.1	−12.0
Utrecht	−8.9	−8.7	−6.8	+2.0	−13.7	−15.6	−13.7	−8.0

housing projects in former harbor areas in Amsterdam and Rotterdam;[2] and (c) the conversion of offices and other buildings to residential dwellings, a process that has been increasing in the past few years.

Furthermore, there are fewer withdrawals from the housing stock because of demolition for traffic purposes or the construction of large office buildings than previously. As a result, changes in the housing stock and in population development in most Dutch inner cities show marked differences between the years 1975–79 and the preceding five-year periods, as illustrated by table 19.2.[3]

During the sixties and the first half of the seventies, there was a large decline in inner-city housing stock, but since 1975 there has been a net increase. In addition, there was less population decline in the second half of the seventies. The decrease in the average number of persons per dwelling assumes a growing importance as a factor in population decline.

We can conclude that the residential function of Dutch inner cities is to a certain extent on its way back. Adding dwellings to the housing stock and improving the residential environment in central urban areas can contribute to reducing the amount of space needed to house the urban population. However, in most cases, this contribution will be modest; the poor quality of many dwellings in these areas leads to the demolition of dwellings, and, in cases of replacement in the same neighborhood, the number of new dwellings is usually smaller. Therefore, policy measures intended to maintain or increase population densities at the urban level should also be oriented toward filling in open spaces in existing residential areas and building dwellings at higher densities in extension plans.

Population structure of central areas

It is difficult to say whether there has been a clear drop in the socio-economic level of the inner-city population in The Netherlands. Certainly this has been the case in those areas into which the expanding center functions have not yet penetrated and where the housing stock is of inferior quality, but the scarce data available for the past decade do not reveal considerable changes in the socioeconomic level of the population of the inner city as a whole.

In this respect, the recent trend of social upgrading is worth mentioning. Some inner-city neighborhoods of large Dutch cities are subject to "gentrification." Two forms of this process can be perceived: (a) old dilapidated houses are demolished and replaced by new dwellings, either by (semi-)public authorities or by private developers. Frequently the former inhabitants cannot pay the much higher rents and middle- and upper-income groups invade the area; and (b) by private, spontaneous revitalization, older houses, especially those of a specific architectural style, such as dwellings along the canals in Amsterdam, are bought and improved by the residents themselves.

This pattern of lower-income households being displaced by higher-income households and a process of housing improvement has also been reported for parts of London (Short, 1982: 45) and for the inner cities of Munich, Hamburg, Wiesbaden, and Heidelberg (Von Einem, 1982: 17). Students who continue living in such areas after their graduation are one population group which contributes to this type of social upgrading in the central parts of some larger cities, e.g., Utrecht.

Gentrification can cause and indeed has caused social conflicts, notably in English cities. Elliot and McCrone (1982: 105) report sharp confrontations between the established locals on the one hand and property owners and newcomers on the other. This is one aspect of a general problem as to whether dwellings in urban renewal areas should be provided for the original population or for newcomers. We will return to this subject in the last part of this chapter.

Thus far, we have provided a short description of some recent trends regarding the recovery of the Dutch inner cities. Important questions concerning the future population composition are: (a) What policy intentions have been formulated by the municipalities? and (b) What relationship exists between residential building density at the neighborhood level and population composition, given the policy goal to increase urban population density?

In regard to the first question, a marked feature of the plans and reports is the widespread objective of a balanced population. "Balanced" can be conceived of as an equivalent of "normal," which means that the intended composition is derived from another, usually larger, geographical unit (for example, the city as a whole). In our view, there are serious objections to this policy objective. Why should the population structure in the inner city be the same as in the whole city or urban region? The inner city must be considered as a residential location with specific characteristics; this holds as much for the existing housing stock and the physical environment as for the proximity to various facilities. As a consequence, this submarket caters to population groups other than, for instance, outer urban districts and suburbs. There is no reason why the inner city or any other part of the town should have a normal, average, or balanced population. In this sense, the concept of balance is not useful. In some cases, policies are directed towards avoiding a one-sided population composition. While conclusions about one-sidedness are a subjective matter, it is not hard to conceive of undesirable effects of a very high and still increasing percentage of nonfamily households (particularly single, mobile persons) upon social integration, use of facilities, and so on. Some municipalities want to create housing opportunities for a wide range of income categories to control socioeconomic one-sidedness resulting from selective migration.

With regard to the second question, concerning building density, policy intentions to slow down a town's population decline by means of increasing the residential density in specific areas have consequences for population composition. Applied to the central parts of the towns, this means that contradictions could arise between the objective of achieving a population density as high as possible and the objective of housing a wide range of demographic categories.

In this respect, some findings of Burgers (1979), based on research in eleven Dutch cities, are relevant. He concludes that demographic one-sidedness will increase with increasing building density. If the primary aim is to attract families with children, a relatively low building density (about forty dwellings per hectare) is desirable. As for towns of medium size, Burgers suggests that, given this aim, residential units with three or more stories should be avoided. In the larger cities (Amsterdam, The Hague), the opportunities for housing families with children in multistory buildings are somewhat better, because of the scarce supply of dwellings in these towns. However, that does not alter the fact that these dwellings are not really attractive to families with children. If, in towns of medium size, the primary aim is to house as many people per hectare as possible, an optimum density is about fifty-five dwellings per hectare in the case of one-family dwellings and about 120 dwellings per hectare in multistory buildings. In larger towns, the average household size in these dwellings will be greater, so population density will be higher despite the same residential density.

The desirability of an urban social impact analysis

Urban policy in general, and specific measures in the field of revitalization and urban renewal in particular, have social effects and may lead to conflicts of interest or values and sometimes to social disintegration and greater social inequality. Therefore, we think that it is necessary to carry out a social impact analysis as part of an overall urban impact analysis preceding political decisions. Nijkamp (1981: 95) argues that "urban impact analysis should contain an assessment of all foreseeable and expected consequences of a change in one or more stimuli which exert effects on the urban welfare profile." One of the three categories of impacts he distinguishes is impacts as a consequence of urban policies. In this framework, we emphasize the necessity of analyzing foreseeable and expected social consequences of policy decisions to increase population densities. This orientation applies to behavioral effects on the individual level, as well as to organizational effects on the community level. Such an analysis should be based on available data of past research, specific data with regard to the existing situation, and the expected consequences of alternative policies. As an example, we point to two policy alternatives in urban renewal areas: either building for the neighborhood population or for newcomers. There can be no question that many interests are involved other than those of the residents in these areas, however important they may be. In our view, it is necessary to consider this problem within the framework of policy objectives for the whole city or urban region.

Along the above lines, we can distinguish between internal effects, i.e., for the neighborhood population, and external effects, i.e., for the whole city or urban region. Internal effects include such issues as the emotional attachment and social ties of residents to their neighborhood, the risks of social deterioration and stigmatization, and the possibility of maintaining the neighborhood as a framework for social and cultural integration. External effects are, among others, intensified segregation processes in several parts of the region and their consequences for the political system, the financial situation of the larger towns, the earning power of center-city retail establishments, and the use of recreational facilities.

In light of the foregoing discussion, it would be inappropriate to make an a priori choice between the population already living in the neighborhood and potential newcomers. Also, decisions may differ for different urban renewal areas. In dealing with these questions, urban planners are confronted with an ever-recurrent problem in urban planning: the contrasts between local, usually short-term, interests and regional, usually long-term, interests. Generally, in a social impact analysis special attention should be given to effects concerning social conflicts, social integration, and social equality. It is unrealistic to expect that all conflicts and contradictions will be solved in this manner, but, with the help of multidimensional evaluation techniques, it will be possible to prepare well-founded political decisions.

Egalitarian Possibilities in Housing:
        Norwegian Housing Policy

        Cedric Pugh

Abstract. In this final chapter Pugh discusses housing policy as a vehicle to achieve broader socioeconomic objectives. Census information and other secondary data in the housing arena are drawn upon to describe and analyze attempts of the Norwegian government to bring about relative equity. Compared with other countries, housing supply has been ample, moderately priced, and characterized by less segregation according to tenure and dwelling type. Overall economic performance has not been hampered by a housing policy which has lessened inequities generated antecedently in the production process.

The Norwegian housing system is comparatively successful when assessed against criteria from egalitarian principles.[1] In respect to egalitarianism in housing, we look at the housing policy in relation to the economic situation and economic policies. Beyond this, we examine the way housing is financed and resourced. Tenure, housing poverty, land policies, and other things will also be evaluated. In an egalitarian housing system, we expect provisions to deal with housing poverty and the housing gap; beyond the antipoverty provisions, we further expect to see some distributive measures to counter horizontal and vertical inequity.[2]

The economic situation in Norway during the seventies compares favorably with that of other developed capitalist countries (OECD, 1981). Per capita income in 1980 stood at a relative high of US$11,357; unemployment was less than 1 percent; and the balance of payments was in credit. Norway experienced steady economic growth until the seventies, and during the seventies its possession of oil and natural gas reserves enabled it to bridge the worst stresses of structural unemployment, inflation, and change experienced worldwide. Between 1974 and 1977, Norway's growth rate was double the average in OECD countries. However, wage and price inflation occurred in 1977 and 1978, and in response the government tightened the money supply and pursued a cooling-off period in wages and prices.

Egalitarian tendencies have operated in various spheres of economic policies: in wage settlements; in government expenditure, which reached 50 percent of GNP in 1974; and in interest rate policy. Some new directions were taken in policy in the capital markets and in interest rates after 1978. Before 1978, policy was to maintain low and stable (nominal) interest rates in order to protect low-income groups, especially in housing, and to stimulate investment. In 1978, policy turned in the direction of partial liberalization, giving more flexibility and economic freedom in bank lending rates and in the workings of the capital market. Nevertheless, the capital market is not completely free, and the change reflected a loosening of some administrative regulations. This has affected housing policy, where the proportion of Housing Bank lending in total State Bank's lending fell from 56.9 percent in 1971 to 38.9 percent in 1981. Also, the share of State Bank's lending in total domestic credit fell from 55 percent in 1978 to 30 percent in 1981. The government, nevertheless, ensured a firm flow of funds into housing. As the private banks increased their supply of credit, a quota of total credit was earmarked for housing. We will return to the role of the Housing Bank a little later. Here, it is sufficient to point out that housing policy has been coordinated with changes in monetary and capital market policies.

Housing has maintained a firm position in relation to other indicators. From an indices base of 100 in 1978, by 1980 the building and construction index had reached 216 (below the consumer price index of 223), but hourly earnings by adult males exceeded these other indicators, attaining 273. The average useful floor space in Housing Bank dwellings continued to increase, from 75 square meters in 1973 to 83 square meters in 1980.

Various social commentators draw attention to the generally egalitarian ethos in Norwegian society. Sieriestad (1974) comments upon the egalitarian ideals in the equalization of some incomes and in the social control of business. Torgensen (1974) identifies a number of characteristics and examples, all tending toward a comparative egalitarianism. Norway has no legacy of conservative aristocracy, and large business is less dominant in domestic politics than in other countries. Public institutions dominate the elite, and Norwegian conservatives tend to be more moderate and stand further left on the political spectrum than conservatives in other European countries. Society is also less stratified and there are no formal barriers to check social mobility. Politically, privileges have been eroded, and social democratic politics was dominant from the thirties until 1979. The welfare state has been firmly established in a context of steady economic growth, comparative social and regional homogeneity, and the absence of major political disturbance.

Norwegian housing policies: A historical and general outline

The major characteristics of Norwegian housing are the expression of social objectives in the financial instruments, openness of tenure choice and dwelling type, and unbureaucratic administration. The financial instruments, affordable loans with housing allowances for low- and moderate-income households, are available on similar terms to all tenure groups—private renters, homeowners, and cooperative societies. Consequently, the system is less fragmented and less exposed to vertical and horizontal inequity than other systems. At the 1980 take-up of State Bank loans, which financed some 80 percent of new housing loans, owner-occupiers absorbed 61 percent, cooperators 23 percent, and private enterprise landlords 9 percent. Some 80 percent of these housing loans were used to develop single- and two-family houses, and 14 percent went to apartments. From the perspective of coherence and continuity in policy development, a useful package of coordinated elements was developed as early as 1916. The Norwegian Labour party had then articulated a policy covering support for homeownership, municipal land acquisition, municipal housing for relieving chronic shortages, support for cooperative housing, and security for tenants.

The principal agencies of central government housing policy are two state housing banks. They have deep historical origins. In 1894, the government created the Housing Loan Fund to provide housing credit for low-income families. This initiative has produced, through successive stages, a modern housing policy dominated by central government housing banks. The changes occurred by consolidating the role of central housing banks, and, since 1946, these instruments have been the Housing Bank and the Smallholders Bank. These banks operate as financial and administrative organizations, reviewing applications for funds and administering the mortgages. Housing credit is available to any adult Norwegian, regardless of income, but with limits on the size and standard of housing which can be permitted, and the allocation of resources to housing has been slotted into a system of national social and economic planning started in 1946. As noted, the banks support owner-occupier, cooperative, and rental tenure. The government has used its dominating economic role so that saving banks buy government bonds and then channel the funds into the housing banks.

In response to the severe inflation of 1973, the government introduced reforms in housing finance aimed at easing repayment burdens and expanding housing allowances inherited from the fifties, so that low-income access was easier. Under the revised housing allowances, those with the lowest incomes spent no more than 15 percent of their incomes on housing. For those with higher incomes, the scale of assistance was reduced to cover 20 percent of housing costs. The scheme was designed to reach those income groups just below the average. Housing allowances were available to owner-occupiers, cooperators, and renters. By 1978, they covered 112,000 households and cost NKr289 million.[3]

In 1973 Norway had achieved reform in response to considerations of inflation and distributional equity in just one step, by simultaneously altering housing allowances and the structure of the bank's loans. This reflects the direct, uncomplicated, and effective approach in Norwegian housing. Homeownership has continued to grow, but it is taxed on grounds of tenure-related equity. Imputed rental value is taxed at 2.5 percent on 30 percent of the value of the dwelling; other assets are subject to the same tax rate, but full value, not just 30 percent of value, is taxed.

The Norwegian housing system in structural perspective

We proceed to interpret the Norwegian housing system in its main structural characteristics. The economy operates from the basis of a production-consumption sector, where goods, factor services, incomes, and spending flow circularly through consumption and production. The production sphere builds, renovates, and provides services to the housing system, and it has inflow and outflow relationships with the government sector. It produces its own capital goods, and funds for new private capital formation originate in household savings and in credit creation in the capital market. The government sector has some influence on the capital market and on its relationship to the housing system. First, its monetary policy will have impacts upon the levels of credit availability, upon the rate of interest and other terms on which credit is available, and upon the degree of liquidity (i.e., the facility with which funds can be used to purchase real resources).

Second, government has the potential to influence the relationship between housing capital and wider capital market. This can be done in various ways. For example, in Norway it has been done through the Housing Bank. Some of the finance is privilege circuit in the sense that it is drawn specifically into housing, sometimes carrying lower rates of interest or deferred payments as compared to nonhousing capital.

A structural interpretation of Norwegian housing can be made by examining the roles of government and its Housing Bank. These two instruments shift resources from the general production-consumption system into the housing system. The Housing Bank has performed this intermediary role since the 1890s, adding supply year by year to the housing stock. In comparative terms, the rates of production in Norway are consistently high. For example, in 1978 Norway completed 9.4 dwellings per 1,000 population, relative to 8.6 in the United States, 8.0 in the Soviet Union, 6.0 in West Germany, and 6.5 in Sweden. Essentially, what happens is that some of the flow of saving from the rich and from the general community is channeled into housing, and, especially through homeownership and cooperative tenure, wealth is spread to some extent. The rich continue to own and to reproduce capital through the production process, but, through financial instruments and resource flows, some wealth (assets) and housing income flows are spread to the not-so-rich, to middle- and moderate-income groups, and to some working-class families. Norway's comparative position in homeownership and cooperative tenure is shown in figure 20.1.

The variations in homeownership among countries arise from a whole configuration of circumstances, including cultural, ideological, and historical factors, but the major explanation is accessibility because of the way financial instruments are designed and constructed. The specifics involve duration of loans, patterns of repayment, amount of

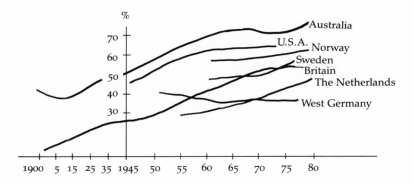

Figure 20.1   Homeownership in the housing stock of selected countries.

Sources: Schriftenreihe *Wohnungsmarkt und Wohungspolitik, Wohneigentumsquote* (07.005), Bundesminister fur Raumordning, Bauwesen und Stadtebau, Bonn, 1979; United Nations (ECE), *A Statistical Survey of the Housing Situation in the ECE Countries Around 1970,* New York, 1978, pp. 80–90, and *Annual Bulletin of Housing and Building Statistics for Europe.* 1979, pp. 37–41., Personal communications: Den Norske Stats Husbank; Riksbyggen; and Jan van der Schaar, Technische Hogeschool Delft. Notes: The Norwegian and Swedish statistical representation includes cooperative (coownership) tenure, which is 14% for Sweden and 10% for Norway.

deposit or own capital, and the loan-to-building cost ratio. Access is easier where loans are of long duration, say fifteen years or more; where deposit requirements are low, say something like less than 20 percent of purchase price; and where loan-to-building cost ratios are high, say about 90 percent of the purchase price. Comparative data are shown in figure 20.2 and figure 20.3.

All the representations in figure 20.2 and figure 20.3 should be interpreted cautiously. They are based upon data from the years 1974–80 with the aim of reflecting "typical" housing costs and tenure "cost/price" (through "typical" instituted financing). This, of course, means that a typical pattern of production and tenure price/cost should be compared with variations and the extent of "untypical" conditions—dwelling form, city-rural context, eligibilities for overt subsidies, waiting time for easier access schemes, and so on. However, the representations do have some use for making very general comparative evaluations and relating tenure proportions to financial structures. Furthermore, they point toward ways in which tenure can be used as a partial equalizer in some income ranges between the

Own-capital as a
% of buying price

Percentage of own-capital and capital costs

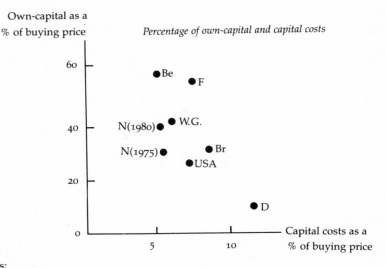

Notes:

Be—Belgium, 54% owner-occupied stock in 1976
Br—Britain, 51% owner-occupied stock in 1976
D—Denmark, 53% owner-occupied stock in 1976
F—France, 45% owner-occupied stock in 1976
USA, 64% owner-occupied stock in 1976
W.G.—West Germany, 34% owner-occupied stock in 1976
N—Norway (Housing Bank housing)
Under income-conditioned subsidy schemes in Belgium and France, the percentage of own-capital is reduced to some 30% and 25% of buying price, respectively.
1. Own-capital: capital contribution from the individual required to cover that part of the value of housing not covered by the loan. This is expressed as a percentage of the total financing.
2. Income: own-capital ratios; "income" is net annual average income.
3. Capital costs: the annual interest and principal repayments. These are expressed variously as a percentage of "income" and as a percentage of total financing.

Figure 20.2 Own capital and capital costs: Typical financial structures for mortgage-financed new one-family homes, 1974–80.

top decile and the bottom three deciles of family income distribution.

   The representations shown in figures 20.2 and 20.3 indicate that Norway has comparatively good access to homeownership and cooperative tenure, though access became more difficult from 1975 to 1980. In fact, most of the points fixed for other countries refer only to earlier 1974–77 data, and access has become more difficult with increasing interest rates and higher prices since 1977. In 1980, a Norwegian family buying a new cottage of some 85 square meters in a large city such as Oslo, would pay NKr330,000 (US$53,140). Median and average annual (individual) incomes were in the range of NKr80,000 to NKr100,000 (US$12,880 to US$16,105).

Land policies influence house prices, and consequently these policies are important in pursuing egalitarian objectives. Our conceptualization of housing includes urban land policies. Norway has followed a policy of public acquisition and sale of land which is planned for urban development. Effectively, this keeps the land price component in housing costs to proportions below 20 percent. Without such public acquisition policies, land prices would rise, with speculative pressures driving them beyond rises in the general consumer price index. More significantly, speculative processes in growing urban economies trans-

Figure 20.3 Income-own capital and capital costs-income: Typical financial structures for mortgage-financed new one-family homes, 1974–80.

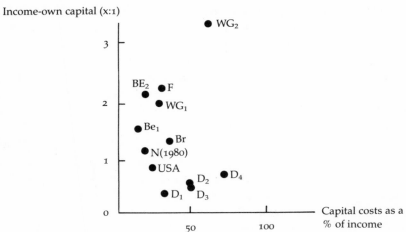

Notes:

Be Belgium; Be_1 = white collar worker; Be_2 = blue collar worker.

Br Britain

D Denmark; D_1, D_2, D_3, D_4—according to rural and urban housing cost and income differences. D_3 and D_4 represent urban and metropolitan housing costs and incomes.

F France

USA

WG West Germany; WG_1 = professional income; WG_2 = blue collar worker income.

N Norway (Housing Bank housing)

France and West Germany support saving for homeownership with grants/premiums and/or tax credits.

fer wealth from moderate- to high-income groups and impede access to housing (Neutze, 1973; Pugh, 1980). The Norwegian land policies have been developed upon the basis and initiative of Swedish policies, which have been effectively egalitarian throughout the twentieth century.

The Norwegian housing system can be related to the profile of Norwegian family income distribution. We first make some general comparative statements about the distribution of family income in Norway. To begin with, in terms of percentage distribution, the bottom 20 percent of households receives some 5.6 percent of total income, compared with the top 20 percent, which receives some 40 percent. With reference to family income distribution, we divide the housing system into two categories. Households in the top 20 percent of the income distribution live mainly in large, non-Housing Bank dwellings. They finance their dwellings directly from the regular capital market, at greater cost than those in the bottom 80 percent of the income distribution, who get housing through the Housing Bank system. Interest rates in commercial and savings banks rose at a rate between 8.0 percent and 13.0 percent in the years 1977–80, which is affordable in terms of ten years or more only to those in the top 20 percent of income distribution. Indeed, since there are no income eligibility limitations on cheaper and more flexible Housing Bank credit, the richest can have access to easier finance. Their option for non-Housing Bank credit or for outright purchase is a preference for larger and more expensive houses.

The housing built or financed in association with the Housing Bank serves the majority of Norwegian households. It is capacious and of more varied design, compared to housing in both the capitalist and socialist countries of Europe. Since 1973, Housing Bank finance has been geared to a capacity to pay, taking as its benchmark some 20 percent of average male blue collar earnings. It is a deferred payments design and construction, available in cooperative (co-owned) tenure, and in private rental. Eligibility for housing allowance is widespread throughout low- and moderate-income households, and it crosses tenure lines. The eligibility is fixed in relation to family income, family size, and housing outlays. Large families with lower incomes and higher housing outlays will receive larger housing allowances. Housing allowances are designed to reach the median-to-average income range.

Other egalitarian aspects of Norwegian housing policy include low rates of tax on imputed rental values of owner-occupied housing and a capital tax. Imputed rental is taxed at 2.5 percent on 30 percent of the value of the dwelling. Interest payments are tax deductible in homeownership and cooperative tenure. In summary, the tax treatments favor housing compared with other assets, but the tax collector gets more revenue from higher-value dwellings than from lower-value dwellings.

We can extend our appreciation of the egalitarian direction of Norwegian housing by looking at the effects on the distribution of wealth and at the allocation of housing allowances to households. Table 20.1 gives some indication of the effects on the distribution of wealth.

Table 20.1 shows that homeownership and cooperative tenures tend to deconcentrate the distribution of wealth to a limited extent. Housing wealth is more significant in the wealth of lower and moderate asset groups. The richest will often have homeownership, but stocks, shares, and business ownership are more important in their total accumulation of assets. Homeownership or cooperative tenure does not fully cover the income profile, since some 35 percent of the households are renters; these renters include some of the poorest population segments, who, although supported by various social income provisions, have been unable to save the deposits necessary for homeownership. Housing allowances will have reduced their rent-income burdens, and in some instances eased access into homeownership or cooperative tenure.

Table 20.1 The housing wealth component in total wealth.

Total wealth (Kr., net worth)	Proportion of housing wealth in total wealth
Negative and Zero	55.2%
1–9,999	48.3
10,000–24,999	47.2
25,000–49,999	53.9
50,000–99,999	48.6
100,000–199,999	37.2
200,000–499,999	33.8
Above 500,000	32.6

Source: Data for 1976 calculated from Table 373. Norway. Central Bureau of Statistics, *Statistical Yearbook*, 1980, Oslo: Central Bureau of Statistics, 1980.

Table 20.2 Allocation of housing allowances, by family income and by housir outlays, April 1982, (in Kr1,000).

Housing Outlays	Income p.a.								
	<10	10–15	15–20	20–25 (US$3,543)	25–30	30–35	35–40	40–45 (US$7,085)	45–5(
<5	36	25	81	535	18				
5–6	52	35	117	1,254	288	14			
6–7	166	75	326	2,597	823	410	38		
7–8	242	124	595	2,964	1,320	953	533	36	1
8–9	281	131	702	3,112	1,501	1,162	847	371	34
9–10 (US$1,610)	419	210	891	3,263	1,629	1,273	965	738	260
10–11	391	193	875	3,047	1,514	1,269	1,001	833	521
11–12	424	212	744	2,403	1,259	1,090	930	812	613
12–13	420	203	576	1,514	995	1,014	861	771	626
13–14	423	222	510	1,091	785	872	740	712	644
14–15 (US$2,415)	486	225	589	1,235	821	738	716	714	610
15–16	282	99	163	288	311	357	370	400	436
16–17	426	171	244	455	464	525	586	651	698
17–18	151	61	61	90	103	110	152	187	239
18–19	213	72	96	142	183	186	188	184	196
19–20 (US$3,220)	52	10	15	21	19	32	33	35	47
20–21	104	22	39	45	55	57	71	77	108
21–22	4				1	3	4	3	
>22 (US$3,543)	13		3	6	3	2	4	7	7
Total	4,585	2,090	6,627	24,062	12,090	10,067	8,039	6,531	5,040

Source: Personal Communication from the Norwegian Housing Bank.

The data in table 20.2 show the allocation of housing allowances. It indicates that the allowances reach to NKr90,000 (US$14,492), being just below average individual incomes, and that, in the higher income ranges, the main factor giving eligibility is the higher housing expense. Most allowances are clustered in the low-income range NKr15,000 per year to NKr45,000 per year (US$2,415 to US$7,246), where housing outlays range from NKr5,000 per year to NKr15,000 per year (US$805 to US$1,169). The redistributional impact is clearly mainly for anti-poverty purposes with some modest egalitarian association.

50–55	55–60	60–65 (US$10,628)	65–70	70–75	75–80 (US$14,171)	80–85	85–90	>40	Total
									695
									1,760
									4,435
									6,768
7									8,148
42	4								9,694
176	35								9,855
438	159	24	1						9,109
535	462	239	17						8,233
640	653	552	166	6					8,016
779	825	851	523	62	1				9,175
553	636	702	671	199	19	1			5,487
871	872	932	758	414	58	6		2	8,133
288	386	449	448	354	95	19		1	3,194
266	334	383	411	422	121	21	3		3,421
56	97	102	131	135	117	33	8	1	944
147	220	285	356	420	438	135	7		2,586
1	5	1	3	9	3	6	4		47
12	5	12	18	15	7	13	20	11	158
,811	4,693	4,532	3,503	2,036	859	234	42	15	99,858

Summary and future issues

The Norwegian housing system works in egalitarian directions in several ways. It tends to deconcentrate wealth by adding asset value to middle-, moderate-, and some low-income households. The housing allowances target through a wide range of income groups across the poor and the mean income sections in the profile. Land pricing and urban investment is influenced by social principles in land policy. More specifically, the government excludes major speculative price impulses by its land acquisition policy, and urban areas are planned to provide accessible services. At a more general level, the Housing Bank acts as an intermediary between the production-consumption process and the capital market on the one hand and the housing system on the other. The Norwegian system expresses social goals through the design and construction of housing finance. Compared with other countries, supply has been maintained at high levels over a long period of time, and the housing system contains less rigid separatism along the lines of tenure, dwelling type, and housing which is stigmatizing and/or identifiably government housing in some countries. In its general economic framework, Norway has maintained better growth rates than many of the modern democracies; levels of employment have been high; and interest rates have risen less steeply than in, for example, the United States or Australia.

Any consideration of using housing as an equalizer has to be set in the context of antecedent societal inequalities. Inequality arises basically in the production process and in the ownership of productive capital in capitalist societies. Socialist societies have their own structural inequalities in general, and the inequalities show up in housing allocations and in underallocation of resources to housing. The Norwegians have some housing egalitarianism, to be interpreted as a moderating influence on basic and fundamental inequalities in the economic system. At least, housing in Norway does not entirely endorse and accentuate prior inequalities. To go further, it would mean that other measures would have to be contemplated, including: (a) counting housing-related activities as production, with financial flows attached to services and to costs; (b) spreading the ownership of capital in manufacturing and commerical activities; and (c) pushing up homeownership and cooperative tenure rates among the low-income groups and/or raising their relative incomes. These matters touch upon institutional matters and upon the access of housewives and househusbands to financial income and to property rights, more than they make a general call for the advent of socialism.

Not everything in the Norwegian housing system is entirely egalitarian. Low-income households cannot always save enough to gain access to homeownership. Also, the low-interest rates policy may exhibit some contradictions. Although low-interest rates ease access, and, through privileged circuiting, housing is firmly resourced, some low-income savers may be penalized. It is often the case that the low-income savers, especially the aged, are not sophisticated in deploying their funds where the returns are highest. Some of their saving is accordingly caught and trapped in low-interest channels, with higher income groups increasing their wealth via cheap housing credit. This is not to argue categorically that housing money should be at the same cost as nonhousing capital; what is needed is an evalution of the incidence of costs and benefits overall. In most countries, housing capital and the financial instruments attached to it were created explicitly and institutionally.

Concluding evaluation

From any modern perspective of social policy, whether in less-developed countries or in developed capitalist and socialist countries, egalitarianism features strongly among the values of social critics and policy makers. Other criteria which normally enter the discussions in social policy development include economic efficiency, political and economic liberty, choice for consumers, and social or community development. In modern economics and social administration, frequently discussions are contentious between those who advocate more liberty and those who favor egalitarian objectives. Sometimes the discussions are conveyed as though either emphasis is absolute, without any details of whose freedoms and whose greater equalities are at stake. Fortunately, in Norwegian housing the discussion does not have to be polarized, nor does it have to proceed from theoretical dogma. We can make relative claims for efficiency, choice, and egalitarianism in Norwegian housing.

Norwegian housing is provided efficiently, in the sense that most economists would want to use the term efficiency. That is to say, housing wants are met at affordable cost, giving expression to individual and to political means of expressing those wants. As in most modern societies, housing is linked to the development of state social policy and to the willingness of households to pay for their housing benefits. Norwegian housing history indicates the use of community power and social cooperation to create an economic framework for housing which fulfills the satisfaction of individual households (Pugh, 1980). The housing provided is neither meager and stigmatizing on the one hand nor dominated by excessively bureaucratic and technocratic preferences on the other. The consumer has choice of dwelling type, location, and tenure. But choice is not without limit; it relates to affordability and to submarket relevance. Nevertheless, compared with

Britain and other modern democratic countries, the housing system has far less fragmented rigidity, held tightly along tenure-design lines. Or, compared with socialist countries, the Norwegians have more choice in dwelling types, and the majority choose not to live in high-rise apartment blocks. Finally, within the framework of national economic and social planning Norway has achieved more compatibility and consistency between housing and nonhousing capital and between private and government-subsidized urban investment. Norwegian society has been comparatively effective at providing jobs and the sorts of housing that people want to pay for and live in. That goes a long way toward establishing the basis for economic and social welfare. General economic well-being is at high levels, with the 1981 per capita income exceeded in Europe by only Switzerland, Denmark, Sweden, West Germany, and Luxembourg. Egalitarian housing does not imply underperformance in key economic indicators; it may enhance the economic performance. The Norwegian example shows that there are limited, but important, egalitarian possibilities in housing.

Notes

2 The Effects of Household Formation on Housing Needs in Britain

1 "Leasehold" here means a form of ownership limited in time. It is favored for the combination of home ownership and welfare services for the elderly because it allows the freeholder to retain some control, e.g., to reserve the housing to the elderly on sale and to ensure that services are provided as specified to purchasers.

3 Rental Housing Practices Affecting Families with Children: Hard Times for Youth

1 Among the 629 managers, 22 percent owned or managed a single-family house; the remaining managers were responsible for complexes or buildings containing an estimated total of 78,600 dwellings. For a detailed description of the sampling and data collection procedures, see Marans et al., 1980.
2 For the analyses reported, we have combined renters living in townhouses and duplexes with those living in apartments.

4 Housing the Extended Family in Sweden

1 By the extended family is meant the group of grandparents, parents, children, and grandchildren who keep in close contact with each other but do not necessarily live in the same household.
It is a matter of definition where to draw the lines for the extended family; for practical reasons it does not include siblings, uncles and aunts, or any other close relatives of the same generation. Also excluded are divorced couples with joint responsibility for the children. Empirically, the extended family can consist of many different types of relations and links: the group that considers themselves as belonging to the same family or makes any kind of joint planning for the group as a whole.
2 The sample consists of every fifteenth married woman in Gävleborg County, forty-five to fifty-four years old, without regard to ethnic or social background. This age group has been chosen because they are the most likely to have both

grandchildren and living parents. They can therefore act as informants of their own situation as well as of the situation of their elders, their children, and their grandchildren. By asking one age group, information is obtained about many, if not all. It must be pointed out that the survey includes no questions about values or preferences, in which case this method would have been unacceptable. The response is somewhat low, 64 percent. However, the nonrespondents have been shown not to differ from the respondents in any way that is of importance to the results.

Gävleborg County is in the central part of Sweden, and it includes rural areas as well as moderate-sized towns. In a second part of the project, the Stockholm metropolitan area will be investigated.

3   The investigated four generations are defined by their relation to the respondent women: the parents, the respondent women, the adult children, and the grand-children. Generally this accounts for the household of each generation. The parents can be both households of the woman's mother and father or only one of them. The women include their own households. Adult children are only the children who have moved away from home and may include a spouse. Thus the figures that are presented only include persons outside the woman's own house-hold. A few (1 percent) have elderly relatives living with them, and of course many still have children at home, but these relations will not be discussed in this chapter.

4   All quotations are from the survey. Many respondents made their own comments and some even wrote long letters explaining their situation. The comments often express strong positive feelings, as "We have a wonderful family," or negative feelings, as "I don't care about my mother-in-law, she interferes too much."

5   Official Statistics of Sweden, National Central Bureau of Statistics. *Living conditions 1976, Report No. 18, Isolation and togetherness—An outlook on social participation.* 1980.

6   G. Sundström, "Caring for the aged in welfare society," dissertation, University of Stockholm, 1983. The author investigated mixed generation households in Sweden and found that much unpaid work is carried out by women who look after their old relatives in such households, but that one cannot assume that this will be a solution for a major part of elderly care.

7   The Danish National Institute of Social Research, Merete Platz. *De aeldres levevilkor 1977* (Living conditions for the elderly) Meddelelse 32, Copenhagen, 1981. Apart from the fewer elderly who share residence with their children, the situation has not changed much from the mid-sixties. About as many live within reach of each other, as documented in Shanas, E., et al. *Old people in three industrial societies.* London: Routledge and Kegan Paul, 1968.

8   Young, M. and Wilmott, P. *Family and kinship in East London.* London: Routledge and Kegan Paul, 1957.

9   One reason may be that the (say) usually monthly visits took place just a few days previously. But—and this is important for the discussion later—the reverse is also possible: Usually frequent visits may have been interrupted at the time of the questionnaire, for one reason or another. Comments by the respondents indicate both possibilities. Cross tabulations made by the author on other material be-tween the question "How often to you meet X?" and the question "When did you

see X last?" show that one can fairly safely assume that the number of people who happened to meet during the previous week who usually do not, are roughly equal to the number of people who usually meet every week but did not during the previous week.

10   Teeland, L. *Keeping in touch: The relation between old people and their adult children.* (Monograph 16) Gothenburg, Sweden: University of Gothenburg, Department of Sociology, 1978.

11   Liljeström, R. and Dahlström, E. *Arbetarkvinnor i hem- arbets och samhällsliv* (Working Class Women at home, at work and in society) Stockholm: Tiden, 1981.

12   Björnberg, U. et al. *Livsformer i en region: En jämförande analys av familje- och samhällsliv i 1970-talets Sverige* (Ways of life in a region: a comparative analysis of family life and society in the 1970's in Sweden). Stockholm: Liber Allmänna, 1982.

13   Daun, Å. and Ehn, S. *Boende och livsform* (Housing and ways of life). Stockholm: Tiden, 1980.

14   Kornhaber, A. and Woodward, K. L. *Grandparents, grandchildren: The vital connection.* Garden City, N.Y.: Anchor Press/Doubleday, 1981.

15   Communal living is a subject which currently concerns many researchers in Sweden. The most recent report on this topic is Gromark, S. *Boendegemenskap* (Community in Housing) Gothenburg: By ACTH, Chalmers Institute of Technology, 1983.

5   Residential Fit and Mobility among Low-Income, Female-Headed Family Households in the United States

1   The research reported in this chapter was supported by a grant from the U.S. Department of Housing and Urban Development (H-5451).

2   The other two parts of the Experimental Housing Allowance Program are the supply experiment and the administrative agency experiment. The supply experiment took place in Green Bay, Wisconsin, and South Bend, Indiana, and it was intended to examine the impact of housing allowances on housing markets. The administrative agency experiment took place in eight sites, and it was intended to evaluate the administration of a housing allowance program and the costs associated with its delivery.

3   Since there were only a small number of male single-parent households (thirty-one at enrollment and sixteen at the final panel interview), they were not included in the analyses.

Part II   Introduction

1   Heady, Bruce. *Housing policy in the developed economy.* New York: St. Martin's Press, 1978, p. 45.

2   *Ibid.*, p. 55.

3   Kemeny, Jim. *The myth of home ownership.* London: Routledge and Kegan Paul, 1981.

6   Restructuring the Welfare State: Privatization of Public Housing in Britain

1   This chapter is based on a research project funded by the Nuffield Foundation.

7   State Intervention in Urban Housing Markets: Melbourne, 1945–80

1   We thank Dr. Leslie Kilmartin for presenting an earlier version of this chapter at the 1982 International Sociological Association Congress. We also thank the editors of *Urban Policy and Research* for permission to reproduce material contained in this chapter.

8   State Intervention and Alternative Tenure Patterns in Montreal

1   This would have been consistent with existing life-style preferences of many upper middle-class households, as expressed notably through the rise in the 1920–30s of a rather luxurious variety of apartment buildings, which preceded the introduction of the cheap walk-up apartment building on the Montreal market (Collin, 1983).

2   This "naturalization" of preferences is characteristic of most urban economic theories, especially "hedonic price" conceptualizations of the housing market (for a critical overview, see Ball, 1973).

3   Summarized in so few words, this is of course a caricature of the neo-Marxist views which have become more or less predominant in explaining the production of urban space during the past decade. Although providing important specifications, the basic thesis has remained that of economic determinism in this school of thought, headed mainly by Castells in Europe and David Harvey in the United States.

4   For example, the "streetcar suburb," created by large landholders who also maintained major interests in local electric power corporations (Goldsmith and Jacobs, 1982); the "automobile suburb," as a result of the collusion of the U.S. federal government with the automobile giants who had succeeded in buying the old transit systems; and the "corporate suburb," as a direct consequence of the growth of the large builder-developer (Lorimer, 1978).

5   Between 1954 and 1978, the proportion of single-family dwellings in new construction in the Montreal area remained constantly well below 40 percent. Since then it has risen to 55–65 percent.

6   One must note, however, that the bias is much less important in Canada than in the United States, where a homeowner can also deduct from his taxable income the interest paid on his home mortgage debt as well as his local property tax payments.

7   These figures, although on the increase, are lower than those in Ontario, where the total number of units for the same period was 63,696, i.e., 7.3 percent of total new construction and 19.4 percent of new apartments.

8 Before renewing a lease, the landlord informs the tenant of the rent increase he wishes to effect for the next year; if the tenant refuses, and no agreement is reached, the landlord must turn to the board for a decision, which is based essentially on increases in operating costs.

9 These disputes have culminated in a challenge of the legal status of most of the Rental Board's powers before the court. A similar law in Ontario was recently declared unconstitutional by the Supreme Court, and the same outcome is expected in Quebec.

10 The total gross population out-migration from the Montreal metropolitan area to other provinces in Canada reached 133,800 between 1976 and 1981 (40 percent to Toronto, 16 percent to Alberta, and 12 percent to British Columbia. The net out-migration has been estimated at 70,000 persons or 23,000 families.

11 The social composition of the cooperatives, on the whole, shows an over-representation of both the lower and higher occupational strata. The latter group's over-representation results from the strong appeal of cooperatives among young intellectual professionals.

9 Housing Young People in Israel

1 An early draft for this chapter was written while the author was on leave of absence from The Pennsylvania State University as an Allon Fellow in the Department of Sociology and the Center for Urban and Regional Studies at Tel-Aviv University. Thanks are due to Gideon Burstein, Ezra Hadar, Etan Sabatello, and Moshe Sicron of the Central Bureau of Statistics for assistance in making available the data, to Ayala Hirsch of the Ministry of Housing for helpful discussion of the early government research on young couples' housing needs, and to Pua Rintel for collecting information on the housing aid program for young couples. Another version will appear in the journal *Urban Studies*.

2 In the Israeli context, the denotation "new town" refers to various types of settlements including, for example, ones that were started from scratch as well as others which are expansions of adjacent existing towns. In this chapter no attempt is made to differentiate between these different types.

3 Young couples refers to couples who married after October, 1970, regardless of their ages.

10 The User's Perspective on Government Housing

1 At several points in this discussion, reference will be made for comparative purposes to the suburbs of Canterbury and Hopper's Crossing, also part of the original study. Canterbury is a leafy, well-established largely middle class suburb located ten kilometers east of the CBD. It is well served by train and tram services and is within easy access of a very wide range of metropolitan services. Hopper's Crossing is a working- and lower-middle-class new suburb on the western metropolitan periphery. It is approximately thirty kilometers from the CBD, poorly served by public transport and is located in what have become known as the

"deprived western suburbs." Thus, the ecological locations under study represent outer eastern, outer western and more central residential locations. Within each location, a census collector's distriction (CD) was selected as the ecological unit of analysis. This selection was on the basis of comparable life-cycle characteristics of residents, namely, English-speaking households with dependent children. Within each CD, households were randomly selected, and the sex of consecutive respondents was alternated by the interviewer. The survey instrument was an interview schedule concerning residential mobility, residential satisfaction, and residential preferences.

2 *Ibid.*

Sweden

1 Gottschalk and Tonboe (1974) have made a detailed analysis of "publicity, secrecy and influence" in planning. For a recent assessment of the limited impact that protests by neighborhood groups have had on planning for a Copenhagen community, see Perlman and Spiegel (1983).

2 In Sweden, the term "flats" is used to refer to dwellings in buildings with fifty or more units, as well as to those in smaller buildings; less than ten percent of the Swedish dwellings fall into the first category.

11 Policy Approaches to Social Housing Problems in Northern and Western Europe

1 Johannes F. Linn, *Cities in the developing world: Policies for their equitable and efficient growth.* New York, Oxford University Press, 1983, p. 170.

2 *Ibid.*, p. 179.

13 Popular Housing in Brazil

1 Thanks to all who gave bibliographical references and made comments on the earlier version of this paper. Ademir Figueiredo was able to collaborate as my research assistant due to funds provided by FINEP (Financiadora de Estudos e Projectos). An extensive bibliography is available upon request from the author.

2 Favela, as defined by the national census bureau, is an urban agglomeration which consists of a minimum of fifty dwellings, most of which lack basic infrastructure, on land that does not belong to the inhabitants.

3 The FGTS is a compulsory savings scheme for workers which is run by the BNH. It collects 8 percent of the monthly wage of each Brazilian worker who is regularly employed.

14   Integrated Kampung Improvement Programs and Mutual Aid in Indonesia

1   This chapter is a revision and condensation by Gulati of contributions to the Tenth ISA Congress by Herlianto and Hofsteede on, respectively, kampung improvement and popular participation in housing in Indonesia.

15   Housing the Poor in a Planned City

1   I am thankful to Professor E. B. Huttman for suggesting that I write on this topic. I am also thankful to professors Sylvia Fava, Willem van Vliet—, and Padmini Gulati for going over the manuscript and giving their comments and suggestions.
2   Scheduled castes is an official term which is used for ex-untouchables. In the traditional caste system, castes are ranked in terms of ritual purity. In this hierarchical system, brahmins occupied the top and untouchables were at the bottom.
3   This act was enacted to provide proper planning and development of Chandigarh. It empowered the Punjab government to issue direction with respect to erecting buildings in the city. This act lays down the building norms and rules applicable to the whole of Chandigarh. Its various sections cover the procedure for submission of building application, planning and architectural controls, materials and structural control, and drainage and administrative control. Therefore, no substandard building can be erected in Chandigarh.
4   Pucca huts are those in which kiln-baked (burnt) bricks are used as a unit of construction. The bricks are of rectangular shape and specified dimensions and made by molding and burning a suitable type of clay.
5   Katcha huts are those in which sun-dried or unburnt bricks are used as a unit of construction.

16   The Squatter's Perspective of Housing

1   Ministry of Housing and Reconstruction and Ministry of Planning, USAID, Immediate action Proposals for Housing in Egypt: Statistical Appendix, June 1976, p. 51.
2   Governor Handy Ashur, cited in al-Ahram, March 15, 1973.
3   "Informal Housing in Egypt," Report presented by Stephen K. Mayo. ABT Associates Inc, USAID Cairo 1981 (unpublished).
4   "Arab Ghoneim," "Kafr el-Elw," "Manshiet Nasser," "Zein," National Center for Social and Criminological Research (NCSCR) Cairo, 1979 (unpublished); "Arab Rashed—Helwan upgrading Project," Report presented by P. B. Sabbour, Ministry of Reconstruction and State Ministry of Housing and Land Reclamation, Cairo, 1982 (unpublished). Wafaa Mabrouk, "Provision for the health needs of a low-socio-economic group," M.A. thesis presented to the Department of Sociology-Anthropology-Psychology, American University in Cairo, 1983.
5   Izbet Zein is one of the six communities identified for an upgrading project. A home improvement loan program started in Izbet Zein as a demonstration project. A socioeconomic survey was conducted in this community for all owners, who

numbered about 300. About 130 of them applied for loans, and seven of this group were selected for case study. The objective of these studies was to understand the life history of residents of the area, their income, and their patterns of expenditure and to assess the impact of the home improvement loan program. The data were gathered through intensive interviews with different members of each household in our sample, participant observation of these cases over a period of about two months, and validating this information through interviews with key informants and other residents in the community. The households were selected for case study on the basis of their being the first settlers and their low-income status.

6   The Joint Housing Projects of the Egyptian Ministry of Housing is carrying out an upgrading program which covers six existing low-income residential communities in Helwan. The project started in 1979, and it is financed by the Egyptian Government and USAID. The program provides environmental improvements, basic infrastructure, services, schools, community facilities, the Home Improvement Loan Program, and the Small Enterprise Loan Program. An estimated 120,000 persons will eventually benefit as the communities and the housing stock expand.

7   The gamciya system is a combination of a loan system and a savings system. Thus two types of participants are needed for the gamciya system to function. Some members enter a gamciya because they are in need of a specific sum of money at that particular time. Others join because they wish to save money and do not trust themselves to do so without the additional incentive of a commitment to the group. The latter group is thus in no hurry to get a return on its investment, which makes the money available to the former as they need it. In a gamciya system, a group of acquaintances, relatives or neighbors pool their surplus money so that each member can have access to a substantial sum without interest.

8   Janet Abu-Lughod, *Cairo, 1001 years of the city victorious*, Princeton, N.J.: Princeton University Press, 1971.

17   Segregation Trends in The Netherlands

1   Increase of social distance is a simplified statement. The mass media have enabled the entire population to see the way of life of others who belong to other strata and even to alien cultures; however, confrontation with pictures is quite different from social intercourse, which also means understanding and emotional involvement.

18   Societal Factors Shaping the Internal Structure of Finnish Cities

1   Sweetser, Frank L., and Sweetser, Dorrian A., 1968, 264–65, Popenoe, David, 1980, 12–19 and Hauser, Francis L., 1968, 213–16.
2   The second largest city in Finland, with a population of approximately 160,000.
3   Ylönen, Ari, 1979, 179–83.
4   Voionmaa, Vaino, 1929, 184–90.

5 *Finland. Ministry of Housing. Urban Study*, 70.

6 Popenoe, David, 1980, 2.

7 When the need for housing was most extensive, the cities and builders made agreements concerning the construction of a certain area to make sure that the whole plan for land use and the entire infrastructure included in it would be realized. The status of builders as landowners has, however, occurred in a way worth noting in the relationship between city and builder. It has been claimed to be a result of the fact that especially those cities where the growth of population and increase in construction have occurred at high rates have not been adequately prepared in regard to public landownership and site planning (*National Housing Program 1976–85, Inventory of Resources*).

8 Kuusi, Pekka, 1961, 137.

9 Alestalo, Matti, 1980, 116.

10 Juntto, Anneli, 1976, 23.

11 *National Housing Program 1976–85, Concluding Report*, 82.

12 Statistical data were collected from *Living Conditions 1950–75*, Central Statistical Office of Finland, Statistical surveys no. 58, 1977 and *Population and Housing Census 1980*, volume IX, Central Statistical Office of Finland 1982.

13 *National Housing Program 1976–85, Concluding Report*, 59.

14 Vance, J. E., 1976, 102.

15 *Ibid.*, 101–2.

16 Smith, Wallace F., 1970, 10.

17 Junkka, Teuvo and Loikkanen, Heikki A. 1975, 27, 97.

18 The city can control construction within its area by site planning, which in Finland is the monopoly of municipalities. The community decides on site planning within its boundaries, while upper-level administration merely can confirm or refuse to confirm decisions made on the local community level about site planning. The municipal council approves the town plan and the Ministry of the Interior ratifies it.

19 Junkka, Teuvo, and Loikkanen, Heikki A., 1975, 19–20.

20 Lankinen, Markku, 1982.

19 Dutch Inner-City Housing in the Context of Revitalization Policies

1 The maximum number of inhabitants was reached by Amsterdam in 1958: 872,500 (on 1.1.1982, 700,750); by Rotterdam in 1964: 732,000 (on 1.1.1982, 568,200); by The Hague in 1958: 607,000 (on 1.1.1982, 454,300); and by Utrecht in 1969: 279,000 (on 1.1.1982, 234,550).

2 The port activities are in the process of relocating from these areas to outlying areas as close as possible to the large rivers and canals (see: Herweijer et al., "Strategies for Urban Policy in The Netherlands," p. 8).

3 The number of dwellings in the historical inner cities of the three larger towns was Amsterdam (1960) 32,569, (1980) 25,431; The Hague (1960) 6,123, (1980) 4,404; and Utrecht (1960) 4,533, (1980) 3,586. The number of inhabitants was Amsterdam (1960) 102,417, (1980) 54,155; The Hague (1960) 21,824, (1980) 9,591; Utrecht (1960)

18,944, (1980) 10,967. (Rotterdam has been left out because of the particular character of its largely rebuilt inner city.)

20 Egalitarian Possibilities in Housing

1 The statistical sources in this chapter are from personal communications with officials from the Norwegian Housing Bank and from the Central Bureau of Statistics, 1980, and Norwegian Housing,1982. Where figures are presented in U.S. dollars, the exchange rate for August 1982 was used.

2 Horizontal inequity occurs when, for arbitrary reasons, households on similar incomes pay widely varying amounts for housing which is of approximately similar standards. Vertical inequity arises when, again for arbitrary reasons, households with lower incomes pay more for their similar standard housing than others with higher incomes. It is not possible to eliminate all horizontal and vertical inequity in housing.

3 The extended housing allowance scheme was coordinated with simultaneous revisions to the bank's loans, where applicants could choose between gearing repayments to annual average earnings ("levelling" loans) or repaying a ratio of the principal of the loan ("nominal" loans). The deferred payments levelling loans have been more popular than nominal loans. The repayments on leveling loans are calculated annually by relating them to the average size bank's loan in the year, and they are fixed in relation to 20 percent of average male blue collar earnings and are assessed independently of interest. The loan accumulates debt in the early years when repayments do not cover interest charges.

References

Aaron, Henry J. *Shelter and subsidies: Who benefits from federal housing policies?* Washington, D.C.: The Brookings Institution, 1972.

Abu-Lughod, J. *Cairo: 1001 years of the city victorious.* Princeton, N.J.: Princeton University Press, 1971.

————. Migrant Adjustment. In G. Breese (ed.), *The city in newly developing countries.* Englewood Cliffs, N.J.: Prentice-Hall, 1969.

Age Concern. "New evidence on hypothermia deaths." Press release. London: Age Concern, October 14, 1983.

Agnew, J. A. "Homeownership and the capitalist social order." In M. Dear and A. Scott (eds.), *Urbanization and urban planning in capitalist society.* New York: Methuen, 1981.

Ahrentzen, S. B. "Women and the housing process: A look at residential fit, adjustments, and constraints of lower-income female-headed households." Ph.D. diss. University of California, Irvine, 1983.

Albrecht, G. *Soziologie der geografischen Mobilität.* Stuttgart: F. Enke, 1972.

Alestalo, M. "Yhteiskuntaluokat ja sosiaaliset kerrostumat toisen maailmansodan jalkeen." In Tapani Valkonen, et al. (eds.), *Social classes and social strata after World War II,* 1980.

Alexander, C. *Notes on the synthesis of form.* Cambridge, Mass.: Harvard University Press, 1964.

Allen, I. L. (ed.). *New towns and the suburban dream: Ideology and Utopia in planning and development.* Port Washington, N.Y.: Kennikat, 1977.

Alonso, W. "What are new towns for?" *Urban Studies,* 1970, *7,* 37–45.

Altman, E. A., and Rosenbaum, B. R. "Principles of planning and zionist ideology: The Israeli development town." *Journal of the American Institute of Planners,* 1973, *39,* 316–25.

Anderson, J., and Weidemann, S. *Planning and monitoring change in multifamily housing: The case of North Chicago, Illinois.* Urbana: University of Illinois, Housing Research and Development Program, 1980.

Anderson, J., Weidemann, S., and Butterfield, D. "Using resident's satisfaction to obtain priorities for housing rehabilitation.: In *Proceedings of the International Council for Building Research Studies and Documentation,* CIB '83 Congress. Gävle, Sweden: National Swedish Institute for Building Research, 1983, pp. 141–50.

Anderson-Khlief, S. "Housing needs of single-parent mothers." In S. Keller (ed.), *Building for women.* Lexington, Mass.: Lexington Books, 1981.

————. *Strategies, problems, and policy issues for single parent housing.* Washington, D.C.:

U.S. Department of Housing and Urban Development, 1979.

Andrusz, G. D. "Housing ideals, structural constraints and the emancipation of women." In J. Brine et al., (eds.), *Home, school, and leisure in the Soviet Union*. Boston: Allen & Unwin, 1980.

Anton, Thomas J. *Governing greater Stockholm*. Berkeley: University of California Press, 1975.

Ash, J. "The effects of household formation and life styles on housing need in Britain." Paper presented at World Congress of Sociology, Mexico, August 1982 (included in this volume).

————. "The progress of new towns in Israel." *The Town Planning Review*, 1974, 45(4), 387–400.

————. "The rise and fall of high rise housing in England." In C. Ungerson and V. Karn (eds.), *The consumer experience of housing*. Farnborough, Eng.: Gower, 1980.

Ashford, D., and Eston, P. *The extent and effects of discrimination against children in rental housing: A study of five California cities*. Santa Monica, Calif.: Fair Housing for Children, Inc., 1979.

Badcock, B. "Removing the spatial bias from state housing provision in Australian cities." *Political Geography Quarterly*, 1982, 1, 195–215.

Baer, W. C. "The evolution of housing indicators and housing standards." *Public Policy*, 1976, 24(3), 361–93.

Balbo, L. "The servicing work of women and the capitalist state." In M. Zeitlin (ed.), *Political power and social theory*. vol. 3. Greenwich, Conn.: Jai Press, 1982, 251–30.

Ball, M. "Recent empirical work on the determinants of relative house price." *Urban Studies*, 1973, 10, 213–33.

Bamberger. "Accion's response to the urban challenge." (Unpublished). Quoted in Lisa Peattie, "The concept of marginality as applied to squatter settlements." In W. A. Cornelius and F. M. Trueblood (eds.), *Latin American Urban Research*. vol. 4. Beverly Hills, Calif.: Sage Publications, 1974.

Barkin, D. "Confronting the separation of town and country in Cuba." In W. K. Tabb and L. Sawers (eds.), *Marxism and the metropolis*. New York: Oxford University Press, 1978.

Basham, R. *Urban anthropology*. Palo Alto, Calif.: Mayfield Publishing Co., 1978.

Bassett, K. "The sale of council houses as a political issue." *Policy and Politics*, 1980, 8(3), 290–307.

Batley, R. *Power through bureaucracy: Urban political analysis in Brazil*. Aldershot, Eng.: Gower, 1983.

Bell, W. "Social choice, life styles and suburban residence." In W. M. Dobriner (ed.), *The suburban community*. New York: Putnams, 1958.

Benson, V. M., Jacobson, J. M., and Margulis, H. L. *Discrimination against families with children in rental housing in Cuyahoga County, Ohio*. Cleveland, Ohio: Cleveland State University, 1981.

Berg, A. *Malnourished people: A policy view*. Washington, D.C.: World Bank, 1981, pp. 64–67.

Berler, A. *New towns in Israel*. Jerusalem: Israel Universities Press, 1970.

————. *Strengthening absorption in development towns and their rural hinterland*. (Publications on problems of regional development, no. 10), Rehovot, Israel: Settlement Study Center, 1972.

Beshers, J. M. *Urban social structure*. New York: Free Press of Glencoe, 1962.

Bigsworth, K. *Public sector housing and distribution of income, Great Britain, 1952–77*. Cambridge, Eng.: Cambridge University, 1981.

Bird, B. E. I., and Palmer, J. A. D. *Housing Association tenants*. London: Building Research Establishment, Department of the Environment and the Housing Corporation, 1979.

Blauw, P. W., and Pastor, C. (Ed.) *Soort bij soort*. Deventer, The Netherlands: Van Loghum Slaterus, 1980.

BMRB. *Housing consumer survey*. National Economic Development Office. London: HMSO, 1977.

Bollinger, S. J. "The historic and proper place of central governments in urban redevelopment: The U.S. view." *Urban Law and Policy*, 1983, *6*, 53–63.

Bourkhov, Eli, and Werczberger, Elia. "Factors affecting the development of new towns in Israel." *Environment and Planning, A*, 1981, *13*, 421–34.

Bourne, L. S., and Hitchcock, J. R. (eds.). *Urban housing markets: Recent directions in research and policy*. Toronto: University of Toronto Press, 1978.

Brasileiro, A. M., et al. "Extending municipal services by building on local initiatives: A project in the favelas of Rio de Janeiro." *Assignment children*, UNICEF, 1982, *57/58*.

Brennan, T. *New community: Problems and policies*. Sydney, Australia: Angus & Robertson, 1973.

Brolin, B. C. "Chandigarh was planned by experts, but something has gone wrong." *Smithsonian*, 1972, *3*(3), 56–63.

Bromilow, F. J. "The supply of land for urban purposes." *Proceedings of the Fifth Australian Building Research Conference*, Melbourne, Australia, 1975.

———. "What is an affordable house?" In *Productivity and the affordable house*, Melbourne, Australia: Housing Industry Association, 1977.

Brouwer, B. F. "Hoe wonen wij het liefst?" *Sociaal-Culturele Kwartaal Berichten C.B.S.*, 1981, *3*(6), 10–21.

Brutzkus, E. "Planning of spatial distribution of population in Israel." *Ekistics*, 1966, pp. 350–55.

Bryson, L., and Thompson, F. *An Australian newtown*. Blackburn, Australia: Penguin, 1972.

Budding, D. W. *Housing deprivation among enrollees in the Housing Allowance Demand Experiment*. Cambridge, Mass.: Abt Associates, 1980.

Bull, D., and Wilding, P. *Thatcherism and the poor*. London: Child Poverty Action Group, 1983.

Burgers, J. P. L. *Nieuwe woningen in oude stadsdelen* (New dwellings in older parts of towns). Tilburg, The Netherlands: IVA, 1979.

———. "Verdichting van oude stadswijken." (Fill-in in old inner city neighborhoods) In *Onderzoeks-programa 1980/1982*, IVA/SSW, Tilburg, The Netherlands: p. 22.

Burke, T., Hancock, L., and Newton, P. W. *A roof over their heads: Housing and the family in Australia*, Melbourne, Australia: Institute of Family Studies, 1983.

Calvin, R. "Children and families: The latest victims of exclusionary land use practices." *Challenge!*, 1979, *10*, 26–28.

Campbell, A., Converse, P. E., and Rodgers, W. L. *The quality of American life: Perceptions, evaluations, and satisfactions*. New York: Russel Sage Foundation, 1976.

Card, E. "Women, housing access, and mortgage credit." Signs, Special supplement on women and the American city, 1980, 5(3), 215–19.

Carmon, N. "Housing policy in western countries: Toward broader social responsibility." *Social Praxis*, 1981, 8(3–4), 53–71.

——., and Manheim, B. "Housing policy as a tool of social policy." *Social Forces*, 1979, 58(1), 336–54.

Castells, M. "Cities and regions beyond the crisis." *International Journal of Urban and Regional Research*, 1980, 1, 128.

Cell, C. P. "The urban-rural contradiction in the Maoist era: The pattern of deurbanization in China." *Comparative Urban Research*, 1980, 7(3), 48–70.

Census of India 1971. Series 25. *Chandigarh*, Parts 1-A and 1-B, General Report.

Census of India 1981. Series-1, *India*, Provisional Population Totals.

Central Bureau of Statistics. *Young couples survey 1971*, Special Series, no. 375. Jerusalem: Central Bureau of Statistics, 1972.

——. *Seker Zugot Tsayirim 1977*, special series no 595. Jerusalem: Central Bureau of Statistics, 1980.

Central Bureau of Statistics. *Statistical Yearbook*, 1980. Oslo: Central Bureau of Statistics, 1980.

Central Bureau of Statistics. *Survey of Housing Conditions 1978*, Special Series, no. 641. Jerusalem: Central Bureau of Statistics, 1981.

——. *Ha-Binui Be-Yisrael 1978–1980*, (Construction in Israel 1978–1980) Special Series, no. 674. Jerusalem: Central Bureau of Statistics, 1981b.

Central Statistical Office. *Social Trends*, No. 13, London: HMSO, 1983.

Centre for Urban Research and Action. *The displaced: A study of housing conflict in Melbourne's inner city*. Melbourne, Australia: Australian Housing Research Council, 1977.

Chavis, D. M., Stucky, P. E., and Wandersman, A. "Returning basic research to the community." *American Psychologist*, 1983, 83(4), 424–34.

Cherki, E. "Populisme et ideologie revolutionaire dans le mouvement des squatters." *Sociologie du Travail*, 18(2), 192–215.

Chirot, D., and Hall, D. "World system theory." In R. Turner and J. F. Short (eds.), *Annual Review of Sociology*. Palo Alto, Calif.: Annual Reviews, Inc., 1982.

Clapp, J. A. *New towns and urban policy: Planning metropolitan growth*. New York: Dunellen, 1971.

Cohen, E. *The city in Zionist ideology*. Jerusalem: The Hebrew University, Institute of Urban and Regional Studies, 1970b.

——. "Development towns–the social dynamics of "planted" urban communities in Israel." In S. N. Eisenstadt et al. (eds.), *Integration and development in Israel*. Jerusalem: Israel Universities Press, 1970a.

Coing, H. *Rénovation urbaine et changement social*. Paris: Les Editions Ouvrières, 1966.

Collin, H. P. *L'histoire de l'urbanisation dans la paroisse de Montreal, 1851–1941*. (forthcoming, 1984), Quebec: Les Presses de l'Université du Quebec.

Collison, P. "British townplanning and the neighbourhood idea." *Housing Centre Review*, 1956, 5.

——. "Class and the neighbourhood." *Town and Country Planning*, 1955, 23(7).

Comay, Y., and Kirschenbaum, A. "The Israeli new town: An experiment at population redistribution." *Economic Development and Cultural Change*, 1973, 22(1), 124–34.

Conn, S. "The squatters rights of favelados." *Ciências Econômicas e Sociais*, 1968, 3(2),

50–142.

Conway, D. "Fact or opinion on uncontrolled peripheral settlement in Trinidad." *Ekistics*, *286*, 37–43.

Cooper-Marcus, C. *Easter Hill Village: Some social implications of design*. New York: The Free Press, 1975.

———. "User needs research in housing." In S. Davis (ed.), *The form of housing*. New York: Van Nostrand Reinhold, 1977.

Csillaghy, J., and Antipas-Schmid, M. Economic Commission for Europe. Working Party on Housing, Ad Hoc Meeting on Housing Management, February, 1982.

Dansereau, F., and Godbout, J. "Cooperative et copropriété: Concurrence ou complementarite?" *L'Actualité Immobilière*, 1981, *5*, 10–15.

Dansereau, F., et al. *La transformation d'imeubles locatifs en copropriété d'occupation*. Montreal: Institut national de la recherche scientifique, 1981.

Dansereau, F., and L'Ecuyer, D. "Le logement neuf en copropriété divise au Quebec: un decollage difficile." *L'Actualité Immobilière*, 1980, *4*, 13–24.

Dansereau, F., and Wexler, M. *Les nouveaux espaces residentiels: D'espaces et indicateurs de qualité*, (forthcoming, 1984).

Danz, M. *Buren*. Meppel, The Netherlands: Krips Repro, 1981.

Great Britain, Department of the Environment. *Housing policy*. Technical volume, Part I. London: HMSO, 1977.

———. *Housing single people* 3 vols. London: HMSO, 1971–78.

———. *National dwelling and housing survey, 1977*. London: HMSO, 1978a.

———. *Housing initiatives for single people of working age*. London: Department of the Environment, 1982a.

———. *English house condition survey 1976, Part 2*. London: HMSO, 1978b.

———. *English house condition survey 1981*. London: HMSO, 1982b.

Department of the Employment & Government Statistical Service. *Family expenditure survey*. London: HMSO, 1981.

Department of Environment, Housing and Community Development. *Urban renewal*, Canberra, Australia: Australian Government Publishing Service, 1978.

Department of Health and Social Security. *Social security statistics*. London, Great Britain: HMSO.

Divay, G., and Gaudreau, M. *La formation des espaces residentiels*. Quebec: Les Presses de l'Université du Quebec (forthcoming, 1983).

———., and Richard, L. *L'aid gouvernementale au logement et sa distribution sociale*. Montreal: Institut national de la recherche scientifique-Urbanisation, (Etudes et documents, No. 26), 1981.

Donnison, D., and Ungerson, C. *Housing policy*. Harmondsworth, Eng.: Penguin Books, 1982.

Downs, A. "The coming crunch in rental housing." *Annals, American Academy of Political and Social Science*, 1983, *465*, 76–85.

Draaisma, J., and Van Hoogstraten, P. "The squatter movement in Amsterdam." *International Journal of Urban and Regional Research*, 1983, *7*(3), 406–16.

Draak, J. Den, and Adel, D. N. Den. *Beleidsvoornemens belicht. Een kritische analyse met betrekking tot de plannen voor de woonfunctie van 14 Nederlandse binnensteden* (An examination of policy aims: A critical analysis of plans dealing with the residential function of the inner city). Delft, The Netherlands: Institute for Town Planning

Research, 1981.

Drake, M., O'Brien, M., and Biebuyck, T. *Single and homeless*. London, Great Britain: HMSO, 1981.

Duncan, G., and Newman, S. "People as planners: The fulfillment of residential mobility expectations." In G. J. Duncan and J. N. Morgan (eds.), *Five thousand American families—patterns of economic progress*. Volume 3. Ann Arbor, Mich.: University of Michigan, Institute for Social Research, 1975.

Duncan, S. S. "Housing policy, the methodology of levels, and urban research: The case of Castells": *International Journal of Urban and Regional Research*, 1981, *5*, 231–54.

Dwyer, D. J. "Attitudes towards spontaneous settlement in Third World Cities." In D. J. Dwyer (ed.), *The city in the Third World*. London: Macmillan, 1974, pp. 204–53.

———. *People and housing in Third World cities: Perspectives on the problem of spontaneous settlements*. London: Longman, 1975.

Economic Commission for Europe. *Annual bulletin of housing and building statistics for Europe*, 1978, 1980.

———. Committee on Housing, Building, and Planning. *Report of the fifty-third session*. October 15, 1982.

———. Committee on Housing, Building, and Planning. Seminar on the Forecasting and Program of Housing. *Report*. Madrid: April 28, 1981.

———. Committee on Housing, Building, and Planning. Seminar on the Relationship between Housing and the National Economy. *Report*. Prague: June 10, 1982.

———. Committee on Housing, Building, and Planning. Working party on Housing. *Report*. November 11, 1982.

———. *Major trends in housing policy in ECE countries*. New York: United Nations, 1980.

Einem, E. Von. "National urban policy: The case of West Germany," *Journal of the American Planning Association*, 1982, *48*, 9–23.

Elliott, B., and McCrone, D. *The city: Patterns of domination and conflict*, London: Macmillan, 1982.

Epstein, D. G. *Brasilia, plan and reality: A study of planned and spontaneous urban settlement*. Berkeley: University of California Press, 1973.

———. "The genesis and function of squatter settlements in Brasilia." In T. Weaver and D. White (eds.), *The anthropology of urban environments*. Washington, D.C.: Society for Applied Anthropology, 1972, p. 260.

Evans, G. W., and Jacobs, S. V. "Air pollution and stress," *Journal of Social Issues*, 1981, *37*(1), 95–125.

Fainstein, "S. S. American policy for housing and community development: A comparative examination." In R. Montgomery and D. R. Marshall (eds.), *Housing policy for the 1980s*. Lexington, Mass.: Lexington Books, 1980.

Faludi, A. "Critical rationalism and planning methodology." *Urban Studies*, 1983, *20*, 265–78.

Faulkner, H. W. *Locational stress on Sydney's metropolitan fringe*. Ph.D. diss., Australian National University, 1978.

Fava, S. F. *Urbanism in world perspective*. New York: Crowell, 1968.

———. "Women's place in the new suburbia." In G. Wekerle, R. Peterson, and D. Morley (eds.), *New space for women*. Boulder, Colo.: Westview Press, 1980.

Firey, W., Loomis, C. P., and Beegle, J. A. "The fusion of urban and rural." In P. Hatt et al. (eds.), *Cities and society*. 2d ed. New York: Free Press, 1957.

Fischer, C. *The urban experience*. New York: Harcourt, Brace Jovanovich, 1976.

Fish, G. S. (ed.). *The story of housing*. New York: Macmillan, 1979.

Forrest, R., and Murie, A. *Right to buy? Issues of equity, need and polarisation in the sale of council houses*. University of Bristol, School for Advanced Urban Studies, 1983a.

——. "Residualization and council housing: Aspects of the changing social relations of housing tenure." *Journal of Social Policy*, 1983b, *12*(4).

——. *Monitoring the right to buy. First report* 1980–1982, University of Bristol, SAUS, 1983c.

Francescato, G., et al. "A systematic method for evaluating multi-family housing." *DMG-DRS Journal*, 1975, *9*(2), 153–58.

Frank, A. G. *Latin America: Underdevelopment or revolution: Essays on the development of underdevelopment and the immediate enemy*. New York: Monthly Review Press, 1969.

Fried, M., and Gleicher, P. "Some sources of residential satisfaction in an urban slum." *Journal of the American Institute of Planners*, 1961, *27*(4), 305–15.

Friedmann, J., and Wulff, G. "World city formation: An agenda for research and action." *International Journal of Urban and Regional Research*, 1982, *6*(3), 309–44.

Friedrichs, J. *Stadtanalyse: Soziale und Raumliche organisation der Gesellschaft*. Reinbek bei Hamburg: Rowohlt, 1977.

Gale, D. E. *Neighborhood revitalization and the postindustrial city*, Lexington, Mass.: Lexington Books, 1984.

Gans, H. J. "The human implications of current redevelopment and relocation planning." *Journal of the American Institute of Planners*, 1959, *25*, 15–25.

——. *The Levittowners*. New York: Vintage Books, 1967.

——. *People and plans: Essays on urban problems and solutions*. Abr. ed. Harmondsworth Eng.: Penguin, 1972.

——. *The urban villagers: Group and class in the life of Italian-Americans*. Glencoe, Ill.: The Free Press, 1962.

Genovese, R. G. "Social factors in planning new suburbs: The Swedish experience." *Sociological Symposium*, Spring 1975, pp. 53–61.

Germanii, G. "Spectos Tercios de la Marginalidad." *Revista Paraguaya de sociologia*, 8. (March). Quoted in Lisa Peattie, "The concept of marginality as applied in squatter settlements." In W. A. Cornelius and F. M. Trueblood (eds.), *Latin American urban research*. vol. 4. Beverly Hills, Calif.: Sage Publications, 1974.

Ghorra-Gobin, C. "The subsidized housing system in France." *Planning and Administration*, 1983, *10*(1), 47–56.

Ginsburg, N. *Class, capital and social policy*, London: Macmillan, 1979.

Godschalk, D. R. "Comparative new community design." *Journal of the American Planning Institute*, 1967, *33*(5), 371–78.

Golany, G. *New-town planning: Principles and practice*. New York: Wiley, 1976.

Golany, G. *International urban growth policies: New town contributions*. New York: Wiley, 1978.

Goldberg, M., and Mercer, J. "Canadian and U. S. cities: Basic differences, possible explanations and their meaning for public policy." *Regional Science Association Papers*, 1980, pp. 159–83.

Goldrich, D. "The political integration of urban settlements in Chile and Peru." (Mimeographed.) Annual Meetings of the Political Science Association, New York City. (Reported in Mangin, 1966.)

Goldsmith, W. W., and Jacobs, H. M. "The improbability of urban policy." *Journal of the American Planning Association*, 1982, *48*, 53–66.

Goodman, J. L. "Causes and indicators of housing quality." *Social Indicators Research*, 1978, *5*, 195–210.

Gordon, D. M. *Problems in political economy*. 2d ed. Lexington, Mass.: D. C. Heath, 1977.

Goss, S., and Lansley, S. *What price housing*, London: SHAC, 1981.

Gottschalk, G., and Jens, Chr. Tonboe. *Offentlighed hemmelighed og medindflydelse i plan-laegningen*. Copenhagen: Statens Byggeforskningsinstitutet, 1974.

Gough, I. *The political economy of the welfare state*, London: Macmillan, 1979.

Gradus, Y., and Stern, E. "Changing strategies of development: Toward a regiopolis in the Negev desert." *Journal of the American Planning Association*, 1980, *46*, 410–23.

Green, D. G. "The spatial sciences and the state." *Environment and Planning, A*, 1982, *14*, 1541–49.

Greene, J. G. "An evaluation of the exclusion of children from apartments in Dallas, Texas." Dallas, Tex.: J. G. & Associates, 1978.

Greene, J. G., and Blake, G. P. *A study of how restrictive rental practices affect families with children*. Washington, D.C.: U.S. Department of Housing and Development, Office of Policy Development and Research, 1980.

Grenell, P. "Planning for invisible people: Some consequences of bureaucratic values and practices." In J. Turner et al. (eds.), *Freedom to build*. New York: Macmillan, 1972.

Greve, J. *Homelessness in London*. Edinburgh: Scottish Academic Press, 1971.

Gribbin, C. C., and Instone, L. H. "Occupying housing commission accommodation as a source of social stigma." Australian Housing Research Council Report, Project 33, Canberra (mimeographed), 1977.

Grigsby, W. G. *Housing markets and public policy*. Philadelphia: University of Pennsylvania Press, 1963.

Grigsby, W. G., and Rosenberg, L. *Urban housing policy*. New York: APS Publications, 1975.

Grimes, O., Jr. *Housing for low-income urban families*. Baltimore, Md.: Johns Hopkins University Press, 1976.

Grünfeld, F. "Eenheid in verscheidenheid." In *Handboek van Bouwen en Wonen*, Deventer, The Netherlands: Kluwer, 1976a.

———. *Gebouwde Omgeving, neerslag van onze samenleving*. Alphen aan den Rijn: Samson, 1979.

———. *Habitat and habitation*. Alphen aan den Rijn, The Netherlands: Samson, 1970.

———. *Leven in een Rotterdamse Randzone*. Rotterdam: Gem. Dienst v. Sociale Zaken, 1957.

———. "Nieuwe steden in Israel: Ontwikkelingen, problemen en mogelijkheden." *Social Wetenschappen*, 1978, *21*(3).

———. *Veenzicht, leven in een na-oorlogse woonwijk*. Rotterdam: Gem. Dienst v. Sociale Zaken, 1958.

Guest, A. M. "Residential segregation in urban areas." In K. F. Schwirian (ed.), *Contemporary topics in urban sociology*. Morristown, N.J.: General Learning Press, 1977.

Department of Housing and Urban Development. Office of Policy Development and Research. *The conversion of rental housing to condominiums and cooperatives*. Washington, D.C.: U.S. Dept. of Housing and Urban Development, Office of Policy Development and Research, June 1980.

Haar, C. *Land-use planning: A casebook on the use, misuse, and re-use of urban land*. 2d Ed. Boston: Little, Brown, 1971.

Haggroth, Soren. "Swedish experiments in citizen participation in local planning." *Studies in Comparative Local Government*, Summer 1973, pp. 57–58.

———. "Public participation in design and management of the residential environment." In *Swedish experiences of self-building, cooperation, consumer research participation*. (A contribution to the United Nations Conference on Human Settlements, Habitat, Vancouver, Canada.) Stockholm: Ministry of Housing and Physical Planning, 1976, pp. 105–42.

Hamnett, C. "Split City." *Roof*. July/Aug. 1983, pp. 13–14.

Handelman, D., and Shamgar-Handelman, L. "Social planning prerequisites for new and expanded communities: The case of Israel." *Contact, Journal of Urban and Environmental Affairs*, 1978, *10*(3), 86–122.

Hansard. *Parliamentary debates*, March 31 and April 18, 1983.

Hapgood, K., and Getzels, J. *Planning, women, and change*. Chicago: American Society of Planning Officials, 1974.

Hargreaves, K. *This house is not for sale*. Melbourne, Australia: Centre for Urban Research and Action, n.d.

Harloe, M. "A multi-national perspective on housing policies." In Gerd-Michael Hellstern, F. Spreer and H. Wollman (eds.), *Applied urban research: Towards an internationalization of research and learning*, vol. 3. Bonn: Bundesforschungsanstalt für Landeskunde und Raumordnung, 1982.

———. "Current trends in housing policy: Some European comparisons." *Royal Society for Housing*, 1980, *6*, 207–13.

———. "The green paper on housing policy." In S. Baldwin (Ed.), *The year book of social policy in Britain 1977*, London: Routledge & Kegan Paul, 1978.

———. *Housing in Denmark*. Copenhagen: Danish Ministry of Housing, 1974.

———. "The recommodification of housing." In M. Harloe and E. Lebas (eds.), *City, class, and capital*. London: Arnold, 1981.

Hartman, C. W. (ed.). *America's housing crisis*, Boston: Routledge & Kegan Paul, 1983.

Hartman, C. W. *Housing and social policy*. Englewood Cliffs, N.J.: Prentice-Hall, 1975.

Harvey, D. "Social processes, spatial form and the redistribution of real income in an urban system." In M. Chisholm et al., *Regional forecasting*. Butterworths, 1971.

Hauser, F. L. "Ecological patterns of European cities." In S. F. Fava (ed.), *Urbanism in world perspective*. New York: Crowell, 1968.

Hauser, P., et al. *Population and the urban future*. Albany, N.Y.: State University of New York Press, (tables 1.1 and 1.2), 1982, p. 70.

Healey, P. "'Rational methods' as a mode of policy formation and implementation in land-use policy." *Environment and Planning*, B, 1983, *10*, 19–39.

Hegedus, J., and Toscis, I. "Housing classes and housing policy: Some change in the Budapest housing market." *International Journal of Urban and Regional Research*, 1983, *7*(4), 467–94.

Henderson, J. "Racial segregation in British public housing." Paper presented at the American Sociological Association meetings, Detroit, 1983.

Heraud, B. J. "Social class and the new towns." *Urban Studies*, *5*(1), 33–58.

Herbert, D. T., and Johnston, R. J. (eds.), *Social areas in cities*. 2 vols. London: Wiley, 1976.

Herbert, J. D., and Hayck, A. P. "The housing threshold for lower-income groups: The case of India." *Urban planning in the developing countries*. New York: Praeger, 1968, pp. 64–107.

Herweijer, S., Leefland, H., and Hardy, D. "Strategies for urban policy in The Netherlands: Alleviating urban fiscal stress." Contribution from The Netherlands to the International Ministerial Colloquium on Urban Policy, September 29–30, 1980, Washington, D.C.

Hirszowicz, M. *The bureaucratic leviathan: A study of the sociology of communism*. New York: New York University Press, 1980.

Hole, W. V. "Housing standards and social trends." *Urban Studies*, 1965, No. 2.

Hole, W. V., and Pountney, M. T. *Trends in population, housing and occupancy rates 1861–1961*. London: HMSO, 1971.

Holmans, A. *Housing careers of recently married couples*. (Population Trends, No. 24 OPCS). London: HMSO, 1981.

Hoorn, F. van, and de Smidt, M. "Ruimtelijke konfiguratie van bevolkingskategorieen" (Unpublished paper Regional Science Association Conference), March 12, 1981.

Hopper, K., and Cox, L. S. "Litigation in advocacy for the homeless: The case of New York City." *Development: Seeds of Change*, 1982, 2, 57–62.

Housing Commission of Victoria (HCV). *The enemy within our gates*. Melbourne, Australia: The Commission, 1967a.

———. *Annual report, 1966–67*. Melbourne: The Commission, 1967b.

———. *Housing is people*. Melbourne: The Commission, 1970.

———. *Annual report 1977–78*. Melbourne: The Commission, 1979.

———. *First twenty-five years*. Melbourne: The Commission, n.d.

Housing Corporation. *Directory of Housing Co-operatives, 1981*. London: Housing Corporation, 1981.

Howenstine, E. J. *Private rental housing in industrialized countries*. Washington, D.C.: United States. Department of Housing and Urban Dvelopment, Office of Policy Development and Research, 1981.

Huttman, E. "New towns grow old: Reshaping of land use, size and transportation in maturing British and Dutch new towns." *Sociological Symposium*, Spring 1975, *13*, 31–34.

———. "Multi-level care facilities for the elderly in Denmark and Holland." *Housing and Society*. 1982, *9*(1), 20.

Ineichen, B. "The housing decisions of young people." *British Journal of Sociology*, 1981, *32*(2), 252–58.

International Bank for Reconstruction and Development. *Urbanization*, (Sector Working Paper), Washington, D.C.: The Bank, 1972, p. 82.

International Federation for Housing and Planning. Special Issue—Sweden. IFHP *News sheet* (1979). (Compiled on the occasion of the IFHP International Congress, Gotteborg, May 14–19, 1979, by Martin Percivall.)

Ipsen, D. "Housing conditions and interests of foreign workers in the Federal Republic of Germany." Paper prepared for the Ninth World Congress of Sociology, Uppsala, Sweden, August 1978.

Isaac, L., and Kelly, W. R. "Racial insurgency, the state and welfare expansion: Local and national evidence from the post-war United States," *American Journal of Sociolo-*

gy, 1981, *86*, 1348–86.

Israel government yearbook. Jerusalem: Central Office of Information, 1980.

Jacobs, J. *The death and life of great American cities.* New York: Random House, 1961.

Jacobs, J. C. "Urban poverty, children and the consumption of popular culture: A perspective on the marginality thesis from a Latin American squatter settlement." *Human Organization*, 1980, *39*(3), 233–41.

Joint Economic Committee, U.S. Congress. *Multifamily housing demand, 1975–2000.* Washington, D.C.: U.S. Government Printing Office, 1980.

Jones, M. A., and Hartnett, B. "The Victorian Housing Commission." *Checkpoint*, 1970, *4*, 10–11.

Jonge, D. de. *Stedelijke structuurbeelden*, Arnhem, The Netherlands: Vuga, pp. 74–75, no date.

Junka, T., and Loikkanen, H. A. *Talonrakennustoiminnan keskittymisaste.* (The degree of concentration in construction of houses). Helsinki: TASKU, 1975.

Juntto, A. "Arava-asukkaiden tulot ja tuen tarve vuonna 1972. (The incomes and need for support of Arava-residents in 1972) Helsinki: "Asuntohallitus, tutkimus -ja suunnitteluosasto," 1976.

Kahane, A. "Aufgaben und Einfluss der raumlichen Planung bei der Wirtschaftlichen und sozialen Entwicklung Israels." *Zeitschrift fur Raumforschung und Raumordnung*, 1963, *21*(2), 93–102.

Kain, J. F. "America's persistent housing crises: Errors in analysis and policy." *Annals of the American Academy of Political and Social Science*, 1983, *465*, 136–48.

Karn, V. "The impact of discretion on allocations." *Housing Review*, 1982, *31*, 141.

———. "Where are present housing policies leading?" *Housing Review*, 1984, *33*, 7.

Kazemi, F. *Poverty and revolution in Iran: The migrant poor, urban marginality, and politics.* New York: New York University Press, 1980.

Keare, D., and Parris, S. *Evaluation of shelter programs for the urban poor: Principal findings..* (World Bank Staff Working Papers, No. 547). Washington, D.C.: World Bank, 1982, p. ix.

Kearns, R. "London's homeless." *Annals of the American Association of Geographers*, 1979, *69*, 393–98.

Kemeny, J. "A political sociology of homeownership in Australia." *Australian and New Zealand Journal of Sociology*, 1977, *13*, 47–59.

———. "The 'Maturation Crisis' of public housing." Birmingham, Eng.: Centre for Urban and Regional Studies, 1980. (mimeographed).

———. *The myth of home-ownership: Private versus public choices in housing tenure.* London: Routledge & Kegan Paul, 1981.

Keren, M. "Barriers to communication between scientists and policy makers." *Knowledge: Creation, diffusion, utilization*, 1983, *5*(1), 84–98.

Kilroy, B. "Misplaced resources in housing." *Housing Review*, 1982, *31*, 203.

Kirby, A. "The Housing Corporation, 1974–1979: An example of state housing policy in Britain." *Environment and Planning, A*, 1981, *13*, 1295–1303.

———. "On society without space: A critique of Saunder's nonspatial urban sociology." *Environment and Planning, D*, 1983, *1*, 226–33.

Kirschenbaum, A. L., and Comay, Y. "Dynamics of population attraction to new towns: The case of Israel." *Socio-economic Planning Sciences*, 1973, *7*, 687–96.

Kneebone, T. "The Panzers, the pansies and the panoply (A chronicle of redevelopment warfare in Melbourne)." Paper presented at the 16th Biennial Congress of the Royal Australian Planning Institute, Canberra, 1980 (mimeographed).

Krohn, R. G., Fleming, B., and Manzer, M. *The other economy: The internal logic of local rental housing*. Toronto: Peter Martin Associates, 1977.

Kruijt, B. "De stedelijke inkomensontwikkeling: een benauwend vooruitzicht" (Development of urban income: An oppressive perspective). *Economisch Statistische Berichten*, (The Netherlands) September 28, 1983, pp. 856–59.

Kuklinski, A., et al. (eds.), *Regional dynamics of socioeconomic change*. Tampere, Finland: Finnpublishers, 1979.

Kuusi, P. 60-luvun sosiaalipolitiikka (Social policy in the 1960s). Porvoo, Finland: W. Söderström, 1962.

Kwok, R. "The role of small cities in Chinese urban development." *International Journal of Urban and Regional Research*, 1982, 6(4), 549–66.

Lane, S., and Kinsey, J. "Housing tenure status and housing satisfaction." *Journal of Consumer Affairs*, 1980, 14(2), 341–65.

Lankinen, M. "Sosiallinen tasapaino Helsingissa." (The social balance in Helsinki) Kaupunkimaisten yhdyskuntien kehittamiskampanja. 3/1982. Helsinki: Valtion painatuskeskus 1982.

Lansing, J. B., Marans, R. W., and Zehner, R. B. *Planned residential environments*. Ann Arbor, Mich.: University of Michigan, Survey Research Center, 1975.

Lawton, M. P. *Environment and aging*. Monterey, Calif.: Brooks/Cole, 1980.

Lea, J. P. "Housing policy and political participation in the Third World" *Social Alternatives*, 1980, 1(8), 65–69.

Leather, P. "Housing and public policy." *Policy and Politics*, 1981, 9(2), 227–41.

Leavitt, J. "Women in planning: There's more to affirmative action than gaining access." In G. R. Wekerle, R. Peterson, and D. Morley (eds.), *New space for women*. Boulder, Colo." Westview, 1980.

Leeds, A. "Political, economic and social effects of producer and consumer orientations toward housing in Brazil and Peru: A systems analysis." In F. Rabinovitz and F. Trueblood (eds.), *Latin American urban research*, vol. 3. Beverly Hills, Calif.: Sage Publications, 1973, pp. 181–215.

———. "The significant variables determining the character of squatter settlements." *America Latina*, 1969, 12(3), 44–86.

Le Grand, J. *The strategy of equality: Redistribution and the social services*. London: Allen & Unwin, 1982.

Lewis, O. "The culture of poverty." *Scientific American*. October 1968, 215 (4), 19–25.

Lichfield, N. *Israel's new towns: A development strategy*. 3 vols. Tel Aviv: Institute for Planning and Development, 1971.

Lidmar, Karin. "Ar samradet bara en bluff?" *att bo* 2, 1982a, pp. 16–17.

———. "Some issues on housing and dwelling." Paper prepared for the Institut national de la recherche scientifique, Université de Quebec, Colloquium on the Dynamics of Residential Areas. Far Hills, Quebec, June 1982b.

Liljeström, Rita. "Are children better off in the 'postindustrial' society?" *Social Change in Sweden*, No. 2, November 1977.

Lindberg, G. "Cooperative housing in Sweden." Paper delivered at the World Congress of Sociology, Uppsala, Sweden, August, 1978.

Lipman, A. "The architectural belief system and social behavior." *British Journal of Sociology*, 1969, *20*(2), 190–204.

Lipman-Blumen, J. "The implications for family structure of changing sex roles." *Social Casework*, 1976, *57*, 67–79.

Lithwick, I. *Macro and micro housing programs in Israel*. (Discussion paper D-47-80), Jerusalem: Brookdale Institute/American Joint Distribution Committee, 1980.

Littlewood, J., and Tinker, A. *Families in flats*. London: HMSO, 1981.

Long, L. H. "The influence of number and ages of children on residential mobility." *Demography*, 1972, *9*, 371–82.

Lorimer, J. *The developers*. Toronto: James Lorimer, 1978.

Lozano, E. "Housing and the urban poor in Chile: Contrasting experiences under Christian Democracy and the Unidad Popular." In Cornelius and Trueblood (Eds.), *Latin American urban research*. Vol. 5. Beverly Hills, Calif.: Sage Publications, 1975.

Lundquist, L. J. "Housing policy and alternative housing tenures: Some Scandinavian examples." *Policy and Politics*, 1984, *12*(1), 1–12.

McEaddy, B. J. "Women who head families: A socioeconomic analysis." *Monthly Labor Review*, 1976, *99*(6), 3–9.

McGee, T. G. *The urbanization process in the Third World*. London: Bell, 1971, p. 197.

McGuire, C. C. *International housing policies*, Lexington, Mass.: Lexington Books, 1981.

McKay, D. "Introduction" (Vol. 3) In Gerd-Michael Hellstern, F. Spreer, and H. Wollmann (eds.), *Applied urban research: Towards an internationalization of research and learning*. Bonn: Bundesforschungsanstalt für Landeskunde und Raumordnung, 1982.

McKelvey, B. *The urbanization of America, 1860–1915*. New Brunswick, N.J.: Rutgers University Press, 1963.

McLaughlin, F. A., Jr. "National growth policy and new communities in the United States: An overview." In G. Golany (ed.), *International urban growth policies: New town contributions*. New York: Wiley, 1978, pp. 277–97.

Mainwaring, R., and Young, E. *Starter homes*. (HDD Occasional Paper, 2/80). London: HMSO, 1980.

Mangin, W. "Squatter settlements." In K. Davis (ed.), *Cities: Their origin, growth and human impact*. San Francisco: W. H. Freeman, 1973.

———. "Latin American squatter settlements: A problem and a solution." *Latin American Research Review*, 1967, *2* (3), 65–98.

———. "Mental health and migration in cities: A Peruvian case." In D. B. Heath and R. N. Adams (eds.) *Contemporary cultures and societies of Latin America*. New York: Random House, 1965, p. 70.

Mann, P. H. "The socially balanced neighbourhood unit." *Town Planning Review*, July, 1958, pp. 91–97.

Marans, R. W., and Rodgers, W. "Toward an understanding of community satisfaction." In A. Hawley and V. Rock (eds.), *Metropolitan America in contemporary perspectives*. Beverly Hills, Calif.: Sage Pubns., 1975.

———., et al. *A report on measuring restrictive rental practices affecting families with children: A national survey*. Washington, D.C.: U.S. Government Printing Office, 1980.

Marcuse, P. "Social indicators and housing policy." *Urban Affairs Quarterly*, 1971, *7*, 193–217.

Margulis, H. L., and Benson, V. M. "Age segregation and discrimination against families with children in rental housing." *Gerontologist*, 1982, *22*, 505–12.

Marschalk, P. "Projections of the population structure and the demand for housing." In D. Eversley and W. Köllmann (eds.), *Population change and social planning*. London: Arnold, 1982.

Martin, R. "Upgrading." In H. J. Simons, et al. *Slums or Self-Reliance? Urban Growth in Zambia*. (Communication, No. 12). Lusaka: University of Zambia, Institute for African Studies, 1976.

Marullo, S. "Racial differences in housing consumption and filtering." In J. S. Pipkin, M. E. La Gory, and J. R. Blau (eds.), *Remaking the city: Social science perspectives on urban design*. Albany: State University of New York Press, 1983.

Masnick, G., et al. *The nation's families: 1960–1990*. Boston: Auburn House, 1980.

Masser, I. *The analysis of planning processes: A framework for comparative research*. (Occasional Paper No. 28), Sheffield, Eng.: University of Sheffield, Department of Town and Regional Planning, 1980.

Mathews, G. *L'évolution de l'occupation du parc residentiel plus ancien de Montreal de 1951 à 1979*. Quebec: Les Presses de l'Université du Quebec (forthcoming, 1984).

Mauduit, J., and Raimond, A.-M. *Ce que les femmes réclament*. Paris: Fayard, 1971.

Melbourne and Metropolitan Board of Works. *Metropolitan planning scheme. Report*. Melbourne: The Board, 1954.

Mellor, J. R. *Urban sociology in an urbanized society*. London: Routledge & Kegan Paul, 1977.

Merlin, P. *Les villes nouvelles*. Paris: Presses Universitaires de France, 1969.

Merrett, S. *State housing in Britain*. London: Routledge & Kegan Paul, 1979.

Meuter, H. "Regional and social effects of changed conditions in housing supply." In Gerd-Michael Hellstern, F. Spreer, and H. Wollmann (eds.), *Applied urban research*. vol. 3. Bonn: Bundesforschungsanstalt für Landeskunde und Raumordnung, 1982.

Michel, S. "Urban squatter organizations as a national government tool: The case of Lima, Peru." In F. F. Rabinowitz and F. M. Trueblood (eds.), *Latin American urban research*. vol. 3. Beverly Hills, Calif.: Sage Publications, 1973, 155–78.

Michelson, W. *Environmental choice, human behavior, and residential satisfaction*. New York: Oxford University Press, 1977.

Migranten in Slotermeer. Samenvattend verslag van een onderzoek, in opdracht van de sociale raad to Amsterdam, ingesteld door het ISONEVO. Amsterdam: Sociale Raad, 1960.

Milone, P. "Housing: The disaster cities." *Far Eastern Economic Review*, October 23, 1971, pp. 57–63.

Ministerie van Volkshuisvesting en Ruimtelijke Ordering. *Kwalitatief Woningonderzoek: eigendomsverhouding en onderhoudstoestand*. Rotterdam: Afdeling Soc. Ec. Onderzoek, 1978.

Ministry of Housing. *Spot purchase program: Policies and procedures manual*. Melbourne: Ministry of Housing, 1982.

Ministry of Housing. *Tenai Ha-Diur Ve-Shefotaihem Shel Zugot Tsairim" Be-Yishuvim Ironiim Be-Yisrael* (Housing conditions and aspirations of young couples in urban settlements in Israel). (Report 19). Jerusalem: Ministry of Housing, Division of Socio-Economic Research, 1967.

———. *Hatsa-at Taktsiv Le Shanat He-Kaspim 1982* (Budget for the fiscal year 1982). Jerusalem: National Accounting Office, 1982.

Ministry of Housing and Local Government. *Homes for today and tomorrow*. London: HMSO, 1961.

———. *Housing planning: A guide to user needs with a checklist* (Design Bulletin 14), London: HMSO, 1968.

———. *Family houses at West Ham* and *The family at home*. (Design Bulletins Nos. 15 and 17). London: HMSO, 1969.

Mitroff, I. I., Quinton, H., and Mason, R. O. "Beyond contradiction and consistency: A design for a dialectical policy system." *Theory and Decision*, 1983, *15*, 107–20.

Montgomery, R., et al. (eds.), *Housing in America: Problems and perspectives*. 2d ed. Indianapolis: Bobbs-Merrill, 1979.

Montgomery, R., and Marshall, D. R. (eds.), *Housing policy for the 1980s*, Lexington, Mass.: D. C. Heath, 1980.

Morris, E. W., and Winter, M. "The status of female-headed households: Another minority in housing." Paper presented at the American Sociological Association Annual Meeting, New York, 1976.

Muhlich, E. "Housing policy and housing research." Paper presented at World Congress of Sociology, Uppsala, Sweden, 1978.

Muller, M. S. "Self-help: A case of water projects in two unauthorized settlements in Lusaka." In Simons, H. J., et al. *Slums or self-reliance? Urban growth in Zambia*. Lukasa: University of Zambia, Institute for African Studies, 1976, p. 114.

Murie, A. *The sale of council houses*. Birmingham, Eng.: University of Birmingham, Centre for Urban and Regional Studies, 1975.

Murie, A., and Forrest, R. "Wealth, inheritance and housing policy." *Policy and Politics*, 1980, *8*(1), 1–20.

Murie, A. *Housing inequality and deprivation*. London: Heinemann, 1983.

Murphey, R. *The fading of the Maoist vision: City and country in China's development*. New York: Methuen, 1980.

National Commission on Urban Problems. *Building the American city*. Washington, D.C.: U.S. Government Printing Office, 1968.

National Resources Committee. "The problems of urban America." In P. Hatt and A. Reiss (eds.), *Cities and society: The revised reader in urban sociology*. 2d ed. Glencoe, Ill.: The Free Press, 1957.

Neilson, L. "New cities in Australia: the Australian government's growth center program." In G. Golany (ed.), *International urban growth policies: New town contributions*. New York: Wiley, 1978, pp. 315–34.

Neutze, G. M. *The price of land and land use planning: Policy instruments in the urban land market*, Paris: OECD, 1973.

———. *Urban development in Australia*. Sydney, Australia: Allen & Unwin, 1977.

———. *Australian urban policy*. Sydney, Australia: Allen & Unwin, 1978.

Nevitt, A. *Housing, taxation and subsidies*. London: Nelson, 1966.

Newsview. "Can housing costs be lowered in Israel?" December 1, 1981, pp. 48–53.

Newton, P., and Wulff, M. "Public housing in Melbourne: Locational implications of policy decisions." In John Dixon and D. L. Jayasuriya (eds.), *Social policy in 1980s*. Canberra, Australia: Canberra College of Advanced Education, 1983, pp. 175–85.

Nijkamp, P. "Perspectives for urban analyses and policies." In P. Nijkamp and P. Rietveld (eds.), *Cities in transition: Problems and policies*, Alphen aan den Rijn, The Netherlands: Sijthoff & Noordhoff, 1981.

Norwegian Housing Bank. *Statistics, 1981*. Oslo: Norwegian Housing Bank, 1982.

Noto, N. A. "Tax and financial policies for owner-occupied housing in the 1980s." In R.

Montgomery and D. R. Marshall (eds.), *Housing policy for the 1980s*, Lexington, Mass.: D. C. Heath, 1980.

OECD. *Economic surveys: Norway*, Paris: OECD, 1981.

Office of Population Censuses and Surveys. *Census 1981 OPCS Monitor*. London: Government Statistical Service, 1982.

———. *General household survey*. London: HMSO, 1983a.

———. *Population projections: Mid-1981 based OPCS Monitor*. London: Government Statistical Service, 1983b.

O'Higgins, M. "Rolling back the welfare state: The rhetoric and reality of public expenditure and social policy under the Conservative Government." In C. Jones and J. Stevenson (eds.). *The yearbook of social policy in Britain*. Henley-on-Thames, Eng.: Routledge & Kegan Paul, 1983.

Pahl, R. "Foreword." In M. Harloe, R. Isaacharoff, and R. Minns *The organization of housing*. London: Heinemann, 1974.

Paley, B. *Attitudes to letting in 1976*. London: HMSO, 1978.

Paris, C. "Whatever happened to urban sociology? Critical reflections on *Social Theory and the Urban Question*." *Environment and Planning, D*, 1983, *1*, 217–25.

Pearse, A. "Quelques characteristiques de l'urbanisation dans la Ville de Rio de Janeiro." In Philip Hauser (ed.), *L'Urbanisation en Amérique Latine*. Paris: UNESCO, 1962, pp. 192–205.

Peattie, L. R. "The concept of marginality as applied to squatter settlements." In W. A. Cornelius and F. M. Trueblood (eds.), *Latin American urban research*. vol. 4. Beverly Hills, Calif.: Sage Publications, 1974.

———. "Some second thoughts on sites-and-services." *Habitat International*, 1982, 6(1–2), 131–39.

———. "Realistic planning and qualitative research." *Habitat International*, 1983, 7(5–6), 227–34.

Perlman, J. *The myth of marginality: Urban poverty and politics in Rio de Janeiro*. Berkeley: University of California Press, 1976.

———., and Spiegel, H. "Copenhagen's black quadrant: The facade and reality of participation." In Lawrence Susskind and Michael Elliott (eds.), *Paternalism, conflict and coproduction: Learning from citizen action and citizen participation in Western Europe*. New York: Plenum, 1983, pp. 35–65.

Perry, C. A. *Housing for the machine age*. New York: Russell Sage Foundation, 1939.

Phillips, B. "5,000m repairs bill for million 10-year old homes." *The Times* (London), July 29, 1983, p. 2.

Pickvance, C. G. (ed.), *Urban sociology: Critical essays*. London: Tavistock Publications, 1976.

Popenoe, David. *The suburban environment: Sweden and the United States*. Chicago: University of Chicago Press, 1977.

———. "Urban form in advanced societies: A cross-national enquiry." In C. Ungerson and V. Karn (eds.), *The consumer experience of housing*. Farnborough, Eng.: Gower, 1980.

Portes, A., and Walton, J. *Labor, class and the international system*. New York: Academic Press, 1981.

Power, A. *Priority estates project*. London: Department of the Environment, 1982.

Presidents' Committee on Urban Housing. *A decent home*. Washington, D.C.: U.S. Government Printing Office, 1969.

Pressmman, N. "Israel's new towns." *Habitat*, 1980, *23*(1), 48–53.

Priemus, H. "Squatters in Amsterdam." *International Journal of Urban and Regional Research*, *7*(3), 417–27.

Pugh, C. *Housing in capitalist societies*. Farnborough, Eng.: Gower, 1980.

Pynoos, J., Schafer, R., and Hartman, C. W. (eds.), *Housing urban America*. 2d ed. New York: Aldine, 1980.

Quigley, J. M. "Housing allowances and demand-oriented housing subsidies." In R. Montgomery and D. R. Marshall (eds.), *Housing policy for the 1980s*, Lexington, Mass.: Lexington Books, 1980.

Ray, T. *"The political life of a Venezuela barrio,"* (mimeograph) 1966.

Reid, C., Keating, A., and Long, L. *Patterns of discrimination against children in the metro-Atlanta area*. Atlanta, Ga.: HOPE for Children, 1979.

Rex, J., and Moore, R. *Race. Community and conflict*. London: Oxford University Press, 1965.

Rigby, A. *Communes in Britain*. London: Routledge & Kegan Paul, 1974.

Roberts, B. *Organizing strangers: Poor families in Guatemala City*, Austin: University of Texas Press, 1978.

Robinson, R., and O'Sullivan, T. "Housing tenure polarization: Some empirical evidence." *Housing Review*, July–August, 1983, 116–17.

Rodwin, L. *Nations and cities: A comparison of strategies for urban growth*. Boston: Houghton Mifflin, 1970.

Roistacher, E. A., and Young, J. S. "Two-earner families in the housing market." In R. Montgomery and D. R. Marshall (eds.), *Housing policy for the 1980s*, Lexington, Mass.: Lexington Books, 1980.

Romberg, R. V., and Vitarello, J. D. "The law as a positive framework for future development: A study of information exchange in the Swedish physical planning process." Thesis, University of Stockholm School of Law, June, 1971.

Ross, M. *The political integration of urban squatters*. Evanston, Ill.: Northwestern University Press, 1973, p. 38.

Rossi, P. *Why families move*. Glencoe, Ill.: The Free Press, 1955.

Rotundo, H. "Adaptability of human behavior." In *Environmental determinants of community well-being*. Washington, D.C.: Pan American Health Organization, 1965.

Roweis, S. T. "Urban planning as professional mediation of territorial politics." *Environment and Planning, D*, 1983, *1*, 139–62.

Rubinstein, A. "Tax incentive for owners to rent out flats." *Jerusalem Post*, January 11–17, 1981.

Russell, E. W. *The slum abolition movement in Victoria 1933–37*. Melbourne: Hornet Publications, 1972.

Salmen, L. "A perspective on the resettlement of squatters in Brazil." *America Latina*, 1969, *12*, 73–93.

———. "Housing alternatives for the Carioca working class: A comparison between favelas and casas de comodos." *America Latina*, 1970, *212*(4), 51–70.

Sandberg, E. *Equality is the goal: A Swedish report*. Stockholm: Swedish Institute, 1975.

Sandhu, R. S. "An evaluation of housing for the poor in Chandigarh—a capital project in India." Paper presented for the International IFHP Congress, Lisbon, May 1983.

———. "The urban poor in a new city—case study Chandigarh experience." Thesis, Guru Nanak Dev University, Amristar (India), September 1976.

Santos, Boaventura de Souza. "The law of the oppressed: The construction and reproduction of legality in Pasargada." *Law and Society Review*, 1977, *12*(1).

Sarin, Madhu. "Planning and the urban poor—the Chandigarh experience." Unpublished report, London: University College, School of Environmental Studies, 1975.

Sarkissian, W. "The idea of social mix in town planning: An historical review." *Urban Studies*, 1976, *13*(3), 231–46.

Saunders, P. "Social theory and the urban question: A reply to Paris and Kirby." *Environment and Planning, D*, 1983, *1*, 234–39.

——. *Urban politics*. London: Hutchinson, 1979.

Sawers, L. "Cities and countryside in the Soviet Union and China." In William K. Tabb and L. Sawers (eds.), *Marxism and the metropolis*, New York: Oxford University Press, 1978.

Schneider, A. L. "Studying policy implementation." *Evaluation Review*, 1982, *6*(6), 715–30.

Schorr, A. L., and Moen, P. "The single parent and public policy." *Social Policy*, 1979, *9*(5), 15–21.

Seeley, J. R. "The slum: Its nature, use, and users." In L. S. Bourne (ed.), *Internal structure of the city*. New York: Oxford University Press, 1971.

Seymour, T. "The causes of squatter settlement: The case of Lusaka." 1976.

Shachar, A. S. "Israel's development towns: Evaluation of a national urban policy." *Journal of the American Planning Institute*, 1971, *37*, 362–72.

——. "New towns in a national settlement policy." *Town and Country Planning*, 1976, *44*(2), 83–87.

Shaham, I. "Public housing in Israel." In J. S. Fuerst (ed.), *Public housing in Europe and America*. New York: Wiley, 1974, pp. 52–66.

Shalala, D. E., and McGeorge, J. A. "The women and mortgage credit project: A government response to the housing problems of women." In S. Keller (ed.), *Building for women*, Lexington, Mass.: Lexington Books, 1981.

Shalala, D. E. "Foreword." In C. R. Stimpson et al. (eds.), *Women and the American city*. Special issue of *Signs, Journal of Women in Culture and Society*, supp. to vol. 5, no. 3 (Spring 1980). Chicago: Signs, 1980.

Shaw, G. "Slum clearance and urban renewal." *Australian Municipal Journal*, 1966, *45*, 401–10.

Short, J. R. "Urban policy and British cities." *Journal of the American Planning Association*, 1982, *48*, 39–52.

Showler, B., and Sinfield, A. (eds.), *The workless state*. Oxford, Eng.: Martin Robertson, 1981.

Shuval, J. T. "The micro neighbourhood: An approach to ecological patterns of ethnic groups." *Social Problems*, 1962, *9*(2): 272–80.

Sieriestad, S. "The Norwegian Economy." In Natalie Rogoff Ramsøy (ed.), *Norwegian society*, New York: Humanities Press, 1974, pp. 76–108.

Silberstein, P. "Favela living: Personal solution to larger problems" *America Latina*, 1969, *12*(3), 183–200.

Simons, H. J., et al. *Slums or self-reliance? Urban growth in Zambia*. (Communication No. 12). Lusaka: University of Zambia, Institute for African Studies, 1976.

Smith, B. N. and Thorns, D. C. "Housing markets and sub-markets: An analysis of the role of financial institutions in the allocation of housing." *Australian and New Zealand Journal of Sociology*, 1980, *16*(1), 4–13.

Smith, W. *Housing: The social and economic elements*. Berkeley: University of California Press, 1970.

Soen, P., and Kipnis, B. "The functioning of a cluster of towns in Israel: An analysis of real and expected zones of influence." *Ekistics*, 1972, *34*, 400–407.

Solomon, A. P. *Housing the urban poor*. Cambridge, Mass.: MIT Press, 1974.

Soper, M. "Housing for single-parent families: A women's design." In G. R. Wekerle, R. Peterson, and D. Morley (eds.), *New space for women*. Boulder, Colo.: Westview Press, 1980.

Spiegel, E. *Neue Städte in Israel* (New towns in Israel). Stuttgart: R. Krämer, 1966.

Stamp, J. "Toward supportive neighborhoods: Women's role in changing the segregated city." In G. R. Wekerle, R. Peterson, and D. Morley (eds.), *New space for women*. Boulder, Colo.: Westview, 1980, pp. 189–201.

Stepick, A., and Murphy, A. D. "Comparing squatter settlements and government self-help projects as housing solutions in Oaxaca, Mexico." *Human Organization*, 1980, *39*(4), 339–43.

Sternlieb, G., and Hughes, J. W. "Housing the poor in a post-shelter society." *Annals of the American Academy of Political and Social Science*, 1983, *465*, 109–22.

Sternlieb, G. et al. *America's housing: Prospects and problems*. New Brunswick, N.J.: Rutgers University, Center for Urban Policy Research, 1980.

Stevenson, A., et al. *High living: A study of family life in flats*. Melbourne: Melbourne University Press, 1967.

Straszheim, M. R. "The section and rental-assistance program: Costs and policy options." In R. Montgomery and D. R. Marshall (eds.), *Housing policy for the 1980s*, Lexington, Mass.: Lexington Books, 1980.

Stretton, H. "Housing policy." In P. Scott (ed.), *Australian cities and public policy*. Melbourne, Australia: Georgian House, 1978.

Struyk, R. J. "Research in housing for the elderly: The U.S. Department of Housing and urban Development." In M. P. Lawton and S. L. Hoover (eds.), *Community housing choices for older Americans*. New York: Springer, 1981.

Studer, R. G., and Van Vliet—, W. "Changing perspectives on the social consequences of and the procedures for organizing the spatial environment." In B. Hamm and B. Jalowiecki (eds.), *The social nature of space*. The Hague: Mouton, forthcoming.

Svennson, R. "Swedish housing policy—not only successes . . . problems too." *Current Sweden*, March 1976, No. 107.

Swedish Association of Municipal Housing Companies (Sveriges Allmannyttiga Bostadsforetag). *Swedish housing 1982*. Stockholm: SABO, 1982.

Swedish Ministry of Housing and Physical Planning. *Swedish experiences of self-building, co-operation, consumer research, participation*. A contribution to the United Nations Conference on Human Settlements HABITAT, Vancouver, Canada. Stockholm: Ministry of Housing and Physical Planning, 1976.

Sweetser, F. L., and Sweetser, D. A. "Social class and single-family housing: Helsinki and Boston." In S. F. Fava (ed.), *Urbanism in world perspective*. New York: Crowell, 1968, pp. 256–66.

Szelenyi, I. "The relative autonomy of the state or state mode of production." In Michael Dear and A. Scott (eds.), *Urbanization and urban planning in capitalist society*. New York: Methuen, 1981a, pp. 565–92.

———. "Structural changes of and alternatives to capitalist development in the contemporary urban and regional system." *International Journal of Urban and Regional Research*, 1981b, 5(1), 1–14.

——. *Urban inequalities under state socialism*. New York: Oxford University Press, 1983.

Tabb, W. K. *U.S. Capitalism in Crisis*. New York: Union for Radical Political Economics Education Project, 1978.

Tacken, M. *Wonen in volte* (Living in New Residential Areas with High Densities), Delft, The Netherlands: Delft University of Technology. Institute for Town Planning Research, 1982. (Report in Dutch, with English summary.).

The tenants' movement in Sweden. Stockholm: Hyresgasternas Riksforbund, 1981.

Timms, D. W. G. *The urban mosaic. Towards a theory of residential differentiation*. Cambridge, Eng.: Cambridge University Press, 1971.

Tinker, A. *The elderly in modern society*. London: Longman, 1981.

Torgensen, Ulf. "Political institutions." In Natalie Rogoff Ramsøy (ed.), *Norwegian society*, New York: Humanities Press, 1974, pp. 194–226.

True, C. "The economic rationale for government intervention in housing." *Social Policy and Administration*, 1979, 13(2), 124–37.

Tucker, S. N. "An analysis of housing subsidy schemes in Australia." *Urban Studies*, 1983, 20, 439–53.

Turner, J. F. "Barriers and channels for housing development in modernizing countries." *Journal of the American Institute of Planners*, 1967, 33, 167–81.

——. *Housing by people: Towards autonomy in building environments*. London: Marion Boyars, 1976.

——. "Uncontrolled urban settlements: Problems and policies." In G. W. Breese (ed.), *The city in newly developing countries*, Englewood Cliffs, N.J.: Prentice-Hall, 1969, p. 61.

Turner, J. F., and Goetze, R. "Environmental Security and Housing Input." *Ekistics*, 1967, 23, pp. 123–82.

Ministry of Housing and Local Government. Research and Development Group. *Families living at high density*. London, Great Britain: HMSO, 1970.

Ungerson, C., and Karn, V. (eds.). *The consumer experience of housing*. Farnborough, Eng.: Gower, 1980.

United Nations. *Annual bulletin of housing and building statistics for Europe, 1978*. New York: United Nations, 1979.

U.N. Department of International Economic and Social Affairs. *World housing survey 1974*. New York: United Nations, 1976.

U.S. Agency for International Development. *Housing guarantee program, annual report, fiscal year 1981*. Washington, D.C.: U.S. AID. Office of Housing and Urban Development, 1982.

U.S. Bureau of the Census. *Households, families, marital status and living arrangements: March 1983*. (Current Population Reports, Population Characteristics, Series P–20, No. 382), Washington, D.C.: U.S. Government Printing Office, 1983.

U.S. Department of Housing and Urban Development. *Planning new towns: national reports of the U.S. and the U.S.S.R.*. Washington, D.C.: U.S. Government Printing Office, 1981.

U.S. Department of Housing and Urban Development. *A report to the secretary on the homeless and emergency shelters*. Washington, D.C.: U.S. Government Printing Office, 1984.

Urban Study 70. *Middle-sized Finnish city.* Helsinki: Finnish National Fund for Research and Development. 1974.

Urbanization Report (Verstedelijkingsnota), The Hague: Staatsuitgeverij, 1976.

United States. Bureau of the Census. *Census of housing: 1970. Subject reports.* "Housing characteristics by household composition." (Final report HC (7)-7). Washington, D.C.: U.S. Government Printing Office, 1973.

U.S. Department of Housing and Urban Development. *How well are we housed? 2. Female-headed households.* Washington, D.C.: U.S. Government Printing Office, 1980.

Valkonen, T., et al. (eds.), *Suomalaiset* (The Finns). Porvool, Finland: Söderström, 1980.

Valladares, Licia do Prado. "Working the system: Squatter response to resettlement in Rio de Janeiro." *International Journal of Urban and Regional Research*, 1978, 2(1), 12–25.

Valtakunnallinen asunto-ohjelma vuosille 1976–1985. Realliresurssijaoston mietinto Helsinki: National Housing Program, Inventory of resources, 1976.

——. Yhteenveto. Komiteamietinto (National Housing Report, Concluding Report). 1976:36.

Vance, J. E., Jr. "Institutional forces that shape the city." In D. T. Herbert and R. J. Johnston (eds.), *Social areas in cities.* 2 vol. London: Wiley, 1976, pp. 84–104.

——. *This scene of man.* New York: Harper's College Press, 1977.

Van der Linden, J. "Squatting by organized invasion: A new reply to a failing housing policy?" *Third World Planning Review*, 1982, 4(4), 400–412.

van Vliet—, W. "Neighborhood evaluations by city and suburban children." *Journal of the American Planning Association*, 1981, 47(4), 458–67.

Varady, D. P. "Indirect benefits of subsidized housing programs." *Journal of the American Planning Association*, vol. 48, 1982, pp. 432–40.

——. "Determinants of residential mobility decisions," *Journal of the American Planning Association*, 1983, 49(2), 184–99.

Vestbro, Dick Urban. "Collective Housing Units in Sweden." *Women and Environments. International Newsletter* (December 1980–Jan. 1981): 8–9. Excerpted from *Current Sweden*, published by the Swedish Institute.

Vint, J., and Bintliff, J. "Tower blocks: The economics of high rise housing." *Social Policy and Administration*, 1983, 17(2), 118–29.

Vogelaar, G. A. M. "Economic Commission for Europe, Seminar on Special Housing Needs." *Report of Dutch statement.* November 1976.

——. "All-day riot in Amsterdam over housing." *San Francisco Chronicle*, October 12, 1982.

Voionmaa, V. *Tampereen kaupungin historia.* Osa I. Tampereen Työvaen Kirjapaino 1929. (The History of the City Tampere)

Von Einem, E. "National urban policy—The case of West Germany." *Journal of the American Planning Association*, 1982, 48, 9–23.

Washington Post, November 20, 1983.

Weber, M. *The city.* Glencoe, Ill.: The Free Press, 1958.

Wegelin, E. A. *Urban low-income housing and development.* Leiden: Nijhoff, 1978.

Weidemann, S., et al. "Residents' perceptions of satisfaction and safety: A basis for change in multifamily housing." *Environment and Behavior*, 1982, 14(6), 695–724.

Weidemann, S., et al. "Predictors of housing satisfaction among the elderly." Paper presented at the American Psychological Association Annual Convention, Chicago, 1975.

————., et al. *Resident safety: Research and recommendations for Longview Place anti-crime program*. Urbana, Ill.: University of Illinois, Housing Research and Development Program, 1981.

Weiss, R. S. "Housing for single parents." In R. Montgomery and D. R. Marshall (eds.), *Housing Policy for the 1980s*. Lexington, Mass.: Lexington Books, 1980.

Weiss, S. and Burby, R. *New communities U.S.A.* Lexington, Mass.: Lexington Books, 1976.

Weitz, R. "A strong stand for decentralization." In R. Weitz (ed.), *Urbanization and the developing countries*. New York: Praeger, 1973, pp. 172–79.

Werczberger, E., and Marcus, M. "Development of a new neighborhood as a contribution toward solving the housing problem of young couples in the Tel-Aviv metroplitan area." (Memorandum), Tel-Aviv: Tel-Aviv University, Center for Urban and Regional Studies, 1981.

Winkler Prins Encyclopedie. Deel 17. Segregatie. Amsterdam-Brussel: Elsevier, 1973.

Winter, M., and Morris, E. "Housing conditions, satisfaction and conventionality: An analysis of the housing of female-headed households." *Housing and Society*, 1981, 8(3).

Wirth, L. "Housing as a field of sociological research." *American Sociological Review*, 1947, 12(2), 137–43.

The World Bank. *Housing: Sector policy paper*. Washington, D.C.: The World Bank, 1975, p. 14.

Wulff, M. G., and Newton, P. W. "Public housing in Melbourne: Locational implications of policy decisions." In J. Dixon and D. Jayasuriya (eds.), *Social policy in the 80s*. Canberra, Australia: Canberra College of Advanced Education, 1983.

Yancey, W. L. "Architecture, interaction and social control." *Environment and Behavior*, 1971, 3(1), 3–21.

Yearns, M. H. "Government housing programs: a brief review." In C. S. Wedin and L. G. Nygren (eds.), *Housing perspectives*. 2d ed. Minneapolis: Burgess, 1979.

Ylönen, A. "The social and spatial constraints as determinants for the urban ways of life." In A. Kuklinski et al. (eds.), *Regional dynamics of socioeconomic change*. Tampere, Finland: Finnpublishers, 1979, pp. 179–94.

Young, M., and Willmott, P. *Family and kinship in East London*. London: Routledge & Kegan Paul, 1957.

————. *The symmetrical family*. London: Routledge & Kegan Paul, 1973.

Zambia Mail, Aug. 29, 1970.

Zube, E. H. "Increasing the effective participation of social scientists in environmental research and planning." *International Social Science Journal*, 1982, 34, 481–94.

Index of Terms

Index of Places

Index of Names

Contributors

Sherry Ahrentzen is an assistant professor in the School of Architecture and Urban Planning at the University of Wisconsin, Milwaukee. She chairs the Committee on the Status of Women of the Environmental Design Association and contributed a chapter on school environments to *Environmental Stress* (1982). Her research concentrates on gender issues in urban and residential design as well as children and the physical environment.

Joan Ash, a sociologist, is a housing consultant and member of the Council of Housing Centre Trust in London, England. As a research officer in the Ministry of Housing and Local Government she has made major contributions to Design Bulletins published by Her Majesty's Stationery Office. She also wrote a chapter for *The Consumer Experience of Housing* (1980). Her interests are in user needs.

Francine Dansereau is a professor at the I.N.R.S.-Urbanisation, Montreal, Canada. She has several French publications on housing policy and urban redevelopment, which are her main areas of interest.

Jan den Draak is director of the Institute for Town Planning Research at Delft University of Technology. He has written articles on housing, planning, and the inner city. An English article of his appeared in *Tijdschrift voor Economische en Sociale Geografie* (1983). His research interests are in the sociology of housing and planning with special reference to central city issues.

Sawsan El-Messiri is a consultant for the Egyptian Ministry of Housing and is affiliated with the Cooperative Housing Foundation in Washington, D.C. She has extensive experience as a researcher and director of field projects on social and urban development. She contributed chapters to *Patron and Clients in Mediterranean Societies* (1977) and *Women in the Muslim World* (1978) and published the book *Ibn al-Balad: A Concept of Egyptian Identity* (1978).

Sylvia F. Fava is a professor of sociology at Brooklyn College and the Graduate Center, City University of New York. She is an author of *Urban Society* (seventh revised edition, in press), coeditor of *The Apple Sliced: Sociological Studies of New York City* (1983), and has contributed widely to professional journals and anthologies. Her diverse interests include suburban environments, women and space, and comparative analysis of new towns and metropolitan developments.

Ray Forrest is a coeditor of *Urban Political Economy and Social Theory* (1982) and has recently published articles on housing in *Sociological Review, Society and Space, Environment and Planning*, and the *Journal of Social Policy*. His interests are in housing policy and the sociology of housing.

Louise Gaunt is a senior research officer at the National Swedish Institute for Building Research. She contributed a chapter to *Innovation in Play Environments* (1980) and is interested in housing conditions of children and multigeneration households.

Rosalie G. Genovese is a consultant on community-based planning and a research associate of the Center for the Study of Women and Society, Graduate Center, City University of New York. She has edited *Families and Change: Social Needs and Public Policies* (1984), wrote a chapter for *Professionals and Urban Form* (1983), and has published in various books and journals. Her interests include the social effects of planning, advocacy planning, housing, and public policy with special reference to families.

Jacques Godbout is a professor at the University of Quebec, Montreal, Canada. He has written in French on housing, political power, and consumer participation.

Frans Grunfeld is professor of urban sociology and planning at Tilburg University, The Netherlands. He has been a lecturer at Amsterdam University and a researcher in the city planning department of Rotterdam. In 1976–77 he was a visiting professor at Ben-Gurion University in Beersheva, Israel. His interests are in urban sociology and housing. He is the author of numerous Dutch publications as well as the English book *Habitat and Habitation* (1970).

Padmini Gulati, assistant professor of sociology at the State University of New York, Plattsburgh, has published articles on consumer participation in decision making in the *Social Service Review* (1982) and *Sociology and Social Work* (1981). Her research interests are in low-income housing, social policy issues in comparative perspective, and population issues in the Third World. Part III of this volume was compiled with her assistance.

Shirley Foster Hartley is chair and professor in the department of sociology at California State University, Hayward. She is on the board of directors of the Population Association of America and has written *Comparing Populations* (1981) as well as two earlier demographic books and numerous chapters and journal articles on population, the status of women, marriage styles, and illegitimacy.

Herlianto is deputy rector for research and development, Maranatha Christian University, Bandung, Indonesia. His previous positions include dean, faculty of architecture, Petra Christian University, Surabaya, and senior researcher for the Institute of Human Settlements. His *Urbanization and Urban Development* appeared in 1984. Among his interests are low-cost housing, slum improvement, and community development.

Wilhelmus Hofsteede, head of the Research Institute of the Catholic University Parahyangan, Bandung, Indonesia, has been guest lecturer at the Goethe Institute in Frankfurt, West Germany, and has authored various publications in German and Dutch. His research interests center on popular participation in rural and urban development.

Elizabeth D. Huttman is a professor of sociology at California State University, Hayward, whose publications have focused on housing and social policy. Her *Introduction to Social Policy* appeared in 1981. Her current interests are on European housing policy and housing for the elderly.

Leslie A. Kilmartin is dean of the faculty of arts at the Swinburne Institute of Technology, Melbourne, Australia. He is a past president of the Sociological Association of Australia and New Zealand and coauthor of *Cities Unlimited* (1978). His most recent book is *Social Theory and the Australian City* (1985). His research interests are in urban planning, residential mobility, and residential satisfaction.

Robert W. Marans is a professor in the College of Architecture and Urban Planning at the University of Michigan and a research scientist at that university's Institute for

Social Research where he directs the Urban Environmental Research Program. He also is a senior research fellow at the Brookdale Institute of Gerontology and Adult Human Development in Jerusalem. He has written extensively on environmental evaluation, the concept and measurement of neighborhood quality, and alternative living arrangements for older people. He is the recipient of a 1982 applied research award for *Progressive Architecture* and a 1983 award for design research excellence from the National Endowment for the Arts. His current research deals with techniques for building diagnostics and lighting in office environments.

William Michelson, professor of sociology, is a past president of the Environmental Section of the American Sociological Association and was director of the Child in the City Programme at the University of Toronto. He is the author of numerous books, most recently of *From Sun to Sun: Daily Obligations and Community Structure in the Lives of Employed Women and Their Families* (1985), and he has written extensively for professional journals. His areas of interest are urban and environmental sociology and time geography.

Alan Murie is author of *Housing Inequality and Deprivation* (1983) and a coauthor of *Housing Policy and Practice* (1982). His research focuses on housing policy.

Peter W. Newton is a principal research scientist with the Commonwealth Scientific and Industrial Research Organization, Melbourne, Australia. He is a coeditor of *The Future of Urban Form: The Impact of New Technology* (1985), *Micro-Computers for Local Government Planning and Management* (1985), and the author of *A Roof Over Their Heads: Housing Issues and Families in Australia* (1984). His interests include urban housing markets and microcomputer-based decision aids for local government planning.

David Popenoe is professor of sociology at Rutgers, the State University of New Jersey, where he is also chairperson and graduate director of the department of sociology. His previous positions include research director of the Rutgers Urban Studies Center; visiting faculty member or research scholar at New York University, the University of Pennsylvania, the University of Stockholm, the National Swedish Institute for Building Research, and the Centre for Environmental Studies, London; and city planning posts in Philadelphia, Pennsylvania, and Newark, New Jersey. During 1972–73 he was a Fulbright senior research scholar in Sweden and visiting Fulbright lecturer in Greece, Israel, and Spain. Also a charter member of the American Institute of Certified Planners, his publications include *Private Pleasure, Public Plight: U.S. Metropolitan Community Life in Comparative Perspective* (1984) and *The Suburban Environment: Sweden and the United States* (1977). He is the author of the leading college textbook *Sociology* and coeditor of *Neighborhood City and Metropolis* (1970) and has written numerous articles on community and urban and comparative sociology.

Cedric Pugh is a senior lecturer at the South Australian Institute of Technology and has been a visiting scholar at the National University of Singapore. His *Housing in Capitalist Societies* appeared in 1980. His interests are in the political economy of housing and public policy.

Ranvinder Singh Sandhu is a lecturer in the Guru Ramdas Post-Graduate School of Planning at Guru Hanak Dev University, Amritsar, India. He has published in the fields of housing and anthropology. His current interests are in urban sociology and planning.

Licia Valladares is head of the research department at IUPERJ, Rio de Janeiro, Brazil. She has been a visiting lecturer at the Centre for Urban Studies, University College, London, England. She has edited books and written articles on housing, mostly in

Portuguese; an English article of hers appeared in the *International Journal of Urban and Regional Research* (1977). Her main research interests are in urban studies, particularly in low-income housing, urban protest movements, and poverty.

Willem van Vliet— is in the department of community studies at The Pennsylvania State University. From 1976 to 1979 he was a fellow of the Social Sciences and Humanities Research Council, representing The Netherlands in a bilateral exchange. He was also awarded a Lady Davis Fellowship and, in 1981, the recipient of an Allon Fellowship in Israel. He is an editor of and a contributor to *Habitats for Children* (1985); with Elizabeth Huttman he is coeditor of a forthcoming *Handbook of Housing and the Built Environment*. His interests are virtually unlimited.

Maryann Griffin Wulff is a senior lecturer in sociology of housing at the Swinborne Institute of Technology, Melbourne, Australia. Her recent publications include "The Two Income Household: Relative Contribution of Earners to Housing Costs," *Urban Studies* (1982) and "Social Indicators for Measuring Residential Satisfaction in Marginal Settlements in Costa Rica" (with Peter Chi), *Social Indicators Research* (1980). Her interests are in public housing, residential mobility, and social demography of the family.

Ari Ylonen is an assistant professor in sociology and regional science at the University of Tampere, Finland. He is the author of several articles on urban sociology and housing, which is where his current research interests lie.